C++ for C Programmers

Third Edition

C++ for C Programmers

Third Edition

Ira Pohl

University of California, Santa Cruz

ADDISON–WESLEY

An Imprint of Addison Wesley Longman, Inc.

Reading, Massachusetts • Harlow, England • Menlo Park,
California • Berkeley, California • Don Mills, Ontario
Sydney • Bonn • Amsterdam • Tokyo • Mexico City

The publisher offers discounts on this book when ordered in quantity for special sales. For more information, please contact:

Corporate, Government, and Special Sales
Addison Wesley Longman, Inc.
One Jacob Way
Reading, Massachusetts 01867
(718) 944-3700

Library of Congress Cataloging-in-Publication Data

```
Pohl, Ira
    C++ for C Programmers / Ira Pohl.–3rd ed.
        p. cm.
    Includes bibliographical references and index.
    ISBN 0-201-39519-3
    1. C++ (Computer program language)  I. Title.
QA76.73.C153P654    1999
005.13'3–dc21                                98-37980
                                                 CIP
```

ISBN 0-201-39519-3
Text printed on recycled and acid-free paper
1 2 3 4 5 6 7 8 9 10—MA—0201009998
First printing, November 1998

To Laura and her mother

Contents

Preface

The book uses an evolutionary teaching process, with C as a starting point and C++ as a destination. It can also be used by those already familiar with other similar programming languages, such as Pascal, PL/1, or BASIC. The reader can stop and use the language facilities at various points in the text.

This book will get the C programmer up and running in C++ in the shortest possible time. The teaching-by-equivalency method used enables the C programmer to immediately convert existing code to C++. Working code is emphasized. A program particularly illustrative of the chapter's themes is analyzed by dissection, which is similar to a structured walk-through of the code. Dissection explains to the reader newly encountered programming elements and idioms.

C is a general-purpose programming language that was originally designed by Dennis Ritchie of Bell Laboratories and implemented there on a PDP-11 in 1972. C was first used as the systems language for the UNIX operating system. Ken Thompson, the developer of UNIX, had been using both an assembler and a language named B to produce initial versions of UNIX in 1970.

C++, invented at Bell Labs by Bjarne Stroustrup in the mid-1980s, is a powerful modern successor language to C. C++ adds to C the concept of *class*, a mechanism for providing user-defined types, also called *abstract data types*. C++ supports *object-oriented* programming by these means and by providing inheritance and run-time type binding. C++ is increasingly the choice of scientists and engineers in developing scientific software.

This book, intended for use in a first course in C++ programming, can be used as a supplementary text in an advanced programming, data structures, software methodology, comparative language, or other course in which the instructor wants C++ to be the language of choice. Each chapter presents a number of carefully explained programs.

All of the major pieces of code were tested. A consistent and proper coding style is adopted from the beginning and is one chosen by professionals in the C++ community. The code is available at the Addison Wesley Longman Web site *(www.awl.com/cseng/titles/0-201-39519-3/)*.

For the programmer who wants C experience, this book could be used in conjunction with *A Book on C, 4th ed.,* by Al Kelley and Ira Pohl (Addison-Wesley, 1998). As a package, the two books offer a unique, integrated treatment of the C and C++ programming languages and their use.

This book incorporates a number of important features.

- **An evolutionary approach.** The C programmer can immediately benefit from programming in C++. Chapter 1, "An Overview of C++ and Object-Oriented Programming," provides an introduction to the use of C++ as an object-oriented programming language. Chapter 2, "Native Types and Statements," reviews the kernel language, which is mostly C with some improvements. Chapter 3, "Functions, Pointers, and Arrays," continues with similarities between functions and complex data types. The middle chapters show how to use classes, which are the basis for abstract data types and object-oriented programming (OOP). The later chapters give advanced details of the use of inheritance, templates, and exceptions. At any point in the text, the programmer can stop and use the new material.

- **Teaching by example.** The book is a tutorial that stresses examples of working code. Right from the start, the student is introduced to full working programs. An interactive environment is assumed. Exercises are integrated with the examples to encourage experimentation. Excessive detail is avoided in explaining the larger elements of writing working code. Each chapter has several important example programs. Major elements of these programs are explained by dissection.

- **Data structures in C++.** The text emphasizes many of the standard data structures from computer science. Stacks, safe arrays, dynamically allocated multidimensional arrays, lists, trees, and strings are all implemented. Exercises extend the student's understanding of how to implement and use these structures. Implementation is consistent with an abstract data type approach to software.

- **Object-oriented programming.** The reader is led gradually to the object-oriented style. Chapter 1, "An Overview of C++ and Object-Oriented Programming," discusses how the C programmer can benefit in important ways from a switch to C++ and object-oriented programming. Object-oriented concepts are defined, and the way in which these concepts are supported by C++ is introduced. Chapter 4, "Classes," introduces classes, which are the basic mechanism for producing modular programs and implementing abstract data types. Class variables are the objects being manipulated. Chapter 8, "Inheritance," develops inheritance and virtual functions, two key elements in this paradigm. Chapter 10, "OOP Using C++," discusses OOP programming philosophy. This book develops in the programmer an appreciation of this point of view.

- **C equivalence.** Where appropriate, C++ code is given with equivalent C code. This gives the experienced C programmer immediate access to idiomatic C++ code.

- **New Java equivalence.** At the end of each chapter is a discussion of how the C++ programmer can very naturally and easily begin programming in Java, a language of interest for work on the Internet. The Java programming language borrows ideas from C++ and is designed to run in a machine- and system-independent manner. This makes it suitable for Internet work, such as writing applets for Web pages that are used by browsers. Because Java is an extension of C++, it is readily learned by the C++ programmer.

- **ANSI C++ language and *iostream*.** For an existing, widely used language, C++ continues to change at a rapid pace. This book is based on the most recent standard: the ANSI C++ Committee language documents. A succinct informal language reference is provided in Appendix C, "Language Guide." Use of the *iostream* library is featured in Appendix D, "Input/Output," and STL is featured in Appendix E, "STL and String Libraries."

- **Standard template library (STL).** STL is explained and used in Chapter 7, "Templates, Generic Programming, and STL," and in Appendix E, "STL and String Libraries." Many of the data structure examples foreshadow its explanation and use. There is a strong emphasis on the template mechanism required for STL and the iterator idiom that STL exploits.

- **Industry- and course-tested.** This book is the basis of many on-site professional training courses given by the author, who has used its contents to train professionals and students in various forums since 1986. The various changes are course-tested and reflect the author's considerable teaching and consulting experience. The text is the basis for Web-based training in C++ available from

  www.digitalthink.com

- **Exercises.** The exercises test and often advance the student's knowledge of the language. Many are intended to be done interactively while reading the text, encouraging self-paced instruction.

■ **Web site.** The examples both within the book and at Addison-Wesley's Web site are intended to exhibit good programming style. The Addison-Wesley Web site for this book contains the programs in the book, as well as adjunct programs that illustrate points made in the book or flesh out short pieces of programs. The programs available at the Web site are introduced by their *.cpp* or *.h* names and can be obtained by referencing

www.awl.com/cseng/titles/0-201-39519-3/

My special thanks go to my wife, Debra Dolsberry, who encouraged me throughout this project. She acted as book designer and technical editor for this edition. She developed appropriate formats and style sheets in FrameMaker 5.5 and guided the transition process from my other books on C++. She also implemented and tested all major pieces of code.

This book was developed with the support of my editor, J. Carter Shanklin, and editorial assistant, Angela Buenning.

Ira Pohl
University of California, Santa Cruz

Chapter 1

An Overview of C++ and Object-Oriented Programming

This chapter gives a brief overview of C++ and provides an introduction to its use as an object-oriented programming language (OOP). Like the rest of the book, it assumes a knowledge of C. The chapter presents a series of programs of increasing complexity and carefully explains the elements of each; program examples in the later sections illustrate some of the concepts of object-oriented programming. This approach should give students or professional C programmers a sense of how C++ works. As an overview, this chapter makes use of advanced material that can be skimmed or skipped by readers who wish to begin with the elementary concepts found in the next chapter.

Each feature of C++ is explained briefly. The examples in this chapter give readers simple, immediate, hands-on experience with key features of the C++ language. The chapter introduces stream I/O, operator and function overloading, classes, constructors, destructors, and inheritance to give programmers the flavor of writing C++. Mastery of individual topics requires a thorough reading of the later chapters.

Object-oriented programming is today's programming methodology of choice. OOP is the product of 30 years of programming practice and experience, going back to Simula 67 and continuing with SmallTalk and, more recently, Eiffel, Java, and C++. The OOP programming style captures the behavior of the real world in a way that hides detailed implementation. When successful, OOP allows the problem solver to think in terms of the problem domain.

C++ was created by Bjarne Stroustrup in the mid-1980s. Stroustrup had two main goals: (1) to make C++ compatible with ordinary C and (2) to extend C with OOP constructs based on the class construct of Simula 67. C, developed by Dennis Ritchie in the early 1970s as a system-implementation language to build UNIX, gradually gained popularity not only as a system-implementation language, but also as a general-purpose language.

C programmers can readily use structured programming methodology, which involves writing large programs as a series of procedure calls on properly structured data. C has a limited form of data abstraction. The C struct declaration allows programmers to declare user-defined aggregates with understandable names. As a powerful extension of these concepts, the C++ `class` declaration provides strong typing, data hiding, and code reuse through inheritance. Also, C++ allows programming teams to program in the large, using the techniques of file encapsulation, function encapsulation, and class encapsulation. As a consequence, C++ can be used to teach modular-programming habits within the object-oriented paradigm.

1.1 Object-Oriented Programming

Object-oriented programming is a data-centered view of programming in that data and behavior are strongly linked. Data and behavior are conceived of as classes whose instances are objects. For example, a polynomial can have a range of legal values that can be affected by such operations as addition and multiplication.

OOP views computation as simulating behavior. What is simulated are objects represented by a computational abstraction. Suppose that we wish to improve our poker play; to do so, we must better understand the odds of obtaining various poker hands. We need to simulate card shuffling and must have appropriate ways to speak about cards and suits. Publicly, we use the suit names: spades, hearts, diamonds, and clubs. Privately, these suits are internally represented as integers. This internal choice is hidden and consequently should not affect our computation. Just as decks of cards can have many physical compositions and still properly behave as cards, so too can computational card decks.

We will be using the terms *abstract data type (ADT)* and *object-oriented programming (OOP)* to refer to a powerful new programming approach. An ADT is a user-defined extension to the existing types available in the language. An ADT consists of a set of values and a collection of operations that can act on those values. For example, C++ does not have a native complex number type but instead uses the class construct to define such a type in the *complex* library. *Objects* are class variables. Object-oriented programming allows ADTs to be easily created and used. OOP uses the mechanism of inheritance to conveniently derive a new type from an existing user-defined type. This mechanism is akin to biological taxonomies. For example, both rodents and cats are mammals; if the category mammal is an encoding of the information and behavior true for all objects in this class, creating the categories cat and rodent from the category mammal is an enormous saving.

In OOP, objects are responsible for their behavior. For example, polynomial objects, complex number objects, integer objects, and floating-point number objects can all be added. Each type has code for executing addition. The compiler provides the right code for integers and floating-point numbers. The polynomial ADT has a function defining addition specific to its implementation. The ADT provider should include code for any behavior the object can be commonly expected to understand. Making an object responsible for its behavior eases the coding task for the user of that object.

Consider a class of objects called shapes. If we want a shape to draw on a screen, we need to know where the shape is to be centered and how to draw. Some shapes, such as polygons, are relatively easy to draw. A general shape-drawing routine can be very expensive, requiring storage for a large number of individual boundary points. Avoiding this in the polygon case is clearly beneficial. If the individual shape object knows best how to draw itself, the programmer using such shapes needs only to invoke the object's drawing function.

The new class construct in C++ provides the *encapsulation* mechanism to implement ADTs. Encapsulation includes both the internal implementation details of a specific type and the externally available operations and functions that can act on objects of that type. The implementation details can be made inaccessible to code that uses the type. For example, a stack might be implemented as a fixed-length array, whereas the publicly available operations would include push and pop. Changing the internal implementation to a linked list should not affect how push and pop are used externally. Code that uses the ADT is called *client* code for the ADT. The implementation of a stack is hidden from its clients. The details of how to provide *data hiding* in classes are introduced here and are developed thoroughly in Chapter 4, "Classes," and in Chapter 8, "Inheritance."

1.2 Why Learn C++?

C++ supports the object-oriented programming style, a major advance over the structured programming style supported by such languages as C, Pascal, and FORTRAN. A chief cost is the increased complexity of the C++ language, however. C++ is a more complex language but better suited to developing large software projects.

C is a procedural, imperative language that has a small set of built-in types and limited forms of type extensibility. These types are well suited to system programming. For many problem domains, however, C's usefulness is hampered by its lack of type extensibility. C++ remedies these limitations by allowing arbitrary user-defined types. The increased complexity of C++ is one of its biggest drawbacks. Although this increase reflects the large number of necessary new ideas, it makes mastery more difficult. To overcome this problem, this book approaches the learning process by gradually transforming the C programmer into a practiced C++ programmer.

1.3 C as a Starting Point

C is the kernel language that C++ was built on. Indeed, most C programs are correct C++ programs as is; in some sense, the C programmer is therefore already a C++ programmer.

C++ is a marriage of the low level and the high level. C was designed to be a systems-implementation language, one close to the machine. C++ adds object-oriented features that are designed to allow a programmer to create or to import a library appropriate to the problem domain. The user can write code at the level appropriate to the problem while maintaining contact with the machine-level implementation details.

The following C program uses a function to perform simple output:

In file hello.c

```
/*     Hello World in C
 * by Charles Codeman
 */
#include <stdio.h>

void pr_message(char* message)
{
    printf("%s\n", message);
}

int main()
{
    pr_message("Hello world!");
}
```

Here is the equivalent C++ program:

In file hello1.cpp

```
//Hello world in C++
// by Olivia Programmer

#include <iostream>      //IO library
#include <string>        //string type
using namespace std;
```

```
inline void pr_message(string s = "Hello world!")
{ cout << s << endl; }

int main()
{
    pr_message();
}
```

When executed, this program prints the following message:

```
Hello world!
```

A C++ program is a collection of declarations and functions that begin executing with the function main(). The C++ program is compiled after the preprocessor executes #-designated directives. The preprocessor precedes the phase during which the compiler translates the resulting program into machine code. The #include directive found in the example program *hello1.cpp* imports any needed files, usually library definitions. In this case, the I/O library for a typical compiler system is found in the file *iostream*. The string type is found in the standard library defined in the file *string*. On new C++ systems, these files are wrapped in namespace std. The using declaration allows such names to be used without std:: prepended to each name. The include files could also have been coded without namespace and using, as follows:

```
#include <iostream.h>      //IO library
#include <string.h>        //C++ string type
```

This text will use the namespace convention for include files. In most instances, the inclusion of the header files will not be shown in program code.

The // symbol is used as a rest-of-line comment symbol. Also, the program text can be placed in any position on the page, with white space between tokens being ignored. White space, comments, and indentation of text are all used to create a humanly readable, well-documented program but do not affect program semantics.

An efficiency concern for the C++ programmer is that the inline modifier of the function pr_message() is used to tell the compiler to compile this function without resort to function call and return instructions, if possible. As written, the pr_message() function had a string parameter s, whose default value was "Hello world!". This means that when passed an empty or a void parameter list, pr_message("Hello world!") is executed.

The identifier cout is defined in *iostream* as the standard output stream connected by most C++ systems to the screen for output. The identifier endl is a standard *manipulator* that flushes the output buffer, printing everything to that point while going to a new line. The operator << is the put to output operator, which writes out what comes after it to cout.

A function in C++ has a return type that can be void, indicating that no value is to be returned, as is the case with pr_message(). The special function main() returns an integer value to the runtime system, which in the implicit case found here, is 0, meaning that termination was normal.

Consider the following variation to main():

In file hello2.cpp

```
int main()
{
    pr_message();
    pr_message("Laura Pohl");
    pr_message("It is dinner time.");
}
```

The program, when executed, prints the following message:

```
Hello world!
Laura Pohl
It is dinner time.
```

1.4 Classes and Abstract Data Types

OOP is a balanced approach to writing software. Data and behavior are packaged together. This encapsulation creates user-defined types, which extend and interact with the native types of the language. *Type extensibility* is the ability to add to the language user-defined types that are as easy to use as native types.

An abstract data type, such as a complex number, is a description of the ideal public behavior of the type. The user of a complex number knows that operations, such as add or print, result in certain public behaviors. Operations add and print are called *methods.* A concrete implementation of the ADT also has implementation limits; for example, complex numbers are limited in precision. These limits affect public behavior. Also, internal, or private, details of the implementation do not directly affect the user's understanding. For example, a complex number is frequently implemented as a set of two floating-point variables; their names should be of no direct consequence to the user.

Encapsulation is the ability to hide internal detail while providing a public interface to a user-defined type. C++ uses declarations class and struct in conjunction with the access keywords `private`, `protected`, and `public` to provide encapsulation. C does not have access modifiers, but its `struct` is the basis for the class extensions in C++.

OOP terminology is strongly influenced by SmallTalk programming. The SmallTalk designers wanted programmers to break with their past habits and to embrace a new programming methodology. They invented such terms as *message* and *method* to replace the traditional terms *function invocation* and *member function.*

Public members are available to any function within the scope of the class declaration. Public members provide the type's interface. Private members are available for use only by other member functions of the class. Privacy allows the implementation of a class type to be hidden, which prevents unanticipated modifications to the data structure. Restricted access, or data hiding, is a feature of object-oriented programming.

Let us write a class called `complex` that will implement a restricted form of complex number.

In file complex1.cpp

```
//An elementary implementation of type complex

class complex {
public:                         //universal access to interface
    void re_assign(double r) { real = r; }
    void im_assign(double im) { imaginary = im; }
    void print() const
        { cout << "(" << real << ","
                << imaginary << "i)" << endl; }
friend complex operator+(complex, complex);
private:                        //restricted access to implementation
    double real, imaginary;
};
```

The hidden representation is two variables of type `double`.

The declaration of member functions allows the ADT to have particular functions act on its private representation. For example, the member function `print()` outputs a complex number as a comma-separated pair of `double`s. The imaginary part of the number has the suffix `i`. The member function `re_assign()` stores the real part of a complex number into the hidden variable `real`, and the member function `im_assign()` stores the imaginary part of a complex number into the hidden variable `imaginary`. Member functions, such as `print()`, that do not modify member variables' values are declared `const`. The `friend` function `operator+()` declaration will be used later to implement the definition of the addition of two complex numbers (see Section 1.6, "Overloading," on page 11). The `friend` designation means that the function, although not a member of class `complex`, has access to all of its members.

We can now use the data type `complex` as if it were a basic type of the language. Code that uses this type is its *client*. The client can use only the public members to act on variables of type `complex`.

In file complex1.cpp

```
//Test of the class complex

int main()
{
    complex x, y, z;

    x.re_assign(9.5);
    x.im_assign(-4.5);
    y.re_assign(4.2);
    y.im_assign(6.0);
    z = x + y;
    x.print();
    y.print();
    z.print();
}
```

Variables x, y, and z are of type `complex`. The member functions are called using the dot, or *structure member*, operator. As is seen from their definitions, these member functions act on the hidden private-member fields of the named variables. The output of this example program is

```
(9.5,-4.5i)
(4.2,6i)
(13.7, 1.5i)
```

1.5 Constructors and Destructors

In OOP terminology, a variable is called an *object*. A *constructor* is a member function that *initializes* an object of its class. In many cases, this involves dynamic storage allocation. Constructors are invoked whenever an object of a particular class is created. A *destructor* is a member function that *finalizes* a variable of its class. As we shall see later, in many cases this involves dynamic storage deallocation. If you are not familiar with these concepts, you may want to skip this material for now and wait until the later chapters, where they are explained in detail.

Let's change our `complex` example by adding a constructor to initialize its value. We will also add a destructor to provide debugging output when a `complex` object is destroyed.

In file complex2.cpp

```
class complex {
public:
   //constructor
   complex(double r=0, double im=0): real(r), imaginary(im) { }
   //destructor
   ~complex() { cout << "destructor called on "; print(); }
   .....
};
```

A constructor's name is the same as the class name and is invoked when declaring variables, as in

```
complex  x(5.5, 1.0), y;
```

Here, the variables are declared and initialized: `x.real` is initialized as 5.5 and `x.imaginary` as 1.0; `y.real` is initialized as 0 and `y.imaginary` as 0. These are the default values of the arguments passed to the constructor.

A destructor is written as a member function whose name is the class name preceded by the tilde symbol ~. The destructor written in `complex` is used for debugging. The destructor calls `print()` to write out the value of the `complex` object being destroyed. For example, if x is not changed during execution, the destructor prints the following on exit from x's scope:

```
destructor called on (5.5,1i)
```

1.6 Overloading

Overloading is the practice of giving several meanings to an operator or a function. The meaning selected depends on the types of arguments used by the operator or the function. Let us overload the function `print()` in the previous example. This will be a second definition of the `print()` function.

In file complex1.cpp

```
class complex {
public:                         //universal access
   .....
   void  print(string var_name) const
      { cout << var_name << " = "; print(); }
   .....
}
```

This version of `print()` takes a single argument of type `string` and is used to print the complex number's variable name and value.

```
complex x(1.5,2);
x.print("x");              //print: x = (1.5,2i)
x.print();                 //print: (1.5,2i)
```

It is possible to overload most of the C++ operators. For example, we will overload + to mean complex addition. To do this, we need two keywords: `friend` and `operator`. The keyword `operator` precedes the operator token and replaces what would otherwise be a function name in a function declaration. The keyword `friend` gives a function access to the private members of a class variable. A `friend` function is not a member of the class but has the privileges of a member function in the class in which it is declared.

In file complex3.cpp

```cpp
complex operator+(complex x, complex y)
{
    complex t;

    t.real = x.real + y.real;
    t.imaginary = x.imaginary + y.imaginary;
    return t;
}

int main()
{
    complex x(9.5, -4.5), y(4.2,6.0), z;

    z = x + y;
    x.print("x");
    y.print("y");
    z.print("z");
}
```

◆◆◆◆◆◆◆◆◆◆◆◆

Dissection of the **operator+()** Function

■ `complex operator+(complex x, complex y)`

The + is overloaded. Both of its arguments are of type `complex`. The return type is `complex`, as expected.

■ `complex t;`

The function needs to return a value of type `complex`. This local variable is initialized to (0,0i) by the constructor.

■ `t.real = x.real + y.real;`
  `t.imaginary = x.imaginary + y.imaginary;`
  `return t;`

The definition adds both the real and the imaginary parts of the complex numbers and returns them as the `complex` variable t.

1.7 Inheritance

A singular concept in OOP is the promotion of code reuse through the *inheritance* mechanism. A new class is derived from an existing, or *base*, class. The derived class reuses the base-class members and can add to or alter them.

Many types are variants of one another, and it is frequently tedious and error prone to develop new code for each. A derived class inherits the description of the base class, thus avoiding redevelopment and testing of the existing code. The inheritance relationship is hierarchical. Hierarchy is a method for coping with complexity, imposing classifications on objects.

For example, the periodic table of elements has elements that are gases. These have properties that are shared by all elements in that classification. The inert gases are an important subclassification. The hierarchy is that an inert gas, such as argon, is a gas, which in turn is an element. The hierarchy provides a convenient way to understand the behavior of inert gases. We know that they are composed of protons and electrons, as this is shared description with all elements. We know that the inert gases are in a gaseous state at room temperature, as this behavior is shared with all gases. We know they do not combine in ordinary chemical reactions with other elements, as this is shared behavior of all inert gases.

As another example, consider designing a database for a college. The registrar must track various types of students. The base class must capture a description of student. Two main categories of student are graduate and undergraduate.

OOP Design Methodology

1. Decide on an appropriate set of types.

2. Design their relatedness into the code, using inheritance.

An example of deriving a class follows.

In file student1.cpp

```
enum support { ta, ra, fellowship, other };
enum year { fresh, soph, junior, senior, grad };
```

```
class student {
public:
   student(char* nm, int id, double g, year x);
   void  print() const;
private:
   int     student_id;
   double  gpa;
   year    y;
   char    name[30];
};

class grad_student : public student {
public:
   grad_student(char* nm, int id, double g,
                year x, support t, char* d, char* th);
   void print() const;
private:
   support  s;
   char     dept[10];
   char     thesis[80];
};
```

In this example, grad_student is the derived class, and student is the base class. The use of the keyword public following the colon in the derived-class header means that the public members of student are to be inherited as public members of grad_student. Private members of the base class cannot be accessed in the derived class. Public inheritance also means that the derived class grad_student is a subtype of student.

An inheritance structure provides a design for the overall system. For example, a database containing all of the people at a college could be derived from the base class person. The student base class could be used to derive law students as a further significant category of objects. Similarly, person could be the base class for a variety of employee categories. The hierarchical inheritance structure is illustrated in the following diagram.

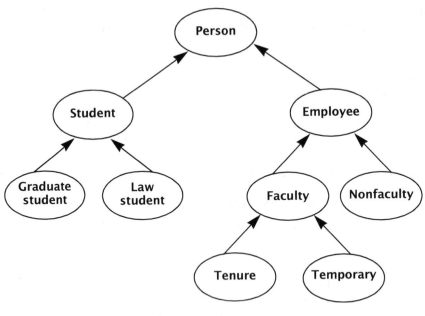

Inheritance Structure

1.8 Moving from C++ to Java

This section introduces Java I/O and classes, as well as Java's use as an object-oriented programming language. Mastery of the individual Java topics requires a thorough reading of a companion book such as *The Java Programming Language* by Arnold and Gosling.

Object-oriented programming is implemented by the class construct. The class construct in Java is based on the class construct in C++. The later examples in this book illustrate how Java implements OOP concepts, such as data hiding, ADTs, inheritance, and type hierarchies. Java, designed to be used on the World Wide Web, has special libraries for graphics and communication across the Net. Java is designed to run in a machine- and system-independent manner. This means that the Java program will execute with the same results on a PC running Windows 95 or on a workstation running Sun Solaris. Java does this by defining its semantics completely in terms of a virtual machine. The job for a system that wants to run Java is to port the virtual machine. This is a trade-off between portability and efficiency. Additional overhead in a machine running a simulator of a different architecture is inevitable. Some of this inefficiency can be overcome by the use of just-in-time compilers or native code written in C. On many platforms, it is also possible to use a direct-to-native code compiler for maximum runtime efficiency.

Programs must communicate to be useful. Our first example is a program that prints on the screen the phrase "Java is an improved C."

In file Improved.java

```java
// A first Java program illustrating output.
//    Title:  Improved
//    Author: Jack Appleteer

class Improved {
    public static void main (String[] args)
    {
        System.out.println("Java is an improved C.");
    }
}
```

The program prints the following on the screen:

```
Java is an improved C.
```

This program is compiled using the command *javac Improved.java*,, resulting in the creation of a code file named *Improved.class*. This file can be run by using the command *java Improved*.

Dissection of the *improved* Program

■ `// A first Java program illustrating output.`

The double slash // is the new symbol for a comment. The comment runs to the end of the line. The old C bracketing comment symbols /*   */ are still available for multiline comments. Java also provides /** */ bracketing comment symbols for a document comment. The program *javadoc* takes these document comments and generates an HTML file.

■ `class Improved {`

Java programs are classes. A `class` has syntactic form that is derived from the C `struct`, which is not in Java. In Java, class identifier names, such as `Improved`, are by convention capitalized. Data and code are placed within classes.

■ `public static void main (String[] args)`

A class executed as a program starts by calling the member function `main()`. In this case, `main()` is a member of `Improved`. In Java, command line arguments are passed in an array of `Strings`. In C, we need an `argc` variable to tell the program the number of command line arguments. In Java, this array length is found by using `args.length`.

■ `System.out.println("Java is an improved C.");`

This statement prints to the screen. The `System.out` object uses the member function `println()` to print. The function prints the string and adds a new line, which moves the screen cursor to the next line. Unlike `printf()` in C, `println()` does not use format controls.

In Java, all functions are contained in classes. In this case, the function `main()` is a member of `class Improved`. A member function is called a *method*.

1.9 Benefits of Object-Oriented Programming

The central element of OOP is the encapsulation of an appropriate set of data types and their operations. The class construct, with its member functions and data members, provides an appropriate coding tool. Class variables are the objects to be manipulated.

Classes also provide data hiding. Access privileges can be managed and limited to whatever group of functions needs access to implementation details. This promotes modularity and robustness.

Another important concept in OOP is the promotion of code reuse through the inheritance mechanism, which derives a new class from an existing, or base, class. The base class can be added to or altered to create the derived class. In this way, a hierarchy of related data types can be created that share code.

The OOP programming task is frequently more difficult than normal procedural programming as found in C. At least one extra design step is needed before one gets to the coding of algorithms. This step involves the design of types that are appropriate for the problem at hand. Frequently, one is solving the problem more generally than is strictly necessary. The belief is that this extra step will pay dividends in several ways. The solution will be more encapsulated and thus more robust and easier to maintain and change. It will also be more reusable. For example, where the code needs a stack, that stack is easily borrowed from existing code. In an ordinary procedural language, such a data structure is frequently "wired into" the algorithm and cannot be exported.

OOP is many things to many people. Attempts at defining it are reminiscent of the blind sages' attempts at describing the elephant. I will offer one more definition, an equation.

OOP = type-extensibility + polymorphism

1.10 Pragmatics

C++ compilers for ANSI C++ as described in this book are still incomplete. Make sure you know what the vendors support, especially when it comes to recent changes in the use of namespaces, exception handling, templates, and libraries, especially the Standard Template Library, or STL.

Revisiting our first example, we can make it compatible with pre-namespace and string library compilers by using char* for our strings and ordinary *.h* header files for including our libraries.

In file hello2.cpp

```
//Hello world in C++ by Older Fogie

#include <iostream.h>

inline void pr_message(char* s = "Hello world!")
{ cout << s << endl;}

int main()
{
   pr_message();
   return 0;
}
```

This version of the program should run correctly with any available compiler. Notice that we explicitly return 0, as we would in a C program. ANSI C++ allows this to be implicit, the style we will use throughout the book.

Summary

1. Object-oriented programming is a data-centered view of programming, meaning that data and behavior are strongly linked. Data and behavior are conceived of as classes whose instances are objects.

2. An *abstract data type (ADT)* is a user-defined extension to the existing types available in the language. An ADT consists of a set of values and a collection of operations that can act on those values. For example, C++ does not have a native complex number type but uses the class construct to define such a type in the *complex* library. *Objects* are class variables.

3. C++ supports the object-oriented programming style. This is a major advance over the structured programming style supported by such languages as C, Pascal, and FORTRAN. C is a procedural, imperative language with a small set of built-in types and limited forms of type extensibility. These types are well suited to system programming. However, for many problem domains, C's usefulness is hampered by its lack of type extensibility.

4. C is the kernel language of C++. C++ is a marriage of C and object-oriented features that are designed to allow a programmer to create or to import a library appropriate to the problem domain. The user can write code at the level appropriate to the problem while maintaining contact with the machine-level implementation details.

5. Encapsulation is the ability to hide internal detail while providing a public interface to a user-defined type. C++ uses the declarations `class` and `struct` in conjunction with the access keywords `private`, `protected`, and `public` to provide encapsulation. C does not have access modifiers, but its `struct` is the basis for the class extensions in C++.

6. In OOP terminology, a variable is called an *object.* A *constructor* is a member function that *initializes* an object of its class. In many cases, this involves dynamic storage allocation. Constructors are invoked whenever an object of a particular class is created. A *destructor* is a member function that *finalizes* a variable of its class.

7. A singular concept in OOP is the promotion of code reuse through the *inheritance* mechanism. A new class is derived from an existing, or *base*, class. The derived class reuses the base-class members and can add to or alter them. The inheritance relationship is hierarchical. Hierarchy, a method for coping with complexity, imposes classifications on objects.

8. Java is an OOP language that also derives from C and C++. It is relatively easy to convert C++ programs to Java. Java is more portable but runs slower than C or C++. Java was developed at a time when the Internet started to flourish and has many features tailored to use on the Internet.

Review Questions

1. Name three object-oriented programming languages.

2. The I/O library in C++ is used by including _____.

3. The rest-of-line comment symbol is _____.

4. The C++ class is an extension of the C _____.

5. C was originally a SIL (systems-implementation language) used to write _____.

6. What does the construct `inline` do?

7. C++ was created by _____ in the mid-1980s.

8. Access keywords are _____, _____, and _____.

Exercises

1. Using stream I/O, write on the screen the words

   `she sells seashells by the seashore`

   (a) all on one line, (b) on three lines, (c) inside a box.

2. Take a working program, omit each line in turn, and run the program through the compiler. Record the error message caused by each deletion. For example, use the following code:

```
#include <iostream>
using namespace std;

main()
{
    int  m, n, k;

    cout << "\nEnter two integers:";
    cin  >> m >> n;
    k = m + n;
    cout << "\nTheir sum is "<< k << ".\n";
}
```

3. Write a program that converts distances measured in yards to distances measured in meters. The relationship is 1 meter equals 1.0936 yards. Write the program to use `cin` to read in distances. The program should be a loop that does this calculation until it receives 0 or a negative number for input. In the previous exercise, we used `cin` and the overloaded operator `>>`, which together replace `scanf()` in C. For example, `cin >> v` is the C++ equivalent to `scanf("%type", &v)`. See Section D.4, "The Input Class `istream`," on page 420, for more information on input in C++.

4. Write a program that interactively asks for your name and age and responds with

```
Hello name, next year you will be next_age.
```

where *next_age* is `age` + 1.

5. Write a program that prints out a table of squares, square roots, and cubes. Use either tabbing or strings of blanks to get a neatly aligned table.

```
i      i * i     square root     i * i * i
-------------------------------------------
1         1    1.00000                  1
. . . . .
```

6. Write a `class person` that contains basic information, such as name, birthdate, and address. Derive `class student` from `class person`. (See Section 1.7, "Inheritance," on page 12.)

7. (S. Clamage) The following three programs behave differently. We start with

```
//Function declarations at file scope

int f(int):

double f(double);          //overloads f(int) double add f()
{
    return(f(1) + f(1.0));       //f(int) + f(double)
}
```

We place one function declaration internally.

```
//Function declaration at local scope

int f(int);
double add f()
{
    double f(double);           //hides f(int)
    return(f(1) + f(1.0));      //f(double) + f(double)
}
```

Now we place the other function declaration internally.

```
double f(double);
double add f()
{
    int f(int);
    return(f(1) + f(1.0));      //What is called here?
}
```

Write some test programs that clearly show the different behaviors.

Chapter 2
Native Types and Statements

This chapter, together with Chapter 3, "Functions, Pointers, and Arrays," will provide an introduction to programming in C++ using its *native types* and its nonOOP features. Since C++ is based on the C language, much of this material is a review of C. A native type is one provided by the language directly. In C++, this includes the simple types, such as character types, integer types, floating-point types, and the boolean type, as well as derived types, such as array types, pointer types, and structure types, which are aggregates of the simple types. This chapter focuses on the native simple data types and statements.

The intent of this chapter, Chapter 3, "Functions, Pointers, and Arrays," and parts of Chapter 4, "Classes," is to enable programmers to program in that subset of C++ that approximates a traditional imperative language, such as C, Pascal, or FORTRAN. This subset is what we are calling the *kernel language*. The improvements to C in the kernel language of C++ are useful enough to prefer C++ over C, even for traditional programming. These enhancements lead to C++ as a better C, independent of the more extensive additional object-oriented features. These chapters also contain examples that will be used throughout the book.

An important feature of OOP is type extensibility, or the ability within the programming language to develop new types suitable to a problem domain. For this extensibility to work properly, the new type should work like the native types of the kernel language. Object-oriented design of user-defined types should mimic the look and feel of the native types.

For the experienced C programmer, most of this chapter's material should be skimmed and read mainly with an eye for differences between C and C++. These differences will be listed in the chapter summary, which the experienced C programmer can use to determine what to selectively read about. For a programmer coming from another language, such as Java or Pascal, or for some C programmers needing a review of C material, this chapter and the next two succinctly review the C++ kernel language.

2.1 Program Elements

A program is composed of elements called *tokens*, which are collections of characters that form the basic vocabulary the compiler recognizes. The C++ character set includes the following:

```
a b c d e f g h i j k l m n o p q r s t u v w x y z
A B C D E F G H I J K L M N O P Q R S T U V W X Y Z
0 1 2 3 4 5 6 7 8 9
+ = _ - () * & % $ # ! | <> . , ; : " ' / ? { } ~ \ [ ] ^
```
white space and nonprinting characters, such as newline, tab, and blank

In C++, tokens can be interspersed with white space and with comment text that is inserted for readability and documentation. There are five kinds of tokens: keywords, identifiers, literals, operators, and punctuators. See Section C.2, "Lexical Elements," on page 348.

C++ distinguishes between upper- and lowercase. As we shall see, C++ uses lowercase in its keyword list.

2.1.1 Comments

C++ has a single-line comment, written as // *rest of line*. This convention has been adopted in many C compilers as well.

```
//C++ for C Programmers - Example 2
#include <vector>     //vector is in STL
```

As in C, a multiline comment is written as /* *possibly multiline comment**/. Everything between /* and */ is a comment. Comments do not nest.

```
/*  Multiline Comments are Frequently Introductory
    Programmer:  Laura Pohl
    Date:        January 1, 1989
    Version:     DJD v4.2
*/
```

2.1.2 Keywords

Keywords in C++ are explicitly reserved words that have a strict meaning and may not be used in any other way. They include words used for type declarations, such as int, char, and float; words used for statement syntax, such as do, for, and if; and words used for access control, such as public, protected, and private. The following table shows the keywords in use in most current C++ systems. Keywords that did not exist in C are bolded.

Keywords			
asm	else	**operator**	**throw**
auto	enum	**private**	**true**
bool	**explicit**	**protected**	**try**
break	extern	**public**	typedef
case	**false**	register	**typeid**
catch	float	**reinterpret_cast**	**typename**
char	for	return	union
class	**friend**	short	unsigned
const	goto	signed	**using**
const_cast	if	sizeof	**virtual**
continue	**inline**	static	void
default	int	**static_cast**	volatile
delete	long	struct	**wchar_t**
do	**mutable**	switch	while
double	**namespace**	**template**	
dynamic_cast	**new**	**this**	

2.1.3 Identifiers

As in C, an identifier in C++ is a sequence of letters, digits, and underscores. An identifier cannot begin with a digit. Uppercase and lowercase letters are treated as distinct. It is bad practice and confusing to use identifiers that are distinguished only by case differences. Although in principle, identifiers can be arbitrarily long, many systems will distinguish only up to the first 31 characters. Some examples of identifiers are as follow:

```
n                //typically an integer variable
count            //meaningful as documentation
buff_size        //C++ style - underscore separates words
buffSize         //Java style - capital separates words
q2345            //obscure
cout             //used in the standard library iostream
_foo             //avoid underscore as a first letter
```

The following are not identifiers:

```
for              //keyword
3q               //cannot start with digit
-count           //do not mistake - for _
too__bad         //double underscore is for system use
_Sysfoo          //underscore capital is for system use
```

2.1.4 Literals

Literals are constant values, such as 1 or 3.14159. There are literals for each C++
data type. String literals are also allowed. Some examples of literals follow.

```
5                //an integer literal
5u               //u or U specifies unsigned
5L               //l or L specifies long
05               //an integer literal written as octal
0x5              //an integer literal written as hexadecimal
true             //a bool literal
5.0              //a floating-point literal treated as double
5.0F             //f or F float - typically single precision
5.0L             //l or L specifies long double
'5'              //a character literal - ASCII value 53
'A'              //letter capital A - ASCII value 65
'a'              //letter small a - ASCII value 97
'\0'             //the null character - terminates strings
'\t'             //the character printing a tab space
'\n'             //the character printing a new line
"5"              //the string consisting of the character '5'
"a string with newline\n"
5555555555555555  //integer too large on most machines
```

String literals are stored as a series of characters terminated with the null
character, whose value is 0. String literals are static char[] constants. Special

characters can be represented inside strings by escaping them with the backslash character \.

```
"a"          //two bytes storing 'a' '\0'
"a\tb\n"     //five bytes 'a' '\t' 'b' '\n' '\0'
"1 \\"       //four bytes '1' ' ' '\\' '\0'
"\""         //two bytes '"' '\0'
```

When printed, these strings would produce effects required by the special characters. Thus, the second string prints an a followed by a number of white-space characters as determined by the tab setting, then a b followed by a newline character.

String literals that are separated only by white space are implicitly concatenated into a single string.

```
"This is a single string, "
"since it is separated only "
"by white space."
```

The character literals are usually given as *symbol.* Some nonprinting and special characters require an escape sequence.

Character Constants	
`'\a'`	alert
`'\\'`	backslash
`'\b'`	backspace
`'\r'`	carriage return
`'\"'`	double quote
`'\f'`	formfeed
`'\t'`	tab
`'\n'`	newline
`'\0'`	null character
`'\''`	single quote
`'\v'`	vertical tab
`'\101'`	octal 101 in ASCII 'A'
`'\x041'`	hexadecimal ASCII 'A'
`L'00'`	wchar_t constant

Floating-point literals can be specified either with or without signed integer exponents.

```
0.1234567              //double constant - the default
3.14f  1.234F          //float constant - smallest fp type
0.123456789L           //long double - either l or L
3.  3.0  0.3E1         //all express double 3.0
300e-2                 //also 3.0
```

2.1.5 Operators and Punctuators

C++, like C, allows operators, punctuators, and white space to separate language elements. C++ gives special meaning to many characters and character sequences. Examples of C++ operators include:

```
+ - * / %              //arithmetic operators
->   ->*               //pointer & pointer-to-member operators
&&     ||              //logical operators
=  +=  *=              //assignment operators
::                     //scope resolution operator
new   delete           //free-store operators
```

Operators are used in expressions and are meaningful when given appropriate arguments. C++ has many operators (see Appendix B, "Operator Precedence and Associativity"). Certain symbols stand for different operators, depending on context; for instance, "–" can be either unary or binary minus. C operators are all available in C++, but C++ has operators that are not found in C, such as the scope resolution operator ::.

Punctuators include parentheses, braces, commas, and colons and are used to structure elements of a program. For example, the following are punctuators in C++:

```
foo(a, 7, b + 8)       //comma-separated argument list
{ a = b; c = d; }      //{ starts statement list or block
```

2.2 Input/Output

C++ input/output is not directly part of the language but rather is added as a set of types and routines found in a standard library. The C++ standard I/O library is *iostream* or *iostream.h*. The file name without the *.h* extension is the official ANSI standard name and is used with the `namespace std`. The ANSI C standard library *stdio.h* or *cstdio* is also in widespread use. The ANSI standard libraries that are C libraries are officially *c* followed by their names without a *.h* extension. We will use *iostream* because we are illustrating current practice. (We leave to Appendix D, "Input/Output," a more complete description of this and other I/O issues.) This section is introductory, intended to give the bare minimum of detail to get the reader up and running.

The *iostream* library overloads the two bit-shift operators.

```
<<          //"put to" output stream, normally left shift
>>          //"get from" input stream, normally right shift
```

This library also declares three standard streams:

```
cout        //standard out
cin         //standard in
cerr        //standard error
```

Their use in conjunction with values and variables is analogous to assignment. C++ can use existing C library functions, such as `printf()` and `scanf()`, but the *iostream* library is type safe and easier to use. It is type safe because in the expression `cout << x`, the type of the variable x determines how it is to be printed. Therefore, one cannot make the annoying formatting mismatch errors found in C, where with `printf("%format", x)`, the expression value x can be printed incorrectly when the format is mismatched.

In file io.cpp

```
cout << "\nEnter a double: ";
cin >> x;
cout << "\nEnter a positive integer: ";
cin >> i;
if (i < 1)
   cerr << "error i = " << i << endl;
cout << "i * x = " << i * x;
```

The first output statement in the preceding code places a string on the screen. The second statement expects the `double` variable x to get a value converted from string input typed at the keyboard. The string represents a value that is either a `double` or assignment convertible to a `double`. Other typed input will fail. Notice how the last two statements allow multiple assignments to their output streams and are executed left to right. For example, if i had received a value of –1, the error message on the screen would be

```
error i = -1
```

The `endl` is a specially recognized identifier, called a *manipulator*, that flushes the `cerr` output stream and adds a newline character. The last statement prints the string i * x = , followed by the `double` value of the expression i * x.

2.3 Program Structure

A *program* in C++ is a collection of functions and declarations. The language is block structured, and variables declared within blocks are allocated automatically on block entry. Unless otherwise specified, parameters are call-by-value. The following C++ program computes the greatest common divisor of two integers:

In file gcd.cpp

```
//GCD greatest common devisor program.
#include <iostream>
using namespace std;

int gcd(int m, int n)       //function definition
{                           //block
   int   r;                 //declaration of remainder

   while (n != 0) {         //not equal
      r = m % n;            //modulus operator
      m = n;                //assignment
      n = r;
   }                        //end while loop
   return m;                //exit gcd with value m
}
```

```
int main()
{
   int  x, y, g;

   cout << "\nPROGRAM Gcd C++";
   do {
      cout << "\nEnter two integers: ";
      cin >> x >> y;
      if (x * y == 0)
         throw new exception();
      cout << "\nGCD(" << x << ", " << y << ") = "
           << (g = gcd(x, y)) << endl;
   } while (x != y);
}
```

As you can see, C++ is very terse. C++ compilers can compile multifile programs. Large C++ programs are prepared as separate files. Each file is conceptually a module that contains related program declarations and definitions. On many systems, C++ source files have the suffix either *.c* or *.cpp*. The GNU C++ translator command is *g++*. So,

   g++ module1.c module2.c my_main.c

is the UNIX C++ compile command *g++*, acting on the three files *module1.c*, *module2.c*, and *my_main.c*. If compilation shows no errors, an executable *a.out* is produced.

Some minor differences from C are easily seen in this C++ version of the greatest common divisor program.

Some Differences Between C++ and C

- The C++ comment symbols are either // or /* */ .

- C++ uses *iostream* for input/output.

- C++ uses namespace std to avoid name collisions among global variables.

- The function main(), used as the starting point for the program's execution, obeys the C++ rules for function declaration. It is ANSI C++ for main() to implicitly return the integer value 0, indicating that the program completed normally. Other return values would indicate an error condition.

- C++ has exceptions. Here, it used a throw for termination on finding errors.

2.4 Simple Types

The *simple native types* in C++ are `bool`, `int`, `double`, `char`, and `wchar_t`. These types have a set of values and representation that is tied to the underlying machine architecture on which the compiler is running. Both the `bool` and the `wchar_t` types are new to C++. The `bool` type provides a native boolean type, and `wchar_t` provides a wide character type, used for representing character sets requiring more than the standard 255 characters. On older C++ systems, as in C, there is no native boolean type. They use the value zero to mean false and nonzero values to mean true.

The `complex` number type in C++ is provided by including the library *complex*. This library provides the nonnative type `complex`, which can be used with the various ordinary arithmetic operators and mixed in expression with other arithmetic types.

C++ simple types can often be modified by the keywords `short`, `long`, `signed`, and `unsigned` to yield further simple types. The following table lists these types shortest to longest. Length here refers to the number of bytes used to store the type. The bolded types are not available in C.

Fundamental Data Types		
bool		
char	signed char	unsigned char
wchar_t		
short	int	long
unsigned short	unsigned	unsigned long
float	double	long double

This list runs from the conceptually shortest type, `bool`, to the conceptually longest type, `long double`. A requirement is that each longer type be at least as long as its predecessor type. On most machines, a `bool` or a `char` is stored in a single byte. On many PCs, `short` and `int` are stored in 2 bytes, whereas `long`, `float`, and `double` are each stored in 4 bytes. The `wchar_t`, or wide character type, can represent distinct codes for any element of the largest extended character set in any language's alphabet, such as Katakana used in Japanese. A `wchar_t` type is the same size as an `int` type.

C++ also has the `sizeof` operator, which is used to determine the number of bytes a particular object or type requires for storage.

```
//determine how many bytes it takes to store type long
cout << sizeof(int) << " <= " << sizeof(long) << endl;
```

The range of integral values representable on your system is defined in the standard header file *limits*. Some examples from our system are

```
#define CHAR_BIT 8                  //bits per char
#define SCHAR_MIN (-128)            //signed char minimum
#define SCHAR_MAX 127               //signed char maximum
#define UCHAR_MAX 255               //unsigned char maximum
#define INT_MAX 2147483647          //int maximum
#define INT_MIN (-2147483648)       //int minimum
#define UINT_MAX 4294967295U        //unsigned int maximum
```

The range of floating-point values representable on your system is defined in the standard header file *float*. Some examples from our system are

```
#define FLT_EPSILON ((float)1.19209290e-07)   //single
#define FLT_MIN ((float)1.17549435e-38)       //float min
#define FLT_MAX ((float)3.40282347e+38)       //float max
#define DBL_EPSILON 2.2204460492503131e-16    //double
#define DBL_MIN 2.2250738585072014e-308       //double min
#define DBL_MAX 1.7976931348623157e+308       //double max
```

On newer systems, the file *limits* contains the template `numeric_limits`, which allows, for example,

```
numeric_limits<type>::max()         //maximum value for type
```

2.4.1 Initialization

A variable declaration associates a type with the variable name. A declaration of a variable constitutes a definition, if storage is allocated for it. Informally, we think of the definition as creating the object.

A definition can also initialize the value of the variable. Syntactically, initialization is expressed by following the identifier name with an initializer. For simple variables, this is usually

type id = expression

Some examples of definitions are

```
{
    int     i = 5;                  //i is initialized to 5
    char    c1, c2 = 'B';           //c1 is uninitialized
    double  x = 0.777, y = x + i;

    cout << x << '\t' << y;         //print 0.777 5.777
    cout << c2;                     //print 'B'
    cout << c1;                     //system dependent
    . . . . .
}
```

Initialization can involve an arbitrary expression, provided that all of the variables and functions used in the expression are defined. In the preceding example, y is initialized in terms of the just-defined x. The uninitialized variable c1 cannot be relied on to have any particular value associated with it. Using it in the computation before a well-defined value is assigned to it is a mistake. As a rule of thumb, when there is a choice, it is preferable to initialize a variable than to define it as uninitialized and to subsequently assign it a value. Initialization makes the code more readable, less error prone, and more efficient.

Note that C++ declarations are themselves statements and can occur intermixed with executable statements. This differs from C, in which declarations are either in global scope or at the head of a block. In the previous code, we could have placed the char declarations after the first cout statement without affecting the output.

```
    . . . . .
    cout << x << '\t' << y;         //print 0.777 5.777
    char    c1, c2 = 'B';           //declaration statement
    cout << c2;                     //print 'B'
    . . . . .
```

2.5 The Traditional Conversions

The expression x + y has both a value and a type. For example, if x and y are both variables of type int, x + y is also an int. However, if x and y are of different types, x + y is a *mixed expression*. Suppose that x is a short and y an int. The value of x is converted, or *coerced*, to an int, and the expression x + y has type int. The value of x as stored in memory is unchanged. It is only a temporary copy of x that is converted during the computation of the value of the expression. Now suppose that both x and y are of type short. Even though x + y is not a mixed expression, automatic conversions again take place; both x and y are promoted to int, and the expression is of type int. The general rules are straightforward.

Automatic Expression Conversions

1. Any bool, char, short, or enum is promoted to int. Integral values unrepresentable as int are promoted to unsigned.

2. If, after the first step, the expression is of mixed type, the following applies, according to the hierarchy of types:

```
int <  unsigned <  long    <  unsigned long
    <  float     <  double <  long double
```

The operand of the lower type is promoted to that of the higher type, and the value of the expression has that type.

To illustrate implicit conversion, we make the following declarations and list a variety of mixed expressions along with their corresponding types:

Declarations			
char c; long lg; double d;			
short s; float f; unsigned u; int i;			
Expression	**Type**	**Expression**	**Type**
c - s / i	int	u * 3 - i	unsigned
u * 3.0 - i	double	f * 3 - i	float
c + 1	int	3 * s * lg	long
c + 1.0	double	d + s	double

An automatic conversion can occur with an assignment. For example, d = i causes the value of i, which is an int, to be converted to a double and then assigned to d; double is the type of the expression as a whole. A promotion, or *widening*, such as d = i, will usually be well behaved, but a demotion, or *narrowing*, such as i = d, can lose information. Here, the fractional part of d will be discarded.

In addition to implicit conversions, which can occur across assignments and in mixed expressions, there are explicit conversions, called *casts*. If i is an int,

```
static_cast<double>(i)
```

will cast the value of i so that the expression has type double. The variable i itself remains unchanged. The static_cast is available for a conversion that is well defined, portable, and invertible. This makes it a safe cast, namely, one with predictable and portable behavior. Some more examples are

```
static_cast<char>('A' + 1.0)
x = static_cast<double>(static_cast<int>(y) + 1)
```

Casts that are representation or system dependent use reinterpret_cast.

```
i = reinterpret_cast<int>(&x)    //system dependent
```

These casts are undesirable and generally should be avoided. They are considered unsafe.

Two other special casts exist in C++: const_cast and dynamic_cast. A useful discussion of dynamic_cast requires understanding inheritance (see Section 8.8, "Runtime Type Identification," on page 295). The const modifier means that a variable's value is nonmodifiable. Very occasionally, it is convenient to remove this restriction. Doing so is known as *casting away constness* and is accomplished with the const_cast, as in

```
foo(const_cast<int>(c_var));    //used to invoke foo
```

Older C++ systems allow an unrestricted form of cast with the following forms:

(*type*) *expression*   or   *type*(*expression*)

Some examples are

```
y = i / double(7);                //would do division in double
ptr = (char*)(i + 88);            //C style int to pointer value
```

The C cast notation (*type*) is considered obsolete and will not be used in the text. The older casts do not differentiate among relatively safe casts, such as static_cast, and system-dependent unsafe casts, such as reinterpret_cast. The newer casts also are self-documenting; for example, a const_cast suggests its intent through its name.

The next program converts miles to kilometers. Miles will be kept as an integer value, and kilometers will be computed in floating point.

In file mi_to_k.cpp

```
//Miles are converted to kilometers

const double  m_to_k = 1.609;    //conversion constant

inline double  mi_to_km(int miles)
{
    return miles * m_to_k;
}

int main()
{
    int  miles;
    double kilometers;

    do {
        cout << "\nEnter distance in miles: ";
        cin >> miles;
        kilometers = mi_to_km(miles);
        cout << "\nThis is approximately " <<
            static_cast<int>(kilometers) << "km." << endl;
    } while (miles > 0);
}
```

This program consists of two functions, each of which has its own local scope in which variables are declared. Each variable has a type. The variable m_to_k is initialized to the value 1.609, and the const modifier ensures that this value is nonmodifiable. This is good programming practice in that the identifier is mnemonic and provides useful documentation. Notice that such a const variable must be initialized on definition. Where the inline keyword modifies a function definition, it suggests to the compiler that when invoked, the code defining it avoid function call by being compiled inline.

The expression miles * m_to_k is widened to a double. Conceptually, the integer valued miles is a narrower type than a double. The input statement cin >> miles expects keyboard input in the form of a string convertible to an integer. For example, the input 5.45 will be converted and assigned to miles as the integer value 5.

The safe cast static_cast<int>(kilometers) truncates the double value to an int value. Without this explicit cast, the variable kilometers would have printed as a double.

2.6 Enumeration Types

The keyword enum is used to declare a distinct integer type with a set of named integer constants called *enumerators*. Consider the declaration

```
enum suit { clubs, diamonds, hearts, spades };
```

This declaration creates an integer type with the four suit names as named integer constants. The enumerators are the identifiers clubs, diamonds, hearts, and spades, whose values are 0, 1, 2, and 3, respectively. These values are assigned by default, with the first enumerator being given the constant integer value 0. Each subsequent member of the list is one more than its left neighbor. In C++, the identifier suit is now its own unique type, distinct from other integer types. This identifier is called *tag name*.

Enumerators can be defined and initialized to arbitrary integer constants.

```
enum ages { laura = 7, ira, harold = 59, philip = harold + 7 };
```

The enumerators can be initialized to constant expressions. Note that the default rule applies when there is no explicit initializer; therefore, in the example, ira is 8.

The tag name and the enumerators must be distinct identifiers within scope. The values of enumerators need not be distinct. Enumerations can be implicitly converted to ordinary integer types but not vice versa.

In file enum_tst.cpp

```
enum signal { off, on } a = on; //a initialized to on
enum answer { no, yes, maybe = -1 } b;
enum neg { no, off} c;             //illegal no and off redeclared
int  i, j = on;                    //legal on is converted to 1

a = off;                           //legal
i = a;                             //legal i becomes 1
b = a;                             //illegal two distinct types
b = static_cast<answer>(a);        //legal explicit cast
b = (a ? no : yes);                //legal enumerators type answers
```

Enumerators can be declared *anonymously*, without a tag name. Some examples are

```
enum { LB = 0, UB = 99 };
enum { lazy, hazy, crazy } why;
```

The first declaration is a common means of declaring mnemonic integer constants. The second declares a variable why of enumerated type, with lazy, hazy, and crazy as its allowable values.

2.6.1 **typedef** Declarations

Synonyms for type declarations can be provided with typedef declarations.

```
typedef int   miles;       //miles a synonym for int
typedef char* cstring;     //pointer to char
typedef void* gen_ptr;     //generic pointer type
typedef point* pPoint;     //pointer to point
```

Besides providing a form of documentation, typedef declarations reduce complicated declarations to simple identifiers. In C, we would use a typedef such as

```
typedef enum suit suit;
```

to avoid the further need to use the keyword enum in subsequent declarations. This is unneeded in C++. Consequently, the use of typdef to provide synonyms for types is rarely used in C++.

2.7 Expressions

C++ has a few more operators and expression forms than does C (see Appendix B, "Operator Precedence and Associativity"). In C++, for example, scope resolution : : is an operator. The following is legal C++:

```
a = ::b ;                  //::b means global b
```

Arithmetic expressions in C++ are consistent with C practice. For example, in both C++ and C, the results of an operator such as the division operator /, depend on its argument types.

```
a = 3 / 2;          //evaluates to integer value 1;
a = 3 / 2.0;        //evaluates to double value 1.5
```

C++ systems use the `bool` values `true` and `false` to direct the flow of control in the various statement types. These values are equivalent to the *nonzero* and *zero* values used in C. The following table contains the C++ operators that are most often used to affect flow of control.

C++ Relational, Equality, and Logical Operators		
Relational operators	less than	<
	greater than	>
	less than or equal to	<=
	greater than or equal to	>=
Equality operators	equal	==
	not equal	!=
Logical operators	(unary) negation	!
	logical and	&&
	logical or	||

Just as with other operators, the relational, equality, and logical operators have rules of precedence and associativity that determine precisely how expressions involving them are evaluated (see Appendix B, "Operator Precedence and Associativity"). The negation operator ! is unary. All of the other relational, equality, and logical operators are binary, operate on expressions, and yield the `bool` value, either `false` or `true`. This replaces the earlier C convention of treating zero as false and nonzero as true when no `bool` type existed in the language. Where a boolean value is expected, an arithmetic expression is automatically converted, following this convention of treating zero as false and nonzero as true. This means that older code still works correctly.

One pitfall in C++ is that the equality operator and the assignment operator are visually similar. The expression a == b is a test for equality, whereas a = b is an assignment expression. One of the more common C++ programming mistakes is to code something like

```
if (i = 1)
    //do something
```

intending

```
if (i == 1)
    //do something
```

The first `if` statement assigns 1 to `i` and evaluates to 1, so it is always true. This error can be very difficult to find.

The logical operators !, &&, and ||, when applied to expressions, yield the `bool` value `true` or `false`. Logical negation can be applied to an arbitrary expression. If an expression has value `false`, its negation will yield `true`.

The precedence of && is higher than ||, but both operators are of lower precedence than all unary, arithmetic, and relational operators. Their associativity is left to right.

In the evaluation of expressions that are the operands of && and ||, the evaluation process stops as soon as the outcome true or false is known. This is called *short-circuit* evaluation. For example, suppose that *expr1* and *expr2* are expressions and that *expr1* has value `false`.

expr1 && *expr2*

The expression *expr2* will not be evaluated, because the value of the logical expression is already determined to be false. Similarly, if *expr1* is `true`, then *expr2* in

expr1 || *expr2*

will not be evaluated, because the value of the logical expression is already determined to be 1.

The following table shows some examples in C++.

Declarations and Initialization		
int a = 1, b = 2, c = 0;		
C++	Parenthesized Equivalent	Value
a + 5 && b	((a + 5) && b)	true
!(a < b) && c	((!(a < b)) && c)	false
(a == b) || c	((a == b)|| c)	false

Of all the operators in C++, the comma has the lowest precedence. It is a binary operator with expressions as operands. In a comma expression of the form

    expr1 , *expr2*

expr1 is evaluated first, then *expr2*. The comma expression as a whole has the value and type of its right operand. For example, in

    `sum = 0, i = 1`

if `i` has been declared an `int`, this comma expression has value 1 and type `int`.

The comma operator typically is used in the control expression part of an iterative statement, when more than one action is required. The comma operator associates from left to right.

The conditional operator `?:` is unusual in that it is a ternary operator. Thus, it takes as operands three expressions.

    expr1 ? *expr2* : *expr3*

In this construct, *expr1* is evaluated first. If it is `true`, then *expr2* is evaluated and that is the value of the conditional expression as a whole. If *expr1* is `false`, *expr3* is evaluated, and that is the value of the conditional expression as a whole.

The following example uses a conditional operator to assign the smaller of two values to the variable `x`:

    `x = (y < z) ? y : z;`

The parentheses are not necessary, because the conditional operator has precedence over the assignment operator. However, parentheses are good style because they make clear what is being tested for.

The type of the conditional expression

    expr1 ? *expr2* : *expr3*

is determined by *expr2* and *expr3*. If they are different types, the usual conversion rules apply. The conditional expression's type cannot depend on which of the two expressions *expr2* or *expr3* is evaluated. The conditional operator `?:` associates right to left.

C++ provides bit-manipulation operators, which operate on the machine-dependent bit representation of integral operands. For example, the operand `~` changes an integral operand bit representation into its one's complement. These operators can be ignored by programmers not interested in manipulating the underlying bit representation of integral values.

Bitwise Operators	Meaning
~	unary one's complement
<<	left shift
>>	right shift
&	and
^	exclusive or
|	or

In C++, we overload the shift operators to perform I/O.

C++ considers *function call* () and *indexing* or *subscripting* [] to be operators. C++ also has an *address &* operation and an *indirection **, or *dereferencing*, operation. The address operator is a unary operator that yields the address, or location, where an object is stored. The indirection operator is a unary operator that is applied to a pointer that retrieves the value from the location being pointed at. This operation is also known as dereferencing (see Section 3.11.1, "Addressing and Dereferencing," on page 83).

C++ also has a sizeof operator, which is used to determine the number of bytes a particular object or type requires for storage. This operator is important for obtaining an appropriate amount of storage for dynamically allocated objects.

2.8 Statements

C++ uses the semicolon as a statement terminator. C++ has a large variety of statement types, including an expression statement. For example, the assignment statement in C++ is syntactically an assignment expression followed by a semicolon. C++ and C both have assignment statements, procedure statements, transfer statements, conditional statements, selection statements, and iterative statements. A key difference is that C++ treats declarations as statements, allowing them to be most anywhere in blocks, but C allows declarations only at the head of blocks, before executable statements. In C++, declarations can also occur in the initializer part of the for loop. (Much of this material is review and may be skipped by the practiced C programmer.)

2.8.1 Assignment and Expressions

In C++, assignment occurs as part of an assignment expression, which can occur in several forms.

    a = b + 1;

This expression evaluates the right-hand side of the assignment and converts it to a value compatible with the variable on the left-hand side. This value is assigned to the left-hand side. The left-hand side must be an *lvalue*, a location in memory where a value can be stored or retrieved. Simple variables are lvalues.

C++ allows multiple assignment in a single statement.

    a = b + (c = 3);

C++ provides assignment operators that combine an assignment and some other operator.

    a += b;   is equivalent to   a = a + b;
    a *= a + b;   is equivalent to   a = a * (a + b);

C++ also provides autoincrement (++) and autodecrement (--) operators in both prefix and postfix form. In prefix form, the autoincrement operator adds 1 to the value stored at the lvalue it acts on. Similarly, the autodecrement operator subtracts 1 from the value stored at the lvalue it acts on.

    ++i;   is equivalent to   i = i + 1;
    --x;   is equivalent to   x = x - 1;

The postfix form behaves differently from the prefix form, changing the affected lvalue after the rest of the expression is evaluated.

    j = ++i;   is equivalent to   i = i + 1; j = i;
    j = i++;   is equivalent to   j = i; i = i + 1;
    i = ++i + i++;   //awful practice is system dependent

Note: These are not exact equivalencies. The compound assignment operators evaluate their left-hand side expressions once. Therefore, for complicated expressions with side effects, results of the two forms can be different.

The null statement is written as a single semicolon and causes no action to take place. A null statement is usually used where a statement is required syntactically but no action is desired. This situation sometimes occurs in statements that affect the flow of control.

2.8.2 The Compound Statement

A compound statement in C++ is a series of statements surrounded by braces { and }. The chief use of the compound statement is to group statements into an executable unit. The body of a C++ function, for example, is always a compound statement. In C, when declarations come at the beginning of a compound statement, the statement is called a *block*. This rule is relaxed in C++, and declaration statements may occur throughout the statement list. Wherever it is possible to place a statement, it is also possible to place a compound statement.

2.8.3 The `if` and `if-else` Statements

The general form of an `if` statement is

```
if (condition)
   statement
```

If *condition* is `true`, then *statement* is executed; otherwise, *statement* is skipped. After the `if` statement has been executed, control passes to the next statement. A *condition* is an expression or a declaration with initialization that selects flow of control.

In file if_test.cpp

```
if (temperature >= 32)
   cout << "Above Freezing!\n";
cout << "Fahrenheit is " << temperature << endl;
```

`Above Freezing!` is printed only when `temperature` is greater than or equal to 32. The second statement is always executed. The expression in an `if` statement is usually a relational, equality, or logical expression.

In file if_test.cpp

```
if (grade > 70 && grade < 80) {
   cout << " you passed ";
   letter_gr = 'C';
}
```

The difference from C is subtle. In C++, *condition* evaluates as a `bool`, but otherwise, the `if` statement behaves the same way.

Closely related to the `if` statement is the `if-else` statement, which has the general form

```
if (condition)
    statement1
else
    statement2
```

If *condition* is `true`, then *statement1* is executed and *statement2* is skipped; if *condition* is `false`, then *statement1* is skipped and *statement2* is executed. After the `if-else` statement has been executed, control passes to the next statement. Consider the following code.

In file if_test.cpp

```
if (x < y)
    min = x;
else
    min = y;
cout << "min = " << min;
```

If `x < y` is `true`, then `min` will be assigned the value of x; if `x < y` is `false`, `min` will be assigned the value of y. After the `if-else` statement is executed, `min` is printed.

2.8.4 The `while` Statement

The general form of a `while` statement is

```
while (condition)
    statement
```

First, *condition* is evaluated. If it is `true`, *statement* is executed, and control passes back to the beginning of the `while` loop. The effect of this is that the body of the `while` loop, namely, *statement*, is executed repeatedly until *condition* is `false`. At that point, control passes to the next statement. The effect of this is that *statement* can be executed zero or more times.

An example of a `while` statement follows.

In file while_t.cpp

```
while (i <= 10) {
    sum += i;
    ++i;
}
```

Assume initially that the value of `i` is 1, and that the value of `sum` is 0. The `while` loop increments the value of `sum` by the current value of `i` and then increments `i` by 1. After the body of the loop has been executed 10 times, the value of `i` is 11, and the value of the condition `i <= 10` is `false`. Thus, the body of the loop is not executed, and control passes to the next statement. When the `while` loop is exited, the value of `sum` is 55.

2.8.5 The for Statement

Consider the general form of a `for` statement:

```
for (for-init-statement; condition; expression)
        statement
    next statement
```

Using the `while` in C++, this becomes

```
for-init-statement;
while (condition) {
        statement
        expression;
}
next statement
```

These two forms are equivalent, provided that *condition* is nonempty and a `continue` statement is not in the body of the `for` loop.

From our understanding of the `while` statement, we can deduce the semantics of the `for` statement. First, the *for-init-statement* is evaluated and is used to initialize a variable used in the loop. Then *condition* is evaluated. If it is `true`, *statement* is executed, *expression* is evaluated, and control passes back to the beginning of the `for` loop again, except that evaluation of *for-init-statement* is skipped. This iteration continues until *condition* is `false`, at which point control passes to *next statement*.

The *for-init-statement* can be an expression statement or a simple declaration. If it is a declaration, the declared variable has the scope of the `for` statement.

The `for` statement is an iterative statement typically used with a variable that is incremented or decremented. As an example, the following code uses a `for` statement to sum the integers from 1 to 10:

In file for_test.cpp

```
sum = 0;
for (i = 1; i <= 10; ++i)
    sum += i;
```

Any or all of the expressions in a `for` statement can be missing, but the two semicolons must remain. If *for-init-statement* is missing, no initialization step is performed as part of the `for` loop. If *expression* is missing, no incrementation step is performed as part of the `for` loop. If *condition* is missing, no testing step is performed as part of the `for` loop. The special rule for when *condition* is missing is that the test is always `true`. Thus, the `for` loop in the code

```
for (i = 1, sum = 0 ; ; ++i )
    sum += i;
```

is an infinite loop.

The `for` statement is one common case in which a local declaration is used to provide the loop control variable, as in

```
for (int i = 0; i < N; ++i)
    sum += a[i];    //sum array a[0] + ... + a[N - 1]
```

The semantics are that the `int` variable `i` is local to the given loop. This form of local declaration is not possible in C but it can be simulated as follows:

```
{
    int i;              /*local to block*/
    for ( i = 0; i < N; ++i)
        sum += a[i];
}
```

2.8.6 The **do** Statement

The do statement can be considered a variant of the while statement. However, instead of making its test at the top of the loop, the do statement makes it at the bottom. An example is the following:

```
do {
    sum += i;
    cin >> i;
} while (i > 0);
```

Consider a construction of the form

```
do
    statement
while (condition);
next statement
```

First, *statement* is executed, and then *condition* is evaluated. If it is true, control passes back to the beginning of the do statement, and the process repeats itself. When the value of *condition* is false, control passes to *next statement*. As an example, suppose that we want to read in an integer and want to insist that it be positive. The following code will accomplish this:

In file do_test.cpp

```
do {
    cout << "\nEnter a positive integer: ";
    cin >> n;
} while (n <= 0);
```

The user will be prompted for a positive integer. A negative or zero value will cause the loop to be executed again, asking for another value. Control will exit the loop only after a positive integer has been entered.

2.8.7 The **break** and **continue** Statements

In C++, the break and continue statements are used to interrupt ordinary iterative flow of control in loops. In addition, the break statement is used within a switch statement, which can select among several cases. To interrupt the normal flow of control within a loop, the programmer can use the two special statements

```
break;      and      continue;
```

The break statement, in addition to its use in loops, can be used in a switch statement, causing an exit from the innermost enclosing loop or switch statement.

The following example illustrates the use of a break statement. A test for a negative value is made. If the test is true, the break statement causes the for loop to be exited. Program control jumps to the statement immediately following the loop.

In file for_test.cpp

```
for (i = 0; i < 10; ++i) {
   cin >> x;
   if (x < 0.0) {
      cout << "All done" << endl;
      break;          //exit loop if value is negative
   }
   cout << sqrt(x) << endl;
}

//break jumps to here
. . . . .
```

This is a typical use of a break statement. When a special condition is met, an appropriate action is taken and the loop is exited.

The continue statement causes the current iteration of a loop to stop and causes the next iteration of the loop to begin immediately. The following code processes all characters except digits.

In file for_test.cpp

```
for (i = 0; i < MAX; ++i) {
   cin.get(c);
   if (isdigit(c))
      continue;
   . . . . .   //process other characters
//continue jumps to here
}
```

When the continue statement is executed, control jumps to just before the closing brace, causing the loop to begin execution at the top again. Notice that the continue statement ends the current iteration, whereas a break statement would end the loop.

A break statement can occur only inside the body of a for, while, do, or switch statement. The continue statement can occur only inside the body of a for, while, or do statement.

2.8.8 The `switch` Statement

The `switch` statement is a multiway conditional statement generalizing the `if-else` statement. The general form of the `switch` statement is given by

    switch (*condition*)
        statement

where *statement* is typically a compound statement containing `case` labels and optionally a `default` label. Typically, a `switch` is composed of many cases, and the *condition* in parentheses following the keyword `switch` determines which, if any, of the cases are executed.

The following `switch` statement counts the number of test scores by category.

In file switch_t.cpp

```
switch (score) {
case 9: case 10:
    ++a_grades; break;
case 8:
    ++b_grades; break;
case 7:
    ++c_grades; break;
default:
    ++fails;
}
```

A `case` label is of the form

    `case` *constant integral expression*:

In a `switch` statement, each `case` label must be unique. Typically, the action taken after each `case` label ends with a `break` statement. If there is no `break` statement, execution "falls through" to the next statement in the succeeding `case` or `default`.

If no `case` label is selected, control passes to the `default` label, if there is one. No `default` label is required, but including one is good practice. If no `case` label is selected and if there is no `default` label, the `switch` statement is exited. The keywords `case` and `default` cannot occur outside a `switch`. To detect errors, programmers frequently include a `default` even when all of the expected cases have been accounted for.

The Effect of a switch Statement

1. Evaluate the integral expression in the parentheses following switch.

2. Execute the case label having a constant value that matches the value of the expression found in step 1. If no match is found, execute the default label. If there is no default label, terminate the switch.

3. Terminate the switch when a break statement is encountered or by "falling off the end."

2.8.9 The goto Statement

The goto statement, the most primitive method of interrupting ordinary control flow, is an unconditional branch to an arbitrary labeled statement in the function. The goto statement is considered a harmful construct in most accounts of modern programming methodology. Thus, the statement can undermine all of the useful structure provided by other flow-of-control mechanisms (for, while, do, if, and switch).

A label is an identifier. By executing a goto statement of the form

goto *label*;

control is unconditionally transferred to a labeled statement. An example is

In file goto_tst.cpp

```
if (d == 0.0)
   goto error;
else
   ratio = n / d;
 .....
error:  cerr << "ERROR:  division by zero" << endl;
```

Both the goto statement and its corresponding labeled statement must be in the body of the same function. In general, goto should be avoided.

2.9 Pragmatics

C++ has greatly improved on C's primitive form of cast. In general, it is best to avoid explicit casting, also known as coercion, or conversion. Type logic is a safety check that the compiler can perform statically to detect coding mistakes. However, if you must cast, try to stay with the most benign form of conversion, `static_cast<>`. A true conversion is performed that will be portable. At the other end of the spectrum is `reinterpret_cast<>`, with nonportable system-dependent effects. This cast should be avoided.

C++ has changed C's rules on where declarations can occur. The `for` loop is one place where local declarations are idiomatically used. Because these rules have changed in C++ since its introduction in 1985, many books, text, and legacy code are wrong and must be updated to conform to ANSI rules. It is perfectly acceptable to declare simple variables at the head of a block, most likely the beginning of a function definition. Following this advice yields code that works in both C and C++. For example, let us write an iterative version of the Fibonacci function this way.

In file fibona1.c

```
//Fibonacci series compatible with C

unsigned fibonacci(unsigned n)
{
   unsigned i, sum = 0, f0 = 0, f1 = 1;

   for (i = 0; i < n - 1; ++i){
      sum = f0 + f1;
      f0 = f1;
      f1 = sum;
   }
   if (n > 1)
      return sum;
   else
      return n;
}
```

Using the fact that declarations are allowed in the *for-init-statement* gives us

In file fibona2.c

```
//Idiomatically correct C++
//Fibonacci series incompatible with C
//This code follows the rule of smallest enclosing scope

unsigned fibonacci(unsigned n)
{
    unsigned sum = 0;
    for (unsigned i = 0, f0 = 0, f1 = 1; i < n - 1; ++i){
        sum = f0 + f1;
        f0 = f1;
        f1 = sum;
    }
    if (n > 1)
        return sum;
    else
        return n;
}
```

Notice what happens if we make the following coding error:

In file fibona3.c

```
//ERROR because of scopes

unsigned fibonacci(unsigned n)
{
    unsigned sum;

    for(unsigned i = 0, f0 = 0, f1 = 1, sum = 0; i < n - 1; ++i){
        sum = f0 + f1;
        f0 = f1;
        f1 = sum;
    }
    if (n > 1)
        return sum;
    else
        return n;
}
```

In this last piece of code, an error was introduced by initializing `sum` in the `for` loop. The program compiles and runs but with system-dependent results because there are two `sum` variables in `fibonacci()`.

2.10 Moving from C++ to Java

The primitive types in a Java program can be `boolean`, `char`, `byte`, `short`, `int`, `long`, `float`, and `double`. These types are always identically defined regardless of machine or system they run on. For example, the `int` type is always a signed 32-bit integer, unlike in C, where this can vary from system to system. The `boolean` type is not an arithmetic type and cannot be used in mixed arithmetical expressions. The `char` type uses 16-bit Unicode values. The `byte`, `short`, `int`, and `long` are all signed integer types, with length in bits of 8, 16, 32, and 64, respectively. Unlike in C++, unsigned types are not provided. The floating types comply with IEEE754 standards and are `float`, a 32-bit size, and `double`, a 64-bit size. The nonprimitive types are class and array types, and variables of these types take references as their values.

Java has the same basic set of operators as C++, with a few exceptions. For example, Java does not have the comma operator, scope resolution operator, or `delete` operator. Java added two operators: the `instanceof` and `>>>` operators.

The flow of control statements—`if`, `if-else`, `while`, `for`, and `switch`—available to C++ are also available in Java. Although `goto` is a reserved word in Java, the `goto` statement was not implemented. However, Java extended the `break` and `continue` statements so that they can use labels.

We will write a program, *Moon*, to convert to kilometers the distance in miles from Earth to the moon. In miles this distance is, on average, 238,857 miles. This number is an integer. To convert miles to kilometers, we multiply by the conversion factor 1.609, a real number.

Our conversion program will use variables capable of storing integer values and real values. The variables in the following program will be declared in `main()`. Java cannot have variables declared as `extern` (in other words, as global or file scope variables).

In file Moon.java

```
// The distance to the moon converted to kilometers

public class Moon {
    public static void main(String[] s) {
        int moon = 238857;
        int moon_kilo;

        System.out.println("Earth to moon = " + moon + " mi.");
        moon_kilo = (int)(moon * 1.609);
        System.out.println("Kilometers = " + moon_kilo +" km.");
    }
}
```

The output of the program is

```
Earth to moon = 238857 mi.
Kilometers = 384320 km.
```

Dissection of the *Moon* Program

■ `int moon = 238857;`

Variables of type `int` are signed 32-bit integers. They can be initialized as in C.

■ `System.out.println("Earth to moon = " + moon + " mi.");`

The `println()` method can discriminate among a variety of simple values without needing additional formatting information. Here, the value of `moon` will be printed as an integer. The symbol `+` represents string concatenation. Using "plus" `println()` can print a list of arguments. What is happening is that each argument is converted from its specific type to an output string that is concatenated together and printed along with a newline character.

■ `moon_kilo = (int)(moon * 1.609);`

The mixed expression `moon * 1.609` is a `double` and must be explicitly converted to `int`. Java cast operators are notationally the same as in C, namely, (*type*).

Note that narrowing conversions that are implicit in C++ are not done in Java. Java in this regard is more type safe than C++. Also in Java all the primitive types are implementation independent. So numerically, a Java program gets the same answer regardless of the system it is running on. C++ continues C's tradition of having implementation-dependent choices of primitive types, so as to optimize performance on a given machine.

Summary

This summary emphasizes in order of appearance changes and differences from C in the C++ language.

1. C++ comments include the //*rest of line comment* while retaining the multiline bracketed comments of C /* *comment here* */.

2. C++ has many new tokens not found in C. In the keyword list in Section 2.1.2, "Keywords," on page 25, new keywords, such as `bool`, `static_cast`, `virtual`, and `private` are bolded to distinguish them from preexisting C keywords. New operators exist in C++, such as the free store operators `new` and `delete` and the scope resolution operator `::`.

3. C++ has the new native types `bool` and `wchar_t` and literals appropriate to each type.

4. The new ANSI header file names, such as *iostream*, are embedded in the namespace `std`. In these cases, the construct `using namespace std;` allows access to the names in this library without the need for scope-resolved names, such as `std::cout`.

5. At the conclusion of the execution of `main()` there is an implicit `return 0`. Thus, it is proper C++ style to omit writing this explicitly, as is required by C.

6. C++ relies on an external standard library to provide input/output. The information the program needs to use this library resides in the *iostream.h* or the *iostream* file. This library is type safe and requires no formatting specifications, as found in C's use of `printf` and `scanf`. In C++, a typical output expression is

```
cout << expression1 << expression2 << endl;
```

7. In addition to implicit conversions, which can occur across assignments and in mixed expressions, there are explicit conversions, called casts. New keywords introduced in C++ for casts are `static_cast`, `reinterpret_cast`, `const_cast`, and `dynamic_cast`. Old-style C casts (*type*) should be avoided.

8. The keyword `enum` is used to declare a distinct integer type with a set of named integer constants, called enumerators. In C++, the enumerator tag name is automatically a user-defined type.

9. Both C++ and C have assignment, procedure, transfer, conditional, selections, and iterative statements. Two important differences are: (1) C++ uses `bool` expressions to control flow-of-control statements; and (2) C++ allows declarations as statements instead of just being at the head of blocks or global.

10. The general form of a `for` statement is different from that in C.

   for (*for-init-statement*; *condition*; *expression*)
       statement
   next statement

   First, the *for-init-statement* is evaluated and is used to initialize a variable used in the loop. Then *condition* is evaluated. It is of type `bool`. If it is `true`, *statement* is executed, *expression* is evaluated, and control passes back to the beginning of the `for` loop again, except that evaluation of *for-init-statement* is skipped. This iteration continues until *condition* is `false`, whereupon control passes to *next statement*. The *for-init-statement* can be an expression statement or a simple declaration. Where it is a declaration, the declared variable has the scope of the `for` statement.

   ```
   for (int i = 0; i < N; ++i)
      sum += a[i];    //sum array a[0] + ... + a[N - 1]
   ```

   The semantics are that the `int` variable i is local to the given loop. This form of local declaration is not possible in C.

Review Questions

1. A type in C++ that C does not have is _____.

2. Three keywords in C++ that are not in C are _____, _____, and _____. Describe their use as far as you currently understand it.

3. What token does the new comment style in C++ involve? Why should it be used?

4. What two literal values does the `bool` type have? Can they be assigned to `int` variables? With what result?

5. What is the distinction between `static_cast<>` and `reinterpret_cast<>`? Which is the more dangerous? Why?

6. C++ uses the semicolon as a statement _____.

7. The general form of a `for` statement is

   `for` (*for-init-statement, condition, expression*)
        statement

   There are two important differences between the C++ `for` and the C `for`. What are they? Explain with an example.

8. The `goto` should _____ be used.

9. What happens when the condition part of the `for` statement is omitted?

10. The Java output library function works by converting its arguments to concatenated strings, as in

    ```
    System.out.println("Earth to moon = " + moon + " mi.");
    ```

    Explain what happens in this statement.

Exercises

1. Rewrite the gcd() function from Section 2.3, "Program Structure," on page 30, with a for loop replacing the while loop.

2. Rewrite the *gcd* program from Section 2.3, "Program Structure," on page 31, to read a value for how_many greatest common divisors will be computed. The variable how_many will be used to exit the for loop.

3. On most systems, input can be *redirected* from a file. Assume that the *gcd* program has been compiled into an executable file called *gcd*. The command

       gcd < gcd.dat

   will take its input from the file *gcd.dat* and will write the answers to the screen. Test this with a file containing

         4   4   6   6   21   8   20   15   20

   On most systems, output can also be redirected to a file. The command

       gcd > gcd.ans

   will place its output in the file *gcd.ans,* taking its input from the keyboard. Enter the same data as previously and check the file *gcd.ans* to see that it has the four correct answers. The two redirections can be combined as follows:

       gcd < gcd.dat > gcd.ans

   This will take its input from the file *gcd.dat* and will place its output in the file *gcd.ans.* Test this on your system.

4. Short-circuit evaluation is an important feature. The following code illustrates its importance in a typical situation:

```
//Compute the roots of: a * x * x + b * x + c

    cin >> a >> b >> c;
    discr = b * b - 4 * a * c;
    if ((discr > 0) && (sq_disc = sqrt(discr))) {
        root1 = (-b + sq_disc) / (2 * a);
        root2 = (-b - sq_disc) / (2 * a);
    }
    else if (discr < 0) {          //complex roots
        .....
    }
    else
        root1 = root2 = -b / (2 * a);
```

The `sqrt()` function would fail on negative values, and short-circuit evaluation protects the program from this error. Complete this program by having it compute roots and print them out for the following values:

```
a = 1.0, b = 4.0, c = 3.0
a = 1.0, b = 2.0, c = 1.0
a = 1.0, b = 1.0, c = 1.0
```

5. Use the *complex* library to provide the C++ `complex` number type, and rewrite the previous root-finding program to print out roots as complex numbers when appropriate. Compare this to a C implementation. In ANSI C++, use `#include <complex>`. In the main program, declare such variables as

```
complex<double> root1, root2;      //complex is a template type
```

6. What will the following program print?

```
//What is printed?

int main()
{
    char  c = 'A';
    int   i = 3, j = 1, k = -2, m = 0;
    bool  p = false, q = true;
```

```
    cout << c << " is integer value " << int(c)
        << "  and !'A' is " << !c << endl;
    cout << "i = " << i << ", !i = " << !i << endl;
    cout << "!!i = " << !!i << ", !m = " << !m
        << endl;
    cout << "p = " << p << ", q = " << q << endl;
    cout << "!p = " << !p << ", !q = " << !q << endl;
    cout << "!(i + j) || m = " << (!(i + j) || m)
        << endl;
    cout << "q || (j / m) = " << (q || (j / m))
        << endl;
    cout << "(j / m) || q = " << ((j / m) || q)
        << endl;
}
```

7. The C++ `switch` statement allows two or more cases to be executed for the same value by allowing the code to "fall through."

```
switch (i) {
case 0: case 1:
   ++hopeless;           // fall through
case 2: case 3:
   ++weak;
case 4: case 5:
   ++fails; break;
case 6: case 7:
   ++c_grades; break;
case 8:
   ++b_grades; break;
case 9:
   ++a_grades; break;
default:
   cout << "incorrect grade " << i << endl;
}
```

Hand simulate this statement for i equals 1. Write the equivalent `if-else` statement.

8. Use `sizeof` to determine the number of bytes each of the following requires on your local system: `bool`, `char`, `short`, `int`, `long`, `float`, `double`, and `long double`. Also do this for the enumerated types

   ```
   enum bounds { lb = -1, ub = 511 };
   enum suit { clubs, diamonds, hearts, spades };
   ```

9. Write a program to convert from Celsius to Fahrenheit. The program should use integer values and print integer values that are rounded. Recall that zero Celsius is 32 degrees Fahrenheit and that each degree Celsius is 1.8 degrees Fahrenheit.

10. Write a program that prints whether water at a given Fahrenheit temperature would be solid, liquid, or gas. In the computation, use an enumerated type:

    ```
    enum state { solid = STMP, liquid = LTMP, gas = GTMP };
    ```

11. Write a program that accepts either Celsius or Fahrenheit and produces the other value as output. For example, input 0C, output 32F; input 212F, output 100C.

12. Simplify the following code:

    ```
    for (sum =i = 0, j = 2, k = i + j; i < 10 || k < 15;
          ++i, ++j, ++k)
       sum += (i < j)? k : i;
    ```

    Remember that comma expressions are sequences of left-to-right evaluations, with each comma-separated subexpression evaluated in strict order.

13. In the C world, more flexible file I/O is available by using the `FILE` declaration and file operations found in *stdio*. The C++ community uses *fstream*, as discussed in Appendix D, "Input/Output." Familiarize yourself with this library. Convert the program in exercise 3 on page 60, to use *fstreams*. The program should get its arguments from the command line, as in

    gcd   gcd.dat   gcd.ans

14. The following code prints 100 random numbers:

```
int main()
{
   int how_many = 100;

   cout << "Print " << how_many
        << "  random integers.\n";
   for (int i = 0; i < how_many; ++i)
      cout << rand() << '\t';
}
```

Add code that determines average, maximum, and minimum values generated. Note that the rand() function is found in *stdlib* library.

15. Alter the previous program to ask the user how many numbers should be generated. Have this be an outer loop. Exit this program when the user answers with zero or a negative number.

16. The constant RAND_MAX is the largest integer that rand() generates. Use RAND_MAX/2 to decide whether a random number is to be heads or tails. Generate 1,000 randomly generated heads and tails. Print out the ratio of heads to tails. Is this a reasonable test to see whether rand() works correctly? Print out the size of the longest number of heads thrown in a row.

17. The conditions in selection and iterative statements can be declaration statements, such as if (bool d = test()) ...., where scope is restricted to the statement. Write a program that tests whether your compiler conforms to this latest ANSI rule change.

18. Rewrite fibonacci() found in Section 2.9, "Pragmatics," on page 54, as a recursive function. Test it against the iterative form to see which is faster. Useful timing functions can be found in *time* library.

19. *(Java)* Rewrite the convert from Celsius to Fahrenheit program in exercise 9 on page 63, in Java.

20. *(Java)* Rewrite the C++ Fibonacci program in Section 2.9, "Pragmatics," on page 54, in Java. Have it print out the first forty Fibonacci numbers. Investigate the for loop scope rules in Java.

Chapter 3
Functions, Pointers, and Arrays

This chapter continues the discussion of the C++ kernel language, focusing on functions, pointers, and arrays. The experienced C programmer can read the chapter quickly, with an eye for differences and extensions to C. These differences will again be stressed in the summary section for easy reference.

In C++, a primary unit for structuring a program is the function. Aggregate data in C++ are either arrays or structures. In both cases, a pointer type is used as a mechanism for accessing such data.

3.1 Functions

A problem in C++ or C can be decomposed into subproblems, each of which can be either coded directly or further decomposed. This is the method of *stepwise refinement*. The *function* construct in C++ is used to write code for these directly solvable subproblems. These functions are combined into other functions and are ultimately used in `main()` to solve the original problem.

The function mechanism is provided in C++ to perform distinct programming tasks. Some functions, such as `strcpy()` and `rand()`, are provided by libraries; others can be written by the programmer. New to C++ are default arguments, function overloading, and inlining of functions. The use of an empty parameter list also differs between C and C++.

3.1.1 Function Invocation

A C++ program is made up of one or more functions, one of which is main(). Program execution always begins with main(). When program control encounters a function name, the function is called, or *invoked*. This means that program control passes to the function. After the function does its work, program control is passed back to the calling environment, which then continues with its work. As a simple example, consider the following program, *echo*, which uses the *string* library and echoes an input word:

In file echo1.cpp

```
//Echo a message

void echo(string message)
{
    cout << message << endl;
}

int main()
{
    string word;

    cout << "Enter your word: ";
    cin >> word;        //reads to white space
    echo(word);
}
```

3.2 Function Definition

The C++ code that describes what a function does is called the *function definition*. Its form is

```
function header
{
    statements
}
```

Everything before the first brace comprises the *header* of the function definition, and everything between the braces comprises the *body* of the function definition.

The function header is

type name(*parameter-declaration-list*)

The *type* specification which precedes the function name is the *return type* and determines the type of the value that the function returns, if any.

In the function definition for `echo()` in the *echo* program, the parameter list has one parameter. The body of the function consists of a block. Since the function does not return a value, the return type of the function is `void`.

Parameters are syntactically identifiers, and they can be used within the body of the function. The parameters in a function definition are called *formal parameters* to emphasize their role as placeholders for the values that are passed to the function when it is called. When the function is invoked, the value of the argument corresponding to a formal parameter is used within the body of the executing function. As in C, such parameters are *call-by-value*.

C and C++ functions have a number of differences which we will point out as we explain various features of using functions. One difference is that a C++ block need not have declarations at the head of the block. So in the *echo* program, `main()` could have been written as

In file echo2.cpp

```
int main()
{
    cout << "Enter your word: ";
    string word;     //place declaration near its use
    cin >> word;
    echo(word);
}
```

In ANSI C++, the empty parameter list is always equivalent to using `void`. Thus, `main()` is equivalent to `main(void)`. The function `main()` implicitly returns the integer value 0 if no explicit `return` expression statement is executed.

3.3 The `return` Statement

The `return` statement is unchanged from its C use. When a `return` statement is executed, program control is immediately passed back to the calling environment. In addition, if an expression follows the keyword `return`, the value of the expression is returned to the calling environment as well. This value must be assignment convertible to the return type of the function definition header.

A `return` statement has one of the following two forms:

```
return;
return expression;
```

Some examples are

```
return;
return 3;
return (a + b);
```

Using parentheses in the `return` expression is optional, a stylistic device that some programmers use to enhance readability.

3.4 Function Prototypes

The syntax of functions in C++ is type safe where the types of parameters are listed inside the header parentheses. By explicitly listing the type and number of arguments, strong type-checking and assignment-compatible conversions are possible.

A function can be declared before it is defined. It can be defined later in the file or can come from a library or a user-specified file. Such a declaration is called a *function prototype* and has the following general form:

type name(argument-declaration-list) ;

The *argument-declaration-list* is typically a comma-separated list of types. If a function has no parameters, the preferred style for such an empty parameter list is *function_name*(). The function's argument list can include the argument identifiers. This information allows the compiler to enforce type compatibility. Arguments are converted to these types as if they were following rules of assignment.

The use of the empty parameter list differs from that in traditional C, in which an empty parameter list can indicate an unknown number of arguments. Frequently, C programmers indicate an empty parameter list by using *function_name*(void). In C++, the empty parameter list is the same as the use of void.

In Section 3.1.1, "Function Invocation," on page 66, we used in the *echo1.cpp* program the function echo(). Its prototype in main() would be

```
void echo(string);
```

Both the function return type and the argument-list types are explicitly mentioned. The definition of echo() that occurs in the file must match this declaration. The function prototype can also include the identifier names of the arguments. In the case of echo(), this would be

```
void echo(string message);
```

C++ uses the ellipsis symbol (. . .) for an argument list that is unspecified. The *stdio* function printf() is declared as the prototype.

```
int printf(const char* cntrl_str, ...);
```

Such a function can be invoked on an arbitrary list of parameters. This practice should be avoided because of loss of type safety.

3.4.1 Recursion

As in C, C++ has recursion. A recursive function calls itself as part of its definition. A simple recursive function has two main parts: the base-case part, where it computes a value and terminates, and the recursive part, where it calls itself. Recursion corresponds to mathematical induction in describing how functions such as factorial are proved correct.

In file factor.cpp

```
//Recursive factorial function

long factorial(int n)
{
    if (n <= 1)
        return 1;
    else
        return n * factorial(n - 1);
}
```

Notice how the recursive call is with the expression n - 1. This guarantees that the function factorial() will terminate. Each recursion will reduce the called expression by 1 until the termination condition n <= 1 is true. In running this computation, be aware that for relatively small values of n (such as 13), the computation will fail because of integer overflow.

A pseudocode prescription for writing a simple recursion is

```
//base-case part

if (base-case condition)
    return base-case computed value;

//general case as a recursion

else
    return recursively computed expression;
```

3.5 Default Arguments

A formal parameter can be given a default argument, usually a constant that occurs frequently when the function is called. Use of a default argument saves writing this default value at each invocation. The ability to provide default values to arguments does not exist in C. The following recursive function illustrates the point.

In file powers.cpp

```
int sqr_or_power(int n, int k = 2)    //k=2 is default
{
    assert(k > 1);  //note asserts are as in C
    if (k == 2)
        return (n * n);
    else
        return (sqr_or_power(n, k - 1) * n);
}
```

We assume that most of time the function is used to return the value of n squared. The assert is discussed later in this chapter.

```
sqr_or_power(i + 5)          //computes (i + 5) * (i + 5)
sqr_or_power(i + 5, 3)       //computes (i + 5) cubed
```

Only trailing parameters of a function can have default values. This rule allows the compiler to know which arguments are defaulted when the function is called with fewer than its complete set of arguments. The rule substitutes for the leftmost arguments with the explicit arguments and then uses defaults for any of the remaining contiguous unspecified arguments. Some examples are

```
void foo(int i, int j = 7);              //legal
void goo(int i = 3, int j);              //illegal
void hoo(int i, int j = 3, int k = 7);   //legal
void moo(int i = 1, int j = 2, int k = 3); //legal
void noo(int i, int j = 2, int k);       //illegal
```

3.6 Functions as Arguments

Functions in C++ can be thought of as the addresses of the compiled code residing in memory. Functions are therefore a form of pointer (see Section 3.11, "Pointer Types," on page 82) and can be passed as a pointer-value argument into another function. Using this idea, we write code that will print n values of a function, starting at an initial value using a specific increment. This form of plotting function can be useful to generate a function map that later will be used to find properties of the function, such as a root of the function.

In file root.cpp

```
double f(double x)
{
    return (x*x + 1.0/x);
}

void plot(double fcn(double), double x0, double incr, int n)
{
    for (int i = 0; i < n; ++i){
        cout << " x :" << x0
             << "    f(x) : " << fcn(x0) << endl;
        x0 += incr;
    }
}
```

```
int main()
{
    cout << "mapping function x*x + 1.0/x " << endl;
    plot(f, 0.01, 0.01, 100);
}
```

Notice that the first argument to `plot()` is a function of a specific type. Functions as arguments are strongly typed. In this case, `plot()` will take only a function returning `double` of one argument that is `double`.

3.7 Overloading Functions

Function overloading is a feature not available in C but is a feature in C++. The usual reason for picking a function name is to indicate the function's chief purpose. Readable programs generally have a diverse and literate choice of identifiers. Sometimes, different functions are used for the same purpose. For example, consider a function that averages the values in an array of `double` versus one that averages the values in an array of `int` (see Section 3.14, "Arrays and Pointers," on page 89). Both are conveniently named `avg_arr()`, as in the following example.

Overloading refers to using the same name for multiple meanings of an operator or a function. The meaning selected depends on the types of the arguments used by the operator or function. Here, we restrict our discussion to function overloading and leave operator overloading to Chapter 6, "Operator Overloading and Conversions," as the operator overloading is used chiefly in the context of classes. In the following code, we overload `avg_arr()`:

In file avg_arr.cpp

```
//Average the values in an array

double avg_arr(const int a[], int size)
{
    int   sum = 0;

    for (int i = 0; i < size; ++i)
        sum += a[i];          //performs int arithmetic
    return static_cast<double>(sum) / size;
}
```

```
double avg_arr(const double a[], int size)
{
   double  sum = 0.0;

   for (int i = 0; i < size; ++i)
      sum += a[i];         //performs double arithmetic
   return (sum / size);
}
```

The following code shows how avg_arr() is invoked:

```
int main()
{
   int     w[5] = { 1, 2, 3, 4, 5 };    //initialization
   double  x[5] = { 1.1, 2.2, 3.3, 4.4, 5.5 };

   cout << avg_arr(w, 5) << " int average" << endl;
   cout << avg_arr(x, 5) << " double average" << endl;
}
```

The compiler chooses the function with matching types and arguments. The *signature-matching algorithm* gives the rules for performing this (see Section 6.2, "Overloading and Function Selection," on page 197). By *signature*, we mean the list of types that are used in the function declaration.

3.8 Inlining

C++ provides the keyword inline to preface a function declaration when the programmer intends the code replacing the function call to be inline.

In file inline.cpp

```
inline double cube(double x)
{
   return (x * x * x);
}
```

The compiler parses this function, providing semantics that are equivalent to a non-inline version. The compiler limits prevent complicated functions, such as recursive functions, from being inlined.

Macro expansion is a scheme for placing code inline that would normally use a function call. The `#define` preprocessor directive supports general macro substitution, as in the following:

```
#define  SQR(X)    ((X) * (X))
#define  CUBE(X)   (SQR(X)*(X))
#define  ABS(X)    (((X) < 0)? -(X) : X)
     . . . . .
    y = SQR(t + 8) - CUBE(t - 8);
    cout << sqrt(ABS(y));
```

The preprocessor expands the macros and passes on the resulting text to the compiler. So the preceding is equivalent to

```
    y = ((t+8) * (t+8)) - ((((t-8)) * (t-8)) * (t-8));
    cout << sqrt(((((y) < 0)? -(y) : y));
```

One reason for all the parentheses is to avoid precedence mistakes, as would occur in the following:

```
#define  SQR(X)   X * X
     . . . . .
    y = SQR(t + 8);       //expands to t + 8 * t + 8
```

Macro expansion provides no type safety as is given by the C++ parameter-passing mechanism. Since the macro argument has no type, no assignment type conversions are applied to it, as they would be in a function. Although careful definition and use of macros can avoid such mistakes, C++ programmers avoid macro definitions by using inlining for purposes of code efficiency.

3.9 Scope and Storage Class

The kernel language has two principal forms of scope: *file scope* and *local scope*. Local scope is scoped to a block. Compound statements that include declarations are blocks. Function bodies are examples of blocks. They contain a set of declarations that include their parameters. File scope has names that are external (global). There is also block scope, which is discussed in the next section. Class scope rules are discussed in Section 4.6, "Class Scope," on page 122.

The basic rule of scoping is that identifiers are accessible only within the block in which they are declared. Thus, they are unknown outside the boundaries of that block. A simple example follows.

In file scope_t.cpp

```
{
    int   a = 2;                //outer block a
    cout << a << endl;          //prints 2
    {                           //enter inner block
        int  a = 7;             //inner block a
        cout << a << endl;      //prints 7
    }                           //exit inner block
    cout << ++a << endl;        //3 is printed
}
```

Each block introduces its own nomenclature. An outer block name is valid unless an inner block redefines it. If redefined, the outer block name is hidden, or masked, from the inner block. Inner blocks may be nested to arbitrary depths that are determined by system limitations.

In C++, declarations can be internal to a block. In C, all block-scope declarations occur at the head of the block. An example shows this.

In file array_mx.cpp

```
//C++ but not C

int max(int c[], int size)
{
    cout << "array size is " << size << endl;

    int  comp = c[0];              //declare comp
    for (int i = 1; i < size; ++i) //declare i
        if (c[i] > comp)
            comp = c[i];
    return comp;
}
```

In C++, the scope of an identifier begins at the end of its declaration and continues to the end of its innermost enclosing block.

Even though C++ does not require that declarations be placed at the head of blocks, it is frequently good practice to do so. Since blocks are often small, this practice provides a good documentation style for commenting on their associated use.

Placing declarations within blocks allows a computed or input value to initialize a variable. Especially for large blocks, it is best to place declarations as close as possible to where they are used.

3.9.1 The Storage Class `auto`

Every variable and function in C++ kernel language has two attributes: *type* and *storage class*. The four storage classes are automatic, external, register, and static, with corresponding keywords

```
auto        extern       register       static
```

Variables declared within function bodies are by default automatic, making automatic the most common of the four storage classes. If a compound statement contains variable declarations, these variables can be acted on within the scope of the enclosing compound statement. Recall that a compound statement with declarations is a *block.*

Declarations of variables within blocks are implicitly of storage class automatic. The keyword `auto` can be used to explicitly specify the storage class. An example is

```
auto int    a, b, c;
auto float  f = 7.78;
```

Because the storage class is automatic by default, the keyword `auto` is seldom used. As in C, blocks are a principal mechanism for the allocation and deallocation of storage.

3.9.2 The Storage Class `extern`

One method of transmitting information across blocks and functions is to use external variables. When a variable is declared outside a function at the file level, storage is permanently assigned to it, and its storage class keyword is `extern`. A declaration for an external variable can look just like a declaration for a variable that occurs inside a function or a block. Such a variable is considered to be global to all functions declared after it. On block exit or function exit, the external variable remains in existence. Such variables cannot have automatic or register storage class. The keyword `static` can be used. (See Section 3.9.4, "The Storage Class `static`," on page 78.)

The keyword `extern` is used to tell the compiler, "Look for it elsewhere, either in this file or in some other file." Thus, two files can be compiled separately. The use of `extern` in the second file tells the compiler that the variable will be *defined* elsewhere, either in this file or in another one. The ability to compile files separately is important for writing large programs.

Since external variables exist throughout the execution life of the program, they can be used to transmit values across functions. They may, however, be hidden if the identifier is redefined. Another way to conceive of external variables is as being declared in a block that encompasses the whole file.

Information can be passed into a function two ways: by external variables and by the parameter mechanism. The parameter mechanism is the preferred method, although there are exceptions. This tends to improve the modularity of the code and reduces the possibility of undesirable side effects.

Here is a simple example of using external declarations for a program that sits in two separate files.

In file circle3.cpp

```
const double  pi = 3.14159;
double circle(double radius)
{
    return (pi * radius * radius);
}
```

In file cir_main.cpp

```
double circle(double);        //functions are of extern scope

int main()
{
    double  x;

    . . . . .
    cout << circle(x) << " is area of circle of radius "
        << x << endl;
}
```

With the GNU system, this is compiled as *g++ circle.c main.c.*

The `const` modifier causes `pi` to have local file scope, so `pi` cannot be directly imported into another file. When such a definition is required elsewhere, it must be modified explicitly with the keyword `extern`.

3.9.3 The Storage Class `register`

The storage class `register` tells the compiler that the associated variables should be stored in high-speed memory registers, provided it is physically and semantically possible to do. Since resource limitations and semantic constraints sometimes make this impossible, the storage class `register` defaults to automatic whenever the compiler cannot allocate an appropriate physical register. When speed is of concern, the programmer may choose a few variables that are most frequently accessed and declare them to be of storage class `register`. Common candidates for such treatment include loop variables and function parameters. Here is an example.

```
{
    for (register i = 0; i < LIMIT; ++i) {
        .....
    }
}
```

The declaration `register i;` is equivalent to `register int i;`. If a storage class is specified in a declaration and the type is absent, the type is `int` by default.

The storage class `register` is of limited usefulness. It is taken only as *advice* to the compiler. Furthermore, contemporary optimizing compilers are often more astute than the programmer.

3.9.4 The Storage Class `static`

Static declarations have two important and distinct uses. The more elementary use is to allow a local variable to retain its previous value when the block is reentered. By contrast, ordinary automatic variables lose their value on block exit and must be reinitialized. The second, more subtle use is in connection with external declarations and will be discussed in the next section.

As an example of the value-retention use of `static`, we will write a function that maintains a count of the number of times it is called.

In file stat_tst.cpp

```
int f()
{
    static int  called = 0;

    ++called;
    .....
    return called;
}
```

The first time the function is invoked, the variable `called` is initialized to 0. On function exit, the value of `called` is preserved in memory. When the function is invoked again, `called` is *not* reinitialized; instead, it retains its value from the previous time the function was called.

In its second, more subtle use, `static` provides a privacy mechanism that is very important for program modularity. By privacy, we mean *visibility*, or *scope*, restrictions on otherwise accessible variables or functions.

This use restricts the scope of the function. Static functions are visible only within the file in which they are defined. Unlike ordinary functions, which can be accessed from other files, a static function is available throughout its own file but in no other. Again, this facility is useful in developing private modules of function definitions. Note that in C++ systems with namespaces, this mechanism should be replaced by anonymous namespaces (see Section 3.10, "Namespaces," on page 80).

```
//C scheme of file privacy using static extern
//C++ should replace this with anonymous namespaces

static int goo(int a)
{
   . . . . .
}

int foo(int a)
{
   . . . . .
   b = goo(a);
   //goo() is available here but not in other files
   . . . . .
}
```

In C++, the system initializes to 0 both external variables and static variables that are not explicitly initialized by the programmer. Such variables include arrays, strings, pointers, structures, and unions. For arrays and strings, this means that each element is initialized to 0; for structures and unions, it means that each member is initialized to 0. In contrast, automatic and register variables usually are not initialized by the system. This means that they can start with "garbage" values.

3.9.5 Linkage Mysteries

Multifile programs require proper linkage. C++ requires some special rules to avoid hidden inconsistencies. As already indicated, a name declared at file scope as explicitly `static` is local and is hidden from other files. This form of linkage is called *internal linkage*. By default, `const` and `typedef` declarations have internal linkage. A `const` variable that is at file scope but is not static can be given external linkage by declaring it `extern`. Finally, linkage to C code is possible using the form

```
extern "C" { code or included file }
```

Linkage to languages other than C is system dependent. For example, some systems might allow `"Pascal"`. (See Section C.11.6, "Type-Safe Linkage for Functions," on page 386.)

It is the coder's responsibility to make sure that all names referring to the identical construct are consistent. It is beyond the scope of this text to discuss all of the nuances of linkage.

Tips for Avoiding Linkage Problems

- Use header files for function prototypes, class definitions, constants, typedefs, templates, inline functions, and named namespaces.

- Use these header files with an `# ifdef` __*filename* as a guard against multiple inclusion.

- Think in terms of the *one-definition rule* (ODR) which states that classes, enumerations, templates, and so forth, must be defined exactly once in the program.

- As a heuristic, envision "writing" the code into one monolithic file and "seeing" whether this causes conflicts.

3.10 Namespaces

C++ inherited C's single global namespace. Programs written by two or more parties can have inadvertent name clashes when combined. C++ encourages multivendor library use. This motivates the addition of a namespace scope to ANSI C++.

```
namespace LMPinc {
   class puzzles { ····· };
   class toys { ····· };
   ·····
}
```

The namespace identifier can be used as part of a scope-resolved identifier, which has the form

namespace_id::*id*

A `using` declaration lets a client have access to all names from that namespace.

```
using namespace LMPinc;
toys  top;                          //LMPinc::toys
```

Namespaces can also nest.

In file namespac.cpp

```
namespace LMPinc{
   int  n;
   namespace LMPdolls {               //inner namespace
      int  sq(){ return n * n; }      //LMPinc::n
      void  pr_my_logo();
   }
   void  LMPdolls::pr_my_logo()
      { cout << "Dolls by Laura" << endl; }
}
```

As mentioned in Section 3.9.4, "The Storage Class `static`," on page 79, namespaces can be used to provide a unique scope that replaces static global declarations. This is done by an anonymous namespace definition, as in

```
namespace { int count = 0; }            //count is unique here
//count is available in the rest of the file
void  chg_cnt(int i) { count = i; }
```

Library headers conforming to ANSI C++ will no longer use the *.h* suffix. Files such as *iostream* and *complex* will be declared with the namespace `std`. Vendors no doubt will continue shipping old-style headers, such as *iostream.h* or *complex.h* as well, so that old code can run without change.

3.11 Pointer Types

C++ *pointers*, used to reference variables and machine addresses, are intimately tied to array and string processing. C++ arrays can be considered a special form of pointer associated with a contiguous piece of memory for storing a series of indexible values.

Pointers are used in programs to access memory and to manipulate addresses. If v is a variable, &v is the *address*, or location in memory, of its stored value. The address operator & is unary and has the same precedence and right-to-left associativity as the other unary operators. Pointer variables can be declared in programs and then used to take addresses as values. The following declares p to be of type "pointer to int":

```
int*  p;
```

The legal range of values for any pointer always includes the special address 0, as well as a set of positive integers that are interpreted as machine addresses on a particular system. Some examples of assignment to the pointer p are

```
p = &i;                  //the address of object i
p = 0;                   //a special sentinel value
p = static_cast<int*>(1507);    //absolute address
```

In the first example, we think of p as "referring to i," "pointing to i," or "containing the address of i." The compiler decides what address to assign the variable i. This will vary from machine to machine and may even differ for various executions on the same machine. The second example is the assignment of the special value 0 to the pointer p. This value is typically used to indicate a special condition. For example, a pointer value of 0 is returned by a call to the operator new when free storage is exhausted. That pointer value is also used to indicate the end of a dynamic data structure, such as a tree or a list. In the third example, the cast is necessary to avoid a type error, and an actual memory address is used.

3.11.1 Addressing and Dereferencing

As in C, *dereferencing*, or *indirection*, operator * is unary and has 1
dence and right-to-left associativity as the other unary operators.
*p is the value of the variable that p points to. The direct value of p is a memory
location, whereas *p is the indirect value of p, namely, the value at the memory location stored in p. In a certain sense, * is the inverse operator to &. Here is code showing some of these relationships.

```
int   i = 5, j;
int*  p = &i;         //pointer init to address of i

cout << *p << " = i stored at " << p << endl;
j = p;                //illegal pointer not convertible to integer
j = *p + 1;           //legal
p = &j;               //p points to j
```

3.11.2 Pointer-Based Call-by-Reference

The *addresses* of variables can be used as arguments to functions so that the stored
values of the variables can be modified in the calling environment to simulate call-
by-reference. Experienced C programmers should skip this discussion and go to the
next section to read about an equivalent C++ technique for call-by-reference parameters. In pointer-based call-by-reference, pointers must be used in the parameter list
in the function definition. Then, when the function is called, addresses of variables
must be passed as arguments. For example, let us code a function order() that
exchanges two values if the first value is greater than the second.

In file order1.cpp

```
//Pointer-based call-by-reference

void  order(int*, int*);

int main()
{
   int   i = 7, j = 3;

   cout << i << '\t' << j << endl;    //7   3 is printed
   order(&i, &j);
   cout << i << '\t' << j << endl;    //3   7 is printed
}
```

```
void order(int* p, int* q)
{
    int   temp;

    if (*p > *q) {
        temp = *p;
        *p = *q;
        *q = temp;
    }
}
```

Most of the work of this program is carried out by the function call to order().
Notice that the addresses of i and j are passed as arguments. As we shall see, this
allows the function call to change the values of i and j in the calling environment.

◆◆◆◆◆◆◆◆◆◆◆◆

Dissection of the **order()** Function

- ```
  void order(int* p, int* q)
  {
      int   temp;
  ```

The parameters p and q are both of type pointer to int. The variable temp is local to
this function and is of type int.

- ```
  if (*p > *q) {
      temp = *p;
      *p = *q;
      *q = temp;
  }
  ```

If the value of what is pointed to by p is greater than the value of what is pointed to
by q, the following is done. First, temp is assigned the value of what is pointed to by
p; second, what is pointed to by p is assigned the value of what is pointed to by q;
and third, what is pointed to by q is assigned the value of temp. This interchanges in
the calling environment the stored values of whatever p and q are pointing to.

The rules for using pointer arguments to achieve call-by-reference can be summarized as follows:

Call-by-Reference Using Pointers

1. Declare a pointer parameter in the function header.

2. Use the dereferenced pointer in the function body.

3. Pass an address as an argument when the function is called.

3.12 Reference Declarations and Call-by-Reference

Reference declarations, a C++ feature not available in C, declare the identifier to be an alternative name, or *alias*, for an object specified in an initialization of the reference. Reference declarations allow a simpler form of call-by-reference parameters. Some examples are

```
int      n;
int&     nn = n          //nn is alternative name for n
double   a[10];
double&  last = a[9];    //last is an alias for a[9]
```

Declarations of references that are definitions must be initialized and are usually initialized to simple variables. The initializer is an lvalue expression, which gives the variable's location in memory. In these examples, the names n and nn are aliases for each other; that is, they refer to the same object. Modifying nn is equivalent to modifying n and vice versa. The name last is an alternative to the single array element a[9]. These names, once initialized, cannot be changed.

When a variable i is declared, it has an address and memory associated with it. When a pointer variable p is declared and initialized to &i, it has an identity separate from i. The pointer p has memory associated with it that is initialized to the address of i. When a reference variable r is declared and initialized to i, it is identical to i. It does not have an identity separate from the other names for the same object.

The following definitions are used to demonstrate the use of pointers, dereferencing, and aliasing. The definitions assume that memory at location 1004 is used for integer variable a and that memory at 1008 is used for pointer variable p.

```
int   a = 5;          //declaration of a
int*  p = &a;         //p points to a
int&  ref_a = a;      //alias for a
*p = 7;               //*p is lvalue of a, so a is assigned 7
a = *p + 1;           //rvalue 7 added to 1 and a assigned 8
```

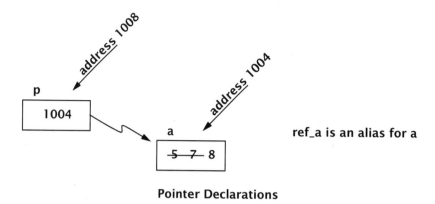

Pointer Declarations

Notice in the figure of pointer declarations that any change to the value of a is equivalent to changing `ref_a`. Such a change affects the dereferenced value of p. The pointer p can be assigned another address and lose its association with a. However, a and `ref_a` are aliases and within scope must refer to the same object. These declarations can be used for call-by-reference arguments, which allows C++ to have call-by-reference arguments directly.

The function `order()` using this mechanism is recoded as follows:

In file order2.cpp

```
void order(int& p, int& q)
{
    int   temp;

    if (p > q) {
        temp = p;
        p = q;
        q = temp;
    }
}
```

The function would be prototyped and invoked in `main()` as follows:

```
void  order(int& p, int& q);

int main()
{
   int  i, j;
   .....
   order(i, j);
   .....
}
```

If i and j are int variables, then order(i, j) will use the reference to i and the reference to j to exchange, if necessary, their two values. In traditional C, this operation must be accomplished by using pointers and dereferencing.

When function arguments are to remain unmodified, it can be efficient and correct to pass them const call-by-reference. This is the case for types that are structures.

```
struct large_size {
   int  mem[N];
   .....
};

void print(const large_size& s)
{
   //since s will not be modified
   //avoid call-by-value copying
   .....
}
```

3.13 The Uses of void

The keyword void is used to declare the *generic* pointer type—pointer to void. The keyword void is also used as the return type of a function not returning a value. In programming, such a function is sometimes called a pure procedure. In addition, void can be used in a cast to indicate that a value is unneeded.

Most interesting is the use of void* as a generic pointer type. A pointer declared as type pointer to void, as in void* gp, may be assigned a pointer value of any underlying base type but may not be dereferenced. Dereferencing is the operation * acting on a pointer value to obtain what is pointed at. It would not make sense to dereference a pointer to a void value.

```
void*   gp;                             //generic pointer
int*    ip;                             //int pointer
char*   cp;                             //char pointer

gp = ip;                                //legal conversion
ip = reinterpret_cast<int*> gp;         //legal conversion
cp = ip;                                //illegal conversion
*ip = 15;                     //legal dereference of pointer to int
*ip = *gp;                    //illegal generic pointer dereference
```

A key use for this type is as a formal parameter. For example, the library function memcpy() is declared in *cstring*.

```
void* memcpy(void* s1, void* s2, size_t n);
```

On older C++ systems or on C systems, this is *string.h*. This function copies n characters from the object based at s2 into the object based at s1. The function works with any two pointer types as arguments. The type size_t is defined in *cstddef* and is often a synonym for unsigned int.

A further use of void given as the parameter list in a function declaration means that the function takes no arguments. Thus, int foo() is equivalent in C++ to int foo(void).

A void cast can inform the compiler that the expression's computed value is to be discarded.

In file voidcast.cpp

```
//Simple use of a void cast

int  foo(int i)
{
    cout << "i is " << i << endl;
    return i;
}

int main()
{
    int  k = 5;

    static_cast<void>(foo(k));          //remove return value
    .....
}
```

This use is a matter of taste, as most compilers will issue a warning only if the return value from a nonvoid function is not being used or tested for.

3.14 Arrays and Pointers

An array is a data type used to represent a large number of homogeneous values. The array is sequential storage. The elements of an array are randomly accessible through the use of subscripts. Arrays of all types are possible, including arrays of arrays. A typical array declaration allocates memory starting from a base address. An array name is, in effect, a pointer constant to this base address. In C++, only one-dimensional arrays are provided, with the first element always indexed as element zero.

To illustrate some of these ideas, let us write a small program that fills an array, prints out values, and sums the elements of the array.

In file sum_arr1.cpp

```
//Simple array processing

const int  SIZE = 5;

int main()
{
   int  a[SIZE];                //get space for a[0],·····,a[4]
   int  i, sum = 0;

   for (i = 0; i < SIZE; ++i) {
      a[i] = i * i;
      cout << "a[" << i << "] = " << a[i] << "    ";
      sum += a[i];
   }
   cout << "\nsum = " << sum << endl;
}
```

The output of this program is

```
a[0] = 0   a[1] = 1   a[2] = 4   a[3] = 9   a[4] = 16
sum = 30
```

The preceding array requires enough memory to store five integer values. Thus, if a[0] is stored at location 1000, the remaining array elements on a system needing 4 bytes for an int are successively stored at locations 1004, 1008, 1012, and 1016. It is considered good programming practice to define the size of an array as a symbolic constant. Since much of the code may depend on this value, it is convenient to be able to change a single #define line to process various size arrays. Notice how the various parts of the for statement are neatly tailored to provide a terse notation for dealing with array computations.

3.14.1 Subscripting

Assume that a declaration has the form

```
int  i, a[size];
```

We can write a[i] to access an element of the array. More generally, we may write a[*expr*], where *expr* is an integral expression, to access an element of the array. We call *expr* a *subscript*, or *index*, of a. The value of a C++ subscript should lie in the range 0 to *size* – 1. An array subscript value outside this range often causes a run-time error. When this happens, the condition is called "overrunning the bounds of the array," or "subscript out of bounds." It is a common programming error. The effect of the error in a C++ program is system dependent and can be quite confusing. One frequent result is that the value of an unrelated variable will be returned or modified. Thus, the programmer must ensure that all subscripts stay within bounds.

3.14.2 Initialization

Arrays can be initialized by a comma-separated list of expressions enclosed in braces.

```
int  array[4] = { 9, 8, 7 };    //a[0]=9, a[1]=8, a[2]=7
```

When the list of initializers is shorter than the size of the array, the remaining elements are initialized to 0. If uninitialized, external and static arrays are automatically initialized to 0. This is not so for automatic arrays, which start with undefined values.

An array declared with an explicit initializer list and no size expression is given the size of the number of initializers. The following two arrays are equivalent:

```
char laura[] = { 'l', 'm', 'p' };
char laura[3] = { 'l', 'm', 'p' };
```

3.15 The Relationship Between Arrays and Pointers

An array name by itself is an address, or *pointer value*, and pointers and arrays are almost identical in terms of how they are used to access memory. However, there are subtle and important differences. A pointer is a variable that takes addresses as values. An array name is a particular fixed address that can be thought of as a constant pointer. When an array is declared, the compiler must allocate a base address and a sufficient amount of storage to contain all of the elements of the array. The base address of the array is the initial location in memory where the array is stored; it is the address of the first element (index 0) of the array. Suppose that we write the declaration

```
const int  N = 100;

int  a[N], *p;
```

and the system causes memory bytes 300, 304, 308, . . . , 696 to be the addresses of a[0], a[1], a[2], . . . , a[99], respectively, with location 300 being the base address of a. We are assuming that each byte is addressable and that 4 bytes are used to store an int. The two statements p = a; and p = &a[0]; are equivalent and would assign 300 to p.

Pointer arithmetic provides an alternative to array indexing. The two statements p = a + 1; and p = &a[1]; are equivalent and would assign 304 to p. Assuming that the elements of a have been assigned values, we can use the following code to sum the array:

In file sum_arr2.cpp

```
sum = 0;
for (p = a; p < &a[N]; ++p)
   sum += *p;
```

is equivalent to

```
sum = 0;
for (i = 0; i < N; ++i)
   sum += a[i];
```

In this loop, the pointer variable p is initialized to the base address of the array a. Then the successive values of p are equivalent to &a[0], &a[1], . . . , &a[N-1]. In general, if i is a variable of type int, p + i is the ith offset from the address p. In a similar manner, a + i is the ith offset from the base address of the array a. Here is another way to sum the array.

```
sum = 0;
for (i = 0; i < N; ++i)
    sum += *(a + i);
```

Just as the expression *(a + i) is equivalent to a[i], the expression *(p + i) is equivalent to p[i].

In many ways, arrays and pointers can be treated alike but there is one essential difference. Because the array a is a constant pointer and not a variable and we cannot change the address of a, expressions such as the following are illegal.

```
a = p           ++a           a += 2
```

3.16 Passing Arrays to Functions

In a function definition, a formal parameter that is declared as an array is a pointer. When an array is being passed, its base address is passed call-by-value. The array elements themselves are not copied. As a notational convenience, the compiler allows array bracket notation to be used in declaring pointers as parameters. This notation reminds the programmer and other readers of the code that the function should be called with an array. To illustrate this, we write a function that sums the elements of an array of type int.

In file sum_arr3.cpp

```
int sum(int a[], int n)         //n is the size of a[]
{
    int  i, s = 0;

    for (i = 0; i < n; ++i)
        s += a[i];
    return s;
}
```

As part of the header of a function definition, the declaration int a[] is equivalent to int *a. In other contexts, the two are not equivalent.

Suppose that v has been declared to be an array with 100 elements of type int. After the elements have been assigned values, we can use the function sum() to add various elements of v. The following table illustrates some of the possibilities.

Summing Elements of an Array	
Invocation	**What Gets Computed and Returned**
sum(v, 100)	v[0] + v[1] + . . . + v[99]
sum(v, 88)	v[0] + v[1] + . . . + v[87]
sum(v + 7, k)	v[7] + v[8] + . . . + v[k+6]

The last function call again illustrates the use of pointer arithmetic. The base address of v is offset by 7, and sum() initializes the local pointer variable a to this address. This causes all address calculations inside the function call to be similarly offset.

In C++, a function with a formal array parameter can be called with an array argument of any size, provided the array has the right base type.

3.17 The char* String: A Kernel Language ADT

The C and C++ communities have "agreed" to treat the type char* as a form of string type. The understanding is that such strings will be terminated by the char value 0, and that the *cstring* (or *string.h* on older systems) package of functions will be called on this abstraction. In ANSI C++, the library *string* provides as a template class a standardized string type that is preferred to this use of char*. The language partly supports this abstraction by defining string literals as being null terminated. A char* or char[] can be initialized with a literal string. Note that the terminating 0 is part of the initializer list.

```
char*  s = "c++";   // s[0] = 'c', s[1] = '+',
                    // s[2] = '+', s[3] = '0';
```

The *cstring* package contains more than 20 functions.

Some Functions in the c*string* Library

- `size_t strlen(const char* s);`
  Computes the string length. The number of characters before 0 is returned.

- `char* strcpy(char* s1, const char* s2);`
  Copies the string s2 into s1. The value of s1 is returned.

- `int strcmp(const char* s1, const char* s2);`
  Returns an integer that reflects the lexicographic comparison of s1 and s2. When the strings are the same, 0 is returned. When s1 is less than s2, a negative integer is returned. When s2 is less than s1, a positive integer is returned.

By adhering to these conventions, the programmer can reuse a lot of string code. The library routines ensure that portable, readily understood code is available.

In file str_func.cpp

```
//string function implementations

size_t strlen(const char* s)
{
    int i;
    for (i = 0; s[i]; ++i)
        ;
    return i;
}

int strcmp(const char* s1, const char* s2)
{
    int i;
    for (i=0; s1[i] || s2[i] || (s1[i]!=s2[i]); ++i)
        ;
    return (s1[i] - s2[i]);
}

char* strcpy(char* s1, const char* s2)
{
    for (int i = 0; s1[i] = s2[i]; ++i)
        ;
    return s1;
}
```

Notice how these functions use the convention that a string is null terminated to end their major loops. The function `strcpy()` terminates when `s2[i] == 0`. It is also good practice to place the `const` keyword in front of those strings whose contents will not be modified.

3.18 Multidimensional Arrays

C++ allows arrays of any type, including arrays of arrays. With two bracket pairs, we obtain a two-dimensional array. This idea can be iterated to obtain arrays of higher dimension. With each bracket pair, we add another array dimension.

Declarations of Arrays	
`int a[100];`	a one-dimensional array
`int b[3][5];`	a two-dimensional array
`int c[7][9][2];`	a three-dimensional array

A k-dimensional array has a size for each of its k dimensions. If we let s_i represent the size of its ith dimension, the declaration of the array will allocate space for $s_1 \times s_2 \times \ldots \times s_k$ elements. In the preceding table, b has 3×5 elements, and c has $7 \times 9 \times 2$ elements. Starting at the base address of the array, all of the array elements are stored contiguously in memory, row by row.

Initialization of multidimensional arrays can be a brace-enclosed list of initializers, where each row is initialized from a brace-enclosed list.

```
int   a[2][3] = { {1, 2, 3,}, {4, 5, 6} } ;
                //same as {1, 2, 3, 4, 5, 6}
char  name[3][9] = { "laura", "michelle", "pohl"};
                //pad with '\0'
```

This last example has `name[][]` representing three strings, each storing nine `char` values. So, `name[0][0]` is `'l'`, `name[0][1]` is `'a'`, `name[0][2]` is `'u'`, `name[0][3]` is `'r'`, `name[0][4]` is `'a'`, `name[0][5]` is `'\0'`, `name[0][6]` is `'\0'`, `name[0][7]` is `'\0'`, and `name[0][8]` is `'\0'`.

3.19 Assertions and Program Correctness

An *assertion* is a program check for correctness that, if violated, forces an error exit. One point of view is that an assertion is a contractual guarantee among the provider of a piece of code, the code's manufacturer, and the code's client or user. In this model, the client needs to guarantee that the conditions for applying the code exist, and the manufacturer needs to guarantee that the code will work correctly under these provisions. In this methodology, assertions provide various guarantees.

Program correctness can be viewed in part as a proof that the computation terminated with correct output dependent on correct input. The user of the computation has the responsibility of providing correct input. This is a *precondition*. The computation, if successful, satisfies a *postcondition*. Such assertions can be monitored at runtime to provide very useful diagnostics. Indeed, the discipline of thinking out appropriate assertions frequently allows the programmer to avoid bugs and pitfalls.

In the C++ community, there is an increasing emphasis on the use of assertions. The standard library *assert* provides the macro `assert` and is invoked as though its function signature were

```
void assert(expression);
```

If the *expression* evaluates as `false`, execution is aborted with diagnostic output. The assertions are discarded if the macro `NDEBUG` is defined.

The following program provides assertions to demonstrate this technique. The program examines a slice of an array for its minimum element and places that minimum element in the first examined array position.

In file order3.cpp

```
//Finding a minimum element in an array slice

void order(int& p, int& q)
{
    int temp = p;

    if (p > q) {
        p = q;
        q = temp;
    }
}
```

```
int place_min(int a[], int size, int lb = 0)
{
   int i, min;
   assert(size >= 0);                        //precondition

   for (i = lb; i < lb + size; ++i)
      order(a[lb], a[i + 1]);
   return a[lb];
}

int main()
{
   int   a[9] = { 6, -9, 99, 3, -14, 9, -33, 8, 11};

   cout << "Minimum = " << place_min(a, 3, 2) << endl;
   assert(a[2]<=a[3] && a[2]<=a[4]);         //postcondition
}
```

The precondition assertion in place_min() guarantees that a nonnegative number of elements will be searched. The postcondition in main() checks that the minimum element was found and placed in the correct position.

3.20 Free-Store Operators new and delete

The unary operators new and delete are available to manipulate *free store*. They are more convenient than and replace the C standard library functions malloc(), calloc(), and free() in most applications. Free store is a system-provided memory pool for objects whose lifetime is directly managed by the programmer. The programmer creates an object using new, and destroys the object using delete. This is important for dynamic data structures, such as lists and trees.

In C++, the operator new is typically used in the following forms:

new *type-name*
new *type-name initializer*
new *type-name*[*expression*]

In each case, there are at least two effects. First, an appropriate amount of store is allocated from free store to contain the named type. Second, the base address of the object is returned as the value of the new expression.

The operator new can either throw a bad_alloc exception or return the value 0, when memory is unavailable. (See Section 9.9, "Standard Exceptions and Their Uses," on page 318.)

The following example uses new:

```
int*  p, *q;
p = new int(5);        //allocation and initialization
q = new int[10];       //gets q[0] to q[9] with q = &q[0]
```

In this code, the pointer to int variable p is assigned the address of the store obtained in allocating an object of type int. The location pointed at by p is initialized to the value 5. This use is not usual for a simple type, such as int, in that it is far more convenient and natural to automatically allocate an integer variable on the stack or globally. Usually, an array of elements is allocated to the pointer q.

The operator delete destroys an object created by new, in effect returning its allocated storage to free store for reuse. The operator delete is used in the following forms:

```
delete expression
delete [ ] expression
```

The first form is used when the corresponding new expression has not allocated an array. The second form has empty brackets, indicating that the original allocation was an array of objects. The operator delete does not return a value. Equivalently, one can say that its return type is void. The following example uses these constructs to dynamically allocate an array.

In file dynarray.cpp

```
//Use of new to dynamically allocate an array
//assumes older-style return of 0 for allocation error

int main()
{
   int*  data;
   int   size;

   cout << "\nEnter array size: ";
   cin >> size;
   assert(size > 0);
```

```
    data = new int[size];        //allocate an array of ints
    assert(data != 0);           //data != 0 allocation succeeds
    for (int j = 0; j < size; ++j)
        cout << (data[j] = j) << '\t';
    cout << "\n\n";
    delete[] data;               //deallocate an array
}
```

◆◆◆◆◆◆◆◆◆◆◆◆

Dissection of the *dynarray* Program

- ```
  int*  data;
  int   size;

  cout << "\nEnter array size: ";
  cin >> size;
  assert(size > 0);

  data = new int[size];        //allocate an array of ints
  assert(data != 0);           //data != 0 allocation succeeds
  ```

  The pointer variable data is used as the base address of a dynamically allocated array whose number of elements is the value of size. The user is prompted for the integer valued size. The new operator is used to allocate storage from free store capable of storing an object of type int[size]. On a system on which integers take 2 bytes, this would allocate 2 × size bytes. At this point, data is assigned the base address of this store. The second assert guarantees that allocation succeeded. In newer C++ systems, if the new operator fails, it can throw an exception of type bad_alloc, automatically aborting the program.

- ```
  for (int j = 0; j < size; ++j)
      cout << (data[j] = j) << '\t';
  ```

  This statement initializes the values of the data array and prints them.

- ```
  delete[] data;               //deallocate an array
  ```

  The operator delete returns the storage associated with the pointer variable data to free store. This can be done only with objects allocated by new. The bracket form is used because the corresponding allocation was of an array.

◆◆◆◆◆◆◆◆◆◆◆◆
  ```

This introductory discussion of the free-store operators treats the basic cases. The free-store operators are addressed in greater detail in Chapter 5, "Constructors and Destructors."

3.21 Pragmatics

It is becoming a standard practice to use C++ libraries for accessing both `char*` arrays and general arrays instead of coding the array functions directly. Here, we discuss two such libraries: one for vectors and one for string processing.

3.21.1 Vector Instead of Array

The standard C++ library contains the template for the vector data structure. We will discuss this in detail later (see Section 7.4, "Parameterizing the Class `vector`," on page 249). In almost all cases, the vector is an improvement over the simple C++ array but can be used essentially as an array. We recommend that the vector be used in place of arrays for most programming. For example, the function in Section 3.16, "Passing Arrays to Functions," on page 92, for summing an array uses `int sum(int a[], int n)`. We can trivially change this to use vector as follows:

```
int sum(vector<int> a, int n)
{
   int  i, s = 0;

   for (i = 0; i < n; ++i)
      s += a[i];
   return s;
}
```

Notice that the only change was to transform the array declaration to a vector declaration. Without investigating the details of template syntax, we can use a simple rule:

    Type id[]   is replaced by   vector<*Type*> *id*

If the declaration requires an array size, we can extend the rule as follows:

    Type id[*size*]   is replaced by   vector<*Type*> *id(size)*

One improvement for `vector` is that it knows the number of elements associated with it. The expression *id*.`size()` gives the current number of elements contained in the vector. Using this information improves the `sum()` function by making it simpler and by avoiding errors that come about in C and C++ when the wrong size is passed as a parameter. This prevents out-of-range errors that are the bane of C array programming.

In file sum_arr4.cpp

```
//sum written to use a.size() in place of N

int sum(vector<int> a)
{
   int  i, s = 0;

   for (i = 0; i < a.size(); ++i)
      s += a[i];
   return s;
}
```

3.21.2 String Instead of `char*`

In C++, the standard library provides both *cstring* and *string*. Both libraries can be used for string processing, and they can be used jointly. However, C++ style is to prefer the use of the `string` type, which is more robust and has a more extensive interface. In certain cases, it is both more efficient and elegant. For a more extended discussion of `string`, see Section 5.4, "An Example: Dynamically Allocated Strings," on page 159, and Section 5.10, "Strings Using Reference Semantics," on page 181.

The following simple program uses `string`. The program is easy to understand and is easy to use because the operator + provides concatenation.

In file string1.cpp

```
//Print strings with line numbers

void pr_line_number(string& line)
{
   static int ln = 0;

   ln++;                    //start the line numbers at 1
   cout << "line " << ln << ":" + line + "\n";
}
```

```
int main()
{
   string s1, s2;

   cin >> s1 >> s1;
   pr_line_number(s1);
   pr_line_number(s2);
   cout << endl;
}
```

3.22 Moving from C++ to Java

Java does not have pointers but instead has nonprimitive variables that are references. Java avoids much of the direct programmer management of memory that causes so many bugs in C and C++. Java does have arrays, which are reference types. Java does not have functions that are outside the scope of a class. Java's term for functions is *methods* to indicate that all functions are members of a class. The closest construct to an ordinary C or C++ function is a static method. Java can overload methods but does not allow default arguments or inlining.

The following program initializes an array, prints its values, and computes its sum and average value:

In file SumArray.java

```
class SumArray {
   public static void main(String[] args)
   {
      int[] data = {1, 2, 3, 4, 5, 6, 7};
      int sum = 0;
      double average;

      for (int i = 0; i < 7; ++i) {
         sum = sum + data[i];
         System.out.print(data[i] + ", ");
      }
      average = sum / 7.0;
      System.out.println("\n\n sum = " + sum
         + " average = " + average);
   }
}
```

Dissection of the *SumArray* Program

- `int[] data = {1, 2, 3, 4, 5, 6, 7};`

The variable data is declared to refer to an array of integers. It is allocated seven integer elements, which are initialized to the values 1 through 7.

- `for (int i = 0; i < 7; ++i) {`

The `for` statement declares the local variable i to be used as an index or a subscript variable. This `for` statement is the most common array code idiom. The initial subscript for array objects in Java is 0, so the subscript variable is usually initialized to 0. The array length is 7, so the terminating condition is usually `i < 7` so that the array index will stop at 7 - 1. The last part of the `for` statement header is the auto-increment of the index variable, so that each array element gets processed in turn.

- ```
      sum = sum + data[i];
      System.out.print(data[i] + ", ");
  }
  ```

The element `data[i]` is selected by computing the index value. A common error that results in an exception is for this to be out of range. These subscripted or indexed elements can be used as simple variables of type `int`. In this code, each element's integer value is added to the variable `sum`. Then, in turn, each element's value is printed.

Note: In this example, `main()` is `static`. The Java `static` method more or less corresponds to an ordinary C function.
  ```

Summary

This summary emphasizes, in order of appearance, changes and differences from C in the C++ language.

1. In ANSI C++, the empty parameter list is always equivalent to using `void`, and so `main()` is equivalent to `main(void)`. The function `main()` implicitly returns the integer value 0 if no explicit `return` expression statement is executed.

2. A formal parameter can be given a default argument, usually a constant that occurs frequently when the function is called. Use of a default argument saves writing this default value at each invocation. The following function header shows the syntax:

   ```
   int sqr_or_power(int n, int k = 2);   //k=2 is default
   ```

3. Overloading refers to using the same name for multiple meanings of an operator or a function. The meaning selected depends on the types of the arguments used by the operator or function. In the following code, we overload `avg_arr()`:

   ```
   //Average the values in an array

   double avg_arr(const int a[], int size);
   double avg_arr(const double a[], int size);{
   ```

4. Reference declarations allow an object to be given an alias, or alternative name. These declarations can be used for call-by-reference arguments. For example, the function `order()`, using this mechanism, is declared as

   ```
   void order(int &p, int &q);
   ```

5. C++ provides the keyword `inline` to preface a function declaration when the programmer intends the code replacing the function call to be inline. In most cases, this should be used in place of `#define` macros.

6. C++ inherited C's single global namespace. Programs written by various parties can inadvertently have name clashes when combined. C++ adds namespace scope, as in

```
namespace StellarSoft {
    class S_widget { ····· };
    int update{ ····· };
    ·····
}
```

The namespace identifier can be used as part of a scope-resolved identifier. This has the form

namespace_id::id

There is also a `using` declaration, which lets a client have access to all names from that namespace.

```
using namespace StellarSoft;
S_widget  w;              //StellarSoft::S_widget
```

Namespaces can be used to provide a unique scope that replaces static global declarations.

7. The declaration `void*` is a generic pointer type. A pointer declared as type pointer to `void`, as in `void* gp`, can be assigned a pointer value of any underlying base type, but it may not be dereferenced. Unlike in C, a generic pointer may not be assigned to a nonvoid pointer type without an explicit cast. In this regard, C++ is again more type safe than C is.

8. The C and C++ communities have "agreed" to treat the type `char*` as a form of string type. The understanding is that these strings will be terminated by the `char` value 0, and that the *cstring* (or *string.h* on older systems) package of functions will be called on this abstraction. In ANSI C++, the library *string* provides as a template class a standardized string type that is preferred to this use of `char*`.

9. The unary operators `new` and `delete` are available to manipulate free store. Free store is a system-provided memory pool for objects whose lifetime is directly managed by the programmer. The programmer creates an object by using `new` and destroys the object by using `delete`. This is important for dynamic data structures, such as lists and trees.

10. The standard library contains the template for the `vector` data structure. In almost all cases, the vector is an improvement over the simple C++ array but can be used essentially as an array. We recommend that it be used in place of arrays for most programming.

Review Questions

1. If not explicitly returned, the value _____ is returned by `main()`.

2. Replace `#define ABS(X)    ((X <0) ? -X: X)` by an inline function.

3. Discuss the difference between using the macro `ABS(f(y))` and the equivalent inline call. Assume that `f(y)` calls a nontrivial function.

4. What is wrong with overloading `int foo();` and `void foo();` in the same scope? Note that the only difference in their declarations is the return types.

5. The C++ STL `vector` can be used to replace _____ in C and C++ programs.

6. In C, control of an `if` statement depends on whether an `if` statement expression is zero or nonzero. In C++, this condition is type _____.

7. In C, the function `strlen()` is found in _____; in C++, it is found in _____. Can you think of a reason for this difference?

8. The _____ exception is thrown when _____ fails to properly allocate memory.

9. The operator _____ is used in place of the *cstdlib* function `free()` to return memory to free store.

10. In C, call-by-reference requires the use of pointers, but in C++, _____ may be used as well.

Exercises

1. Pointers to `char` strings are by convention terminated with the value 0. The following function implements a string-equality test. Note its use of pointer arithmetic. The construct `*s1++` means "dereference the pointer `s1`, and after using this value in the expression, add 1 to its pointer value."

```
bool streq(const char* s1, const char* s2)
{
    while ( *s1 != 0 && *s2 != 0)
        if ( *s1++ != *s2++)
            return false;
    return (*s1 == *s2);
}
```

Write and test a function

```
bool strneq(const char* s1, const char* s2, int n);
```

that returns `true` if the first *n* characters of the two strings are the same and that otherwise returns `false`.

2. Reimplement the preceding functions using array notation.

```
bool streq(char s1[], char s2[]);
```

3. The standard header file *cstring* contains the prototypes for a number of useful string functions found in the standard library. Among them is:

```
size_t strlen(const char* s);
```

This returns the length of a string. The text in Section 3.17, "The `char*` String: A Kernel Language ADT," on page 94, gave a terse definition of this function; here is another way to code it:

```
//iterative string length
size_t strlen(const char *s)
{
    size_t  len = 0;

    while (*s != '\0') {        //string terminator
        ++len;                  //increment length
        ++s;                    //advance pointer
    }
    return len;
}
```

This algorithm marches the pointer s down the string, looking for the termination character. External to the function, the pointer value has not been changed, because it is call-by-value. Write a recursive version of this function.

4. The greatest common divisor of two integers is recursively defined in pseudocode as follows:

```
GCD(m,n) is:
    if m mod n equals 0 then n;
    else GCD(n, m mod n);
```

Recall that the modulo operator in C++ is %. Code this routine in C++.

5. We wish to count the number of recursive function calls by gcd(). It is generally bad practice to use globals inside functions. In C++, we can use a local static variable instead of a global. Complete and test the following C++ gcd() function:

```
int gcd(int m, int n)
{
    static int  fcn_calls = 1;    //happens once
    int         r;                //remainder

    fcn_calls++;
    .....
}
```

6. The following C program uses traditional C function syntax:

```
/* Compute a table of cubes. */

#define  N    15
#define  MAX  3.5

int main()
{
    int     i;
    double  x, cube();

    printf("\n\nINTEGERS\n");
    for (i = 1; i <= N; ++i)
        printf("cube(%d) = %d\n", i, cube(i));
    printf("\n\nREALS\n");
    for (x = 1; x <= MAX; x += 0.3)
        printf("cube(%f) = %f\n", x, cube(x));
}

double cube(x)
double  x;
{
    return (x * x * x);
}
```

The program gives the wrong answers for the integer arguments because integer arguments are passed as if their bit representation were double. It is unacceptable as C++ code. Recode, as a proper function prototype, and run, using a C++ compiler. C++ compilers enforce type compatibility on function argument values. Therefore, the integer values are properly promoted to double values.

7. Predict what the following program prints:

```
int foo(int n)
{
    static int  count = 0;

    ++count;
    if ( n <= 1) {
        cout << " count = " << count << endl;
        return n;
    }
    else
        foo(n / 3);
}

int main()
{
    foo(21);
    foo(27);
    foo(243);
}
```

8. The `static` storage class is useful in multifile compilation. Predict what the following program prints:

```
//  file A.c

static int  foo(int i)
{
    return (i * 3);
}

int  goo(int i)
{
    return (i * foo(i));
}

//  file B.c

int foo(int i)
{
    return (i * 5);
}
```

```
int  goo(int i);          //imported from file A.c

int main()
{
    cout << "foo(5) = " << foo(5) << endl;
    cout << "goo(5) = " << goo(5) << endl;
}
```

The program is compiled as follows: *g++ A.c B.c.* File-scope functions are by
default `extern`. The `foo()` in file *A.c* is private to that file, but `goo()` is not.
Thus, redefining `foo()` in file *B.c* does not cause an error. Try this again, this
time dropping `static`, to see what error message your compiler gives. Then try
a third time, making `goo()` `inline` in *A.c*, to see what error message your compiler gives. Recode these files, using anonymous namespaces to replace the
`static extern` declarations.

9. C++ provides a method to pass command-line arguments into the function
`main()`. The following code prints its command-line arguments:

```
//Print command-line arguments rightmost first

int main(int argc, char **argv)
{
    for (--argc; argc >= 0; --argc)
        cout << argv[argc] << endl;
}
```

Compile this into an executable called *echo*. Run it with the following command-
line arguments:

> *echo a man a plan a canal panama*

The argument `argc` is passed the number of command-line arguments. Each
argument is a string placed in the two-dimensional array `argv`.

10. Modify the previous program to print the command-line arguments from left to
right and to number each of them.

11. One advantage of C++ over traditional languages is type extensibility. Using the
complex library, you can import a complex number type that can be mixed and
matched with the native arithmetic types. Overload and test

```
complex<double> avg_arr(const complex<double> a[], int size)
```

12. Redo the previous exercise and use `vector<complex<double> > a` as the argument. Overload and test, using the fact that vectors maintain their own size:

    ```
    complex<double> avg_arr(const vector< complex<double> > a)
    ```

13. The problem with using `void*` is that it cannot be dereferenced. Thus, to perform useful work on a generic pointer, one must cast it to a standard working type, such as a `char*`. Write and test

    ```
    void* memcpy(void* s1, const void* s2, unsigned n)
    {
       char*  from = s2, *to = s1;    //uses char type
       .....
    }
    ```

14. Write a program that performs string reversal. Assume that `s1` ends up with the reverse of the string `s2` and that `s1` points at enough store that is adequate for reversal. (See Section 3.17, "The `char*` String: A Kernel Language ADT," on page 94, for some examples of string-handling functions.)

    ```
    char* strrev(char* s1, const char* s2);
    ```

15. Write a program that performs string reversal, using storage allocated with new. Assume that `s1` ends up with the reverse of the string `s2`, and use new to allocate `s1` of length `strlen(s2) + 1`, which is adequate store for `s1`.

    ```
    char* strrev(char*& s1, const char* s2);
    ```

16. Write a program that allocates a one-dimensional array from free store, using user-provided lower and upper bounds. The program should check that the upper bound exceeds the lower bound. If that is not the case, perform an error exit, using the *assert* library, as follows:

    ```
    //input lower bound and upper bound

    assert(ub - lb > 0);
       .....
    ```

    The size of this array will be (*upper bound – lower bound + 1*) elements. Given a standard C++ array of this many elements, write a function that uses the standard array to initialize the dynamic array. Test this by writing out in a nicely formatted style both arrays before and after initialization.

17. Write a function

    ```
    double findmin(double fcn(double), double x0,
                   double x1, double incr, double& xmin)
    ```

    that returns the value at `fcn(xmin)`, where `xmin` is the minimum value of `fcn(x)` in the interval `(x0, x1)`, evaluated at increments of `incr`.

18. Rewrite the function `findmin()` so that the range (0, 1.0) and the increment 0.00001 is used by default, unless explicitly passed in. Note that to do this, the preceding function arguments should be used but in a different order. Why?

19. Write a function

    ```
    double plot(double y[], double fcn(double), double x0,
                double x1, double incr)
    ```

    that computes $y[i] = fcn(x_i)$, where x_i is in the interval `(x0, x1)`, evaluated at increments of `incr`. Use the defaults (0, 1.0) and an increment of 0.001, with `y` expected to have 1,000 elements.

20. Redo the previous exercise to use `vector<double>` `y`.

21. Write a function `findzero()` that finds `xzero`, the value closest to zero in a specified interval. The function should have the same arguments as `findmin()`. Again write it to have standard default values for its parameters.

22. Modify the dynamic array program in Section 3.20, "Free-Store Operators `new` and `delete`," on page 98, so that it is initialized by pseudorandom numbers in the range (0, `RAND_MAX`). For 5,000 such random numbers, find their average value. See whether, while using the operator `new`, you can do this problem for 50,000, 500,000, 5,000,000, . . ., until you find a value on your system that causes `new` to fail. If you rewrote this code to use ordinary stack-allocated arrays, at what size on your system will it fail to allocate the array? Also try the same problem, using `vector<int>`, and see how large a problem can be run.

23. Write a function index (BMI) to compute body mass as follows:

    BMI = (*weight in kilograms*) / (*height in meters*)^2

    If the BMI is over 25, you are considered overweight; if it is over 40, you are considered obese. Test the program on data taken from at least five individuals, printing out for each name a weight, height, BMI, and BMI category of normal, overweight, or obese.

24. *(Java)* Recode the BMI program in Java. Use Java arrays to store values for each individual.

Chapter 4
Classes

This chapter introduces the reader to structures and classes. The original name given by Stroustrup to his language was "C with classes." A *class* is an extension of the idea of `struct` found in C. A class packages a data type with its associated functions and operators. User-defined data types, such as stacks, complex numbers, and card decks are examples of classes. In C++, structures may have member functions and also may have parts of their descriptions hidden. Both of these extensions will be described here.

C++ classes bundle data declarations with function declarations, thereby coupling data with behavior. The class description also has access modifiers that allow data hiding. Access that is public is available to any part of the code. Access that is private is restricted principally to use by the class code itself.

Allowing private and public *visibility* for members gives the programmer control over what parts of the data structure are modifiable. The private parts are hidden from client code, and the public parts are available. It is possible to change the hidden representation, but not to change the public access or functionality. If this is done properly, client code need not change when the hidden representation is modified. A large part of the OOP design process involves thinking up the appropriate ADTs for a problem. Good ADTs not only model key features of the problem but also are frequently reusable in other code.

4.1 The Aggregate Type `struct` and `class`

The structure type allows the programmer to aggregate components into a single named variable. A structure has components, called *members*, that are individually named. Since the members of a structure can be of various types, the programmer can create aggregates that are suitable for describing complicated data.

As a simple example, let us define a structure that will describe a point. We can declare the structure type as follows:

```
struct point {
    double x, y;
}
```

In C++, the structure name, or *tag name*, is a type. In the preceding declaration, `struct` is a keyword, `point` is the structure tag name, and the variables x and y are members of the structure. The declaration `point` can be thought of as a blueprint; it creates the type `point`, but no instances are allocated. The declaration

```
point   pt;
```

allocates storage for the variable pt. To access the members of pt, we use the structure member operator, represented by a period, or dot. It is a construct of the form

structure_variable.member_name

and is used as a variable in the same way that a simple variable or an element of an array is used. Suppose that we want to assign to pt the value (-1, +0.5). To do this, we can write

```
pt.x = -1;
pt.y = 0.5;
```

The member name must be unique within the specified structure. Since the member must always be prefaced or accessed through a unique structure variable identifier, there is no confusion between two members that have the same name in different structures. An example is

```
struct fruit {
   char   name[15];
   int    calories;
};

struct vegetable {
   char   name[15];
   int    calories;
};

fruit      a;        //struct fruit     a; in C
vegetable  b;        //struct vegetable b; in C
```

Having made these declarations, we can access a.calories and b.calories without ambiguity.

In general, a structure is declared with the keyword `struct`, followed by an identifier (tag name), followed by a brace-enclosed list of member declarations. The tag name is optional but should be expressive of the ADT concept being modeled.

When the tag name is not present, the structure declaration is anonymous and can be used only to declare variables of that type immediately, as in

```
struct {
    int a, b, c;
} triples [2] = { {3, 3, 6}, {4, 5, 5} };
```

4.2 Structure Pointer Operator

We have already seen the use of the member operator in accessing members. Now we introduce the structure pointer operator ->, which provides access to the members of a structure via a pointer. This operator is typed on the keyboard as a minus sign followed by a greater-than sign. If a pointer variable is assigned the address of a structure, a member of the structure can be accessed by a construct of the form

pointer_to_structure -> *member_name*

An equivalent construct is given by

(*pointer_to_structure*) . *member_name*

The operators -> and ., along with () and [], have the highest precedence, and they associate left to right. In complicated situations, the two accessing modes can be combined. The following table illustrates their use.

Declarations and Assignments		

point w, *p = &w;
point v[5];
w.x = 1;
w.y = 4;
v[0] = w;		

Expression	**Equivalent Expression**	**Value**
w.x	p -> x	1
w.y	p -> y	4
v[0].x	v -> x	1
(*p).y	p -> y	4

4.3 Member Functions

The concept of `struct` or `class` is augmented in C++ to allow functions to be members. The function declaration is included in the structure declaration and is invoked by using access methods for structure members. The idea is that the functionality required by the structure or class should be directly included in the `struct` declaration. This construct improves the encapsulation of the ADT `point` operations by packaging it directly with its data representation. Let us add a printing operation and an initializing operation to the ADT `point`.

In file point1.cpp

```
struct point {
    double x, y;
    void print() { cout << "(" << x << "," << y << ")"; }
    void init(double u, double v) { x = u; y = v; }
};
```

The member functions are written in much the same way that other functions are. One difference is that they can use the data member names directly. Thus, the member functions in `point` use x and y in an unqualified manner. When invoked on a particular object of type `point`, they act on the specified member in that object.

Let us use these member functions in an example.

```
int main()
{
    point w1, w2;

    w1.init(0, 0.5);
    w2.init(-0.5, 1.5);
    cout << "\npoint w1 = ";
    w1.print();
    cout << "\npoint w2 = ";
    w2.print();
}
```

This prints

```
point w1 = (0,0.5)
point w2 = (-0.5,1.5)
```

Member functions that are defined within the `struct` are implicitly inline. As a rule, only short, heavily used member functions should be defined within the `struct`, as in the example just given. To define a member function outside the `struct`, the scope resolution operator is used (see Section 4.6, "Class Scope," on page 122). Let us illustrate this by adding a member function, `point::plus()`. We write it out fully, using the scope resolution operator. In this case, the function is not implicitly inline.

In file point1.cpp

```
struct point {
.....
   void  plus(point c);          //function prototype
   .....
};

void point::plus(point c)     //definition not inline
{
//offset the existing point by point c
   x += c.x;
   y += c.y;
}
```

Member functions within the same `struct` can be overloaded. Consider adding to the data type `point` a print operation that has a string parameter printed as the name of the point. The print operation could be added as the following function prototype within the `struct`:

In file point1.cpp

```
struct point {
   .....
   void print(string name);
   .....
};

void point::print(string name)
{
   cout << name << " (" << x << "," << y << ")";
}
```

The definition that is invoked depends on the arguments to `print()`:

```
w1.print();                  //invokes standard print
w1.print("point w = ");      //invokes print with name
```

A member function is conceptually part of the type. The `inline` specification can be used explicitly, with member functions defined at file scope, which avoids having to clutter the class definition with function bodies. The grouping of operations with data emphasizes their "objectness." Objects have a description and behavior. Think of an object as a noun and its behavior as the verbs that are most often associated with that noun. OOP is a data-centered design approach.

4.4 Access: Private and Public

In C++, structures have public and private members. Inside a `struct` or a `class`, the use of the keyword `private` followed by a colon restricts the access to the members that follow this construct. The private members can be used by only a few categories of functions, those whose privileges include access to these members. These functions include the member functions of the structure. Other categories of functions that have access will be discussed later.

We modify our example of `point` to hide its data representation, as follows:

In file point2.cpp

```
struct point {
public:
   void print(){ cout << "(" << x << "," << y << ")";}
   void init(double u, double v) { x = u; y = v; }
   void plus(point c);
private:
   double x, y;
};
```

An attempt by a nonmember function to access the now private members will result in a syntax error.

```
void foo(point w)
{
   .....
   cout << " x coordinate = " << w.x ;    //syntax error
   .....
}
```

Hiding data is an important component of OOP. It allows for more easily debugged and maintained code, because errors and modifications are localized. Client programs need be aware only of the type's interface specification.

4.5 Classes

Classes in C++ are introduced by the keyword `class`. A form of `struct`, classes have a default privacy specification of `private`. Thus, `struct` and `class` can be used interchangeably, with the appropriate access specifications. In the following example, we modify `point` to use `class`:

In file point3.cpp

```
class point {
   double x, y;          //implicitly private
public:
   void print() { cout << "(" << x << "," << y << ")"; }
   void init(double u, double v) { x = u; y = v; }
   void plus(point c);
};
```

Contemporary C++ style is to use access specifiers explicitly rather than to rely on defaults. The use of implicit features is labor saving but error prone. Therefore, it is better style to declare `point` as follows:

In file point4.cpp

```
class point {
public:                   //place public members first
   void print() { cout << "(" << x << "," << y << ")"; }
   void init(double u, double v) { x = u; y = v; }
   void plus(point c);
private:
   double x, y;
};
```

When access keywords are used, `struct` and `class` are interchangeable. Stylistically, professional C++ programmers use `class` in preference to `struct` unless the `struct` has only public data members.

As a second example, let us write an ADT for complex numbers, which many scientific computations require. Let us recode complex numbers from Section 1.4, "Classes and Abstract Data Types," on page 7.

In file complex4.cpp

```
class complex {
public:                        //need to know style - our preference
    void   assign(double r, double i) { real = r;   imag = i; }
    void   print() { cout << real << " + " << imag << "i "; }
private:
    double   real, imag;
};
```

This text uses access keywords explicitly and places public members first and private members last. In this "need-to-know" style, everyone needs to know the public interface, but only the class provider needs to know the private implementation details.

The presence of member functions within the class shows the clear relationship of the data type `complex` and its associated operations `assign()` and `print()`. There is also less likelihood of a misuse of the representation, since the implementation details `real` and `imag` are private. An attempt to directly alter these members would result in the syntactic error access violation, so a client of this version of `complex` must use member functions that properly act on complex variables.

4.6 Class Scope

Class adds new scope rules to those of the kernel language. (See Section 3.9, "Scope and Storage Class," on page 74.) One point of classes is to provide an encapsulation technique. Conceptually, it makes sense that all names declared within a class be treated within their own scope as distinct from external names, function names, and other class names. This creates a need for the scope resolution operator.

4.6.1 Scope Resolution Operator

The scope resolution operator, the highest-precedence operator in the language, comes in two forms:

```
::i              //unary operator  - refers to external scope
foo_bar::i       //binary operator - refers to class scope
```

Its unary form is used to uncover or to access a name that has external scope and has been hidden by local or class scope.

In file how_many1.cpp

```
int  count = 0;                       //global count

void how_many(double w[], double x, int& count)
{
   for (int i = 0; i < N; ++i)
      count += (w[i] == x);           //local count
   ++ ::count;                        //global count tracks calls
}
```

To understand this program fragment, change the parameter `int& count` to `int& cnt`. Now there is no need for the scope resolution operator, as the two identifiers are distinct.

In file how_many2.cpp

```
int  count = 0;                       //global count

void how_many(double w[], double x, int& cnt)
{
   for (int i = 0; i < N; ++i)
      cnt += (w[i] == x);
   ++count;                           //global count tracks calls
}
```

Binary scope resolution is used to clarify names that are reused within classes:

```
class widgets { public: void f(); };
class gizmos  { public: void f(); };

void f() { ····· }                    //ordinary external f
void widgets::f() { ····· }           //f scoped to widgets
void gizmos::f() { ····· }            //f scoped to gizmos
```

One way to think about the scope resolution operator is to view it as providing a path to the identifier. If there is no scope modifier, normal scope rules apply. Continuing with the previous example:

```
widgets  w;
gizmos   g;

g.f();
w.f();
g.gizmos::f();     //legal but redundant
g.widgets::f();    //illegal; widgets::f() cannot act on a gizmo
```

4.6.2 Nested Classes

Like blocks and namespaces, classes are scopes and can nest. Nesting allows local hiding of names and local allocation of resources. This is often desirable when a class is needed as part of the implementation of a larger construct. The following nested classes illustrate current C++ rules.

In file nested.cpp

```
char  c;                //external scope  ::c

class X {               //outer class declaration  X::
public:
   char  c;             //X::c
   class Y {            //inner class declaration  X::Y::
   public:
      void foo(char e) { X t; ::c = t.X::c = c = e; }
   private:
      char  c;          //X::Y::c
   };
};
```

In class Y, the member function foo(), when using ::c, references the global variable c; when using X::c, it references the outer class variable; when using c, it references the inner class variable X::Y::c. All three variables named c are accessible by using the scope resolution operator.

Furthermore, purely locally scoped classes can be created within blocks. Their definitions are unavailable outside their local block context.

```
void foo()
{
   class local { ····· } x;
}

local y;          //illegal:local is scoped within foo()
```

Notice that C++ allows you to nest function definitions by using class nesting, which is a restricted form of function nesting. The member functions must be defined inside the local class and cannot be referred to outside this scope. As in C, ordinary nested functions are not possible.

4.7 An Example: Flushing

We want to estimate the probability of being dealt a flush in poker. A flush occurs when at least five cards are of the same suit. We simulate shuffling cards by using a random-number generator. This is a form of *Monte Carlo* calculation. The program uses classes to represent the necessary data types and functionality.

In file poker.cpp

```
//A poker calculation on flushing

enum suit { clubs, diamonds, hearts, spades };

class pips {
public:
   void   assign(int n) { p = n % 13 + 1; }
   int    getpip() { return p; }
   void   print() { cout << p; }
private:
   int  p;
};

class card {
public:
   suit  s;
   pips  p;
   void  assign(int n)
      { cd = n; s = static_cast<suit>(n/13); p.assign(n); }
   void  pr_card();
private:
   int  cd;        //a cd is from 0 to 51
};
```

```
class deck {
public:
   void  init_deck();
   void  shuffle();
   void  deal(int, int, card*);
   void  pr_deck();
private:
   card  d[52];
};
```

The clustering of member functions and the data members they act on improves modularity. Behavior and description are logically grouped together. Each level of declaration hides the complexity of the previous level.

```
void deck::init_deck()
{
   for (int i = 0; i < 52; ++i)
      d[i].assign(i);
}

void  deck::shuffle()
{
   for (int i = 0; i < 52; ++i) {
      int  k = i + (rand() % (52 - i));
      card  t = d[i];              //swap cards
      d[i] = d[k];
      d[k] = t;
   }
}

void deck::deal(int n, int pos, card* hand)
{
   for (int i = pos; i < pos + n; ++i)
      hand[i - pos] = d[i];
}
```

The init_deck() function calls card::assign() to map the integers into card values. The shuffle() function uses the library-supplied pseudo-random-number generator rand() in *stdlib* to exchange two cards for every deck position. The deal() function takes cards in sequence from deck and arranges them into hands.

```cpp
int main()
{
    card one_hand[9];          //max hand is 9 cards
    deck dk;
    int  i, j, k, fcnt = 0, sval[4];
    int  ndeal, nc, nhand;

    do {
        cout << "\nEnter no. cards in a hand (5-9):";
        cin  >> nc;
    } while (nc < 5 || nc > 9);
    nhand = 52 / nc;
    cout << "\nEnter no. of hands to deal: ";
    cin  >> ndeal;
    srand(time(NULL));          //seed rand() from time()
    dk.init_deck();
    for (k = 0; k < ndeal; k += nhand) {
        if ((nhand + k) > ndeal)
            nhand = ndeal - k;
        dk.shuffle();
        for (i = 0; i < nc * nhand; i += nc) {
            for (j = 0; j < 4; ++j)      //zero suit counts
                sval[j] = 0;
        dk.deal(nc, i, one_hand);        //deal next hand
        for (j = 0; j < nc; ++j)
            sval[one_hand[j].s]++;       //increment suit count
        for (j = 0; j < 4; ++j)
            if (sval[j] >= 5)            //5 or more is flush
                fcnt++;
        }
    }
    cout << "\n\nIn " << ndeal << " ";
    cout << nc << "-card hands there were ";
    cout << fcnt << " flushes\n    ";
}
```

4.8 `static` and `const` Members

C++ allows both static and constant members. Using the modifier `static` in declaring a data member means that the data member is independent of any given class variable. The data member is part of the class but separate from any single class object. Nonstatic data members are created for each instance of the class. Using static data allows class data not specific to any instance to be scoped to the class but still require only one object for its storage. Without static data members, data required by all instances of a class would have to be global, thereby decoupling the relationship between the data and the class.

Since a static member is independent of a particular instance, it can be accessed in the form

   class-name `::` *identifier*

Note the use of the scope resolution operator. A static member of a global class must be explicitly declared and defined in file scope. For example, if we want a counter to keep track of how many points are declared at any time, we can add to class `point` as follows:

```
class point {
public:
    static int how_many;        //declaration
    .....
};

int point::how_many = 0;        //initialization
    .....
++point::how_many;              //use independent of any instance
```

The static member `point::how_many` needs a definition separate from an ordinary `point` variable, since it exists independent from these variables. The static member can be used with scope resolution, since it exists independent of `point` objects. Syntactically, a `static` member function has the modifier `static` precede the return type inside the class declaration. The preferred style for accessing static members is to use scope resolution. Pointer and dot operator access are misleading and give no indication that the member is static. A definition outside the class must not have this modifier.

```
class foo {
.....
    static int  foo_fcn();      //static goes first
.....
};

int foo::foo_fcn()              //no static keyword here
{  /* definition */ }
```

A data member declared with the const modifier cannot be modified after initialization. To use const properly, you need to understand constructors (see Chapter 5, "Constructors and Destructors"). Syntactically, a const member function has the modifier const follow the argument list inside the class declaration. A definition outside the class must also have this modifier.

```
class foo {
.....
    int  foo_fcn() const;
.....
};

int foo::foo_fcn() const        //const keyword needed
{  /* definition */ }
```

The const and static member function implementation can be understood in terms of this pointer access. An ordinary member function invoked as

```
x.mem(i, j, k);
```

has an explicit argument list i, j, k and an implicit argument list that includes the members of x. The implicit arguments can be thought of as a list of arguments accessible through the this pointer. In contrast, a static member function does not get the implicit arguments. A const member function cannot modify its implicit arguments. Writing out const member functions and parameter declarations is called *const-correctness* and is an important aid in writing code. In effect, it is an assertion that the compiler should check that an object will not have its values modified. Const-correctness can also allow the compiler to apply some special optimizations, such as placing a const object in read-only memory.

The following example illustrates these differences.

In file salary.cpp

```
//Calculate salary using static members

class salary {
public:
    void init(int b) { b_sal = b; your_bonus = 0; }
    void  calc_bonus(double perc) { your_bonus = b_sal * perc; }
    static void  reset_all(int p) { all_bonus = p; }
    int  comp_tot() const
       { return (b_sal + your_bonus + all_bonus); }
private:
    int        b_sal;
    int        your_bonus;
    static int  all_bonus;      //declaration
};

//declaration and definition
int salary::all_bonus = 100;

int main()
{
    salary  w1, w2;

    w1.init(1000);
    w2.init(2000);
    w1.calc_bonus(0.2);
    w2.calc_bonus(0.15);
    salary::reset_all(400);
    cout << " w1 " << w1.comp_tot() << "    w2 "
         << w2.comp_tot() << endl;
}
```

Dissection of the *salary* Program

- ```
  class salary {
      .....
  private:
      int        b_sal;
      int        your_bonus;
      static int all_bonus;        //declaration
  };
  ```

There are three private data members. The static member all_bonus requires a file-scope declaration and can exist independent of any specific variables of type salary being declared.

- ```
  void init(int b) { b_sal = b; your_bonus = 0; }
  ```

This assigns the value of b to the member b_sal. This member function initializes the base salary. The variable your_bonus is also initialized. Although our small example did not require this, it is a good habit to initialize all member variables. As we will see in Chapter 5, "Constructors and Destructors," special functions called constructors are used when initialization and object creation are needed.

- ```
  static void  reset_all(int p) { all_bonus = p; }
  ```

The modifier static must come before the function return type.

- ```
  int  comp_tot() const
     { return (b_sal + your_bonus + all_bonus); }
  ```

The const modifier comes between the end of the argument list and the beginning of the code body. This modifier indicates that no data member will have its value changed. Thus, it makes the code more robust. In effect, the self-referential pointer is passed as const salary* const this.

- ```
  salary::reset_all(400);
  ```

A static member function can be invoked by using the scope resolution operator. The member function could also have been invoked as w1.reset_all(400) but this is misleading, since there is nothing special about the class variable w1.
  ```

Note: The `static` keyword is used only in the class definition and must be omitted when the data or function member is defined outside the class.

Newly allowed in C++ is `static const` initialization within a class declaration.

```
class ch_stack {
.....
private:
   static const int max_len = 10000;        //initializer
.....
};

const ch_stack::int max_len;                //declaration required
```

4.8.1 Mutable Members

The keyword `mutable` allows data members of class variables that have been declared `const` to remain modifiable. This reduces the need to cast away constness using `const_cast<>`. The keyword is used as follows.

In file mutable.cpp

```
//class with mutable members

class person {
public:
   person(const char* pname, int page, unsigned long ssno);
   void bday() { ++age; }
   .....
private:
   const char*     name;
   mutable int     age;        //always modifiable
   unsigned long   soc_sec;
};
.....
const person ira("ira pohl", 38, 1110111);
.....
ira.bday();                    //okay, ira.age is mutable
```

4.9 The this Pointer

The keyword this denotes an implicitly declared self-referential pointer that can be used only in a nonstatic member function. In a static member function, the implicit arguments are not available. A simple illustration of the pointer's use follows.

In file point5.cpp

```
//The this pointer

class point {
public:                     //place public members first
   void    print() { cout << "(" << x << "," << y << ")"; }
   void    init(double u, double v) { x = u; y = v; }
   void    plus(point c);
   point   inverse() { x = -x; y = -y; return (*this); }
   point*  where_am_I() { return this; }
private:
   double x, y;
};

int main()
{
   point   a, b;

   a.init(1.5, -2.5);
   a.print();
   cout << "\na is at " << a.where_am_I() << endl;
   b = a.inverse();
   b.print();
   cout << "\nb is at " << b.where_am_I() << endl;
}
```

The output on our system is

```
(1.5,-2.5)
a is at 0x0064fdd4
(-1.5,2.5)
b is at 0x0064fdc4
```

Note that machine addresses are displayed in hexadecimal and are system dependent. In this case, the two addresses differ by 0 x 10, or 16 bytes, the size of the two `doubles` required to represent a point.

The member function `inverse()` uses the implicitly provided pointer `this` to return the newly inverted value of a. The member function `where_am_I` returns the address of the given object. The `this` keyword provides for a built-in self-referential pointer, as if `point` implicitly declared the private member `point* const this`.

4.10 Unions

A *union* is a derived type whose syntax is the same as for structures except that the keyword `union` replaces `struct`. The member declarations share storage, and their values will be overlaid. Therefore, a union allows its value to be interpreted as a set of types that correspond to the member declarations.

A union initializer is a brace-enclosed value for its first member. Consider the following declaration.

In file union.cpp

```
union int_dbl {
    int    i;
    double x;
} n = { 0 };              //i member is init to zero
```

The variable n can be used as either an integer type or a double type:

```
n.i  = 7;                 //int value 7 is stored in n
cout << n.i << " is integer. ";
cout << n.x << " is double - machine dependent.";
n.x  = 7.0;               //double value 7.0 is stored in n
```

This example also illustrates why unions can be dangerous and are often system dependent. On some systems, it is possible that not all bit patterns are legal values for the overlaid types. In that case, a legal value with one type might, when accessed as the other type, lead to an exception.

A union can be anonymous, as in the following code:

In file weekend.cpp

```
enum week { sun, mon, tues, weds, thurs, fri, sat };

static union {
    int   i;
    week  w;
};

i = 5;

if (w == sat || w == sun)
    cout << " It's the weekend! ";
```

The anonymous union allows the individual member identifiers to be used as variables. The member names must be unique within scope, and no variables of the anonymous type can be declared. Note that an anonymous union declared in file scope must be static.

4.11 Bit Fields

A member that is an integral type can consist of a specified number of bits. Such a member is called a *bit field*, and the number of associated bits is called its *width*. The width is specified by a nonnegative constant integral expression following a colon.

```
struct pcard {            //packed representation of card
    unsigned  s : 2;
    unsigned  p : 4;
};
```

The compiler will attempt to pack the bit fields sequentially within memory but it is at liberty to skip to a next byte or word for purposes of alignment. Arrays of bit fields are not allowed. Also, the address operator & cannot be applied to bit fields.

Bit fields are used to address information conveniently in packed form. On many machines, words are 32 bits, and bit operation can be performed in parallel. In this case, bit manipulation is an implementation technique for sets that contain up to 32 elements, as shown next.

In file set.cpp

```
struct word {
unsigned w0:1,w1:1,w2:1, w3:1, w4:1, w5:1, w6:1, w7:1,
   w8:1, w9:1,w10:1,w11:1, w12:1, w13:1, w14:1, w15:1,
  w16:1,w17:1,w18:1,w19:1, w20:1, w21:1, w22:1, w23:1,
  w24:1,w25:1,w26:1,w27:1, w28:1, w29:1, w30:1, w31:1;
};
```

We can overlay word and unsigned within a union to create a data structure for manipulating bits.

```
union set {
   word      m;
   unsigned  u;
};

int main()
{
   set  x, y;

   x.u = 0x0f100f10;
   y.u = 0x01a1a0a1;
   x.u = x.u | y.u;              //set union
   cout << "element 9 ="
        << ((x.m.w9)? "true" : "false") << endl;
}
```

The set operation union is performed as a word-parallel operation on most systems.

4.12 A Container Class Example: ch_stack

A *container* is a data structure whose main purpose is to store and retrieve a large number of values. In the kernel language, an array acts as such a structure. In this section, we develop code that is used to store character values in a *stack*, which is a *last-in-first-out* (LIFO) container, using ch_stack to store characters.

In file ch_stac1.h

```
class ch_stack {
public:
   void   reset() { top = EMPTY; }
   void   push(char c) { top++; s[top] = c; }
   char   pop() { return s[top--]; }
   char   top_of() const { return s[top]; }
   bool   empty() const { return (top == EMPTY);}
   bool   full() const { return (top == FULL); }
private:
   enum { max_len = 100, EMPTY = -1, FULL = max_len-1 };
   char   s[max_len];
   int    top;
};
```

The basic operations on a stack are push and pop. The push operation places a value on the top of the stack, and the pop operation removes the value at the top of the stack. We use a fixed-length char array to implement the stack. Later, we will talk about other, more flexible implementations.

We now write main() to test the same operations.

In file ch_stac1.cpp

```
//Reverse a string with a ch_stack

int main()
{
   ch_stack  s;
   char    str[40] = { "My name is Don Knuth!" };
   int     i = 0;

   cout << str << endl;
   s.reset();                        //s.top = EMPTY; would be illegal
   while (str[i] && !s.full())
      s.push(str[i++]);
   while (!s.empty())                //print the reverse
      cout << s.pop();
   cout << endl;
}
```

The output from this version of the test program is

```
My name is Don Knuth!
!htunK noD si eman yM
```

As the comment in `main()` states, access to the hidden variable `top` is controlled. The variable can be changed by the member function `reset()` but cannot be accessed directly. Also, notice how the variable `s` is passed to each member function, using the structure member operator form.

The `ch_stack` class has a private part that contains its data description and a public part that contains member functions to implement `ch_stack` operations. It is useful to think of the private part as restricted to the implementor's use and the public part as an interface specification that clients may use. The implementor could change the private part without affecting the correctness of a client's use of the `ch_stack` type.

4.13 Pragmatics

The access order for classes has traditionally been private first, as in

```
class ch_stack {
private:
   int    top;
   enum { max_len = 100, EMPTY = -1, FULL = max_len-1 };
   char   s[max_len];
public:
   void   reset() { top = EMPTY; }
   void   push(char c) { top++; s[top] = c; }
   char   pop() { return s[top--]; }
   char   top_of() const { return s[top]; }
   bool   empty() const { return (top == EMPTY); }
   bool   full() const { return (top == FULL); }
};
```

The reason is that, in the original form of C++, the access keywords `private` and `protected` did not exist. By default, member access for `class` was `private`; therefore, the private members had to come first.

The style of public first is becoming the norm. It follows the rule that the widest audience needs to see the public members. More specialized information is placed later in the class declaration.

Data members should in general be private. This is an important coding heuristic. Generally, data are part of an implementation choice and should be accessed through public member functions. Such member functions are called *accessor functions* when they do not change, or mutate, the data. This is not necessarily inefficient, because simple accessor member functions can be inline. In the class `ch_stack`, the member functions `top_of()`, `empty()`, and `full()` are all inline accessor functions. Accessor functions should be declared `const`. The member function `reset()` is a *mutator*. It allows a constrained action on the hidden variable `top`. Notice how much safer such a design is. If `top` were directly accessible, it would be easy for it to be inappropriately changed.

In OOP design, the public members are usually functions and are thought of as the type's *interface*. These are the actions, or behaviors, publicly expected of an object. If we think of the object type as a noun, the behaviors are verbs. In the implementation, data members are generally placed in private access. This is a key data-hiding principle, namely, that implementation is kept inside a black box that cannot be directly exploited by the object's user.

4.14 Moving from C++ to Java

Java classes are based on the C++ aggregate type `class`. A `class` provides the means for implementing a user-defined data type and associated functions. Therefore, a `class` can be used to implement an ADT. Unlike in C++, however, functions, or methods as they are called in Java, cannot exist outside a class construct. Let us write a `class` called `Person` that will be used to store information about people.

In file Person1.java

```
// An elementary implementation of type Person
class Person {
   private String name;
   private int age;
   private char gender;            //male == 'M' , female == 'F'
   public void assignName(String nm) { name = nm; }
   public void assignAge(int a) { age = a; }
   public void assignGender(char b) { gender = b; }
   public String toString(
       return (name + " age is " + age +
       " sex is " + gender );
   }
};
```

As with C++ classes, Java has the two important additions to the structure concept of traditional C. First, Java has members called *class methods* that are functions, such as `assignAge()`. Second, Java has both public and private members. The keyword `public` indicates the visibility of the members that follow it. Without this keyword, the members are private to the class. Private members are available for use only by other member functions of the class. Public members are available anywhere the class is available. Privacy allows part of the implementation of a class type to be "hidden" and prevents unanticipated modifications to the data structure. Restricted access, or *data hiding*, is a feature of object-oriented programming.

The declaration of methods inside a class allows the ADT to have actions, or behaviors, that can act on its private representation. For example, the member function `toString()` has access to private members and gives `Person` a string representation used in output. This method is common to many class types.

We can now use this data type `Person` as if it were a basic type of the language. Other code that uses this type is a *client*. The client can use only the public members to act on variables of type `Person`.

```
//PersonTest.java uses Person

public class PersonTest {
    public static void main (String[] args )
    {
        System.out.println("Person test:");
        Person p1 = new Person();    //create a Person object
        p1.assignAge(20);
        p1.assignName("Alan Turing");
        p1.assignGender('M');
        System.out.println(p1.toString());
    }
}
```

The output of this example program is

```
Person test:
Alan Turing age is 20 sex is M
```

Notice the use of `new Person()` to create an instance of `Person`. The new operator goes off to the heap, as it does in C++, and obtains memory for creating an instance of object `Person`. The value of `p1` is a reference to this object. In effect, this is the address of the object.

Summary

1. The original name Stroustrup gave to his language was "C with classes." A class is an extension of the idea of structure in traditional C. A class is a way of implementing a data type and associated functions and operators, the mechanism in C++ for implementing ADTs, such as complex numbers and stacks.

2. The structure type allows the programmer to aggregate components into a single named variable. A structure has components, called members, that are individually named. Critical to processing structures is the accessing of their members. This is done with either the member operator . or the structure pointer operator -> . These operators, along with () and [], have the second-highest precedence. Highest precedence belongs to scope resolution, : :.

3. The concept of structure or class is augmented in C++ to allow functions to be members. The function declaration is included in the structure declaration and is invoked by using access methods for structure members. The idea is that the functionality required by the `struct` data type should be directly included in the `struct` declaration.

4. Member functions that are defined within the structure or class are implicitly inline. As a rule, only short, heavily used member functions should be defined within the structure. To define a member function outside the structure, the scope resolution operator is used.

5. The scope resolution operator allows member functions of various structure types to have the same names. In this case, which member function is invoked depends on the type of object it acts on. Member functions within the same `struct` can be overloaded.

6. Structures have public and private members that provide data hiding. Inside a structure or class, the keyword `private` followed by a colon restricts the access of the members that follow it. The private members are used by only a few categories of functions, whose privileges include access to these members. These functions include the member functions of the class.

7. Classes in C++ are a form of `struct` whose default access specification is private. Thus, `struct` and `class` can be used interchangeably, with the appropriate access specification.

8. Data members can be declared with the storage class modifier `static`. A data member that is declared `static` is shared by all variables of that class and is stored in one place only. Therefore, the data member can be accessed in the form

    class-name `::` *identifier*

9. Classes can be nested. The inner class is inside the scope of the outer class. This is not in accordance with C semantics.

Review Questions

1. In C++, the structure name, or _____, is a type.

2. Member functions that are defined within `class` are implicitly _____.

3. A function invocation `w1.print();` means that print is a _____ function.

4. A private member (can or cannot)_____ be used by a member function of that class.

5. The keyword _____ allows data members of class variables that have been declared `const` to remain modifiable. This reduces the need to cast away const-ness using _____ <>.

6. The `static` modifier used in declaring a data member means that the data member is _____.

7. The preferred style is to have members of _____ access first and members of _____ access declared last in a class declaration.

8. A *stack* is a LIFO container. A *container* is a data structure whose main purpose is _____.

9. LIFO means _____.

Exercises

1. Design a C++ structure to store a dairy product name, portion weight, calories, protein, fat, and carbohydrates. Twenty-five grams of American cheese have 375 calories, 5 grams of protein, 8 grams of fat, and 0 carbohydrates. Show how to assign these values to the member variables of your structure. Write a function that, given a variable of type `struct dairy` and a weight in grams (portion size), returns the number of calories for that weight.

2. Write a struct `point` that has three coordinates x, y, and z. How can you access the individual members?

3. Use the struct `card` defined in the *poker* program in Section 4.7, "An Example: Flushing," on page 125, to write a hand-sorting routine. In card games, most players keep their cards sorted by pip value. The routine will place aces first, kings next, and so forth, down to twos. A hand will be five cards.

4. The following declarations do not compile correctly. Explain what is wrong.

```
struct brother {
    char          name[20];
    int           age;
    struct sister sib;
} a;

struct sister {
    char           name[20];
    int            age;
    struct brother sib;
} a;
```

5. In this exercise, use the class `ch_stack`, defined in Section 4.12, "A Container Class Example: ch_stack," on page 137. Write the function

```
void reverse(char s1[], char s2[]);
```

The strings s1 and s2 must be the same size. String s2 should become a reversed copy of string s1. Internal to `reverse`, use a `ch_stack` to perform the reversal.

6. Rewrite the functions push() and pop() discussed in Section 4.12, "A Container Class Example: ch_stack," on page 137, to test that push() is not acting on a full ch_stack and that pop() is not acting on an empty ch_stack. If either condition is detected, print an error message, using cerr, and use exit(1) (in *stdlib*) to abort the program. Contrast this to an approach using asserts.

7. Write reverse() as a member function for type ch_stack, discussed in Section 4.12, "A Container Class Example: ch_stack," on page 137. Test it by printing normally and reversing the string

   Gottfried Leibniz wrote Toward a Universal Characteristic

8. For the ch_stack type in Section 4.4, "Access: Private and Public," on page 120, write as member functions

   ```
   //push n chars from s1 onto the ch_stack

   void  pushm(int n, const char s1[]);

   //pop n chars from ch_stack into char string
   void  popm(int n, char s1[]);
   ```

   Hint: Be sure to put a terminator character into the string before outputting it.

9. Explain the difference in meaning between the structure

   ```
   struct a {
       int i, j, k;
   };
   ```

   and the class

   ```
   class a {
       int i, j, k;
   };
   ```

   Explain why the class declaration is not useful. How can you use the keyword public to change the class declaration into a declaration equivalent to struct a?

10. Recode as a class the data type deque, which is a double-ended queue that allows push and pop at both ends.

```
class deque {
public:
   void reset() { top = bottom = max_len / 2; top--; }
   .....
private:
   char  s[max_len];
   int   bottom, top;
};
```

Declare and implement push_t, pop_t, push_b, pop_b, out_stack, top_of, bottom_of, empty, and full. The function push_t() stands for push on top and pop_t() for pop on top; push_b() stands for push on bottom and pop_b() for pop on bottom. The out_stack() function should output the stack from bottom to top. An empty stack is denoted by having the top fall below the bottom. Test each function.

11. Extend the data type deque by adding a member function relocate(). If the deque is full, relocate() is called, and the contents of the deque are moved to balance empty storage around the center max_len/2 of array s. Its function declaration header is

```
//returns true if it succeeds, false if it fails

bool deque::relocate()
```

12. Write a function that swaps the contents of two strings. If you pushed a string of characters onto a ch_stack and popped them into a second string, they would come out reversed. In a swap of two strings, we want the original ordering. Use a deque to do the swap. The strings will be stored in character arrays of the same length, but the strings themselves may be of differing lengths. The function prototype is

```
void swap(char s1[], char s2[]);
```

13. Write the member functions

```
void  pips::print();
void  card::pr_card();
void  deck::pr_deck();
```

and add them to the *poker* program found in Section 4.7, "An Example: Flushing," on page 125. Let pr_deck() use pr_card() and pr_card() use print(). Print the deck after it is initialized.

14. Write a function pr_hand() that prints out card hands. Add it to the *poker* program, and use it to print out each flush.

15. In Section 4.7, "An Example: Flushing," on page 125, main() detects flushes. Write a function

    ```
    bool  isflush(const card hand[], int nc);
    ```

    that returns true if a hand is a flush.

16. Write a function

    ```
    bool  isstraight(const card hand[], nc);
    ```

    that returns true if a hand is a straight. A straight is five cards that have sequential pip values. The lowest straight is ace, two, three, four, five, and the highest straight is ten, jack, queen, king, ace. Run experiments to estimate the probability that dealt cards will be a straight, and compare the results of five-card hands with results of seven-card hands. *Hint:* You may want to set up an array of 15 integers to correspond to counters for each pip value. Be sure that a pip value of 1 (corresponding to ace) is also counted as the high card corresponding to a pip value of 14.

17. Use the previous exercises to determine the probability that a poker hand will be a straight flush. This is the rarest poker hand and has the highest value. Note that, in a hand of more than five cards, it is not sufficient to merely check for the presence of both a straight and a flush to determine that the hand is a straight flush.

18. Change the `suit` declaration from an enumerated type to a class as follows:

    ```
    enum  suit_val { clubs, diamonds, hearts, spades };

    class suit {
    public:
       void  assign(int n) { s = n / 13; }
       int   getsuit() const { return s; }
       void  print() const;
    private:
       suit_val  s;
    };
    ```

    We add the member function `getsuit()` to access the hidden integer value of a `suit` variable. Now recode all references to `suit` throughout the program.

19. Change class `ch_stack` to `int_stack` by substituting type `int` for type `char` in the class definition as appropriate. Later, we will see how to use templates to automate this process.

20. *(Java)* Recode `point` in Section 4.9, "The `this` Pointer," on page 133, as a Java class.

21. *(Java)* Recode and test `ch_stack` in Section 4.12, "A Container Class Example: `ch_stack`," on page 137, as a Java class. Add a method `reverse()` that does the same basic operation as the code in `main()` in Section 4.12, "A Container Class Example: `ch_stack`," on page 137 and test it.

22. *(Java to C++)* Recode the Java program *PersonTest.java* in Section 4.14, "Moving from C++ to Java," on page 139, to run as C++.

Chapter 5
Constructors and Destructors

An *object* requires memory and an initial value, which C++ provides through declarations that are definitions. Variables are objects. For example, in

```
void foo()
{
    int     n = 5;
    double  z[10] = { 0.0 };
    struct  gizmo { int i, j; } w = { 3, 4 };
    .....
}
```

all of the objects are created at block entry when foo() is invoked. A typical implementation uses a runtime system stack. Thus, the int object n on a system with 4-byte integers gets this allocated off the stack and initialized to the value 5. The gizmo object w requires 8 bytes to represent its two integer members. The array of double object z requires 10 times sizeof(double) to store its elements. In each case, the system provides for the construction and initialization of these objects. On exit from foo(), deallocation occurs automatically.

In creating complicated aggregates, the user will expect similar management of a class-defined object. The class needs a mechanism to specify object creation and destruction so that a client can use objects like native types.

A *constructor* is a member function whose name is the same as the class name; it constructs values of the class type. This process involves initializing data members and, frequently, allocating free store by using new. A *destructor* is a member function whose name is the class name preceded by the tilde character ~. A destructor's usual purpose is to finalize objects of the class type, typically by using delete to deallocate store assigned the object.

Constructors, the more complicated of these two specially named member functions, can be overloaded and can take arguments, whereas destructors can do neither. A constructor is invoked when its associated type is used in a definition, when call-by-value is used to pass a value to a function, or when the return value of a function must create a value of associated type. Destructors are invoked implicitly when an object goes out of scope. Constructors and destructors do not have return types and cannot use `return` *expression* statements.

5.1 Classes with Constructors

The simplest use of a constructor is for initialization. In this and later sections, we will develop some examples that use constructors to initialize the values of the data members of the class. Our first example is an implementation of a data type `mod_int` to store numbers that are computed with a modulus.

In file modulo.cpp

```
//Modulo numbers and constructor initialization

class mod_int {
public:
    mod_int(int i);                  //constructor declaration
    void  assign(int i) { v = i % modulus; }
    void  print() const { cout << v << '\t'; }
    const static int modulus;
private:
    int  v;
};

//constructor definition
mod_int::mod_int(int i) { v = i % modulus; }
const int mod_int::modulus = 60;
```

The integer v is restricted in value to 0, 1, 2, . . . , `modulus` – 1. It is the programmer's responsibility to enforce this restriction by having all member functions guarantee this behavior.

The member function `mod_int::mod_int(int)` is a constructor. It does not have a return type. This constructor is invoked when objects of type `mod_int` are declared. It is a function of one argument. When invoked, the constructor requires an expression that is assignment compatible with its `int` parameter. It then creates and initializes the declared variable.

Some examples of declarations using this type are

```
mod_int  a(0);       //a.v = 0;
mod_int  b(61);      //b.v = 1;
```

but not

```
mod_int  a;        //illegal:no parameter list
```

Since this class has only the one constructor of argument list `int`, a `mod_int` declaration must have an integral expression passed as an initializing value. Not allowing a `mod_int` variable to be declared without an initializing expression prevents run-time errors due to uninitialized variables.

5.1.1 The Default Constructor

A constructor requiring no arguments is called the *default* constructor. It can be a constructor with an empty argument list or one whose arguments all have default values. It has the special purpose of initializing arrays of objects of its class.

It is often convenient to overload the constructor with several function declarations. In the preceding example, it could be desirable to have the default value of `v` be 0. If the default constructor

```
mod_int() { v = 0; }
```

is added as a member function of `mod_int`, the following declarations are possible:

```
mod_int  s1, s2;  //both init private member v to 0
mod_int  d[5];    //arrays are properly initialized
```

In both of these declarations, the empty parameter-list constructor is invoked.

If a class does not have a constructor, the system provides a default constructor. If a class has constructors but not a default constructor, array allocation causes a syntactic error.

In our `mod_int` example, the following constructor could serve as both a general initializer and a default constructor:

```
inline  mod_int::mod_int(int i = 0)
        { v = i % modulus; }
```

5.1.2 Constructor Initializer

A special syntax is used for initializing subelements of objects with constructors. *Constructor initializers* for structure and class members can be specified in a comma-separated list that follows the constructor parameter list and that precedes the code body. The previous example can be recoded as

```
//Default constructor for mod_int
mod_int::mod_int(int i = 0) : v(i % modulus){}
```

Notice that initialization replaces assignment. The individual members must be initializable as

> *member-name* (*expression list*)

It is not always possible to assign values to members in the body of the constructor. An initializer list is required when a nonstatic member is either a const or a reference type.

5.1.3 Constructors as Conversions

Constructors of a single parameter are used automatically for conversion unless declared with the keyword explicit. For example, T1::T1(T2) provides code that can be used to convert a T2 object to a T1 object. Consider the following class, whose purpose is to print invisible characters with their ASCII designation; for example, the code 07 (octal) is alarm or bel.

In file printabl.cpp

```
//ASCII printable characters

class pr_char {
public:
    pr_char(int i = 0) : c(i % 128) { }
    void  print() const { cout << rep[c]; }
private:
    int  c;
    static const char*  rep[128];
};

const char*  pr_char::rep[128] = { "nul", "soh", "stx",
    .....
    "w", "x", "y", "z","{", "|", "}", "~", "del" };
```

```
int main()
{
   pr_char  c;

   for (int i = 0; i < 128; ++i) {
      c = i;                  //or: c = static_cast<pr_char>(i);
      c.print();
      cout << endl;
   }
}
```

The constructor creates an automatic conversion from integers to pr_char. Notice that c = i implies this conversion. It is also possible to explicitly use a cast. Conversions are covered in detail in Section 6.1, "ADT Conversions," on page 196. One reason OOP has implicit conversions for ADTs is that it is desirable for them to have the look and feel of the native types.

5.1.4 Improving the point Class

The class point from Section 4.5, "Classes," on page 121, is readily improved by adding constructors. Notice that the class contains the member function point::init(), which is similar to a constructor.

In file point5.cpp

```
class point {
public:
   point() { x = 0; y = 0; }                   //default
   point(double u) { x = u; y = 0;}            //double to point
   point(double u, double v) { x = u; y = v; }
   void print() { cout << "(" << x << "," << y << ")"; }
   void init(double u, double v) { x = u; y = v; }
   void plus(point c);
.....
private:
   double x, y;
};
```

Many scientific problems require producing a table of points or a graph by using a function. For example, a parabola can be coded as

```
double parabola(double x, double p) { return(x * x) / p; }
```

Let us use this function to produce a table of points that graphs the parabola from 0 to 2 in increments of 0.1.

In file parabola.cpp

```
void graph(double a, double b, double incr,
    double f(double, double), double p, point gr[])
{
    double x = a;
    for (int i = 0; x <= b; ++i, x += incr)
        gr[i].init(x, f(x, p));
}

int main()
{
    point g[1000];              //uses the default constructor

    graph(0, 2, 0.1, parabola, 5, g );
```

5.2 Constructing a Dynamically Sized Stack

A constructor can also be used to allocate space from free store. We shall modify the ch_stack type from Section 4.12, "A Container Class Example: ch_stack," on page 137, so that its maximum length is initialized by a constructor.

The design of the object ch_stack includes hidden implementation detail. Data members are placed in the private access region of class ch_stack. The public interface provides clients with the expected stack abstraction. These are all public member functions, such as push() and pop(). Some of these functions are *accessor functions* that do not change the stack object, such as top_of() and empty(). It is usual to make these const member functions. Some of these functions are *mutator functions* that do change the ch_stack object, such as push() and pop(). The constructor member functions have the job of creating and initializing ch_stack objects.

In file ch_stac2.h

```
class ch_stack {
public:
//the public interface for the ch_stack
    explicit ch_stack(int size): max_len( size), top(EMPTY)
       { assert(size > 0); s = new char[size]; assert(s != 0); }
    void   reset() { top = EMPTY; }
    void   push(char c) { s[++top]= c; }
    char   pop() { return s[top--]; }
    char   top_of() const { return s[top]; }
    bool   empty() const { return (top == EMPTY); }
    bool   full() const { return (top == max_len - 1); }
private:
    enum   { EMPTY = -1 };
    char*  s;                     //changed from s[max_len]
    int    max_len;
    int    top;
};
```

In the preceding code and in the rest of this chapter, we use assertions to test whether a pointer value is 0. This is done after calling new and indicates that new has failed. In ANSI C++ compiler, this will be an alternative to the bad_alloc exception being thrown.

Now a client using ch_stack can decide on the size requirement. An example of a ch_stack declaration invoking this constructor is

```
ch_stack   data(1000);        //allocate 1000 elements
ch_stack   more_data(2 * n);  //allocate 2 * n elements
```

Two additional constructors would be a default constructor to allocate a specific-length ch_stack and a two-parameter constructor whose second parameter would be a char* to initialize the ch_stack. The two constructors could be written as follows:

```
//default constructor for ch_stack
ch_stack::ch_stack():max_len(100),top(EMPTY)
{
    s = new char[100];
    assert(s != 0);
}
```

```
//copy a char* string into the ch_stack
ch_stack::ch_stack(int size, const char str[]):
   max_len(size)
{
   int i;
   assert(size > 0);
   s = new char[size];
   assert(s != 0);
   for (i = 0; i < max_len && str[i] != 0; ++i)
      s[i] = str[i];
   top = --i;
}
```

The corresponding function prototypes would be included as members of the class ch_stack. These constructors are used in the following:

```
ch_stack  data;            //creates s[100]
ch_stack  d[N];            //creates N 100 element ch_stacks
ch_stack  w(4, "ABCD");    //w.s[0]='A'...w.s[3]='D'
```

5.2.1 The Copy Constructor

Suppose that we wish to examine our stack and to count the number of occurrences of a given character. We can repeatedly pop the stack, testing each element in turn, until the stack is empty. But what if we want to preserve the contents of the stack? Call-by-value parameters accomplish this.

In file ch_stac2.cpp

```
//count the number of c's found in s
int cnt_char(char c, ch_stack s)
{
   int  count = 0;

   while (!s.empty()) //done when empty
      count += (c == s.pop()); //found a c
   return count;
}
```

The semantics of call-by-value require that a local copy of the argument type be created and initialized from the value of the expression passed as the actual argument. This requires a *copy constructor*. The compiler provides a copy constructor whose signature is

```
ch_stack::ch_stack(const ch_stack&);
```

The compiler copies by *memberwise initialization*. This may not work in all circumstances, such as for complicated aggregates with members that are themselves pointers. In many cases, the pointer is the address of an object that is deleted when it goes out of scope. However, the act of duplicating the pointer value but not the object pointed at can lead to anomalous code. This deletion affects other instances that still expect the object to exist. It is appropriate for the class to explicitly define its own copy constructor.

In file ch_stac4.h

```
//Copy constructor for ch_stack of characters

ch_stack::ch_stack(const ch_stack& str):
   max_len(str.max_len), top(str.top)
{
   s = new char[str.max_len];
   assert(s != 0);
   memcpy(s, str.s, max_len);
}
```

The *stdlib* routine memcpy() copies max_len characters from the base address str.s into memory, starting at base address s. This is called a *deep copy*. The character arrays are distinct because they refer to different memory locations. If, instead, the body of this routine were

```
s = str.s;
```

this would be a *shallow copy*, with the ch_stack variables sharing the same representation. Any change to one variable would change the other.

5.3 Classes with Destructors

A destructor is a member function whose name is the class name preceded by a tilde. Destructors are almost always called implicitly, usually at the exit of the block in which the object was declared. They are also invoked when a delete operator is called on a pointer to an object having a destructor or where they are needed to destroy a subobject of an object being deleted.

Let us augment our ch_stack example with a destructor.

In file ch_stac2.h

```
//ch_stack implementation with constructors and destructor

class ch_stack {
public:
   ch_stack();                               //default constructor
   explicit ch_stack(int size) : max_len(size), top(EMPTY)
      { assert(size > 0); s = new char[size]; assert(s != 0); }
   ch_stack(const stack& str);               //copy constructor
   ch_stack(int size, const char str[]);
   ~ch_stack() { delete []s; }               //destructor
   . . . . .
private:
   enum    { EMPTY = -1 };
   char*   s;
   int     max_len;
   int     top;
};
```

The addition of the destructor allows the class to return unneeded heap-allocated memory during program execution. All of the public member functions perform in exactly the same manner as before. However, the destructor will be implicitly invoked on block and function exit to clean up storage no longer accessible. This is good programming practice and allows programs to execute using less memory.

5.4 An Example: Dynamically Allocated Strings

C++ lacks a native string type. The standard library provides a string template class, which is increasingly the normally used string type. An older style of string representation is as pointer to char. An important drawback of this representation, the end-of-string is denoted by the null character \0. This convention is that many basic string manipulations are proportional to string length. This use is reflected by the library *string.h* (or *cstring* in modern C++). In that library, the standard function int strlen(const char*) is used to compute the length of the character array delimited by the null character. In modern C++, the standard library *string* provides a string type that stores string length as part of its hidden implementation.

In this section, we develop some of the ways in which such a type can be implemented. We want our type to be dynamically allocated and able to represent arbitrary-length strings. A variety of constructors will be coded to initialize and to allocate strings, and a set of operations on strings will be coded as member functions. The implementation will use the *string* library functions to manipulate the underlying pointer representation of strings.

In file string2.cpp

```cpp
//An implementation of dynamically allocated strings

class my_string {
public:
   my_string() : len(0)
      { s = new char[1];assert(s != 0); s[0] = 0; }
   my_string(const my_string& str);      //copy constructor
   my_string(const char* p);             //conversion constructor
   ~my_string() { delete []s; }
   void assign(const my_string& str);
   void print() const { cout << s << endl; }
   void concat(const my_string& a,const my_string& b);
private:
   char*   s;
   int     len;
};

my_string::my_string(const char* p)
{
   len = strlen(p);
   s = new char[len + 1];
   assert(s != 0);
   strcpy(s, p);
}

my_string::my_string(const my_string& str) : len(str.len)
{
   s = new char[len + 1];
   assert(s != 0);
   strcpy(s, str.s);
}
```

```
void my_string::assign(const my_string& str)
{
    if (this == &str)          //a = a; do nothing
        return;
    delete []s;
    len = str.len;
    s = new char[len + 1];
    assert(s != 0);
    strcpy(s, str.s);
}

void my_string::concat(const my_string& a, const my_string& b)
{
    char*  temp = new char[a.len + b.len + 1];

    len = a.len + b.len;
    strcpy(temp, a.s);
    strcat(temp, b.s);
    delete []s;
    s = new char[len + 1];
    assert(s != 0);
    strcpy(s, temp);
}
```

This type allows you to declare my_strings, assign by copying one my_string to another, print a my_string, and concatenate two my_strings. The hidden representation is pointer to char, and it has a variable len in which to store the current my_string length.

◆◆◆◆◆◆◆◆◆◆◆◆

Dissection of the my_string Class

■ my_string() : len(0)
        { s = new char[1]; assert(s != 0); s[0] = 0; }
    my_string(const my_string& str);   //copy constructor
    my_string(const char* p);   //conversion constructor

The class has three overloaded constructors. The first is the default constructor, needed when declaring an array of my_strings. The second is the copy constructor. The third has a pointer to char argument that can be used to convert the char* representation of strings to our my_string type. The class uses two library functions: strlen and strcpy. We allocate one additional character to store the end-of-string character \0, although this character is not counted by strlen. The copy constructor will be explained later.

- ~my_string() { delete []s; }

The destructor automatically returns memory allocated to my_strings back to free store for reuse. The empty bracket-pair form of delete is used because array allocation was used. The operator delete[] knows the amount of memory associated with the pointer s.

- ```
  my_string::my_string(const my_string& str) : len(str.len)
  {
      s = new char[len + 1];
      assert(s != 0);
      strcpy(s, str.s);
  }
  ```

This form of copy constructor is used to copy one my_string into another.

Copy Constructor Use for my_string

1. A my_string is initialized by another my_string.

2. A my_string is passed as an argument in a function.

3. A my_string is returned as the value of a function.

In C++, if this constructor is not present explicitly, the compiler creates one that uses member-by-member initialization.

- ```
  void my_string::assign(const my_string& str)
  {
      if (this == &str)          //a = a; do nothing
          return;
      delete []s;    len = str.len;
      s = new char[len + 1];
      assert(s != 0);
      strcpy(s, str.s);
  }
  ```

The assignment semantics are based on deep-copy semantics, whereby the entire aggregate must be replicated and the data values copied into its representation. The copying requires a check against copying over the same my_string. This is the case with a = a. If we had not tested for this case and had performed deletion on the left-hand argument, the value of a would have disappeared. Each time the value of a my_string is copied, the value is physically recopied using strcpy(). This is in distinction to a later implementation that will show how to use shallow-copy semantics, which sets a pointer to an existing value without replicating the aggregate. As we shall see, this can be very efficient.

■
```
void my_string::concat(const my_string& a, const my_string& b)
{
    char   temp[a.len + b.len + 1];

    len = a.len + b.len;
    strcpy(temp, a.s);
    strcat(temp, b.s);
    delete []s;
    s = new char[len + 1];
    assert(s != 0);
    strcpy(s, temp);
}
```

This is a form of concatenation. Neither my_string argument is modified. The implicit argument, whose hidden member variables are s and len, is modified to represent the my_string a followed by the my_string b. Note that in this member function, the use of len, a.len, and b.len is possible. Member functions have access not only to the private members of the implicit argument but also to the private representation of any of the arguments of type my_string.

◆◆◆◆◆◆◆◆◆◆◆◆

The following code tests class my_string by concatenating several my_strings:

In file string2.cpp

```
int main()
{
    char* str = "The wheel that squeaks the loudest\n";
    my_string  a(str), b, author("Josh Billings\n"), both, quote;

    b.assign("Is the one that gets the grease\n");
    both.concat(a, b);
    quote.concat(both, author);
    quote.print();
}
```

The printout from this program is

```
The wheel that squeaks the loudest
Is the one that gets the grease
Josh Billings
```

We deliberately used a variety of declarations to show how various constructors would be called. The `my_string` variables b, both, and quote all use the default constructor. The declaration for author uses the constructor whose argument type is char*. The concatenation takes place in two steps. First, `my_string`s a and b are concatenated into both. Next, `my_string`s both and author are concatenated into quote. Finally, the quotation is printed out.

The constructor `my_string::my_string(const char*)` is invoked to create and to initialize objects a and author. This constructor is also called implicitly as a conversion operation when invoking `my_string::assign()` on the literal "Is the one that gets the grease\n".

5.5 The Class dbl_vect

The one-dimensional array in C++ is a very useful and efficient aggregate type. In many ways, it is the prototypical container: easy to use and highly efficient. However, it is error prone. A common mistake is to access elements that are out of bounds. In C++, this problem can be controlled by defining an analogous container type in which bounds can be tested. This type can also be used as a mathematical vector type.

In file dbl_vect1.h

```
//Implementation of a safe array type dbl_vect
class dbl_vect {
public:
    explicit dbl_vect(int n = 10);
    ~dbl_vect() { delete []p; }
    double& element(int i);                 //access p[i]
    int  ub() const { return (size - 1); }  //upper bound
    void print() const;
private:
    double*  p;
    int      size;
};
```

```
dbl_vect::dbl_vect(int n) : size(n)
{
    assert(n > 0);
    p = new double[size];
    assert(p != 0);
}

double& dbl_vect::element(int i)
{
    assert (i >= 0 && i < size);
    return p[i];
}
```

The constructor dbl_vect::dbl_vect(int n) allows the user to build dynamically allocated arrays. Such arrays are much more flexible than those in such languages as FORTRAN, Pascal, and C, in which array sizes must be constant expressions. The constructor also initializes the variable size, whose value is the number of elements in the array. Note that this one-argument constructor is declared explicit because it is not intended as an implicit conversion from int to dbl_vect.

The print() function outputs tab-separated elements of the vector.

```
void dbl_vect::print()const
{
    cout << " vector of size " << size << endl;
    for (int i = 0; i <size; ++i)
        cout << p[i] << "\t";
}
```

Access to individual elements is through the safe-indexing member function

```
double& dbl_vect::element(int i)
```

An index that is outside the expected array range 0 through ub will cause an assertion failure. This safe-indexing member function returns a reference to int that is the address of p[i] and that can be used as the left operand of an assignment, or lvalue. The technique is often used in C++ and is an efficient mechanism for operating on complicated types.

As an example, the declarations

```
dbl_vect a(10), b(5);
```

construct arrays of 10 and 5 integers, respectively. Individual elements can be accessed by the member function `element`, which checks whether the index is out of range. The statements

```
a.element(1) = 5;
b.element(1) = a.element(1) + 7;
cout << a.element(1) - 2;
```

are all legal. In effect, we have a safe dynamic array type.

Classes with default constructors use them to initialize a derived array type. For example, the declaration

```
dbl_vect a[5];
```

uses the default constructor to create an array `a` of five objects, each of which is a size 10 `dbl_vect`. The `i`th element's address in the `j`th array would be given by `a[j].element(i)`.

Chapter 9, "Exceptions," discusses how exceptions can be used to check on error conditions. With this more powerful methodology,

```
assert(n > 0);
```

is replaced by

```
if (n < 1)
    throw(vect_allocation_error(n));
```

5.5.1 `dbl_vect` as a Linear Vector Type

The basic type in linear algebra is the vector, which allows a description of many scientific and engineering problems. To use `dbl_vect` effectively as a linear vector, we need to add mathematical operations, such as vector addition, vector subtraction, and vector scalar product. We can do this as a set of functions that use `dbl_vect::element()`, but this does not allow efficient access to the underlying representation. Including these operations as part of the class `dbl_vect` supports an efficient implementation and appropriate encapsulation. We display the `dot_prod()` function, leaving the others as exercises.

In file dbl_vect1.h

```
double dbl_vect::dot_prod(const dbl_vect& v) const
{
    assert(size == v.size);
    double sum = 0.0;

    for (int i = 0; i < size; ++i)
        sum += p[i] * v.p[i];
    return sum;
}
```

In file dbl_vect1.cpp

```
int main()
{
    dbl_vect c(6);
    for (int i = 0; i <= c.ub(); ++i)
        c.element(i) = i + 0.1;
    c.print();
    cout << " dot product = " << c.dot_prod(c) << endl;
}
```

5.6 Members That Are Class Types

In this section, the type dbl_vect is used as a member of the class pair_vect. In OOP methodology, this is known as the *has-a relationship*. Complicated objects can be designed from simpler ones by incorporating them with the has-a relationship.

In file pairvect.cpp

```
#include "dbl_vect1.h"

class pair_vect {
public:
   pair_vect(int i) : a(i), b(i), size(i) { }
   double& first_element(int i);
   double& second_element(int i);
   int ub()const { return size -1; }
private:
   dbl_vect a, b; //pair_vect has a dbl_vect
   int size;
};

double& pair_vect::first_element(int i)
{   return a.element(i); }

double& pair_vect::second_element(int i)
{   return b.element(i);}
```

Notice that the pair_vect constructor is a series of initializers. The initializers of the dbl_vect members a and b invoke dbl_vect::dbl_vect(int). Let us use this data type to build a table of age and weight relationships.

```
int main()
{
   int     i;
   pair_vect age_weight(5);        //age and weight

   cout << "table of age, weight\n";
   for (i = 0; i <= age_weight.ub(); ++i) {
      age_weight.first_element(i) = 21 + i;
      age_weight.second_element(i) = 135 + i;
      cout << age_weight.first_element(i) << ","
           << age_weight.second_element(i) << endl;
   }
}
```

5.7 Example: A Singly Linked List

In this section, we develop a singly linked list data type, the prototype of many useful dynamic ADTs called *self-referential structures*. These data types have pointer members that refer to objects of their own type and are the basis of many useful container classes. The following declaration implements such a type:

In file slist.cpp

```cpp
struct slistelem {
    char       data;
    slistelem*  next;
};

class slist {                    //a singly linked list
public:
    slist() : h(0) { }           //0 denotes empty slist
    ~slist() { release(); }
    void  prepend(char c);       //adds to front of slist
    void  del();
    slistelem*  first() const { return h; }
    void  print() const;
    void  release();
private:
    slistelem*  h;               //head of slist
};
```

Singly Linked List

List Operations

1. prepend: adds to front of list

2. first: returns first element

3. print: prints list contents

4. del: deletes first element

5. release: destroys list

The link member `next` points to the next `slistelem` in the list. In this example, `data` is a simple variable, but it could be replaced by a complicated type capable of storing a range of information. The constructor initializes the head of `slist` pointer `h` to the value 0, which is called the *null-pointer constant* and can be assigned to any pointer type. In linked lists, this constant typically denotes the empty list or end-of-list value. The member function `prepend()` builds the list structure as follows:

```
void slist::prepend(char c)
{
    slistelem*  temp = new slistelem;   //create element
    assert(temp != 0);
    temp -> next = h;                   //link to slist
    temp -> data = c;
    h = temp;                           //update head of slist
}
```

A list element is allocated from free store, and its data member is initialized from the single argument c. Its link member `next` is set to the old list head. The head pointer `h` is updated to point at this element as the new first element of the list.

The member function `del()` has the inverse role.

```
void slist::del()
{
    slistelem*  temp = h;

    h = h -> next;                //presumes a nonempty slist
    delete temp;
}
```

This function returns the first element of the list to free store by using the `delete` operator on the head of `slist` pointer h. The new head-of-list is the value of the `next` member. This function can be modified to work on the empty list without aborting (see exercise 16 on page 193).

Much of list processing consists of repetitively chaining down the list until the null-pointer value is found. The following two functions use this technique:

In file slist.cpp

```
void slist::print() const               //object is unchanged
{
   slistelem*  temp = h;

   while (temp != 0) {                   //detect end of slist
       cout << temp -> data << " -> ";
       temp = temp -> next;
   }
   cout << "\n###" << endl;
}


//elements returned to free store

void slist::release()
{
   while (h != 0)
       del();
}
```

◆◆◆◆◆◆◆◆◆◆◆◆

Dissection of the `print()` and `release()` Functions

- ```
  void  slist::print() const            //object is unchanged
  {
     slistelem*  temp = h;
  ```

An auxiliary pointer `temp` will be used to chain down the list. The pointer is initialized to the address of the `slist` head h. The pointer h cannot be used, because its value would be lost, in effect destroying access to the list.

- ```
  while (temp != 0) {                   //detect end of list
     cout << temp -> data << " -> ";
     temp = temp -> next;
  }
  ```

The value 0 is guaranteed to represent the end-of-list value, because the constructor `slist::slist()` initialized it as such and the `slist::prepend()` function maintains it as the end-of-list pointer value. Notice that the internals of this loop could be changed to process the entire list in another manner.

■   `void slist::release()`

The `release` function is used to return all list elements to free store and marches down the list, doing so.

■   ```
    while (h != 0)
       del();
    ```

Each element of the list must be returned to free store in sequence. This is done for a single element by `slist::del()`, which manipulates the hidden pointer h. Since we are destroying the list, it is unnecessary to preserve the original value of pointer h. This function's chief use is as the body of the destructor `slist::~slist()`. We could not use a destructor written

```
slist::~slist()
{
    delete h;
}
```

because it deletes only the first element in the list.

The following code demonstrates the use of this type. The destructor has been modified to print a message.

In file slist.cpp

```
slist:: ~slist()
{
    cout << "destructor invoked" << endl;
    release();
}
```
```

```
int main()
{
   slist*  p;
   {
      slist  w;

      w.prepend('A');
      w.prepend('B');
      w.print();
      w.del();
      w.print();
      p = &w;
      p -> print();
      cout << "exiting inner block" << endl;
   }
   //p -> print();  gives system-dependent behavior
   cout << "exiting outer block" << endl;
}
```

Notice that main() contains an inner block, which is included to test that the destructor is invoked on block exit, returning storage associated with w to free store. The output of this program is

```
B -> A ->
###
A ->
###
A ->
###
exiting inner block
destructor invoked
exiting outer block
```

The first print() call prints the two-element slist, which stores B and A. After a del operation is performed, the list contains one element, which stores A. The outer block pointer to slist p is assigned the address of the slist variable w. When the list is accessed through p in the inner block, it prints A. This output shows that the destructor works at block exit on the variable w.

The commented-out invocation of slist::print() is system dependent. It is a runtime error to dereference p here, because the address it refers to may have been overwritten at block exit by the deletion routine.

5.8 Two-Dimensional Arrays

Standard C does not have authentic multidimensional arrays. Instead, the programmer must be careful to map such an abstract data structure into a pointer to pointer to base type. In C++, the programmer can implement flexible, safe, dynamic multidimensional arrays. We shall demonstrate this by implementing a two-dimensional array type matrix. Notice its similarity to the class dbl_vect.

In file matrix1.cpp

```
//A two-dimensional safe array type matrix

class matrix {
public:
   matrix(int d1, int d2);
   ~matrix();
   int  ub1() const { return(s1 - 1); }
   int  ub2() const { return(s2 - 1); }
   double&  element(int i, int j);
private:
   double**  p;
   int     s1, s2;
};
```

The type matrix has a size for each dimension and a corresponding public upper bound. The hidden representation uses the pointer to pointer to double type. This will store the base address of an array of pointers to double, which in turn store a base address for each row of the matrix type.

```
matrix::matrix(int d1, int d2) : s1(d1), s2(d2)
{
   assert(d1 > 0 && d2 > 0);
   p = new double*[s1];
   assert(p != 0);
   for (int i = 0; i < s1; ++i){
      p[i] = new double[s2];
      assert(p[i] != 0);
   }
}
```

```
matrix::~matrix()
{
   for (int i = 0; i <= ub1(); ++i)
      delete []p[i];
   delete []p;
}
```

The constructor allocates an array of pointers to `double`. The number of elements in this array is the value of `s1`. Next, the constructor iteratively allocates an array of `double` pointed at by each element `p[i]`. Therefore, there is space for `s1 × s2` doubles allocated from free store; additionally, the space for `s1` pointers is allocated from free store. The destructor deallocates store in reverse order. This scheme generalizes to higher dimensions.

Obtaining the lvalue of an element in this two-dimensional array requires two index arguments, as follows:

```
double& matrix::element(int i, int j)
{
   assert(i >= 0 && i <= ub1() && j >= 0 && j <= ub2());
   return p[i][j];
}
```

Both are tested to see that they are in range. This is a generalization of the one-index case.

5.9 Polynomials as a Linked List

A polynomial is *sparse* when it has relatively few nonzero coefficients in comparison to its degree. The degree of the polynomial is simply the highest exponent of a nonzero term. For example, the degree-1,000 polynomial $P(x) = x^{1000} + x^1 + 1$ has only three nonzero terms. When large sparse polynomials are being manipulated, it is often efficient to base the representation on a linked list. In such a representation, each list element contains a nonzero term of the polynomial.

The next routine manipulates such polynomials and does polynomial addition, allowing only one term per exponent. The list is sorted with terms in descending order of their exponents.

In file poly1.cpp

```
//A polynomial represented as a singly linked list

struct term {
   int        exponent;
   double     coefficient;
   term*      next;
   term(int e, double c, term* n = 0)
       : exponent(e), coefficient(c), next(n) { }
   void print()
     { cout << coefficient << "x^" << exponent << " "; }
};

class polynomial {
public:
   polynomial(): h(0), degree(0) { }
   polynomial(const polynomial& p);
   polynomial(int size, double coef[], int expon[]);
   ~polynomial() { release(); }
   void print() const;
   void plus(polynomial a, polynomial b);
private:
   term*      h;
   int        degree;
   void       prepend(term*  t);              //add term to front
   void       add_term(term*& a, term*& b);
   void       release();                      //garbage collect
   void       rest_of(term* rest);            //add remaining terms
   void       reverse();                      //reverse terms
};
```

In this representation, a polynomial is coded as a list of terms where each term is a coefficient-exponent pair. A polynomial's terms will be listed in decreasing order by exponent. This canonical form makes addition and other operations simpler. A polynomial will be empty, initialized using the copy constructor, or constructed from a pair of arrays that contains a properly ordered sequence of coefficient-exponent pairs.

Several important auxiliary member functions manipulate the underlying list representation. The prepend() function links a term to the head of the list. The reverse() function reverses a list in place. The add_term() function is used by plus() to add a next term and to properly advance pointers within the two polynomials being added.

```
inline void polynomial::prepend(term*  t)
   { t -> next = h; h = t; }

void polynomial::reverse()          //in place
{
   term*  pred, *succ, *elem;

   if (h && (succ = h -> next)) {
      pred = 0;
      elem = h;
      while (succ) {
         elem -> next = pred;
         pred = elem;
         elem = succ;
         succ = succ -> next;
      }
      h = elem;
      h -> next = pred;
   }
}
```

The following figure shows a graphic representation of both the prepend and reverse operations.

prepend()

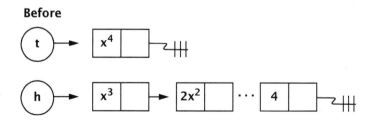

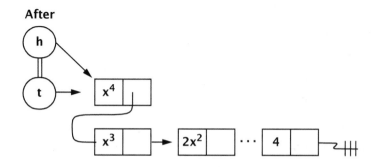

reverse()

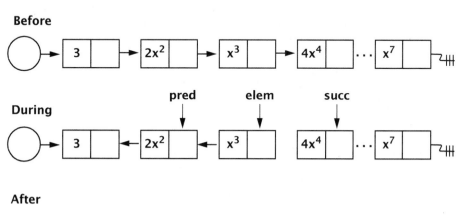

Prepend and Reverse Operations

The constructors build an explicit list for each polynomial. It would be incorrect to rely on the compiler-generated default copy constructor.

```
//assumes ordering is correct expon[i] < expon[i+1]

polynomial::polynomial(int size, double coef[], int expon[])
{
    term* temp = new term(expon[0], coef[0]);
    assert(temp != 0);

    h = 0;
    prepend(temp);                              //create initial term
    for (int i = 1; i < size; ++i) {
        assert(expon[i - 1] < expon[i]);
        temp = new term(expon[i], coef[i]);
        assert(temp != 0);
        prepend(temp);                          //add term
    }
    degree = h -> exponent;
}

polynomial::polynomial(const polynomial& p) : degree(p.degree)
{
    term* elem = p.h, *temp;

    h = 0;
    while (elem) {                              //term-by-term copying
        temp = new term(elem -> exponent, elem -> coefficient);
        assert(temp != 0);
        prepend(temp);
        elem = elem -> next;
    }
    reverse();
}
```

The next set of functions implements a merge-sort polynomial addition.

```
void polynomial::add_term(term*& a, term*& b)
{
    term*   c;

    if (a -> exponent > b -> exponent) {                      //add a
        c = new term(a -> exponent, a -> coefficient) ;
        assert(c != 0);
        a = a -> next;
        prepend(c);
    }
    else if (a -> exponent < b -> exponent){                  //add b
        c = new term(b -> exponent, b -> coefficient);
        assert(c != 0);
        b = b -> next;
        prepend(c);
    }
     else {                                        //check on cancellation
        if (a -> coefficient + b -> coefficient != 0) {
            c = new term( a -> exponent,
                            a -> coefficient + b -> coefficient);
            assert(c != 0);
            prepend(c);
        }
        a = a -> next;
        b = b -> next;
    }
}
```

This code merges the terms at the head of the two lists. The exponents can be of the same or different values. If the exponents are of different values, the larger term is the result, and only its list pointer is advanced. If the exponents are the same, both list pointers are advanced. Cancellation occurs when both exponents are the same and their coefficients sum to 0; no term is produced. Otherwise, zero terms might proliferate, thus defeating our attempt at an efficient representation of a sparse polynomial.

When one list of terms is exhausted by the merge, the terms from the remaining list are added to the front of the list by rest_of().

```
void polynomial::rest_of(term* rest)
{
    term* temp;

    while (rest) {
        temp  = new term(rest -> exponent, rest -> coefficient);
        assert(temp != 0);
        prepend(temp);
        rest = rest -> next;
    }
}

//c.plus(a,b) means c = a + b;

void polynomial::plus(polynomial a, polynomial b)
{
    term*    aterm = a.h, *bterm = b.h;

    release();              //garbage collect c, assumes not a or b
    h = 0;
    while (aterm && bterm)      //merge step
        add_term(aterm, bterm);
    if (aterm)
        rest_of(aterm);
    else if (bterm)
        rest_of(bterm);
    reverse();
    degree = ((h) ? h -> exponent: 0);
}
```

The function polynomial::plus() uses add_term() and rest_of() to put the terms in the reverse order to the expected representation and uses reverse() to correct this. The print() and release() functions for polynomial are needed to test this code (see exercise 20 on page 194).

5.10 Strings Using Reference Semantics

Allocation at runtime of large aggregates can readily exhaust memory resources. The list example in Section 5.7, "Example: A Singly Linked List," on page 169, shows one scheme for handling this; the system reclaims memory by traversing each list and disposing of each element. This model of reclamation is a form of *garbage collection*. In such languages as LISP and SmallTalk, the system itself is responsible for this reclamation. Such systems periodically invoke a garbage collector to identify all cells that are currently accessible and to reclaim those that are inaccessible. Most such schemes require traversal and marking of cells accessible from pointers with a computationally expensive procedure.

A disposal scheme that avoids this is *reference counting*, whereby each dynamically allocated object tracks its active references. When an object is created, its reference count is set to 1. Every time the object is newly referenced, the reference count is incremented; every time it loses a reference, the count is decremented. When the reference count becomes 0, the object's memory is disposed of.

The following example creates a `my_string` class that has reference semantics for copying. The class uses both the *string* and the *assert* libraries. This class has shallow-copy semantics because pointer assignment replaces copying. The techniques illustrated are common for this type of aggregate. We use the class `str_obj` to create object values. The type `str_obj` is a required implementation detail for `my_string`. The detail could not be directly placed in `my_string` without destroying the potential many-to-one relationship between objects of type `my_string` and referenced values of type `str_obj`. The values of `my_string` are in the class `str_obj`, which is an auxiliary class for `my_string`'s use only. The publicly used class `my_string` handles the `str_obj` instances and is called a *handler* class.

In file string2.cpp

```
//Reference counted my_strings
class str_obj {
public:
   int    len, ref_cnt;
   char*  s;
   str_obj() : len(0), ref_cnt(1)
      { s = new char[1]; assert(s != 0); s[0] = 0; }
   str_obj(const char* p) : ref_cnt(1)
      { len = strlen(p); s = new char[len + 1];
        assert(s != 0); strcpy(s, p); }
   ~str_obj() { delete []s; }
};
```

The str_obj declares objects that are used by my_string. We will explain later how these can be made private and accessed using the friend mechanism (see Section 6.3, "Friend Functions," on page 200). Notice how the str_obj class is used for construction and destruction of objects using free store. On construction of a str_obj, the ref_cnt variable is initialized to 1.

```
class my_string {
public:
   my_string() { st = new str_obj; assert(st != 0);}
   my_string(const char* p)
      { st = new str_obj(p); assert(st != 0);}
   my_string(const my_string& str)
        { st = str.st; st -> ref_cnt++; }
   ~my_string();
   void  assign(const my_string& str);
   void  print() const { cout << st -> s; }
private:
   str_obj*  st;
};
```

The client will use objects of type my_string. These objects are implemented as pointers st to values of type str_obj. Notice how the copy constructor for this class uses reference semantics to produce a copy.

The semantics of assign() show some of the subtleties of using reference counting.

```
void my_string::assign(const my_string& str)
{
   if (str.st != st) {
      if (--st -> ref_cnt == 0)
         delete st;
      st = str.st;
      st -> ref_cnt++;
   }
}
```

The assignment occurs if the my_string is not being assigned its same value. The assignment causes the assigned variable to lose its previous value. This is equivalent to decrementing the reference count of the pointed-at str_obj value. Whenever an object's reference count is decremented, it gets tested for deletion.

The advantage of this over normal copying is clear. A very large aggregate is copied by reference, using a few operations and a small amount of storage for the reference counter. Also, each possible change to a pointer adds a reference-count operation. The destructor must also test the reference count before deletion.

```
my_string:: ~my_string()
{
    if (--st -> ref_cnt == 0)
        delete st;
}
```

5.11 No Constructor, Copy Constructor, and Other Mysteries

Object creation for native types is usually the task of the compiler. The writer of a class wishes to achieve the same ease of use for the class. Let us reexamine some issues in simple terms.

Does every class need an explicitly defined constructor? Of course not. If no constructor is written by the programmer, the compiler provides a default constructor, if needed.

In file tracking.cpp

```
//personal data tracking

struct pers_data {
    int    age;          //in years
    int    weight;       //in kilograms
    int    height;       //in centimeters
    char   name[20];     //last name
};

void print(pers_data d)
{
    cout << d.name << " is " << d.age
         << " years old\n";
    cout << "weight : " << d.weight << "kg,  height : "
         << d.height << "cm." << endl;
}
```

```
int main()
{
    pers_data  laura = { 3, 14, 88, "POHL" };
                            //construction off the stack

    print(laura);          //calls copy constructor
}
```

What if we use constructors and allow the copy constructor to be provided by the compiler? Recall that this means that the copy constructor does member-by-member copy, which can result in the wrong semantics—namely, shallow-copy semantics—in which no new value is created; instead, a pointer variable is assigned the address of the existing value.

Take the case of reference semantics, whereby a copy implies that the reference counter is incremented. This would not happen with the compiler-provided copy constructor. Thus, objects copied in this manner would be undercounted and prematurely returned to free store. As a rule of thumb, the class provider should explicitly write out the copy constructor unless it is self-evident that memberwise copy is safe. Always be cautious if the aggregate has any pointer-based members.

Are there special rules for unions? Yes. This should not be surprising, since unions are a technique for having various objects share space. Unions cannot have members that have constructors or destructors; nor can they have `static` data members. Anonymous unions can have only public data members, and a global anonymous union must be declared `static`.

5.11.1 Destructor Details

A destructor is implicitly invoked when an object goes out of scope. Common cases include block exit and function exit.

```
my_string sub_str(char c, my_string b)
{
    my_string  temp;
    .....
    return temp;
}
```

In `sub_str()`, we have b, a call-by-value argument of type `my_string`. Therefore, the copy constructor is invoked to create a local copy when the function is invoked. Correspondingly, a destructor is called on function exit. A local `my_string` variable, `temp`, is constructed on block entry to this function and therefore must have its destructor invoked on block exit. Finally, the `return` argument must be constructed and passed back into the calling environment. The corresponding destructor will be invoked, depending on the scope of the object to which it is assigned.

It is possible to explicitly call a destructor.

```
p = new my_string("I don't need you long");
    //invokes my_string::my_string(const char*);
.....
p -> ~my_string();        //or p -> my_string::~my_string()
.....                     //but delete p is strongly preferred
```

5.12 Pragmatics

In constructors, initialization is preferred to assignment. For example,

```
ch_stack::ch_stack(int size)
   { s = new char[size]; assert(s != 0);
     max_len = size; top = EMPTY; }
```

is better written as

```
ch_stack::ch_stack(int size) : max_len(size), top(EMPTY)
   { s = new char[size]; assert(s != 0); }
```

As mentioned, data members that are reference declarations or const declarations must be initialized. Also, the compiler is often more efficient about initialization.

In classes that use new to construct objects, a copy constructor should be explicitly provided. The default compiler-provided copy constructor usually has the wrong semantics for such an object. Usual practice is to provide a default and a copy constructor with any class that uses pointers in its implementation. As we shall see in Section 6.7, "Overloading Assignment and Subscripting Operators," on page 209, such classes should have their own explicit definition of operator=(). This ensures that copying and assignment will be done safely.

In cases where constructors of one argument are not intended as conversions, C++ has the recently added keyword explicit to disable its conversion semantics.

```
class ch_stack {
public:
   explicit ch_stack(int n);    //not used for conversion
.....
};
```

5.13 Moving from C++ to Java

Like a C++ constructor, a Java *constructor* is a function whose job is to *initialize* an object of its class. Constructors are invoked after the instance variables of a newly created class object have been assigned default initial values and any explicit initializers are called. Constructors are frequently overloaded.

In both C++ and Java, the term *overloading* refers to the practice of giving several meanings to a method. The meaning selected depends on the types of the arguments passed to the method, called the method's *signature*.

A constructor is a member function whose name is the same as the class name. The constructor is not a method and does not have a return type. Let us change our `Person` example in Section 4.14, "Moving from C++ to Java," on page 139, to have constructors initialize the name-instance variable.

In file Person2.Java

```
//constructor to be placed in Person

public Person() {name = "Unknown";}
public Person(String nm) { name =nm;}
public Person(String nm, int a, char b)
   { name =nm; age =a; gender = b;}
```

These constructors would be invoked when new gets used to associate a created instance with the appropriate type reference variable. For example,

```
p1 = new Person();                 //creates "unknown 0 M
p1 = new Person("Laura Pohl");     //creates Laura Pohl 0 M
p1 = new Person("Laura Pohl" 9, 'F'); //creates Laura Pohl 9 F
```

The overloaded constructor is selected by the set of arguments that matches the constructor's parameter list.

Destruction is done automatically by the system, using automatic garbage collection. This differs from C++, in which the programmer must provide the destructor. When the object can no longer be referenced—for example, when the existing reference is given a new object—the now inaccessible object is called garbage. Periodically, the system sweeps through memory and retrieves these "dead" objects. The programmer need not be concerned with such apparent memory leaks.

Summary

1. A constructor, a member function whose name is the class name, constructs objects of its class type. This process may involve initializing data members and allocating free store, using the operator new. A constructor is invoked when its associated type is used in a definition.

   ```
   TYPE_foo y(3);              //invoke TYPE_foo::TYPE_foo(int)
   extern TYPE_foo x;          //declaration but not definition
   ```

   Again, not all declarations are definitions. In those cases, no constructor is invoked.

2. A destructor is a member function whose name is the class name preceded by the tilde character ~. Its usual purpose is to destroy values of the class type, typically by using delete.

3. A constructor requiring no arguments is called the default constructor. It can be a constructor with an empty argument list or one whose arguments all have default values. It has the special purpose of initializing arrays of objects of its class.

4. A copy constructor of the form

   type::*type*(const *type*& *x*)

   is used to copy one type value into another when

   - A type variable is initialized by a type value.
   - A type value is passed as an argument in a function.
   - A type value is returned from a function.

   If the copy constructor is not present, the compiler provides one that does member-by-member initialization of value.

5. A class having members whose type requires a constructor uses initializers, a comma-separated list of constructor calls following a colon. The constructor is invoked by using the member name followed by an argument list in parentheses. The initialization is in the order of the declaration of the members.

6. An efficient disposal scheme for large aggregates is reference counting. Here, each dynamically allocated object tracks its active references. When an object is created, its reference count is set to 1. Every time the object is newly referenced, its reference count is incremented. Every time the object loses a reference, its count is decremented. When the reference count becomes 0, the object's memory is disposed of.

7. Constructors of a single parameter are automatically conversion functions. They convert from the parameter type to the class type. For example, `my_type::my_type(int);` is a conversion from `int` to `my_type`. This property can be disallowed by declaring the constructor `explicit`.

Review Questions

1. The default constructor requires _____ arguments.

2. If a class does not have an explicit copy constructor, it is provided by the _____.

3. A constructor is used for _____.

4. A destructor is used for _____.

5. *Constructor initializers* for class members can be specified in a comma-separated list after the punctuation character _____.

6. Constructor initializers are needed when a member was declared _____.

7. A conversion constructor is one whose signature has _____.

8. A linked list data type is an example of a _____ class.

9. A linked list has pointer members that refer to objects of their own type. This is called a _____.

10. Shallow-copy semantics means that copying is performed by _____.

Exercises

1. Discuss why constructors are almost always public member functions. What goes wrong if they are private?

2. Write a member function for the class `mod_int`:

   ```
   void add(int i);    //add i to v modulo 60
   ```

   The function should add the number i to the current value of v while retaining the modulo 60 feature of v.

3. Run the following program and explain its behavior. Placing debugging information inside constructors and destructors is a very useful step in developing efficient and correct classes.

   ```
   //Constructors and destructors invoked

   class A {
   public:
      A(int n) : xx(n)
         { cout << "A(int " << n << ") called" << endl;}
      A(double y) : xx(y + 0.5)
         { cout << "A(fl " << y << ") called" << endl; }
      ~A()
         { cout << "~A() with A::xx = " << xx << endl; }
   private:
      int  xx;
   };
   ```

```
int main()
{
    cout << "enter main\n";
    int    x = 14;
    float  y = 17.3;
    A      z(11), zz(11.5), zzz(0);

    cout << "\nOBJECT ALLOCATION LAYOUT\n";
    cout << "\nx is at " << &x;
    cout << "\ny is at " << &y;
    cout << "\nz is at " << &z;
    cout << "\nzz is at " << &zz;
    cout << "\nzzz is at " << &zzz;
    cout << "\n_____\n";
    zzz = A(x);    zzz = A(y);
    cout << "exit main" << endl;
}
```

Add a default constructor for class A:

```
A::A() : xx(0) { cout << "A() called" << endl; }
```

Now modify the program by declaring an array of type A:

```
A  d[5];    //declares array of 5 elements of type A
```

Assign the values 0, 1, 2, 3, and 4 to the data member xx of each d[i]. Run the program and explain its behavior.

4. Using the ch_stack type discussed in Section 5.2, "Constructing a Dynamically Sized Stack," on page 155, add a default constructor to allocate a ch_stack of 100 elements. Write a program that swaps the contents of two ch_stacks, using an array of ch_stacks to accomplish the job. The ch_stacks will be the first two stacks in the array. One method would be to use four ch_stacks: st[0], st[1], st[2], and st[3]. Push the contents of st[1] into st[2], of st[0] into st[3], of st[3] into st[1], and of st[2] into st[0]. To verify that the contents of the ch_stacks are in the same order, implement a print() function that outputs all elements in the ch_stack. Can this be done with only three ch_stacks?

5. Add a constructor to the type ch_stack with the following prototype:

   ```
   ch_stack::ch_stack(const char* c);
   //initialize from char array
   ```

   When does this provide a conversion? Is this desirable? How can the conversion be avoided?

6. Using the my_string type discussed in Section 5.4, "An Example: Dynamically Allocated Strings," on page 159, code the following member functions:

   ```
   //strcmp is negative if s < s1,
   //        is 0 if s == s1,
   //        and is positive if s > s1
   //        where s is the implicit argument

   int my_string::strcmp(const my_string& s1);

   //strrev  reverses the my_string
   void my_string::strrev();

   //print overloaded to print the first n characters
   void my_string::print(int n);
   ```

7. Write a function that swaps two my_strings. Use it and my_string::strcmp from the previous exercise to write a program that will sort an array of my_strings.

8. Using the dbl_vect type in Section 5.5, "The Class dbl_vect," on page 163, code the following member functions:

   ```
   //adds all the element values and returns their sum
   double dbl_vect::sumelem();

   //prints all the elements
   void dbl_vect::print();

   //adds two vectors into a third  v(implicit) = v1+v2
   void dbl_vect::add(const dbl_vect& v1, const dbl_vect& v2);

   //adds two vectors and returns  v(implicit) + v1
   dbl_vect dbl_vect::add(const dbl_vect& v1);
   ```

9. Write a further constructor for db1_vect that accepts an int array and its size and that constructs a db1_vect with these initial values:

```
dbl_vect::dbl_vect(const dbl_vect* d, int sz);
```

10. Try to benchmark the speed differences between safe arrays, as represented by class db1_vect, and ordinary integer arrays. Repeatedly run an element summation routine, using int a[10000], and one using the db1_vect a(10000). Time your trials. Useful timing functions can be found in the *time* library.

11. Using the class db1_vect in Section 5.5, "The Class db1_vect," on page 163, define the class multi_v as follows:

```
class multi_v {
public:
    multi_v(int i) : a(i), b(i), c(i), size(i) {}
    void  assign(int ind, int i, int j, int k);
    void retrieve(int ind, int& i,
                  int& j, int& k) const;
    void  print(int ind) const;
    int  ub() const { return (size - 1); }
private:
    dbl_vect     a, b, c;
    int    size;
};
```

Write and test code for the member functions assign(), retrieve(), and print(). The function assign() should assign i, j, and k to a[ind], b[ind], and c[ind], respectively. The function retrieve() does the inverse of assign(). The function print() should print the three values a[ind], b[ind], and c[ind].

12. Use the slist type discussed in Section 5.7, "Example: A Singly Linked List," on page 168, to code the following member functions:

```
//slist constructor whose initializer is a char* string
slist::slist(const char* c);

//length returns the length of the slist
int slist::length();

//return number of elements whose data value is c
int slist::count_c(char c);
```

13. Write a member function `append()` that will add a list to the end of the implicit list argument; then clear the appended `slist` by zeroing the head:

    ```
    void slist::append(slist& e);
    ```

14. Write a member function `copy()` that will copy a list:

    ```
    //the implicit argument ends up a copy of e
    void slist::copy(const slist& e);
    ```

    Be sure to destroy the implicit list before you do the copy. You want a special test to avoid the list's copying to itself.

15. Use the `slist` type in Section 5.7, "Example: A Singly Linked List," on page 168, and add the equivalent member functions that give you stack functions:

    ```
    reset    push    pop   top_of   empty
    ```

    Using one data structure as the implementation for another data structure is known as *adapting* it. This idea is used extensively by the standard template library.

16. As written, `slist::del()` expects a nonempty list. What goes wrong if it is passed an empty list? See the effect on your system. Modify this routine to test for this condition and continue. Note that this can be tested as an assertion but will then abort on the empty list.

17. Add a constructor to `slistelem` and use it to simplify the coding of the member function `slist::prepend(char c)`.

18. Modify the `matrix` class to have a constructor that performs a transpose (see Section 5.8, "Two-Dimensional Arrays," on page 173). The second argument of the constructor will be an enumerated type that indicates what transformation should be made on the array.

    ```
    enum transform { transpose, negative, upper };

    matrix::matrix(const matrix& a, transform t)
    {
    //transpose  base[i][j] = a.base[j][i]
    //negative   base[i][j] = -a.base[i][j]
    //upper      base[i][j] = a.base[i][j] i <= j else 0
    }
    ```

19. Write a member function that will return the eigen values of a `matrix`.

20. Complete the polynomial package by writing the code for the routines `void polynomial::release()` and `void polynomial::print()`, which are not found in the text. (See Section 5.9, "Polynomials as a Linked List," on page 175.)

21. Write code for the polynomial addition routine `void polynomial::plus()`. (See Section 5.9, "Polynomials as a Linked List," on page 180.)

22. Rewrite the function from the preceding exercise `void polynomial::plus()`, so that `c.plus(c, c)` works correctly.

23. Make the constructor for `polynomial` more robust. Assume that the coefficient-exponent pairs are not necessarily in sorted order, and take this into account when writing the constructor. (See Section 5.9, "Polynomials as a Linked List," on page 178.)

24. Improve the reference-counted form of class `my_string` by asserting in appropriate member functions that `ref_cnt` is not negative. Why would you want to do this? (See Section 5.10, "Strings Using Reference Semantics," on page 181.)

25. *(Java)* Recode `mod_int` in Section 5.1, "Classes with Constructors," on page 150, as a Java class.

26. *(Java)* Recode `ch_stack` in Section 5.2, "Constructing a Dynamically Sized Stack," on page 155, as a Java class.

27. *(Java: Project)* Recode `polynomial` in Section 5.9, "Polynomials as a Linked List," on page 175, as a Java class. Evaluate the C++ and Java implementations as to simplicity and efficiency.

Chapter 6
Operator Overloading and Conversions

Polymorphism is a means of giving different meanings to the same function name or operator, dependent on context. The appropriate meaning is selected on the basis of the type of data being processed. Object orientation takes advantage of polymorphism by linking behavior to the object's type. Operators, such as + and <<, have distinct meanings overloaded by operand type. For example, the expression cout << x is by convention expected to display an appropriate representation of x, depending on the type of object x.

Conversion is the explicit or implicit change of value between types. Conversions provide a form of polymorphism. Overloading of functions gives the same function name different meanings. The name has several interpretations that depend on function selection. This is called *ad hoc polymorphism*. This chapter discusses overloading, especially operator overloading, and conversions of data types.

Operators are overloaded and selected based on the signature-matching algorithm. Overloading operators gives them new meanings. For example, the meaning of the expression a + b differs, depending on the types of the variables a and b. Overloading the operator + for user-defined types allows them to be used in addition expressions in much the same way native types would be used. The expression a + b could mean string concatenation, complex-number addition, or integer addition, depending on whether the variables were the ADT complex, the ADT my_string, or the native type int. Mixed-type expressions are also made possible by defining conversion functions. This chapter also discusses friend functions and their importance to operator overloading.

One principle of OOP is that user-defined types must enjoy the same privileges as native types. Where C++ adds the complex number type, the programmer expects the convenience of using it without regard to a native/nonnative distinction. Operator overloading and user-defined conversions let us use complex numbers in much the same way as we can use int or double.

6.1 ADT Conversions

Explicit type conversion of an expression is necessary when either the implicit conversions are not desired or the expression will not otherwise be legal. One aim of OOP using C++ is the integration of user-defined ADTs and built-in types. To achieve this, there is a mechanism for having a member function provide an explicit conversion.

Section 5.1.3, "Constructors as Conversions," on page 152, discusses a constructor of one argument as being a de facto type conversion from the argument's type to the constructor's class type. For example,

```
point::point(double u);
```

is automatically a type conversion from `double` to `point` unless it is disabled by declaring such a conversion constructor with the modifier `explicit`. The conversion is available both explicitly and implicitly. Explicitly, it is used as a conversion operation in either cast or functional form. Thus,

```
point s;
double  d = 3.5;

s = static_cast<point>(d);
```

and

```
s = d;          //implicit invocation of conversion
```

both work.

These are conversions from an already defined type to a user-defined type. However, it is not possible for the user to add a constructor to a built-in type such as `int` or `double`. A conversion function for a user-defined type can be created by defining a special conversion function inside the class. The general form of such a member function is

```
operator type() { ····· }
```

Such a member function must be nonstatic, cannot have parameters, and does not have a declared return type. It must return an expression of the designated type.

In the `point` example, one may want a conversion from `point` to `double`. This can be done for the `point` class, as follows.

In file point6.cpp

```
point::operator double()        //use distance from origin
{
    return sqrt(x * x + y * y);
}
```

Notice that we used a commonly accepted conversion that is by no means unique. Another possibility would have been to return the x value only. Unless there is universal agreement on a conversion, it is best to omit such functions, as they can readily lead to unintended results.

6.2 Overloading and Function Selection

Overloaded functions are an important addition in C++. The overloaded meaning is selected by matching the argument list of the function call to the argument list of the function declaration. When an overloaded function is invoked, the compiler must have a selection algorithm with which to pick the appropriate function. The algorithm that accomplishes this depends on what type conversions are available. A best match must be unique, must be best on at least one argument, and must be as good as any other match on all other arguments. The following list shows the matching algorithm for each argument.

Overloaded Function Selection Algorithm

1. Use an exact match if found.

2. Try standard type promotions.

3. Try standard type conversions.

4. Try user-defined conversions.

5. Use a match to ellipsis if found.

Standard promotions—conversions from float to double and from bool, char, short, or enum to int—are better than other standard conversions. Standard conversions also include pointer conversions.

   An exact match is clearly best. Casts can be used to force such a match. The compiler will complain about ambiguous situations. Thus, it is poor practice to rely on subtle type distinctions and implicit conversions that obscure the overloaded function. When in doubt, use explicit conversions to provide an exact match.

Let us write an overloaded function `greater()` and follow our algorithm for various invocations. In this example, the user type `rational` is available.

In file rational.cpp

```
//Overloading functions

class rational {
public:
   rational(int n = 0) : a(n),q(1){}
   rational(int i, int j) : a(i), q(j){}
   rational(double r) : q(BIG), a(r * BIG){}
   void  print() const { cout << a << " / " << q ; }
   operator double() { return static_cast<double>(a)/q; }
private:
   long  a, q;
   enum { BIG = 100 };
};

inline int     greater(int i, int j)
      { return ( i > j ? i : j); }
inline double  greater(double x, double y)
       { return ( x > y ? x : y); }
inline rational greater(rational w, rational z)
      { return ( w > z ? w : z); }

int main()
{
   int    i = 10, j = 5;
   float  x = 7.0;
   double y = 14.5;
   rational w(10), z(3.5), zmax;

   cout << "\ngreater(" << i << ", " << j << ") = "
        << greater(i, j);
   cout << "\ngreater(" << x << ", " << y << ") = "
        << greater(x, y);
   cout << "\ngreater(" << i << ", " ;
   z.print();
   cout << ") = " << greater(static_cast<rational>(i), z);
   zmax = greater(w, z);
   cout << "\ngreater(";
```

```
            w.print();
            cout << ", ";
            z.print();
            cout << ") = ";
            zmax.print();
        }
```

The output from this program is

```
greater(10, 5) = 10
greater(7, 14.5) = 14.5
greater(10, 350 / 100) = 10
greater(10 / 1, 350 / 100) = 10 / 1
```

A variety of conversion rules, both implicit and explicit, are being applied. We explain these in the following dissection of the *rational* program.

◆◆◆◆◆◆◆◆◆◆◆◆◆

Dissection of the *rational* Program

■   `rational(double r) : q(BIG), a(r * BIG){}`

This constructor converts from `double` to `rational`.

■   `operator double() { return static_cast<double>(a)/q; }`

This member function converts from `rational` to `double`.

■   ```
    inline int   greater(int i, int j)
                   { return (i > j ? i : j); }
    inline double greater(double x, double y)
                   { return (x > y ? x : y); }
    inline rational greater(rational w, rational z)
                   { return (w > z ? w : z); }
    ```

Three distinct functions are overloaded. The most interesting has `rational` type for its argument list variables and its return type. The conversion member function `operator double()` is required to evaluate `w > z`. Later, we shall show how to overload `operator>()` to take `rational` types directly.
    ```

```
■   cout << "\ngreater(" << i << ", " << j << ") = "
        << greater(i, j);
    cout << "\ngreater(" << x << ", " << y << ") = "
        << greater(x, y);
```

The first statement selects the first definition of `greater()` because of the exact-match rule. The second statement selects the second definition of `greater()` because of the use of a standard widening conversion `float` to `double`. The value of variable x is widened to `double`.

```
■   << greater(static_cast<rational>(i), z);
```

The second definition of `greater()` is selected because of the exact-match rule. The explicit conversion of i to a `rational` is necessary to avoid ambiguity.

```
■   zmax = greater(w, z);
```

This is an exact match for the third definition.

See exercise 3 on page 230 for more on the *rational* program.

6.3 Friend Functions

The keyword `friend` is a function specifier, giving a nonmember function access to the hidden members of the class and providing a method of escaping the data hiding restrictions of C++. However, we must have a good reason for escaping these restrictions, as they are important to reliable programming.

One reason for using friend functions is that some functions need privileged access to more than one class. A second reason is that friend functions pass all of their arguments through the argument list, and each argument value is subject to assignment-compatible conversions. Conversions would apply to a class variable passed explicitly and would be especially useful in cases of operator overloading, as seen in the next section.

A friend function must be declared inside the class declaration to which it is a friend. The function is prefaced by the keyword `friend` and can appear in any part of the class without affecting its meaning. The preferred style is to place the `friend` declaration in the public part of the class. Since access has no effect on `friend` declarations, they are conceptually public. Member functions of one class can be friend functions of another class. In this case, they are written in the friend's class, using the scope resolution operator to qualify its function name. In order to specify that all member functions of one class are friend functions of a second class, write friend class *class-name.*

The following declarations illustrate the syntax.

```
void alice()
{
  //use some private stuff from tweedledee
    . . . . .
    cout << "Have some more tea.\n";
}

class tweedledee {
    . . . . .
    friend void  alice();          //friend function
    int  cheshire();               //member function
    . . . . .
};

class tweedledum {
    . . . . .
    friend int  tweedledee::cheshire();
    . . . . .
};

class tweedledumber {
    . . . . .
    friend class tweedledee;       //all member functions of
    . . . . .                      //tweedledee have access
};
```

The global function alice() is given access to all members of tweedledee. The member function tweedledee::cheshire() is given access to all members of tweedledum. The member functions of tweedledee are given access to all members of tweedledumber.

Consider the classes matrix (see Section 5.8, "Two-Dimensional Arrays," on page 173) and dbl_vect (see Section 5.5, "The Class dbl_vect," on page 163). A function multiplying a vector by a matrix as represented by these two classes could be written efficiently if it had access to the private members of both classes. The function would be a friend function of both classes. In our discussion, safe access was provided to the elements of dbl_vect and matrix with the member function element(). One could write a multiply function using element() without requiring

friend status. However, the price in function-call overhead and array-bounds
checking would make such a matrix multiply unnecessarily inefficient.

In file matrix2.cpp

```
class matrix;         //forward reference

class dbl_vect {
public:
   friend dbl_vect mpy(const dbl_vect& v, const matrix& m);
   .....
private:
   double*  p;
   int    size;
};

class matrix {
public:
   friend dbl_vect  mpy(const dbl_vect& v, const matrix& m);
   .....
private:
   double**   p;
   int      s1, s2;
};

   //use privileged access to p in both classes
dbl_vect mpy(const dbl_vect& v, const matrix& m)
{
   assert(v.size == m.s1);            //check sizes

   dbl_vect  ans(m.s2);
   int   i, j;

   for (i = 0; i <= m.ub2(); ++i) {
      ans.p[i] = 0;
      for (j = 0; j <= m.ub1(); ++j)
         ans.p[i] += v.p[j] * m.p[j][i];
   }
   return ans;
}
```

A minor point is that a forward declaration of the class `matrix` is necessary. The reason is that the function `mpy()` must appear in both classes, using each class as an argument type.

The OOP paradigm is that objects (in C++, class variables) should be accessed through their public members. Only member functions should have access to the hidden implementation of the ADT. This is a neat, orderly design principle. The friend function, however, straddles this boundary. The friend function has access to private members but is not itself a member function. The friend function can be used to provide quick fixes to code that needs access to the implementation details of a class. But the mechanism is easily abused.

6.4 Overloading Operators

The keyword `operator` is used to define a type-conversion member function, as well as to overload the built-in C++ operators. Just as a function name, such as `print()`, can be given a variety of meanings, depending on its arguments, so can an operator, such as +, be given additional meanings. *Overloading operators* allows infix expressions of both ADTs and built-in types to be written. In many instances, this important notational convenience leads to shorter, more readable programs.

Unary and binary operators can be overloaded as nonstatic member functions. Implicitly, they are acting on a class value. Most unary operators can be overloaded as ordinary functions, taking a single argument of class or reference to class type. Most binary operators can be overloaded as ordinary functions, taking one or both arguments of class or reference to class type. The operators =, (), [], and -> must be overloaded with a nonstatic member function.

```
class foo {
public:
    foo  operator-();          //overload unary minus
    foo  operator-(int);       //binary minus foo-int
    foo  operator-(foo);       //binary minus foo-foo
};

foo operator-(int, foo);       //binary minus int-foo
foo operator-(int, foo*);      //illegal:need foo or foo&
```

The previous section's `mpy()` function could have been written as

```
dbl_vect operator*(const dbl_vect& v, const matrix& m)
    . . . . .
```

If this had been done, if r and s were `dbl_vect`, and if t were a `matrix`, the natural-looking infix expression

```
r = s * t;
```

would invoke the multiply function, replacing the functional notation

```
r = mpy(s, t);
```

Although meanings can be added to operators, their associativity and precedence remain the same. For example, the multiplication operator will remain of higher precedence than the addition operator. The operator precedence table for C++ is included in Appendix B, "Operator Precedence and Associativity." Almost all operators can be overloaded. The exceptions are the member operator `.`, the member object selector operator `.*`, the ternary conditional expression operator `? :`, the `sizeof` operator, and the scope resolution operator `::`. (See Section C.12.5, "Operator Overloading," on page 390.)

Available operators include all of the arithmetic, logical, comparison, equality, assignment, and bit operators. Furthermore, the autoincrement and autodecrement operators, `++` and `--`, can have distinct prefix and postfix meanings. (See exercise 24 on page 236.) The subscript or index operator `[]` and the function call `()` can also be overloaded. The structure pointer operator `->` and the member pointer selector operator `->*` can be overloaded. (See exercise 25 on page 236.) It is also possible to overload `new` and `delete`. The assignment, function call, subscripting, and class pointer operators can be overloaded only by nonstatic member functions.

6.5 Unary Operator Overloading

To continue the discussion of operator overloading, we demonstrate how to overload unary operators, such as `!`, `++`, `~`, and `[]`. For this purpose, we develop the class `clock`, which can be used to store time as days, hours, minutes, and seconds. We shall develop familiar operations on `clock`.

In file clock.cpp

```
class clock {
public:
   clock(unsigned long i);       //construct & conversion
   void  print() const;          //formatted printout
   void  tick();                 //add one second
   clock  operator++() { tick(); return *this; }
private:
   unsigned long  tot_secs, secs, mins, hours, days;
};
```

This class overloads the prefix autoincrement operator; the class is a member function and can be invoked on its implicit single argument. The member function tick adds one second to the implicit argument of the overloaded ++ operator.

```
inline clock::clock(unsigned long i)
{
   tot_secs = i;
   secs = tot_secs % 60;
   mins = (tot_secs / 60) % 60;
   hours = (tot_secs / 3600) % 24;
   days = tot_secs / 86400;
}

void clock::tick()
{
   clock  temp = clock(++tot_secs);

   secs = temp.secs;
   mins = temp.mins;
   hours = temp.hours;
   days = temp.days;
}
```

The constructor performs the usual conversions from tot_secs to days, hours, minutes, and seconds. For example, a day has 86,400 seconds; therefore, integer division by this constant gives the whole number of days. The member function tick() constructs clock temp, which adds 1 second to the total time. The constructor acts as a conversion function that properly updates the time.

The overloaded operator++() also updates the implicit clock variable and returns the updated value as well. It could have been coded in the same way as tick(), except that the statement

```
    return temp;
```

would be added.

Adding the following code, we can test our functions:

```
void clock::print() const
{
    cout << days << " d :" << hours << " h :"
         << mins << " m :" << secs << " s" << endl;
}

//Clock and overloaded operators

int main()
{
    clock  t1(59), t2(172799); //172799 = 2 days-1 sec

    cout << "initial times are" << endl;
    t1.print();
    t2.print();
    ++t1;   ++t2;
    cout << "after one second times are" << endl;
    t1.print();
    t2.print();
}
```

The output is

```
initial times are
0 d :0 h :0 m :59 s
1 d :23 h :59 m :59 s
after one second times are
0 d :0 h :1 m :0 s
2 d :0 h :0 m :0 s
```

It is also possible to overload prefix ++, using an ordinary function.

```
clock operator++(clock& cl)
{
    cl.tick();
    return cl;
}
```

Notice that the clock variable must advance by 1 second; we use call-by-reference.

The decision to choose between a member function representation and a nonmember function typically depends on whether implicit conversion operations are available and desirable. Explicit argument passing allows the argument to be automatically coerced, if necessary and possible. When overloaded as a member function, +c is equivalent to `c.operator++()`. When overloaded as a nonmember function, ++c is equivalent to `operator++(c)`.

6.6 Binary Operator Overloading

We continue with our `clock` example and show how to overload binary operators. The same principles hold: When a binary operator is overloaded using a member function, it has as its first argument the implicitly passed class variable and as its second argument the lone argument-list parameter. Friend functions and ordinary functions have both arguments specified in the parameter list. Of course, ordinary functions cannot access private members.

Let us create an operation for type `clock` that will add two values.

In file clock.cpp

```
class clock {
   .....
   friend clock  operator+(clock c1, clock c2);
};

clock operator+(clock c1, clock c2)
{
   return (c1.tot_secs + c2.tot_secs);
}
```

The integer expression is implicitly converted to a `clock` by the conversion constructor `clock::clock(unsigned long)`. Both `clock` values are passed as function arguments, and both are candidates for assignment conversions. Because `operator+()` is a symmetric binary operator, the arguments should be treated identically. Thus, it is normal for symmetric binary operators to be overloaded by friend functions.

In contrast, let us overload binary minus with a member function.

```
class clock {
   .....
   clock  operator-(clock c);
};

clock clock::operator-(clock c)
{
   return (tot_secs - c.tot_secs);
}
```

Remember that there is an implicit first argument. This takes some getting used to. It would have been better to use a friend function for binary minus, because of the symmetric treatment of the arguments.

We shall define a multiplication operation as a binary operation, with one argument an `unsigned long` and the second a `clock` variable. The operation will require the use of a friend function. It cannot be done with a member function because, as already stated, member functions have as their implicit first argument the `this` pointer.

```
clock operator*(unsigned long m, clock c)
{
   return (m * c.tot_secs);
}
```

This requirement forces the multiplication to have a fixed ordering that is type dependent. In order to avoid this, it is common practice to write a second overloaded function.

```
clock operator*(clock c, unsigned long m)
{
   return (m * c.tot_secs);
}
```

The second function is defined in terms of the first, as follows:

```
clock operator*(clock c, unsigned long m)
{
   return (m * c);
}
```

Defining the second implementation in terms of the first implementation reduces code redundancy and maintains consistency.

6.7 Overloading Assignment and Subscripting Operators

The assignment operator for a class type is by default generated by the compiler to have member-by-member assignment. This is fine for many user-defined types, such as `rational` or `point`. For types, such as `my_string` and `dbl_vect`, that need deep copying, this is incorrect. As a rule of thumb, any time a class needs an explicit copy constructor defined, it also needs an assignment operator defined. As we have seen with copy constructors, this is usually the case when the object allocates its own memory.

The subscripting operator is usually overloaded where a class type represents an aggregate for which indexing is appropriate. The index operation is expected to return a reference to an element contained within the aggregate. Overloading assignment and subscripting share several characteristics. Both must be done as nonstatic member functions, and both usually involve a reference return type.

We shall reimplement the class `dbl_vect`, extending its functionality by applying operator overloading. (See Section 5.5, "The Class `dbl_vect`," on page 163.) The reimplemented class will have several improvements to make it both safer and more useful. A constructor that converts an ordinary integer array to a safe array will be added, allowing us to develop code using safe arrays and to later run the same code efficiently on ordinary arrays. The public data member `ub` has been changed to a member function, which prevents a user from inadvertently introducing a program error by modifying the member. Finally, the subscript operator is overloaded and replaces the member function `element`.

In file dbl_vect2.h

```
//A safe array type dbl_vect with [] overloaded

class dbl_vect {
public:
   //constructors and destructor
   explicit dbl_vect(int n = 10);
   dbl_vect(const dbl_vect& v);
   dbl_vect(const double a[], int n);       //initialize by array
   ~dbl_vect() { delete []p; }
   //other member functions
   int  ub()const { return (size-1); }      //upper bound
   double& operator[](int i) ;              //range checked
   dbl_vect& operator=(const dbl_vect& v); //assignment
private:
   double*  p;                              //base pointer
   int  size;                               //number of elements
};

dbl_vect::dbl_vect(int n) : size(n)
{
   assert(n > 0);
   p = new double[size];
   assert(p != 0);
}

dbl_vect::dbl_vect(const double a[], int n) : size(n)
{
   assert(n > 0);
   p = new double[size];
   assert(p != 0);
   for (int i = 0; i < size; ++i)
      p[i] = a[i];
}

dbl_vect::dbl_vect(const dbl_vect& v) : size(v.size)
{
   p = new double[size];
   assert(p != 0);
   for (int i = 0; i < size; ++i)
      p[i] = v.p[i];
}
```

```
double& dbl_vect::operator[](int i)
{
   assert(i >= 0 && i < size);
   return p[i];
}
```

An overloaded subscript operator can have any return type and any argument list type. However, it is good style to maintain the consistency between a user-defined meaning and standard usage. Thus, the most common function prototype is

element-type& operator[](*integral type*);

Such functions can be used on either side of an assignment.

It is also convenient to be able to assign one array to another. The user can specify the behavior of assignment by overloading it. It is good style to be consistent with standard usage. The following member function overloads assignment for class dbl_vect:

```
dbl_vect& dbl_vect::operator=(const dbl_vect& v)
{
   if (this != &v) {              //do nothing if assigned to self
      assert(v.size == size);
      for (int i = 0; i < size; ++i)
         p[i] = v.p[i];
   }
   return *this;
}
```

Dissection of **dbl_vect::operator=()** Function

■ dbl_vect& dbl_vect::operator=(const dbl_vect& v)

The operator=() function returns reference to dbl_vect and has one explicit argument of type reference to dbl_vect. The first argument of the assignment operator is the implicit argument. If the function had been written to return void, it would not have allowed multiple assignment.

■ if (this != &v) {

Don't do anything if assignment is to the current variable.

■ `assert(v.size == size);`

This is a guarantee that the sizes are compatible.

■ ```
for (int i = 0; i < size; ++i)
   p[i] = v.p[i];
return *this;
```

The explicit argument `v.p[]` will be the right-hand side of the assignment; the implicit argument `p[]` will be the left-hand side. The self-referential pointer is dereferenced and passed back as the value of the expression. This allows multiple assignment with right-to-left associativity to be defined.

◈◈◈◈◈◈◈◈◈◈◈◈◈◈

Expressions of type `dbl_vect` can be evaluated by overloading in appropriate ways the various arithmetic operators. As an example, let us overload binary + to mean element-by-element addition of two `dbl_vect` variables.

```
dbl_vect dbl_vect::operator+(const dbl_vect& v)
{
   assert(size == v.size);
   dbl_vect sum(size);
   for (int i = 0; i < size; ++i)
      sum.p[i] = p[i] + v.p[i];
   return sum;
}
```

The following expressions are now meaningful with the class `dbl_vect`:

```
a = b;                    //a, b are type dbl_vect
a = b = c;                //a, b, c are type dbl_vect
a = dbl_vect(data, DSIZE); //convert array data[DSIZE]
a = b + a;                //assignment and addition
a = b + (c = a) + d;      //complicated expression
```

The class `dbl_vect` is a full-fledged ADT, behaving and appearing in client code much as any built-in type behaves and appears.

Notice that overloading both the assignment and plus operators does not imply that `operator+=` is overloaded. Indeed, it is the class designer's responsibility to make sure that the various operators have consistent semantics. It is customary to overload related sets of operators consistently.
```

6.8 Polynomial: Type and Language Expectations

A type's behavior is dictated largely by expectations found in the community that uses it. So how a polynomial behaves is determined by the mathematical community's definitions. In writing a polynomial type, one expects that the basic mathematical operations, such as +, -, *, and /, are available and work appropriately. Furthermore, one expects that assignment operators, equality operators, and increment and decrement operators provided are consistent with the C++ community's expectations. A class provides a public interface that is easy to use insofar as it meets both expectations. Operators for which there is no normal expectation should not be overloaded.

A more realistic polynomial class based on the representation in Section 5.9, "Polynomials as a Linked List," on page 175, could have the following declaration:

In file poly2.cpp

```cpp
//Polynomials with overloaded arithmetic operators

class polynomial {
public:
   polynomial();
   polynomial(const polynomial& p);
   polynomial(int size, double coef[], int expon[]);
   ~polynomial() { release(); }
   void print() const;
   double operator()(double x) const;  //evaluate P(x)
   polynomial& operator=(const polynomial& a);
   friend polynomial& operator+(const polynomial& a,
                                const polynomial& b);
   friend polynomial& operator-(const polynomial& a,
                                const polynomial& b);
   friend polynomial& operator*(const polynomial& a,
                                const polynomial& b);
   friend polynomial& operator/(const polynomial& a,
                                const polynomial& b);
   friend polynomial& operator-(const polynomial& a);
```

```
    friend polynomial& operator+=(polynomial& a,
                                  const polynomial& b);
    friend bool operator==(const polynomial& a,
                           const polynomial& b);
    friend bool operator!=(const polynomial& a,
                           const polynomial& b);

private:
    term*   h;
    int     degree;
    void    prepend(term* t);
    void    add_term(term*& a, term*& b);
    void    release();
    void    rest_of(term* rest);
    void    reverse();
};
```

The basic mathematical operations should work, and the basic relationships among C++ operators should hold. It would be very undesirable to have `operator=()`, `operator+()`, and `operator+=()` all defined and not have a = a + b give the same result as a += b.

The code for overloading `operator=` is as follows:

In file poly2.cpp

```
polynomial& polynomial::operator=(const polynomial& a)
{
    if (h != a.h) {                      //avoid a = a case
        release();                       //garbage collect old value
        polynomial* temp = new polynomial(a);
        h = temp -> h;
        degree = temp -> degree;
    }
    return *this;
}
```

The implementation of the other operators is left as an exercise (see exercise 28 on page 237).

6.9 Overloading I/O Operators << and >>

In keeping with the spirit of OOP, it is important to overload << to output user-defined types, as well as native types. The operator << has two arguments—an ostream& and the ADT—and must produce an ostream&. Whenever overloading << or >>, you want to use a reference to a stream and return a reference to a stream, because you do not want to copy a stream object. Let us write these functions for the type rational:

In file rational.cpp

```
class rational {
public:
   friend ostream&
      operator<<(ostream& out, rational x);
   friend istream&
      operator>>(istream& in, rational& x)
.....
private:
   long  a, q;
};

ostream& operator<<(ostream& out, rational x)
{
    return (out << x.a << " / " << x.q << '\t');
}
```

When the operator >> is overloaded to produce input to a user-defined type, its typical form is

```
istream& operator>>(istream& p, user-defined type& x)
```

If the function needs access to private members of x, it must be made a friend of its class. A key point is to make x a reference parameter so that its value can be modified. To do this for rational would require placing a friend declaration for this operator in the class rational and providing its function definition.

```
istream& operator>>(istream& in, rational& x)
{
    return (in >> x.a >> x.q);
}
```

6.10 Overloading Operator () for Indexing

A matrix type that provides dynamically allocated two-dimensional arrays can be designed with the function call operator overloaded to provide element selection. This is a good example of a container class that is useful with both scientific and nonscientific computation.

The function call operator () can be overloaded as a nonstatic member function with respect to various signatures. It is frequently used to provide an iterator operation (see exercise 12 on page 232 through exercise 14 on page 233) or an operation requiring multiple indices.

In file matrix3.cpp

```cpp
//dynamic matrix type

class matrix {
public:
   matrix(int c, int r);
   ~matrix();
   int ub1() const { return(c_size - 1); }
   int ub2() const { return(r_size - 1); }
   double& operator()(int i, int j);
   matrix& operator=(const matrix& m);
   matrix& operator+=(matrix& m);
private:
   int c_size, r_size;
   double  **p;
};

matrix:: matrix(int c, int r):c_size(c), r_size(r)
{
   p = new double*[c];
   assert(p != 0);
   for (int i = 0; i < c; ++i){
      p[i] = new double[r];
      assert(p[i] != 0);
   }
}
```

```
matrix:: ~matrix()
{
   for (int i = 0; i < c_size; ++i)
      delete [] p[i];
   delete [] p;
}

inline double& matrix::operator()(int i, int j)
{
   assert( i >= 0 && i < c_size &&
           j >= 0 && j < r_size);
   return p[i][j];
}

matrix& matrix::operator=(const matrix& m)
{
   assert(m.c_size == c_size && m.r_size == r_size);
   int i, j;

   for (i = 0; i < c_size; ++i)
      for (j = 0; j < r_size; ++j)
         p[i][j] = m.p[i][j];
   return *this;
}

matrix& matrix::operator+=(matrix& m)
{
   assert(m.c_size == c_size && m.r_size == r_size);
   int i, j;

   for (i = 0; i < c_size; ++i)
      for (j = 0; j < r_size; ++j)
         p[i][j] += m.p[i][j];
   return *this;
}
```

◆◆◆◆◆◆◆◆◆◆◆◆

Dissection of the Class `matrix`

- ```
  inline double& matrix::operator()(int i, int j)
  {
      assert( i >= 0 && i < c_size &&
              j >= 0 && j < r_size);
      return p[i][j];
  }
  ```

This member function gives a convenient multiple-argument notation for element access. This results in client code using expressions of the form `m(i, j)` to access explicit matrix elements. Notice how matrix indices are bounds tested through an assertion.

- ```
  matrix& matrix::operator+=(matrix& m)
  {
      assert(m.c_size == c_size && m.r_size == r_size);
  ```

The assertion macro is used with a testable precondition for arguments needed by this member function. The matrix being assigned to must be the same size as the matrix expression being computed. The code replaces an `if-else` statement that would perform an error exit. Compare this to the code written for class `dbl_vect` (see Section 5.5, "The Class `dbl_vect`," on page 163).

- ```
      for (i = 0; i < c_size; ++i)
          for (j = 0; j < r_size; ++j)
              p[i][j] += m.p[i][j];
  ```

This inner loop is efficient and transparent. Elementwise addition is being accomplished without overhead.

- ```
      return *this;
  ```

The return type is a *reference* to `matrix`. Dereferencing the `this` pointer causes the lvalue of the `matrix` object to be returned. This is the usual trick that allows multiple assignment to occur.

◆◆◆◆◆◆◆◆◆◆◆◆

This code is expanded in exercise 30 on page 238.

6.11 Overloading the Pointer Operator ->

The structure pointer operator -> is overloaded as a nonstatic class member function. The overloaded structure pointer operator is a unary operator on its left operand. The argument must be either a class object or a reference of this type. The function can return a pointer to a class object, an object of a class for which operator -> is defined, or a reference to a class for which operator -> is defined.

In the following example, we overload the structure pointer operator inside the class t_ptr. Objects of type t_ptr act as controlled-access pointers to objects of type triple.

In file triple.cpp

```
// Overloading the structure pointer operator

class triple {
public:
    triple(int a, int b, int c) { i = a; j = b; k = c; }
    void print() { cout << "\ni = " << i << ", j = "
                        << j << ", k = " << k; }
private:
    int     i, j, k;
};

triple   unauthor(0, 0, 0);

class t_ptr {
public:
    t_ptr(bool f, triple* p) { access = f; ptr = p; }
    triple*  operator ->() ;
private:
    bool   access;
    triple*  ptr;
};
```

```
triple* t_ptr::operator->()
{
    if (access)
        return ptr;
    else {
        cout << "\nunauthorized access";
        return &unauthor;
    }
}
```

The variable t_ptr::access is tested by the overloaded operator ->. If it is true, access is granted. The following code illustrates this:

```
int main()
{
    triple  a(1, 2, 3), b(4, 5, 6);
    t_ptr ta(false, &a), tb(true, &b);

    ta -> print();          //access denied
    tb -> print();          //access granted
}
```

6.12 Overloading new and delete

Most classes involve free-store memory allocation and deallocation. Sometimes, more sophisticated use of memory than is provided by simple calls to operators new and delete is needed for efficiency or robustness.

Operator new has the general form

$::_{opt}$ new $placement_{opt}$ type $initializer_{opt}$

Some examples are

```
::new char[10];         //insist on global new
new(buff) X(a);         //call with buff using X::X(a)
```

Up to now, we have been using the global operator new() to allocate free store. The system provides a sizeof(type) argument to this function implicitly. Its function prototype is

```
void* operator new(size_t size);
```

The operators new and delete can be overloaded. This feature provides a simple mechanism for user-defined manipulation of free store. For example, traditional C programming uses malloc() to access free store and to return a void* pointer to the allocated memory. In this scheme, memory is deallocated by the *stdlib* function free(). We use operator overloading of new and delete to allow an X object to use C's traditional free-store management.

```
class X {
public:
   void* operator new(size_t size) { return (malloc(size)); }
   void  operator delete(void* ptr) { free(ptr); }
   X(unsigned size) { new(size); }
   ~X() { delete(this); }
   .....
};
```

In this example, the class X has provided overloaded forms of new() and delete(). When a class overloads operator new(), the global operator is still accessible using the scope resolution operator ::.

One reason to overload these operators is to give them additional semantics, such as providing diagnostic information or being more fault tolerant. Also, the class can have a more efficient memory-allocation scheme than that provided by the system.

The *placement* syntax provides a comma-separated argument list used to select an overloaded operator new() with a matching signature. These additional arguments are often used to place the constructed object at a particular address. This form of operator new uses the *new* library.

In file over_new.cpp

```
//Placement syntax and new overloaded

char*  buf1 = new char[1000];       //in place of free store
char*  buf2 = new char[1000];

class object {
public:
   .....
private:
   .....
};
```

```
int main()
{
   object *p = new(buf1) object;    //allocate at buf1
   object *q = new(buf2) object;    //allocate at buf2
   .....
}
```

Placement syntax allows the user to have an arbitrary signature for the overloaded new operator. This signature—which is distinct from the initializer arguments—calls to new use to select an appropriate constructor.

The delete operator comes in two flavors. It can have as signatures

```
void operator delete(void* p);
void operator delete(void* p, size_t);
```

The first signature makes no provision for the number of bytes to be returned by delete; in this case, the programmer provides code that supplies this value. The second signature includes a size_t argument passed to the delete invocation. This argument is provided by the compiler as the size of the object pointed at by p. Only one form of delete can be provided as a static member function in each class.

The *new* library has the function pointer _new_handler(), which calls the error handler for operator new(). If memory is exhausted, the function pointer _new_handler is used to call a default system routine. The user can specify an explicit *out-of-free-store* routine, which can replace the default function by using set_new_handler(). The exit() function is provided in the *stdlib* library.

In file new_hdlr.cpp

```
//Simple fault tolerance using _new_handler

void heap_exhausted()    //user-defined error handling
{
   cerr << "HEAP EXHAUSTED" << endl;
   exit(1);
}

int main()
{
   set_new_handler(heap_exhausted);
   ..... //memory exhaustion is like heap_exhausted()
}
```

These class `new()` and `delete()` member functions are always implicitly `static`. The `new()` is invoked before the object exists and therefore cannot have a `this` yet. The `delete()` is called by the destructor, so the object is already destroyed.

6.13 Pragmatics

Explicitly casting arguments can be both an aid to documentation and a useful way to avoid poorly understood conversion sequences. It is not an admission of ignorance to cast or to parenthesize arguments or expressions that otherwise could be converted or evaluated properly.

Operator overloading is easily misused. Do not overload operators when doing so can lead to misinterpretation. The domain of use should have a widely used notation that conforms to your overloading. Also, overload related operators in a manner consistent with C++ community expectations. For example, the relational operators `<`, `>`, `<=`, and `>=` should all be meaningful and provide expected inverse behaviors.

Generally speaking, overload symmetric binary operators, such as `+`, `*`, `==`, `!=`, and `&&`, with friend functions. Both arguments are then passed as ordinary parameters, which subjects them to the same rules of parameter passing. Recall that using a member function to provide overloading for symmetric binary operators causes the first argument to be passed via the `this` pointer.

Any time a class uses `new` to construct objects, it should provide an explicitly overloaded `operator=()`. This advice is analogous to our rule that such a class provide an explicit copy constructor. (See Section 5.2.1, "The Copy Constructor," on page 156.) The compiler-provided default assignment operator semantics would in most cases result in spurious behavior. This leads to a suggested normal form for classes with heap-managed memory.

```
//Normal form for heap-managed classes illustrated

class dbl_vect {
public:
   dbl_vect();                        //default constructor
   dbl_vect(const dbl_vect&);         //copy constructor
   .....
   dbl_vect&  operator=(const dbl_vect&);   //returns lvalue
   .....
};
```

This normal-form rule also applies to reference-counted classes, such as the `my_string` type. (See Section 5.4, "An Example: Dynamically Allocated Strings," on page 159.) The `operator=()` returns a reference to allow assignment to work efficiently. This requires lvalue semantics.

6.13.1 Signature Matching

Rules for signature matching are given in simplified form in Section 6.2, "Overloading and Function Selection," on page 197. A further clarification of these rules with examples is given here.

For a given argument, a best match is always an exact match. An exact match also includes *trivial conversions*. These are shown in the following table for type T:

Trivial Conversions	
From	**To**
T*	const T*
T*	volatile T*

The use of `volatile` is specialized. It means that a variable can be modified external to the program code. So, a variable representation of an address that gets data from an external device, such as a real-time clock, would be `volatile`. Also, `volatile` is used to suppress compiler optimizations that involve such variables.

These additional modifiers can be used in overloading resolution. Thus,

```
void   print(int i);
void   print(const int& i);
```

can be unambiguously overloaded.

It is important to remember that user-defined conversions include constructors of a single argument. These constructors can be implicitly called to perform conversions from the argument type to their class type. This can happen for assignment conversions, as in the argument-matching algorithm. The following example is modified from the one in Section 6.5, "Unary Operator Overloading," on page 205:

In file clock.cpp

```
//modify clock program

class clock {
public:
   clock(unsigned long i);      //construct & conversion
   void  print() const;         //formatted printout
   void  tick();                //add one second
   clock  operator++()  { this -> tick(); return *this; }
   void  reset(const clock& c);
private:
   unsigned long  tot_secs, secs, mins, hours, days;
};


void clock::reset(const clock& c)
{
   tot_secs = c.tot_secs;
   secs = c.secs;
   mins = c.mins;
   hours = c.hours;
   days = c.days;
}

int main()
{
   clock  c1(900), c2(400);
   .....
   c1.reset(c2);
   c2.reset(100);
   .....
}
```

The call to reset(100) involves an argument match between int and clock that is a user-defined conversion invoking the constructor clock(unsigned). Where these conversions are unintended, a new keyword explicit can be used in declaring the constructor to disable its use as an implicit conversion.

6.14 Moving from C++ to Java

Unlike C++, Java does not have operator overloading. Also, Java uses garbage collection instead of explicit deallocation. Java's use of new is similar to that in C++ but does not allow for overloading of the new operator. In general, this simplifies and restricts what the Java programmer can do and needs to worry about. Java allows ordinary casts but does not allow nonportable casts.

Java will perform an automatic conversion only if the conversion does not result in any information loss. The exception is that some numeric conversions from integer types to floating-point types can result in loss of precision, but the most significant digits of the result will be unchanged. For example, the following will result in an automatic conversion when n is assigned to f:

```
int n = 2;
float f;

f = n;
```

Trying to assign f to n would require a cast.

```
n = (int)f;
```

In this case, the floating-point value stored in f will be rounded *toward zero*, and the resulting value will be stored in n.

A *widening primitive conversion* is a conversion from one primitive type to another that loses at most some precision but otherwise does not lose information. The following are the Java widening primitive conversions:

From	To
byte	short, int, long, float, or double
short	int, long, float, or double
char	int, long, float, or double
int	long, float, or double
long	float or double
float	double

Widening primitive conversions are also applied automatically in assignment statements, as shown in the preceding example and in method invocations.

A *narrowing primitive conversion*, between primitive numeric types, may result in significant information loss. The following are narrowing primitive conversions:

From	To
byte	char
short	byte or char
char	byte or short
int	byte, short, or char
long	byte, short, char, or int
float	byte, short, char, int, or long
double	byte, short, char, int, long, or float

The only automatic narrowing primitive conversions are in assignment statements when the expression is a constant of type int; the variable is type byte, char, or short; and the value of the expression is representable by the type of the variable. Because the expression is a constant, it is possible to determine at compile time whether the conversion is legal.

Other than for assignment of constant expressions as just described, narrowing primitive conversions result only from an explicit cast. If the cast is between two integral types, the most significant bits are simply discarded in order to fit into the resulting format. Here is an example that shows how a narrowing conversion can cause a change of sign:

```
int i = 127, j = 128;
System.out.println((byte)i);
System.out.println((byte)j);
```

The output is

```
127
-128
```

The largest positive value that can be stored in a byte is 127. Attempting to force a narrowing conversion on a value greater than 127 will result in the loss of significant information. In this case, the sign is reversed.

String conversion is used in println():

```
System.out.println("x = " + x);
```

where x is a numeric primitive type variable. String conversion occurs when exactly one operand of the operator + is a string. In this case, the nonstring operand is converted to a string. For the primitive types, the result of string conversion is a value of type String that represents the primitive value. For example, the result of doing a string conversion on the int value 123 is the String "123".

Summary

1. Overloading operators gives them new meanings. For example, the meaning of the expression a + b depends on the types of the variables a and b. The expression could mean string concatenation, complex number addition, or integer addition, depending on whether the variables were the ADT my_string, the ADT complex, or the built-in type int, respectively.

2. A nonexplicit constructor of one argument is de facto a type conversion from the argument's type to the constructor's class type. A conversion from a user-specified type to a built-in type can be made by defining a special conversion function. The general form of such a member function is

   ```
   operator type() { ····· }
   ```

   These conversions occur implicitly in assignment expressions, arguments to functions, and values returned from functions.

3. The overloaded meaning is selected by matching the argument list of the function call to the argument list of the function declaration. A best match must be unique. It must be best on at least one argument and must be as good as any other match on all other arguments.

4. The keyword friend is a function specifier that allows a nonmember function access to the nonpublic members of the class of which it is a friend.

5. The keyword operator is also used to overload the built-in C++ operators. Just as a function name, such as print(), can be given a variety of meanings that depend on its arguments, so can an operator, such as +, be given additional meanings. Overloading operators allows infix expressions of both user and built-in types to be written. Operator precedence and associativity remain fixed.

6. Operator overloading typically uses either member functions or friend functions, because both have privileged access. When a unary operator is overloaded

using a member function, it has an empty argument list because the single operator argument is the implicit argument. When a binary operator is overloaded using a member function, it has as its first argument the implicitly passed class variable and as its second argument the lone argument-list parameter.

7. An overloaded subscript operator can have any return type and any argument-list type. However, it is good style to maintain the consistency between a user-defined meaning and standard usage. Thus, a common function prototype is

   element-type&   operator[] (*integral type*) ;

   This is an lvalue that can be used on either side of an assignment.

Review Questions

1. What is the signature in the following declaration: `void f(int x, double y);`?

2. How can you disable a conversion constructor?

3. How many arguments can a user-defined conversion have?

4. Outline the signature-matching algorithm.

5. Explain how `cout << x` uses overloading and why this was important.

6. The keyword `friend` is a function specifier. It gives a nonmember function _____.

7. One reason for using friend functions is _____.

8. Binary operators, such as +, should be overloaded by _____ functions because _____.

9. When a pointer operator is overloaded, it must be a _____ function.

10. Some operators can be overloaded only as nonstatic member functions. Name three such operators.

Exercises

1. The following table contains a variety of mixed-type expressions. Fill in both the type the expression is converted to and its value when well defined.

Declarations and Initializations		

`int    i = 3, *p = &i;`
`char c = 'b';`
`float x = 2.14, *q = &x;`		

Expression	**Type**	**Value**
`i + c`		
`x + i`		
`p + i`		
`p == & i`		
`* p - * q`		
`static_cast<int>(x + i)`		

2. For the type `rational` in Section 6.2, "Overloading and Function Selection," on page 198, explain why the conversions of integer 7 and double 7.0 lead to different internal representations.

3. The following line of code is from the *rational* program in Section 6.2, "Overloading and Function Selection," on page 198.

   ```
   cout << ") = " << greater(static_cast<rational>(i), z);
   ```

   If that line is replaced by

   ```
   cout << ") = " << greater(i, z);
   ```

   what goes wrong?

4. Write a `rational` constructor that, given two integers as dividend and quotient, uses a greatest common divisor algorithm to reduce the internal representation to its smallest a and q value. (See Section 6.2, "Overloading and Function Selection," on page 198.)

5. Overload the equality and comparison operators for `rational`. Notice that two `rationals` are equal in the form given by the previous exercise if and only if their dividends and quotients are equal. (See Section 6.2, "Overloading and Function Selection," on page 198.)

6. Write a function that adds a `dbl_vect` v to a `matrix` m. The prototype to be added to class `matrix` and class `dbl_vect` is

```
friend dbl_vect  add(const dbl_vect& v, matrix& m);
```

The `dbl_vect` v will be added element-by-element to each row of m. (See Section 6.3, "Friend Functions," on page 202.)

7. Define class `complex` as

```
class complex {
public:
    complex(double r) { real = r; imag = 0; }
    void  assign(double r, double i)
       { real = r; imag = i; }
    void  print()
       { cout << real << " + " << imag << "i "; }
    operator double()
       { return (sqrt(real * real + imag * imag));}
private:
    double real, imag;
};
```

We wish to augment the class by overloading a variety of operators. For example, the member function `print()` could be replaced by creating the friend function `operator<<()`:

```
ostream& operator<<(ostream& out, complex x)
{
    out << x.real << " + " << x.imag << "i ";
    return out;
}
```

Also, code and test a unary minus operator. It should return a `complex` whose value in each part is negated.

8. For the type `complex`, write the binary operator functions add, multiply, and subtract. Each should return `complex`. Write each as a friend function. Why not write them as member functions?

9. Write two friend functions:

   ```
   friend complex  operator+(complex, double);
   friend complex  operator+(double, complex);
   ```

   In the absence of a conversion from type `double` to type `complex`, both types are needed to allow completely mixed expressions of `complex` and `double`. Explain why writing one with an `int` parameter is unnecessary when these friend functions are available.

10. Overload assignment for `complex`:

    ```
    complex complex::operator=(complex c) { return c; }
    ```

    If this definition were omitted, would this be equivalent to the default assignment that the compiler generates? In the presence of the conversion operator for converting `complex` to `double`, what is the effect of assigning a `complex` to a `double`? Try to overload assignment with a friend function in class `complex`.

    ```
    friend double  operator=(double d, complex c);
    //assign d = real_part(c)
    ```

    Why won't this work?

11. Program a class `vec_complex` that is a safe array type whose element values are `complex`. Overload operators + and * to mean, respectively, element-by-element `complex` addition and dot-product of two `complex` vectors. For added efficiency, you can make the class `vec_complex` a friend of class `complex`.

12. The following member function is a form of iterator:

    ```
    double& dbl_vect::iterate()
    {
        static int  i = 0;
        i = i % size;
        return p[i++];
    }
    ```

It is called an *iterator* because it returns each element value of a db1_vect in sequence. Use this iterator to write a print function that is not a member function and that writes out all element values of a given db1_vect. Modify class db1_vect given in Section 6.7, "Overloading Assignment and Subscripting Operators," on page 210.

13. The previous exercise has a serious limitation. By providing an iterator that is contained in the class, it does not allow the element sequencing to depend on the individual db1_vect variable. Thus, if a and b are both db1_vect variables, the first call of a.iterate() will get the first element of a, and a subsequent call of b.iterate() will get the second element of b. Therefore, we shall define a new class db1_vect_iterator, as follows:

```
class db1_vect_iterator {
public:
   db1_vect_iterator(db1_vect& v) : p(&v), position(0) { }
   double& iterate() const;
private:
   db1_vect  *p;
   int    position;
};
```

This class must be a friend of db1_vect. Write the code for iterate. Then, for each declaration of a db1_vect, there will be a corresponding declaration of its iterator. For example,

```
db1_vect          a(5), b(10);
db1_vect_iterator  it_a(a), it_b(b);
```

Use this to write a function that finds the maximum element value in a db1_vect.

14. Define a new class matrix_iterator as an iterator class that sequences through all elements of a matrix. (See Section 6.10, "Overloading Operator () for Indexing," on page 216.) Use the new class to find the maximum element in a matrix.

15. Redo the my_string ADT by using operator overloading. (See Section 5.4, "An Example: Dynamically Allocated Strings," on page 159.) The member function assign() should be changed to become operator=. The member function concat() should be changed to become operator+. Also, overload operator[] to return the ith character in the my_string. If there is no such character, the value –1 is to be returned.

16. Explain why friendship to `str_obj` was required when overloading `<<` to act on objects of type `my_string`. (See Section 5.10, "Strings Using Reference Semantics," on page 181.) Rewrite `my_string` by adding a conversion member function `operator char*()`. This now allows `<<` to output objects of type `my_string`. Discuss this solution.

17. What goes wrong with the following client code when the overloaded definition of `operator=()` is omitted from `my_string`? (See Section 5.10, "Strings Using Reference Semantics," on page 181.)

```
//Swapping my_strings that are reference counted

class my_string {
   .....
};

void swap(my_string x, my_string y)
{
   my_string temp;

   temp = x;
   x = y;
   y = temp;
}

int main()
{
   my_string  b("do not try me "), c(" try me");

   cout << b << c << endl;
   swap(b, c);
   cout << b << c << endl;
}
```

18. We can develop our my_string class with a substring operation by overloading function call. The notation is my_string(from, to), where from is the beginning of the substring and to is the end.

```
my_string my_string::operator()(int from, int to)
{
    my_string temp(to - from + 1);

    for (int i = from; i < to + 1; ++i)
        temp.st -> s[i - from] = st -> s[i];
    temp.st[to - from + 1] = 0;
    return temp;
}
```

Use this substring operation to search a string for a given character sequence and to return true if the subsequence is found.

19. Rewrite the substring function, using a char* constructor. Is this better or worse? If you have a profiler, run this example with both forms of substring creation on the following client code:

```
int main()
{
    my_string large("A verbose phrase to search");

    for (i = 0; i < MANY; ++i)
        count += (large(i, i + 3) == "ver");
}
```

For this exercise, code operator==() to work on my_strings.

20. Write the function

```
void reverse(double data[], int size);
//data[size] will be reversed
//internally declare a stack of generic pointers
//push values onto stack, pop them back into data[]
```

21. Use a stack to write out subsequences in increasing order by value. In the sequence (7, 9, 3, 2, 6, 8, 9, 2), the subsequences are (7, 9), (3), (2, 6, 8, 9), (2). Use a stack to store increasing values. Pop the stack when a next sequence value is no longer increasing. Keep in mind that the stack pops values in reverse order. Redo this exercise, using a queue, thus avoiding this reversal problem.

22. For the stack of generic pointers, add the constructor

    ```
    stack::stack(int size, generic_ptr[]);
    ```

23. Redo the list ADT by using operator overloading. (See Section 5.7, "Example: A Singly Linked List," on page 168.) The member function prepend() should change to operator+(), and del() should change to operator--(). Also, overload operator[]() to return the ith element in the list.

24. The postfix operators ++ and -- can be overloaded distinct from their prefix meanings. Postfix can be distinguished by defining the postfix overloaded function as having a single unused integer argument, as in

    ```
    class T {
    public:
        //postfix invoked as t.operator++(0);
        void  operator++(int);
        void  operator--(int);
    };
    ```

    There will be no implied semantic relationship between the postfix and prefix forms. Add postfix decrement and increment to class clock in Section 6.5, "Unary Operator Overloading," on page 205. Have them subtract a second and add a second, respectively. Write these operators to use an integer argument n that will be subtracted or added as an additional argument.

    ```
    clock c(60);

        c++;                    //adds a second
        c--;                    //subtracts a second
        c.operator++(5);        //adds 1 + 5 seconds
        c.operator--(5);        //subtracts 6 seconds
    ```

25. The operator -> is overloadable provided it is a nonstatic member function returning either a pointer to a class object or an object of a class for which operator-> is defined. Such an overloaded structure pointer operator is called a *smart-pointer operator*. It usually returns an ordinary pointer after doing some initial computation. One use could be as an iterator function.

    ```
    dbl_vect* dbl_vect::operator->();
    //maintain an internal i
    //increment and return &p[++i]
    ```

Modify class `dbl_vect` in Section 6.7, "Overloading Assignment and Subscripting Operators," on page 210, to code and test this idea.

26. *(Difficult)* It is a better idea to make a smart-pointer class.

```
class dbl_vect {
public:
   friend class smart_ptr_dbl_vect; //add to dbl_vect
   .....
};

class smart_ptr_dbl_vect {
public:
   smart_ptr_dbl_vect(const dbl_vect& v);
   smart_ptr_dbl_vect&  operator->();
private:
   int*  ptr;
   int   position;
};

smart_ptr_dbl_vect::
   smart_ptr_dbl_vect(const dbl_vect& v) :
               position(0), ptr(v.p) { }
smart_ptr_dbl_vect& smart_ptr_dbl_vect::operator->()
{
   //write this code to access and test that
   //p[position] is not out of range
}
```

Modify class `dbl_vect` in Section 6.7, "Overloading Assignment and Subscripting Operators," on page 210, to test this idea.

27. Take the `polynomial::plus()` member function found in Section 5.9, "Polynomials as a Linked List," on page 180, and convert that member function to code for overloading `operator+`.

```
polynomial operator+(const polynomial&, const polynomial&)
```

This should be a friend of the class `polynomial`.

28. *(Project)* Write code to implement a polynomial multiplication operator. The code can repeatedly call the polynomial addition routine. Did you make sure that intermediate results would be properly garbage collected? Write a full-

blown polynomial package that is consistent with community expectations. You could include differentiation and integration of polynomials as well.

29. Use a conditional compilation flag NDEBUG to signal the compiler whether to include assertions. This simple mechanism allows both safe and unsafe classes to be compiled from the same source code. Run an application, such as a large matrix addition, with both forms of code, and measure the runtime overhead required by the assertion statements.

30. Write a matrix_iterator class with the same interface as dbl_vect_iterator from exercise 13 on page 233. The class should contain the member functions successor(), predecessor(), reset(), and item(). If you want, you can extend this with member functions int row() and int column(). (See Section 6.3, "Friend Functions," on page 202, for class matrix.)

31. Rewrite the matrix class to have row and column indices that go from 1 instead of 0.

32. *(Project)* Write code that fleshes out the rational type of Section 6.9, "Overloading I/O Operators << and >>," on page 215. Have the code work appropriately for all major operators. Allow it to properly mix with other number types, including integers, floats, and complex numbers. There are several ways to improve the rational implementation. You can try to improve the precision of going from double to rational. Also, many algorithms are more convenient when the rational is in a canonical form in which the quotient and divisor are relatively prime. This can be accomplished by adding a greatest common division algorithm to reduce the representation to the canonical form.

33. *(Java)* Rewrite in Java the class rational in Section 6.2, "Overloading and Function Selection," on page 198. You must substitute ordinary methods for any operator overloading.

Chapter 7
Templates, Generic Programming, and STL

C++ uses the keyword `template` to provide *parametric polymorphism*, which allows the same code to be used with respect to various types, where the type is a parameter of the code body. This is a form of generic programming. Many of the classes used in the text so far contained data of a particular type, although the data have been processed in the same way regardless of type. Using templates to define classes and functions allows us to reuse code in a simple, type-safe manner that lets the compiler automate the process of type *instantiation*, or when a type replaces a type parameter that appeared in the template code.

Polymorphic Genie: Capable of Assuming Various Forms

7.1 Template Class **stack**

We shall modify the `ch_stack` type from Section 5.2.1, "The Copy Constructor," on page 157, to have a parameterized type.

In file stack_t1.cpp

```
//template stack implementation

template <class TYPE>
class stack {
public:
   explicit stack(int size = 100)
      : max_len(size), top(EMPTY),s(new TYPE[size])
       { assert(s != 0); }
   ~stack() { delete []s; }
   void   reset() { top = EMPTY; }
   void   push(TYPE c) { s[++top] = c; }
   TYPE   pop() { return s[top--]; }
   TYPE   top_of()const { return s[top]; }
   bool   empty()const { return top == EMPTY;}
   bool   full()const { return top == max_len - 1;}
private:
   enum   { EMPTY = -1 };
   TYPE*   s;
   int     max_len;
   int     top;
};
```

The syntax of the class declaration is prefaced by

```
template <class identifier>
```

This identifier is a template argument that essentially stands for an arbitrary type. Throughout the class definition, the template argument can be used as a type name. This argument is instantiated in the declarations. A template declaration usually has global or namespace scope, can be a member of a class, or can be declared within another template class. An example of a **stack** declaration using this is

```
stack<char>      stk_ch;            //100 char stack
stack<char*>     stk_str(200);      //200 char* stack
stack<complex>   stk_cmplx(500);    //500 complex stack
```

This mechanism saves us rewriting class declarations where the only variation would be the type declarations, providing a type-safe, efficient, and convenient way to reuse code.

When a template class is used, the code must always use the angle brackets as part of the declaration.

In file stack_t1.cpp

```
//Reversing an array of char* represented strings

void reverse(char* str[], int n)
{
   stack<char*>  stk(n);
   int i;

   for (i = 0; i < n; ++i)
      stk.push(str[i]);
   for (i = 0; i < n; ++i)
      str[i] = stk.pop();
}

//Initializing stack of complex numbers from an array

void init(complex c[], stack<complex>& stk, int n)
{
   for (int i = 0; i < n; ++i)
      stk.push(c[i]);
}
```

Member functions, when declared and defined inside the class, are, as usual, inline. When defining them externally, you must use the full angle bracket declaration. So, when defined outside the template class,

```
TYPE  top_of() const { return s[top]; }
```

would be written as

```
template<class TYPE> TYPE stack<TYPE>::top_of() const
   { return s[top]; }
```

Yes, this is ugly and takes some getting used to, but the compiler otherwise would not know that TYPE was a template argument. As another example, we write the file scope definition of the destructor for `template<class TYPE> stack`.

```
template<class TYPE> stack<TYPE>::~stack()
    { delete []s; }
```

A C++ programmer would use the STL class `std::stack`. The code presented in this section will allow you to better appreciate the container classes provided by the standard library.

7.2 Function Templates

Many functions have the same code body, regardless of type; for example, initializing the contents of one array from another of the same type uses the same code body. The essential code is

```
for (i = 0; i < n; ++i)
    a[i] = b[i];
```

Most C programmers automate this with a simple macro.

```
#define  COPY(A, B, N) \
    { int i; for(i = 0; i < (N); ++i) (A)[i] = (B)[i]; }
```

Programming that works regardless of type is a form of generic programming. Using `define` macros can often work but is not type safe. Another problem with `define` macros is that they can lead to repeated evaluation of a single parameter (see exercise 3 on page 270). A user could readily mix types among which conversions were inappropriate. C++ programmers can make use of various forms of conversion and overloading to achieve similar effects. However, in the absence of appropriate conversions and signatures, no action would be taken. Templates provide a further generic programming mechanism for this.

In file copy1.cpp

```
template<class TYPE>
void copy(TYPE a[], TYPE b[], int n)
{
   for (int i = 0; i < n; ++i)
      a[i] = b[i];
}
```

The invocation of copy() with specific arguments causes the compiler to generate the function based on those arguments. If it cannot, a compile-time error results. What are the effects of the following calls?

In file copy1.cpp

```
double  f1[50], f2[50];
char    c1[25], c2[50];
int     i1[75], i2[75];
char*   ptr1, *ptr2;
copy(f1, f2, 50);
copy(c1, c2, 10);
copy(i1, i2, 40);
copy(ptr1, ptr2, 100);
copy(i1, f2, 50);
copy(ptr1, f2, 50);
```

The last two invocations of copy() fail to compile because their types cannot be matched to the template type. This is called a unification error. The types of the arguments do not conform to the template. How the compiler generates this matching is discussed in the next section. If we were to cast f2 as

```
copy(i1, static_cast<int* >(f2), 50);
```

compilation would occur. However, the result would be an inappropriate form of copying. Instead, we need to have a generic copying procedure that accepts two distinct class type arguments.

In file copy2.cpp

```
template<class T1, class T2>
void copy(T1 a[], T2 b[], int n)
{
    for (int i = 0; i < n; ++i)
        a[i] = b[i];
}
```

This form has an element-by-element conversion. This is usually the appropriate and safer conversion.

7.2.1 Signature Matching and Overloading

A generic routine often cannot work for special cases. The following form of swapping template works on basic types.

In file swap.cpp

```
//generic swap

template <class T>
void swap(T& x, T& y)
{
    T  temp;

    temp = x;
    x = y;
    y = temp;
}
```

A function template is used to construct an appropriate function for any invocation that matches its arguments unambiguously:

```
int       i, j;
char      str1[100], str2[100], ch;
complex   c1, c2;

swap(i, j);                //i j int - okay
swap(c1, c2);              //c1, c2 complex - okay
swap(str1[50], str2[33]);  //both char variables - okay
swap(i, ch);               //i int ch char - illegal
swap(str1, str2);          //illegal
```

In the last case, `str1` and `str2` are array names. They are pointer values that cannot be modified.

To have `swap()` work for strings represented as character arrays, we write the following special case:

```
void swap(char* s1, char* s2)
{
    int  max_len;

    max_len = (strlen(s1) >= strlen(s2)) ?
                  strlen(s1) : strlen(s2);
    char* temp = new char[max_len + 1];

    strcpy(temp, s1);
    strcpy(s1, s2);
    strcpy(s2, temp);
    delete []temp;
}
```

With this specialized case added, an exact match of this nontemplate version to the signature of a `swap()` invocation takes precedence over the exact match found by a template substitution.

Overloaded Function-Selection Algorithm

1. Exact match with some trivial conversions on nontemplate functions

2. Exact match using function templates

3. Ordinary argument resolution on nontemplate functions

7.3 Class Templates

In the `stack<T>` example given in Section 7.1, "Template Class `stack`," on page 240, we have an ordinary case of class parameterization. In this section, we wish to discuss various special features of parameterizing classes.

7.3.1 Friends

Template classes can contain friends. A friend function that does not use a template specification is universally a friend of all instantiations of the template class. A friend function that incorporates template arguments is specifically a friend of its instantiated class.

```
template <class T>
class matrix {
public:
   friend void  foo_bar();              //universal
   friend vect<T>  product(vect<T> v);  //instantiated
   .....
};
```

7.3.2 Static Members

Static members are not universal but are specific to each instantiation.

```
template <class T>
class foo {
public:
   static int  count;
   .....
};


   .....
foo<int>    a;
foo<double> b;
```

The static variables foo<int>::count and foo<double>::count are distinct.

7.3.3 Class Template Arguments

Both classes and functions can have several class template arguments. Let us write a function that will convert one type of value to a second type, provided the first type is at least as wide as the second type.

In file coerce.cpp

```
template <class T1, class T2>
bool coerce(T1& x, T2 y)
{
    if (sizeof(x) < sizeof(y))
        return false;
    x = static_cast<T1>(y);
    return true;
}
```

This template function has two possibly distinct types as template arguments.

Other template arguments include constant expressions, function names, and character strings.

In file array_tm.cpp

```
template <class T, int n>
class assign_array {
public:
    T  a[n];
};

.....
assign_array<double,50>  x, y;
.....
x = y;          //should work efficiently
```

The benefits of this parameterization include allocation off the stack, as opposed to allocation from free store. On many systems, the former is the more efficient regime. The type is bound to the particular integer constant; thus, operations involving compatible-length arrays are type safe and are checked at compile time.

7.3.4 Default Template Arguments

In the standard library, the `class complex` is now a template class. The normal instantiation would be to `double`, as in `complex<double> x, y, z[10]`. A template provider can decide that this is such a common case that it can be provided as a default.

```
template<class T = double>
class complex{
...
private:
    T real, imaginary;
}
```

7.3.5 Member Templates

Members may themselves be templates inside the template class. This feature of the ANSI standard has yet to be implemented on many compilers.

```
template <class T1>
class foo {
public:
    //class member template
    template <class T2>
    class fooprime {
    .....
    //can use T1 and T2 in fooprime
    };
    //can only use T1 in foo
    .....
};

foo<int>::fooprime<char>    a;
```

There can also be function member templates. Check your local compiler documentation to see whether these constructs are available.

7.4 Parameterizing the Class vector

The class dbl_vect from Section 5.5.1, "dbl_vect as a Linear Vector Type," on page 166, is a natural candidate for parameterization. It is a form of container class. It improves on the primitive container that is the array. The defects of the array are found in C and C++: Namely, it is easy to have out-of-bounds errors resulting in difficult to find runtime bugs. We will parameterize the class, renaming it vector in anticipation of discussing and understanding the STL class std::vector. The new class is used in conjunction with *iterators* and algorithms. An iterator is a pointer or a pointer-like variable used for traversing and accessing container elements.

In file vect_it.h

```
//Template-based vector type

template <class T>
class vector {
public:
   typedef T* iterator;
   explicit vector(int n = 100);      //create a size n array
   vector(const vector<T>& v);        //copy vector
   vector(const T a[], int n);        //copy an array
   ~vector() { delete []p; }
   iterator begin(){ return p;}
   iterator end(){ return p + size;}
   T& operator[](int i);              //range-checked element
   vector<T>& operator=(const vector<T>& v);
private:
   T* p;                              //base pointer
   int size;                          //number of elements
};
```

Basically, everywhere the previous dbl_vect class used double as the value to be stored in individual elements, the template definition uses T. Thus, the declaration of the private base pointer p is now of type T.

The definition of member functions in file scope includes the scope-resolved label *classname*<T>. The following constructors for vector<T> use T as the type specification to new:

```
template <class T>
vector<T>::vector(int n = 100): size(n)
{
   assert(n > 0);
   p = new T[size];
   assert(p != 0);
}
```

This is the default constructor, because of the default argument of 100. We use the keyword explicit to disallow its use as a conversion from int to vector. Assertions are used to guarantee that the constructor performs its contractual obligations when given appropriate input.

```
template <class T>
vector<T>::vector(const T a[], int n)
{
    assert(n > 0);
    size = n;
    p = new T[size];
    assert(p != 0);
    for (int i = 0; i < size; ++i)
        p[i] = a[i];
}
```

This constructor converts an ordinary array to a vector. The copy constructor defines a deep copy of the vector v.

```
template <class T>
vector<T>::vector(const vector<T>& v)
{
    size = v.size;
    p = new T[size];
    assert(p != 0);
    for (int i = 0; i < size; ++i)
        p[i] = v.p[i];
}
```

The following code defines vector indexing by overloading the bracket operator. The return type for the bracket operator is reference to T, as this is an alias for the item stored in the container. Using this return type allows the bracket operator to access the item in the container as an lvalue.

```
template <class T> T& vector<T>::operator[](int i)
{
    assert (i >= 0 && i < size );
    return p[i];
}
```

Notice that we can test to make sure that the array bounds are not exceeded. With operator[] overloaded, we can access vectors as if they were native C++ arrays. We also need to provide an overloaded assignment operator (see exercise 7 on page 270).

```
template <class T>
vector<T>& vector<T>::operator=(const vector<T>& v)
{
    assert(v.size == size);
    for (int i = 0; i < size; ++i)
        p[i] = v.p[i];
    return *this;
}
```

Client code is almost as simple as with nonparameterized declarations. To use these declarations, you simply add within angle brackets the specific type that instantiates the template. These types can be native types, such as int in the example, or user-defined types. The following code uses these templates.

In file vect_it.cpp

```
int main()
{
    vector<double> v(5);
    vector<double>::iterator p ;
    int i = 0;

    for (p = v.begin() ; p != v.end(); ++p)
        *p = 1.5 + i++;

    do {
        --p;
        cout << *p << " , ";
    } while (p != v.begin());
    cout << endl;
}
```

The output from this program is

```
5.5, 4.5, 3.5, 2.5, 1.5,
```

The values are in reverse order to how they are stored. This is a consequence of iterating back from the iterator value v.end().

7.5 STL

The standard template library (STL) is the C++ library providing generic programming for many standard data structures and algorithms. The STL provides three components—containers, iterators, and algorithms—that support a standard for generic programming.

The library is built using templates and is highly orthogonal in design. Components can be used with one another on native and user-provided types through proper instantiation of the various elements of the STL. The following sections serve only as an overview and brief introduction to STL, which is large and complicated. Many newer systems have important further extensions to the STL.

7.5.1 STL Example Code

One of the most effective uses of the STL is to replace the use of ordinary C++ arrays with STL vectors. The STL vector type has many important advantages over the array, such as dynamic expansion, thus avoiding overflow. Further, it can be readily navigated with both iterators and indices, and has a rich interface of built-in operations. .

In file stl_vec1.cpp

```
//Simple STL vector program
#include <iostream>
#include <vector>
using namespace std;

int main ()
{
   vector<int> v(100); //100 is the vector's size

   for (int i = 0; i < 100; i++)
      v[i] = i;
   for (vector<int>::iterator p = v.begin(); p != v.end(); p++)
      cout << *p << '\t';
}
```

The STL container `vector` is used in place of an ordinary `int` array. The first for-statement is written in exactly the same manner as a C++ loop on ordinary data. The second for-statement is written using the iterator p. An iterator behaves as a pointer. STL provides the member functions `begin()` and `end()` as initial and terminal position values for the container. Note that end() returns the iterator position (or address) one past the last element of the container. Thus, end() is a guard location, or value signaling that you are finished traversing the container.

The next example uses the list container, an iterator, and the generic algorithm accumulate() in our first example program using STL. The *list* and *numeric* libraries are required.

In file stl_cont.cpp

```
//Using the list container

void print( list<double> &lst)
{                   //using an iterator to traverse lst
   list<double>::iterator p;

   for (p = lst.begin(); p !=lst.end(); ++p)
      cout << *p << '\t';
   cout << endl;
}

int main()
{
   double w[4] = { 0.9, 0.8, 88, -99.99 };
   list<double> z;
   for (int i = 0; i < 4; ++i)
      z.push_front(w[i]);
   print(z);
   z.sort();
   print(z);
   cout << "sum is "
        << accumulate(z.begin(), z.end(), 0.0) << endl;
}
```

In this example, a list container is instantiated to hold doubles. An array of doubles is pushed into the list. The print() function uses an iterator to print each element of the list in turn. Notice again that iterators work like pointers. Both the list and the vector have the standard begin() and end() member functions for starting and ending locations of the container. Also, the list interface includes a stable sorting algorithm, the sort() member function. The accumulate() function is a generic function in the *numeric* package that uses 0.0 as an initial value and computes the sum of the list container elements by going from the starting location z.begin() to the ending guard location z.end().

Notice that `print()` itself could be parameterized and made a generic algorithm. Try to do this in a most general way (see exercise 13 on page 272).

7.6 Containers

Containers come in two major families: sequence and associative. Sequence containers (vectors, lists, and deques) are ordered by having a sequence of elements. Associative containers (sets, multisets, maps, and multimaps) have keys for looking up elements. The map container is a basic associative array and requires that a comparison operation on the stored elements be defined. The two varieties of container share a similar interface.

STL Typical Container Interfaces

- Constructors, including default and copy constructors

- Element access

- Element insertion

- Element deletion

- Destructor

- Iterators

Containers are traversed using iterators, pointer-like objects that are available as templates and optimized for use with STL containers.

In file stl_deq.cpp

```
//A typical container algorithm

double sum(deque<double> &dq)
{
   deque<double>::iterator p;
   double s = 0.0;

   for (p=dq.begin(); p != dq.end(); ++p)
      s += *p ;
   return s;
}
```

The deque (double-ended queue) container is traversed using a iterator. The iterator p is dereferenced to obtain each stored value in turn. This algorithm will work with sequence containers and with all types that have operator+=() defined. Containers allow equality and comparison operators. They also have an extensive list of standard data and function members. (See Section E.1, "Containers," on page 431.)

7.6.1 Sequence Containers

Sequence containers (vector, list, and deque) have a sequence of accessible elements. In many cases, the C++ array type can also be treated as a sequence container. The *deque* and *vector* libraries are used.

In file stl_vec2.cpp

```
//Sequence Containers - insert a vector into a deque

int main()
{
   int data[5] = { 6, 8, 7, 6, 5 };
   vector<int> v(5, 6);              //5 element vector
   deque<int> d(data, data + 5);
   deque<int>::iterator p;
   cout << "\nDeque values" << endl;
   for (p = d.begin(); p != d.end(); ++p)
      cout << *p << '\t';            //print:6 8 7 6 5
   cout << endl;
   d.insert(d.begin(), v.begin(), v.end());
   for (p = d.begin(); p != d.end(); p++)
      cout << *p << '\t';            //print:6 6 6 6 6 8 7 6 5
}
```

The five-element vector v is initialized with the value 6. The deque d is initialized with values taken from the data array. The insert() member function places the v values in the specified range v.begin() to v.end(), at the location d.begin().

Dissection of the *stl_vect* Program

- ```
  int data[5] = { 6, 8, 7, 6, 5 };
  vector<int> v(5, 6);              //5 element vector
  deque<int> d(data, data + 5);
  deque<int>::iterator p;
  ```

The vector v initializes a five-element int container to value 6. The deque d uses the iterator values data and data + 5 to initialize a five-element double-ended queue container. This is one of the standard container class constructors. Notice how it uses an iterator range to pass in arguments for the constructor. Many of the STL functions use iterator ranges as arguments. Ordinary array pointers can be used as iterators. The iterator p is declared but is not initialized.

- ```
  for (p = d.begin(); p != d.end(); ++p)
      cout << *p << '\t';        //print:6 8 7 6 5
  ```

This is a standard traversal idiom when using containers and iterators. Notice that d.end() is used to terminate the loop, because it is in effect the end-of-container iterator value. Also notice that the ++ autoincrement has pointer semantics advancing the iterator to the next container position. Dereferencing also works analogously to pointer semantics.

- ```
  d.insert(d.begin(), v.begin(), v.end());
  ```

The insert() member function places the range of iterator values v.begin() up to but not including v.end() at the position d.begin(). The insert() member function is very typical of member functions in STL, using the first iterator value as an insertion point and an iterator range for the values to be inserted.

- ```
  for (p = d.begin(); p != d.end(); ++p)
      cout << *p << '\t'; //print:6 6 6 6 6 8 7 6 5
  ```

As a consequence of inserting five new elements of value 6 at the front of the deque d, the output of the traversal loop for d is now the 10 elements, as shown in the comment.

Some sequence container member functions are given in Section E.1.1, "Sequence Containers," on page 433.

7.6.2 Associative Containers

The associative containers (set, map, multiset, and multimap) have key-based accessible elements and an ordering relation `Compare`, which is the comparison object for the associative container. The *map* and *string* libraries are required.

In file stl_age.cpp

```
//Associative Containers - looking up ages

int main()
{
   map<string, int, less<string> > name_age;

   name_age["Pohl,Laura"] = 7;
   name_age["Dolsberry,Betty"] = 39;
   name_age["Pohl,Tanya"] = 14;
   cout << "Laura is " << name_age["Pohl,Laura"]
        << " years old." << endl;
}
```

The `map` `name_age` is an associative array where the key is a `string` type and the `Compare` object is `less<string>`.

The associative containers have several standard constructors for initialization. What distinguishes these constructors from sequence container constructors is the use of a comparison object. The insertions work when no element of the same key is already present. Some member functions are listed in Section E.1.1, "Sequence Containers," on page 434.

7.6.3 Container Adapters

Container adapter classes modify existing containers to produce various public behaviors based on an existing implementation. Three provided container adapters are `stack`, `queue`, and `priority_queue`.

The `stack` can be adapted from `vector`, `list`, and `deque` and needs an implementation that supports `back`, `push_back`, and `pop_back` operations. The `queue` can be adapted from `list` or `deque` and needs an implementation that supports `empty`, `size`, `front`, `back`, `push_back`, and `pop_front` operations. This is a first-in-first-out data structure

We adapt the `stack` from an underlying `vector` implementation. Notice that the STL ADTs replace our individually designed implementations of these types. The *stack*, *vector*, and *string* libraries are required.

In file stl_stak.cpp

```
//Adapt a stack from a vector

int main()
{
   stack<string, vector<string> > str_stack;
   string quote[3] =
     { "The wheel that squeaks the loudest\n",
       "Is the one that gets the grease\n",
       "Josh Billings\n" };

   for (int i =0; i < 3; ++i)
      str_stack.push(quote[i]);
   while (!str_stack.empty()) {
      cout << str_stack.top();
      str_stack.pop();
   }
}
```

Container adapter functions are given in Section E.1.3, "Container Adapters," on page 436.

7.7 Iterators

Navigation over containers is by iterator. Iterators can be thought of as an enhanced pointer type, templates that are instantiated according to the container class type they iterate over. There are five iterator types: input, output, forward, bidirectional, and random access. Not all iterator types may be available for a given container class. For example, random-access iterators are available for vectors but not for maps.

Input iterators support equality operations, dereferencing, and autoincrement. An iterator that satisfies these conditions can be used for one-pass algorithms that read values of a data structure in one direction. A special case of the input iterator is the istream_iterator.

Output iterators support dereferencing restricted to the left-hand side of assignment and autoincrement. An iterator that satisfies these conditions can be used for one-pass algorithms that write values to a data structure in one direction. A special case of the output iterator is the ostream_iterator.

Forward iterators support all input/output iterator operations, as well as unrestricted use of assignment. This allows position within a data structure to be retained from pass to pass. Therefore, general one-directional multipass algorithms can be written with forward iterators.

Bidirectional iterators support all forward iterator operations, as well as both autoincrement and autodecrement. Therefore, general bidirectional multipass algorithms can be written with bidirectional iterators.

Random-access iterators support all bidirectional iterator operations, as well as address arithmetic operations, such as indexing. Also, random-access iterators support comparison operations. Therefore, algorithms, such as `quicksort`, that require efficient random access in linear time can be written with these iterators.

Container classes and algorithms dictate the category of iterator available or needed, so `vector` containers allow random-access iterators, but `lists` do not. Sorting generally requires a random-access iterator, but finding requires only an input iterator.

7.7.1 The `istream_iterator` and `ostream_iterator`

An `istream_iterator` is derived from an input iterator to work specifically with reading from streams. An `ostream_iterator` is derived from an output iterator to work specifically with writing to streams. We will write a program that prompts for five numbers, reads them, and computes their sum, where I/O uses these iterators. The template for `istream_iterator` is instantiated with a *<type, distance>*. This distance is usually specified by `ptrdiff_t`. As defined in *cstddef* or *stddef,* it is an integer type representing the difference between two pointer values. Both *vector* and *iterator* libraries are needed.

In file stl_io.cpp

```
//Use of istream_iterator and ostream_iterator

int main()
{
   vector<int> d(5);
   int   i, sum ;
   istream_iterator<int, ptrdiff_t> in(cin);
   ostream_iterator<int> out(cout, "\t");
```

```
   cout << "enter 5 numbers" << endl;
   sum = d[0] = *in;                    //input first value
   for (i = 1; i < 5; ++i) {
      d[i] = *++in;                     //input consecutive values
      sum += d[i];
   }
   for (i = 0; i < 5; ++i)
      *out = d[i] ;                     //output consecutive values
   cout << " sum = " << sum << endl;
}
```

The `istream_iterator` `in` is instantiated with type `int` and parameter `ptrdiff_t`. The `ptrdiff_t` is a distance type that the iterator uses to advance in getting a next element. In the preceding declaration, `in` is constructed with the input stream `cin`. The autoincrement operator advances `in` and reads a next value of type `int` from the designated input stream. The `ostream_iterator` `out` is constructed with the output stream `cout` and the `char*` delimiter `"\t"`. Thus, the tab character will be issued to the stream `cout` after each `int` value is written. In this program, the iterator `out`, when it is dereferenced, writes the assigned `int` value to `cout`.

7.7.2 Iterator Adapters

Iterators can be adapted to provide backward traversal and traversal with insertion. Reverse iterators reverse the order of iteration; with insert iterators, insertion takes place instead of the normal overwriting mode. The following example uses a reverse iterator to traverse a sequence. The *vector* library is required.

In file stl_iadp.cpp

```
//Use of the reverse iterator

template <class ForwIter>
void print(ForwIter first, ForwIter last, const char* title)
{
   cout << title << endl;
   while ( first != last)
      cout << *first++ << '\t';
   cout << endl;
}
```

```
int main()
{
   int     data[3] = { 9, 10, 11};
   vector<int> d(data, data + 3);
   vector<int>::reverse_iterator p = d.rbegin();

   print(d.begin(), d.end(), "Original");
   print(p, d.rend(), "Reverse");
}
```

This program uses a reverse iterator to change the direction in which the `print()` function prints the elements of vector d.

Other algorithms in the *iterator* library are discussed in Section E.2.2, "Iterator Adapters," on page 438.

7.8 Algorithms

The STL algorithms library contains the following four categories.

Categories of STL Algorithms Library

- Sorting algorithms
- Nonmutating sequence algorithms
- Mutating sequence algorithms
- Numerical algorithms

These algorithms generally use iterators to access containers instantiated on a given type. The resulting code can be competitive in efficiency with special-purpose codes.

7.8.1 Sorting Algorithms

Sorting algorithms include general sorting, merges, lexicographic comparison, permutation, binary search, and similar operations. These algorithms have versions that use either `operator<()` or a `Compare` object and often require random-access iterators.

The following program uses the quicksort function `sort()` from the STL *algorithm* library to sort over elements d to e.

In file stl_sort.cpp

```
//Using sort() from STL
const int N = 5;

int main()
{
    int     d[N], i, *e = d + N;

    for (i = 0; i < N; ++i)
        d[i] = rand();
    sort(d, e);
    for (i = 0; i < N; ++i)
        cout << d[i] << '\t';
}
```

This is a straightforward use of the library sort algorithm operating on the built-in array d[]. Ordinary pointer values can be used as iterators. Some algorithm prototypes are found in Section E.3.1, "Sorting Algorithms," on page 440.

7.8.2 Nonmutating Sequence Algorithms

Nonmutating algorithms do not modify the contents of the containers they work on. A typical operation is searching a container for a particular element and returning its position.

In the following program, the nonmutating library function find() in the *algorithm* library is used to locate the element t.

In file stl_find.cpp

```
//Use of the find function

int main()
{
    string words[5] = { "my", "hop", "mop", "hope", "cope"};
    string*    where;

    where = find(words, words + 5, "hop");
    cout << *++where << endl;                    //mop
    sort(words, words + 5);
    where = find(words, words + 5, "hop");
    cout << *++where << endl;                    //hope
}
```

This program uses find() to look for the position of the word *hop*. We print the word following *hop* before and after sorting the array words[]. Some mutating function algorithm prototypes are given in Section E.3.2, "Nonmutating Sequence Algorithms," on page 442.

7.8.3 Mutating Sequence Algorithms

Mutating algorithms can modify the contents of the containers they work on. A typical operation is reversing the contents of a container.

In the following program, the mutating library functions reverse() and copy() are used. The *vector, string*, and *algorithm* libraries are required.

In file stl_revr.cpp

```
//Use of mutating copy and reverse

int main()
{
   string first_names[5] = {"laura", "ira",
       "buzz", "debra", "twinkle"};
   string last_names[5] = {"pohl", "pohl",
       "dolsberry", "dolsberry", "star"};
   vector<string> names(first_names, first_names + 5);
   vector<string> names2(10);
   vector<string>::iterator p;

   copy(last_names, last_names + 5, names2.begin());
   copy(names.begin(), names.end(), names2.begin()+5);
   reverse(names2.begin(), names2.end());
   for (p = names2.begin(); p != names2.end(); ++p)
      cout << *p <<'\t';
}
```

The first invocation of the mutating function copy() places last_names in the container vector names2. The second call to copy() copies in the first_names that had been used in the construction of the vector names. The function reverse() reverses all the elements, which are then printed out. Some algorithms are given in Section E.3.3, "Mutating Sequence Algorithms," on page 444.

7.8.4 Numerical Algorithms

Numerical algorithms include sums, inner product, and adjacent difference. In the following program, the function `accumulate()` from the *numeric* library performs a vector summation, and `inner_product()` performs a vector inner product.

In file stl_numr.cpp

```
//Vector accumulation and inner product

int main()
{
   double v1[3] = { 1.0, 2.5, 4.6 },
          v2[3] = { 1.0, 2.0, -3.5 };
   double sum, inner_p;

   sum = accumulate(v1, v1 + 3, 0.0);
   inner_p = inner_product(v1, v1 + 3, v2, 0.0);
   cout << "sum = " << sum
        << ",product = " << inner_p << endl;
}
```

These functions behave as expected on numerical types, where + and * are defined. The `accumulate` algorithm has the starting and ending positions and, as a third argument, the initial value, normally 0.0, to start accumulating the sum with. Some library prototypes for numerical algorithms are given in Section E.3.4, "Numerical Algorithms," on page 446.

7.9 Numerical Integration Made Easy

STL provides the basic computations for many more sophisticated algorithms. By using STL, programmers can easily implement them. We will use numerical integration as an example. The idea is to generate a series of points, using a *generator*. A generator is a class that defines the function by overloading `operator()`, the function call operator. The STL algorithm

```
generate(iterator b, iterator e, generator g)
```

is used to produce a `vector` of values in the range (0, 1) for the function. The *algorithm, numeric,* and *vector* libraries are all required.

In file stl_int1.cpp

```
//Simple integration routine for x*x over (0, 1)
//The function is represented in class gen

class gen {            //generator for function to be integrated
public:
   gen(double x_zero, double increment) : x(x_zero),
   incr(increment) { }
   double operator()() { x += incr; return x*x; }
private:
   double x, incr;
};

double integrate( gen g, int n)    //integrate on (0,1)
{
   vector<double> fx(n);

   generate(fx.begin(),fx.end(), g );
   return(accumulate(fx.begin(), fx.end(), 0.0) / n );
}

int main()
{
   const int n = 10000;

   gen g(0.0, 1.0/n);
   cout << "integration program x**2" << endl;
   cout << integrate(g, n) << endl;
}
```

We approximate the area under the curve by a sequence of rectangles whose
height is the value of the function and whose width is the increment. An increment
gives us two choices for a height. We could improve the numerical accuracy of integration by bounding the area between rectangles based on the smaller heights and
one based on the larger heights.

In file stl_int2.cpp

```
double integrate( gen g, int n, double& diff)
{
   vector<double> fx(n), sm(n), lg(n);
   double s, l;

   generate(fx.begin(),fx.end(), g );
   for (int i = 0; i < n - 1; ++i)
      if (fx[i] > fx[i + 1]) {
         sm[i] = fx[i + 1]; lg[i] = fx[i];
      }
      else {
         sm[i] = fx[i]; lg[i] = fx[i + 1];
      }
   s = accumulate(sm.begin(), sm.end(), 0.0)/n ;
   l = accumulate(lg.begin(), lg.end(), 0.0)/n ;
   diff = l - s;
   return ( s + l ) / 2;
}
```

The preceding code produces a more reliable estimate, with an error estimate calculated in diff. The estimate can be further improved by being adaptive, as discussed in the exercises (see exercise 17 on page 272).

7.10 Pragmatics

Many current C++ template implementations make a distinction between template parameters for functions and those for classes. Functions allow only class arguments, which must occur in the template function as part of the type description of at least one of the function parameters.

The following is okay:

```
template <class TYPE>
void  maxelement(TYPE a[], TYPE& max, int size);

template <class TYPE>
int  find(TYPE* data);
```

The following was previously illegal but is now legal according to the proposed ANSI standard:

```
template <class TYPE>
TYPE  convert(int i) { TYPE temp(i); return temp; }
```

In the ANSI standard, the function is invoked as follows:

```
convert<double>(i + j);        //newly allowed explicit
                               //function instantiation
```

Since it was previously illegal, the function instantiation may not work on many current systems. The restriction exists because current compilers must use the arguments at function invocation to deduce which functions will be created. A workaround is possible by creating a class whose sole member is a parameterized static function, as follows:

```
template <class TYPE>        //other arguments are possible
class convert_it {
   static TYPE  convert(int i)
      { TYPE  temp(i); return temp; }
};
```

7.11 Moving from C++ to Java

Unlike C++, Java does not have templates. Instead, each class in Java can be viewed as an extension of the superclass Object. This is done implicitly. The Object super-class provides for a type of generic programming and achieves some of the ideas of polymorphism accomplished by the use of templates in C++.

JGL (Java generic library) corresponds roughly to STL (standard template library) for C++. The use of Object in writing generic code is based on inheritance and is discussed in Section 8.10, "Moving from C++ to Java," on page 298.

Summary

1. C++ uses templates to provide parametric polymorphism. The same code is used with different types, where the type is a parameter of the code body.

2. Both classes and functions can have several class template arguments. In addition to class template arguments, class template definitions can include constant expressions, function names, and character strings as template arguments. A common case is to have an `int` argument that parameterizes a size characteristic.

3. A nontemplate, specialized version of a function may be needed when the generic routine will not work. When multiple functions are available, an algorithm determines which to use.

4. The standard template library (STL) is the C++ library that provides generic programming for many standard data structures and algorithms.

5. Containers come in two major families: sequence and associative. Sequence containers (vectors, lists, and deques) are ordered by having a sequence of elements. Associative containers (sets, multisets, maps, and multimaps) have keys for looking up elements.

6. Container adapter classes modify existing containers to produce different public behaviors, based on an existing implementation. Three provided container adapters are `stack`, `queue`, and `priority_queue`.

7. Iterators can be thought of as an enhanced pointer type. The five iterator types are input, output, forward, bidirectional, and random access. Not all iterator types may be available for a given container class. For example, random-access iterators are available for vectors but not for maps.

8. The STL algorithms library contains the following four categories: sorting algorithms, nonmutating sequence algorithms, mutating sequence algorithms, and numerical algorithms. These algorithms generally use iterators to access containers instantiated on a given type. The resulting code can be competitive in efficiency with special-purpose codes.

Review Questions

1. In C, one can use `void*` to write generic code, such as `memcpy()`. In C++, writing generic code uses the keyword _____.

2. Rewrite as a template function the macro

   ```
   #define  SQ(A) ((A) * (A))
   ```

   Mention a reason why this is preferable.

3. The three components of STL are _____, _____, and _____.

4. An iterator is like a _____ type in the kernel language.

5. The member _____ is used as a guard for determining the last position in a container.

6. Name two STL sequence container classes.

7. Name two STL associative container classes.

8. Can STL be used with ordinary array types? Explain.

9. True or false: A template argument can be only a type.

10. A nonmutating STL algorithm, such as `find()`, has the property _____.

Exercises

1. Rewrite `stack<T>` in Section 7.1, "Template Class `stack`," on page 240, to accept an integer value for the default size of the stack. Now client code can use such declarations as

   ```
   stack<int, 100>    s1, s2;
   stack<char, 5000>  sc1, sc2, sc3;
   ```

   Discuss the pros and cons of this additional parameterization.

2. Define a template for fixed-length stacks that allocates a compile-time-determined size array to store the stacked values.

3. The code

   ```
   #define CUBE(X) ((X)*(X)*(X))
   ```

   behaves differently from the code

   ```
   template<class T> T cube (T x){ return x * x * x;}
   ```

   Explain the difference when `cube(sqrt(7))` is invoked. When would the two coding schemes give different results?

4. Write a generic `cycle()` function with the following definition, and test it:

   ```
   template<class TYPE>
   void cycle(TYPE& a, TYPE& b, TYPE& c)
   {
   // replace a's value by b's and b's by c's
   // and c's by a's
   }
   ```

5. Write a generic function that, given an arbitrary array and its size, rotates its values with

   ```
   a[1] = a[0] , a[2] = a[1], ·····,
   a[size - 1] = a[size - 2], a[0] = a[size - 1]
   ```

6. Write the member function template

   ```
   <class T> void vector<T>::print()
   ```

   This function prints the entire vector range.

7. Rewrite the overloaded assignment operator to be more general:

   ```
   template <class T>
   vector<T>& vector<T>::operator=(const vector<T>& v)
   //allow different size vectors to be assigned
   //must delete and reallocate storage for left-hand
   //argument and avoid in a = a
   ```

8. Write a generic function that requires swapping of two vector<T>s of different types. (See Section 7.4, "Parameterizing the Class vector," on page 249.) Assume that both array types have elements that are assignment convertible.

9. Using vector<T> and its associated iterator class, code a generic vector internal sorting routine of your choice, but not quicksort (see Section 7.4, "Parameterizing the Class vector," on page 249). Compare its running time with the STL sort routine for vectors of 100, 1,000, and 10,000 elements.

10. *(Project)* Create a parametric string type. The basic type is to act as a container class that contains a class T object. In the prototype case, the object is a char. The normal end-of-string sentinel will be 0. The standard behavior should model the functions found in the *string* library. The class definition could parameterize the sentinel as well. Such a type exists in the standard library *string*.

11. Sorting functions are natural candidates for parameterization. The following is a generic bubble sort:

```
template <class T>
void bubble(T d[], int how_many)
{
    T  temp;

    for (int i = 0; i < how_many - 2;  ++i)
        for (int j= 0; j < how_many - 1 - i; ++j)
            if (d[j] < d[j+1]) {
                temp = d[j];
                d[j ]= d[j + 1];
                d[j+1] = temp;
            }
}
```

What happens if this is instantiated with a class in which operator<() is not defined?

12. Using a random-number generator, generate 10,000 integers between 0 and 9,999. Place them in a list<int> container. (See Section 7.5.1, "STL Example Code," on page 253.) Compute and print the median value. What did you expect? Compute the frequencies of each value; in other words, how many 0s were generated, how many 1s were generated, and so forth. Print the value with the greatest frequency. Use a vector<int> to store the frequencies.

13. Recode `print(const list<double> &lst)` to be a template function that is as general as possible. (See Section 7.5.1, "STL Example Code," on page 253.)

14. For `list<T>`, write the member function

    ```
    iterator list<T>::insert(iterator w_it, T v);
    ```

    which inserts v before `w_it` and returns an iterator pointing at the inserted element. (See Section 7.5.1, "STL Example Code," on page 253.)

15. For `list<T>`, write the member function

    ```
    void list<T>::erase(iterator w_it);
    ```

    which erases the element pointed at by `w_it`. (See Section 7.5.1, "STL Example Code," on page 253.)

16. Write an algorithm to find the second-largest element stored in an arbitrary container class. Use STL containers `vector<T>`, `list<T>`, and `set<T>` to test that it works regardless of the container. Write the algorithm, assuming that a forward iterator is available and comparison is understood.

17. We wish to perform simple numerical integration using STL containers and algorithms. Write a function that, given

    ```
    double f(double x);
    ```

    generates a vector of `doubles` from a to b, with an interval of s. Then accumulate the values s times `f(x)` over this interval. (See Section 7.9, "Numerical Integration Made Easy," on page 264.)

Chapter 8
Inheritance

Inheritance is the powerful code-reuse mechanism of deriving a new class from an old one. That is, the existing class can be added to or altered to create the derived class. Through inheritance, a hierarchy of related types that share code and interfaces can be created.

Many useful types are variants of one another, and it is frequently tedious to produce the same code for each. A derived class inherits the description of the *base* class, which can then be altered by adding members, modifying existing member functions, and modifying access privileges. The usefulness of this concept can be seen by examining how taxonomic classification compactly summarizes large bodies of knowledge. For example, knowing the concept "mammal" and knowing that an elephant and mouse are both mammals allows our descriptions of them to be considerably more succinct than they would be otherwise. The root concept contains the information that mammals are warm-blooded, higher vertebrates, and that they nourish their young through mammary glands. This information is inherited by the concept of both "mouse" and "elephant," but it is expressed only once: in the root concept. In C++ terms, both elephant and mouse are derived from the base class mammal.

C++ supports *virtual member functions*: functions declared in the base class and redefined in a derived class. A class hierarchy that is defined by public inheritance creates a related set of user types, all of whose objects may be pointed at by a base-class pointer. By accessing the virtual function through this pointer, C++ selects the appropriate function definition at runtime. The object being pointed at must carry around type information so that this distinction can be made dynamically, a feature typical of OOP code. Each object "knows" how it is to be acted on. This is a form of polymorphism called *pure polymorphism*.

Inheritance should be designed into software to maximize reuse and to allow a natural modeling of the problem domain. With inheritance, the key elements of the OOP design methodology are as follows:

OOP Design Methodology

1. Decide on an appropriate set of types.

2. Design in their relatedness, and use inheritance to share code.

3. Use virtual functions to process related objects polymorphically.

8.1 A Derived Class

A class can be derived from an existing class by using the form

> class *class-name* : (public|protected|private)_{opt}*base-name*
> {
>   *member declarations*
> };

As usual, the keyword class can be replaced by the keyword struct, with the implication that members are by default public. One aspect of the derived class is the visibility of its inherited members. The keywords public, protected, and private are used after the colon to specify how the base-class members are to be accessible to the derived class. This will be discussed in a later section.

The keyword protected is introduced to allow data hiding for members that must be available in derived classes but that otherwise act like private members. It is an intermediate form of access between public and private.

Consider developing a class to represent students at a college or university.

In file student2.h

```
class student {
public:
    enum year { fresh, soph, junior, senior, grad };
    student(char* nm, int id, double g, year x);
    void  print() const;
protected:
    int     student_id;
    double  gpa;
    year    y;
    char    name[30];
};
```

We could write a program that lets the registrar track such students. Although the information stored in student variables is adequate for undergraduates, it omits crucial information needed to track graduate students. Such additional information might include their means of support, their department affiliations, and their thesis topics. Inheritance lets us derive a suitable grad_student class from the student base class as follows:

In file student2.h

```
class grad_student : public student {
public:
    enum support { ta, ra, fellowship, other };
    grad_student(char* nm, int id, double g, year x,
            support t, char* d, char* th);
    void  print() const;
protected:
    support  s;
    char     dept[10];
    char     thesis[80];
};
```

In this example, `grad_student` is the derived class, and `student` is the base class. The use of the keyword `public` following the colon in the derived-class header means that the protected and public members of `student` are to be inherited as protected and public members of `grad_student`. Private members are inaccessible. Public inheritance also means that the derived class `grad_student` *is a* subtype of `student`. Thus, a graduate student *is a* student, but a student does not have to be a graduate student. This subtyping relationship is called the *is-a* relationship, or *interface inheritance.*

A derived class is a modification of the base class, inheriting the public and protected members of the base class. Only constructors, destructors, and member function `operator=()` cannot be inherited. Thus, in the example of `grad_student`, the `student` members `student_id`, `gpa`, `name`, `y`, and `print()` are inherited. Frequently, a derived class adds new members to the existing class members. This is the case with `grad_student`, which has three new data members and a redefined member function `print()`, which is *overridden*. The function definitions of `student::print()` and `grad_student::print()` appear in the next section. Implementation of the member function of the derived class is different from that of the base class. This is different from overloading, in which the same function name can have different meanings for each unique signature.

Benefits of Using a Derived Class

- Code is reused: `grad_student` uses existing, tested code from `student`.

- The hierarchy reflects a relationship found in the problem domain. When speaking of students, the special grouping "graduate student" is an outgrowth of the real world and its treatment of this group.

- Various polymorphic mechanisms will allow client code to treat `grad_student` as a subtype of `student`, simplifying client code while granting it the benefits of maintaining these distinctions among subtypes.

8.2 Typing Conversions and Visibility

A publicly derived class is a *subtype* of its base class. This means that a variable of the derived class can in many ways be treated as if it were the base-class type. A pointer whose type is pointer to base class can point to objects that have the derived-class type. Public derivation is far more important than private or protected derivation. As such, it should be considered the normal form of inheritance.

We shall examine our example of student and grad_student. Let us first examine the base- and derived-class constructors.

In file student2.h

```
student::student(char* nm, int id, double g,
    year x):student_id(id), gpa(g), y(x)
{
    strcpy(name, nm);
}
```

The constructor for the base class does a series of simple initializations. The constructor then calls strcpy() to copy over the student's name.

```
grad_student::grad_student (char* nm, int id,    double g, year
x, support t, char* d,
    char* th):student(nm, id, g, x), s(t)
{
    strcpy(dept, d);
    strcpy(thesis, th);
}
```

Notice that the constructor for student is invoked as part of the initializer list. This is usual, and, logically, the base-class object needs to be constructed before the object can be completed.

The grad_student is a publicly derived type whose base class is student. In the class student, the members student_id and gpa are protected. This makes them visible to the derived class but otherwise treated as private.

Because grad_student is a subtype of student, a reference to the derived-class grad_student may be implicitly converted to a reference to the public base-class student. For example,

```
grad_student gs("Morris Pohl", 200, 3.2564, grad, ta,
                "Pharmacy", "Retail Pharmacies");
student& rs = gs;
```

In this case, the variable rs is a reference to student. The base class of grad_student is student. Therefore, this reference conversion is appropriate.

The print() member functions are implemented as follows:

In file student2.h

```
void student::print() const
{
   cout << name << " , " << student_id
        << " , " << y << " , " << gpa << endl;
}

void grad_student::print() const
{
   student::print(); //base class info is printed
   cout << dept << " , " << s << '\n'
        << thesis << endl;
}
```

For grad_student::print() to invoke student::print(), the scope-resolved identifier student::print() must be used. Otherwise, there will be an infinite loop caused by a recursive call to grad_student::print(). To see which versions of these functions get called and to demonstrate some of the conversion relationships between base and publicly derived classes, we write a simple test.

In file student2.cpp

```
//Test pointer conversion rules

#include  "student2.h"       //include relevant declarations

int main()
{
   student  s("Mae Pohl", 100, 3.425, student::fresh), *ps = &s;
   grad_student  gs("Morris Pohl", 200, 3.2564,
       student::grad, grad_student::ta, "Pharmacy",
       "Retail Pharmacies"), *pgs;
```

```
    ps -> print();              //student::print
    ps = pgs = &gs;
    pgs -> print();             //grad_student::print
    ps ->print();               //student::print
}
```

This function declares both class variables and pointers to them. The conversion rule is that a pointer to a publicly derived class may be converted implicitly to a pointer to its base class. In our example, the pointer variable ps can point at objects of both classes, but the pointer variable pgs can point only at objects of type grad_student.

We wish to study how various pointer assignments affect the invocation of a version of print(). The first instance of the statement

```
    ps -> print();
```

invokes student::print(), which is pointing at the variable s of type student. The multiple assignment statement

```
    ps = pgs = &gs;
```

has both pointers pointing at an object of type grad_student. The assignment to ps involves an implicit conversion. The statement

```
    pgs -> print();         //grad_student::print
```

invokes the grad_student::print() function. The variable pgs is of type pointer to grad_student and, when invoked with an object of this type, selects a member function from this class.

The second instance of the statement

```
    ps -> print();
```

invokes student::print(). That this pointer is pointing at a grad_student variable gs is not relevant. In the next section, we explain how to use virtual member functions to make function invocation a runtime property, depending on what is being pointed at.

8.3 Virtual Functions

Overloaded member functions are invoked by a type-matching algorithm that includes having the implicit argument matched to an object of that class type. All this is known at compile time, and it allows the compiler to select the appropriate member directly. As will become apparent, it would be nice to dynamically select at runtime the appropriate member function from among base- and derived-class functions. The keyword virtual, a function specifier that provides such a mechanism, may be used only to modify member function declarations. The combination of *virtual functions* and public inheritance will be our most general and flexible way to build a piece of software. This is a form of pure polymorphism.

An ordinary virtual function must be executable code. When invoked, its semantics are the same as those of other functions. In a derived class, it can be overridden, and the function prototype of the derived function must have a matching signature and return type. The selection of which function definition to invoke for a virtual function is dynamic. In the typical case, a base class has a virtual function, and derived classes have their versions of this function. A pointer to base class can point at either a base-class object or a derived-class object. The member function selected will depend on the class of the object being pointed at, not on the pointer type. In the absence of a derived type member, the base-class virtual function is used by default.

Note the difference in selection of the appropriate overridden virtual function from an overloaded member function. The overloaded member function is selected at compile time, based on its signature, and it can have distinct return types. A virtual function is selected at runtime, based on the object's type, which is passed to it as its this pointer argument. Also, once it is declared virtual, this property is carried along to all redefinitions in derived classes. It is unnecessary in the derived class to use the function modifier virtual.

Consider the following example.

In file virt_sel.cpp

```
//virtual function selection

class B {
public:
    int  i;
    virtual void  print_i() const
       { cout << i << " inside B" << endl; }
};
```

```
class D : public B {
public:
    //virtual as well
    void  print_i() const
        { cout << i << " inside D" << endl; }
};

int main()
{
    B    b;
    B*   pb = &b;                //points at a B object
    D    f;

    f.i = 1 + (b.i = 1);
    pb -> print_i();            //call B::print_i()
    pb = &f;                    //points at a D object
    pb -> print_i();            //call D::print_i()
}
```

The output of this program is

```
1 inside B
2 inside D
```

Compare this behavior to the program *student*, shown in Section 8.2, "Typing Conversions and Visibility," on page 277. There, the selection of print() is based on the pointer type, known at compile time. Here, print_i() is selected on the basis of what is being pointed at. In this case, a different version of print_i() is executed. In OOP terminology, the object is *sent the message* print_i(), and it selects its own version of the corresponding method. Thus, the pointer's base type is not the determining method (function) selection. Different class objects are processed by different functions, determined at runtime. Facilities that allow the implementation of ADTs, inheritance, and the ability to process objects dynamically are the essentials of OOP.

Virtual functions and member function overloading cause confusion. Consider the following.

In file virt_err.cpp

```
class B {
public:
   virtual void foo(int);
   virtual void foo(double);
};

class D : public B {
public:
   void foo(int);
};

int main()
{
   D  d;
   B  b, *pb = &d;

   b.foo(9);              //selects B::foo(int);
   b.foo(9.5);            //selects B::foo(double);
   d.foo(9);              //selects D::foo(int);
   d.foo(9.5);            //selects D::foo(int);
   pb -> foo(9);          //selects D::foo(int);
   pb -> foo(9.5);        //selects B::foo(double);
}
```

The base-class member function B::foo(int) is overridden, and the base-class member function B::foo(double) is hidden in the derived class. In the statement d.foo(9.5), the double value 9.5 is converted to the integer value 9. We could have used d.B::foo(double) to call the hidden member function.

The declaration of an identifier in a scope hides all declarations of that identifier in outer scopes. A base class is an outer scope of any class derived from it. This rule is independent of whether the names are declared virtual. Access restrictions (private, protected) are orthogonal to function selection. If the selected function is inaccessible, that is a compile-time error.

Only nonstatic member functions can be virtual. The virtual characteristic is inherited. Thus, the derived-class function is automatically virtual, and the presence of the virtual keyword is usually a matter of taste. Constructors cannot be virtual, but destructors can be. As a rule of thumb, any class having virtual functions should have a virtual destructor.

Virtual functions allow runtime decisions. Consider a computer-aided design application in which the area of the shapes in a design has to be computed. The various shapes will be derived from the shape base class.

In file shape1.cpp

```
class shape {
public:
   virtual double  area() const { return 0; }
   //virtual double area is default behavior
protected:
   double  x, y;
};

class rectangle : public shape {
public:
   double  area() const { return (height * width); }
private:
   double  height, width;
};

class circle : public shape {
public:
   double  area() const
       { return (PI * radius * radius);}
private:
   double  radius;
};
```

In such a class hierarchy, the derived classes correspond to important, well-understood types of shapes. The system is readily expanded by deriving further classes. The area calculation is a local responsibility of a derived class.

Client code that uses the polymorphic area calculation looks like this:

```
shape*  p[N];

. . . . .
for (i = 0; i < N; ++i)
   tot_area += p[i] -> area();
```

A major advantage here is that the client code will not need to change if new shapes are added to the system. Change is managed locally and propagated automatically by the polymorphic character of the client code.

8.4 Abstract Base Classes

A type hierarchy usually has its base class contain a number of virtual functions. They provide for dynamic typing. In the base class, virtual functions are often dummy functions and have an empty body. In the derived classes, however, virtual functions will be given specific meanings. In C++, the *pure virtual function* is introduced for this purpose. A pure virtual function is one whose body is normally undefined. Notationally, such a function is declared inside the class, as follows:

```
virtual function prototype = 0;
```

The pure virtual function is used to defer the implementation decision of the function. In OOP terminology, it is called a *deferred method*.

A class that has at least one pure virtual function is an *abstract class*. In a type hierarchy, it is useful for the base class to be an abstract class. This base class has the basic common properties of its derived classes but cannot itself be used to declare objects. Instead, it is used to declare pointers that can access subtype objects derived from the abstract class.

We will explain this concept while developing a primitive form of ecological simulation. OOP was originally developed as a simulation methodology using Simula 67. Hence, many of its ideas are easily understood as an attempt to model a particular reality.

The world in our example will have various forms of life interacting, which will inherit the interface of an abstract base class called living. Each position in a grid defined to be the world can either have a life-form or be empty. We shall have foxes as an archetypal predator, with rabbits as prey. The rabbits will eat grass. Each of these life-forms will live, reproduce, and die each iteration of the simulation.

In file predator.cpp

```
//Predator-Prey simulation using class living

const int  N = 40;                      //size of square board
enum state { EMPTY , GRASS , RABBIT , FOX, STATES };
const int DRAB = 3, DFOX = 6, CYCLES = 5;

class living;                           //forward declaration
typedef living* world[N][N];
```

```
class living {                          //what lives in world
public:
   virtual state  who() = 0;           //state identification
   virtual living*  next(world w) = 0;
protected:
   int  row, column;                   //location
   void sums(world w,int sm[]);
};

void living::sums(world w, int sm[])
{
   int  i, j;

   sm[EMPTY] = sm[GRASS] = sm[RABBIT] = sm[FOX] = 0;
   for (i = -1; i <= 1; ++i)
      for ( j = -1; j <= 1; ++j)
         sm[w[row + i][column + j] -> who()]++;
}
```

There are two pure virtual functions and one ordinary member function, sums(). Virtual functions incur a small added runtime cost over normal member functions. Therefore, we use virtual functions only when necessary to our implementations. Our simulation will have rules for deciding who goes on living, based on the populations in the neighborhood of a given square. These populations are computed by sums(). (This is akin to Conway's "Game of Life" simulation.)

The inheritance hierarchy will be one level deep.

```
//currently only predator class

class fox : public living {
public:
   fox(int r, int c, int a = 0) : age(a)
      { row = r; column = c; }
   state  who() { return FOX; }   //deferred method for foxes
   living*  next(world w);
protected:
   int  age;                       //used to decide on dying
};
```

```
//currently only prey class

class rabbit : public living {
public:
    rabbit(int r, int c, int a = 0) : age(a)
        { row = r; column = c; }
    state  who() { return RABBIT; }
    living*  next(world w);
protected:
    int  age;
};


//currently only plant life

class grass : public living {
public:
    grass(int r, int c) { row = r; column = c; }
    state who() { return GRASS; }
    living* next(world w);
};


//nothing lives here

class empty : public living {
public:
    empty(int r, int c) { row = r; column = c; }
    state  who() { return EMPTY; }
    living*  next(world w);
};
```

Notice that the design allows other forms of predator, prey, and plant life to be developed, using a further level of inheritance. The characteristics of how each life-form behaves are captured in its version of next().

Grass can be eaten by rabbits. If there is more grass than the rabbits in the neighborhood can eat, the grass remains; otherwise, it is eaten up. (Feel free to substitute your own rules, as these are highly limited and artificial.)

```
living* grass::next(world w)
{
   int  sum[STATES];

   sums(w, sum);
   if (sum[GRASS] > sum[RABBIT])            //eat grass
      return (new grass(row, column));
   else
      return (new empty(row, column));
}
```

Rabbits die of old age if they exceed a defined limit DRAB; they are eaten if there are an appropriate number of foxes in the neighborhood.

```
living* rabbit::next(world w)
{
   int  sum[STATES];

   sums(w, sum);
   if (sum[FOX] >= sum[RABBIT] )            //eat rabbits
      return (new empty(row, column));
   else if (age > DRAB)                     //rabbit is too old
      return (new empty(row, column));
   else
      return (new rabbit(row, column, age + 1));
}
```

Foxes die of overcrowding or old age.

```
living* fox::next(world w)
{
   int  sum[STATES];

   sums(w, sum);
   if (sum[FOX] > 5)                        //too many foxes
      return (new empty(row, column));
   else if (age > DFOX)                     //fox is too old
      return (new empty(row, column));
   else
      return (new fox(row, column, age + 1));
}
```

Empty squares are competed for by the various life-forms.

```
living* empty::next(world w)        //how to fill an empty square
{
   int  sum[STATES];
   sums(w, sum);
   if (sum[FOX] > 1)
      return (new fox(row, column));
   else if (sum[RABBIT] > 1)
      return (new rabbit(row, column));
   else if (sum[GRASS])
      return (new grass(row, column));
   else
      return (new empty(row, column));
}
```

The rules in the various versions of next() determine a possibly complex set of interactions. Of course, to make the simulation more interesting, other behaviors, such as sexual reproduction, whereby the animals have gender and can mate, could be simulated.

The array type world is a container for the life-forms. The container will have the responsibility of creating its current pattern. The container needs to have ownership of the living objects so as to allocate new ones and to delete old ones.

```
//world is all empty

void init(world w)
{
   int  i, j;

   for (i = 0; i < N; ++i)
      for (j = 0; j < N; ++j)
         w[i][j] = new empty(i,j);
}

//new world w_new is computed from old world w_old

void update(world w_new, world w_old)
{
   int  i, j;

   for (i = 1; i < N - 1; ++i)            //borders are taboo
      for (j = 1; j < N - 1; ++j)
         w_new[i][j] = w_old[i][j] -> next(w_old);
}
```

```
//clean world up

void dele(world w)
{
   int  i, j;

   for (i = 1; i < N - 1; ++i)
      for (j = 1; j < N - 1; ++j)
         delete(w[i][j]);
}
```

The simulation will have odd and even worlds, which alternate as the basis for the next cycle's calculations.

```
int main()
{
   world  odd, even;
   int    i;

   init(odd);  init(even);
   eden(even);                     //generate initial world
   pr_state(even);                 //print Garden of Eden state

   for (i = 0; i < CYCLES; ++i) {     //simulation
      if (i % 2) {
         update(even, odd);
         pr_state(even);
         dele(odd);
      }
      else {
         update(odd, even);
         pr_state(odd);
         dele(even);
      }
   }
}
```

We leave as exercises the writing of pr_state() and eden() (see exercise 8 on page 305).

8.5 Templates and Inheritance

Templates and inheritance are jointly an extremely powerful reuse technique. Parameterized types can be reused through inheritance. Such use parallels that of inheritance in deriving ordinary classes. Templates and inheritance are both mechanisms for code reuse, and both can involve polymorphism. They are distinct features of C++ and, as such, combine in various forms. A template class can derive from an ordinary class, an ordinary class can derive from an instantiated template class, and a template class can derive from a template class. Each of these possibilities leads to different relationships.

In some situations, templates lead to unacceptable cost in the size of the object module. Each instantiated template class requires its own compiled object module. This can be remedied by using a template to inherit the base class.

The derivation of a class from an instantiated template class is basically no different from ordinary inheritance. In the following example, we reuse stack<char> as a base class for a safe character stack.

In file stack_t2.cpp

```
//safe character stack

class safe_char_stack : public stack<char> {
public:
   // test push and pop
   void  push(char c)
     { assert (!full()); stack<char>::push(c); }
   char  pop()
     { assert (!empty()); return (stack<char>::pop()); }
};
```

The instantiated class stack<char> is generated and reused by safe_char_stack. This example can be usefully generalized to a template class.

In file stack_t3.cpp

```
//parameterized safe stack

template <class TYPE>
class safe_stack : public stack<TYPE> {
public:
   void  push(TYPE c)
     { assert (!full()); stack<TYPE>::push(c); }
   TYPE  pop()
     { assert (!empty()); return (stack<TYPE>::pop()); }
};
```

It is important to notice the linkage between the base class and the derived class. Both require the same instantiated type. Each pair of base and derived classes is independent of all other pairs.

8.6 Multiple Inheritance

The examples in the text thus far require only single inheritance; that is, they require that a class be derived from a single base class. This feature can lead to a chain of derivations wherein class B is derived from class A, class C is derived from class B, . . . , and class N is derived from class M. In effect, N ends up being based on A, B, . . . , M. This chain must not be circular, however; a class cannot have itself as an ancestor.

Multiple inheritance allows a derived class to be derived from more than one base class. The syntax of class headers is extended to allow a list of base classes and their privacy designations. For example,

```
class student {
   . . . . .
};

class worker {
   . . . . .
};

class student_worker: public student, public worker {
   . . . . .
};
```

In this example, the derived class `student_worker` publicly inherits the members of both base classes. This parental relationship is described by the inheritance *directed acyclic graph* (DAG). The DAG is a graph structure whose nodes are classes and whose directed edges point from base to derived class. To be legal, a DAG cannot be circular; thus, no class may, through its inheritance chain, inherit from itself.

When identically named members are derived from different classes, ambiguities may arise. These derivations are allowed, provided the user does not make an ambiguous reference to such a member. For example,

```
class worker {
public:
   const int  soc_sec;
   const char* name;
   .....
};

class student {
public:
   const char* name;
   .....
};

class student_worker: public student, public worker {
public:
   void print() { cout << "ssn: " << soc_sec << "\n" ;
      cout << name; ..... }                    //error
   .....
};
```

In the body of `student_worker::print()`, the reference to `soc_sec` is fine, but the reference to `name` is inherently ambiguous. The problem can be resolved by properly qualifying `name`, using the scope resolution operator.

With multiple inheritance, two base classes can be derived from a common ancestor. If both base classes are used in the ordinary way by their derived class, it will have two subobjects of the common ancestor. If this duplication is not desirable, it can be eliminated, using virtual inheritance. An example is

```
class student: virtual public person {
   .....
};
```

```
class worker: virtual public person {
    .....
};

class student_worker: public student, public worker {
    .....
};
```

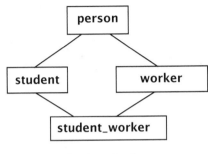

Multiple Inheritance

Without the use of `virtual` in this example, `class student_worker` would have objects of `class student::person` and `class worker::person`. The order of execution for initializing constructors in base and member constructors is given in the following list.

Constructor Execution Order

1. Base classes initialized in declaration order

2. Members initialized in declaration order

3. The body of the constructor

Virtual base classes are constructed before any of their derived classes and before any nonvirtual base classes. Construction order depends on their DAG. It is a depth-first, left-to-right order. Destructors are invoked in the reverse order of constructors. These rules, although complicated, are intuitive.

On many systems, a concrete example of multiple inheritance can be found in the *iostream* library. This library contains the class `iostream`, which can be derived from `istream` and `ostream`. However, it is an interesting comment on multiple inheritance that more recent implementations have gone back to single-inheritance designs.

8.7 Inheritance and Design

At one level, inheritance is a code-sharing technique. At another level, it reflects an understanding of the problem and relationships between parts of the problem space. Much of public inheritance is the expression of an is-a relationship between the base and derived classes. The rectangle is a shape. This is the conceptual underpinning for making shape a superclass and allowing the behavior described by its public member functions to be interpretable on objects within its type hierarchy. In other words, subclasses derived from the superclass share its interface.

A design cannot be specified in a completely optimal way. Design involves trade-offs between the various objectives one wishes to achieve. For example, generality is frequently at odds with efficiency. Using a class hierarchy that expresses is-a relationships increases our effort to understand how to compartmentalize coding relationships and potentially introduces coding inefficiencies by having various layers of access to the (hidden) state description of an object. However, a reasonable is-a decomposition can simplify the overall coding process. For example, a shape-drawing package need not anticipate shapes that might be added in the future. Through inheritance, the class developer imports the base-class "shape" interface and provides code that implements operations, such as "draw." What is primitive or shared remains unchanged. Also unchanged is the client's use of the package.

An undue amount of decomposition imposes its own complexity and ends up being self-defeating. There is a granularity decision, whereby highly specialized classes do not provide enough benefit and are better folded into a larger concept.

Single inheritance (SI) conforms to a hierarchical decomposition of the key objects in the domain of discourse. Multiple inheritance (MI) is more troubling as a modeling or problem-solving concept. In MI, the new object is composed of several preexisting objects and is usefully thought of as a form of each. The term *mixin* is used to mean a class composed using MI, with each base class orthogonal. Much of the time, there is an alternative has-a formulation. For example, is a vampire bat a mammal that happens to fly, a flying machine that happens to be a mammal, or both a flying machine and a mammal? Depending on what code is available, developing a proper class for vampire bat might involve an MI derivation or an SI with appropriate has-a members.

MI presents problems for the type theorist: student might be derived from person, and employee might be derived from person. But what about a student-employee? Generally, types are best understood as SI chains.

None of this diminishes the attraction of MI as a code-reuse technique. It is clearly a powerful generalization of SI. As such, it probably fits in with the style of some programmers. Just as some programmers prefer iteration to recursion, some prefer SI and aggregation to MI and composition.

8.7.1 Subtyping Form

ADTs are successful insofar as they behave like native types. Native types, such as the integer types in C, act as a subtype hierarchy. This is a useful model for publicly derived type hierarchies and promotes ease of use through polymorphism. Here is a recipe for building such a type hierarchy. The base class is made abstract and is used for interface inheritance. The derived classes will implement this interface concretely.

```
class Abstract_Base {
public:
   //interface - largely virtual
   Abstract_Base();                      //default constructor
   Abstract_Base(const Abstract_Base&); //copy constructor
   virtual ~Abstract_Base() = 0;        //pure virtual
      . . . . .
protected:
   //used in place of private because of inheritance
   . . . . .
private:
   //often empty - else it constrains future designs
   . . . . .
};

class Derived: virtual public Abstract_Base {
public:
   //Concrete instance
   Derived();                           //default constructor
   Derived(const Derived&);             //copy constructor
   ~Derived();                          //destructor
   Derived& operator=(const Derived&);  //assignment
      . . . . .
protected:
   //used in place of private if inheritance expected
   . . . . .
private:
   //used for implementation details
   . . . . .
};
```

It is usual to leave the base class of the hierarchy abstract, yielding the most flexible design. Generally, no concrete implementation is developed at this point. By using pure virtual functions, we are precluded from declaring objects of this type. Notice that the ~`Abstract_Base`() function is pure. This level of the design focuses on public interface. These are the operations expected of any subtype in the hierarchy. In general, basic constructors are expected and may not be virtual. Also, most useful aggregates require an explicit definition of assignment that differs from default assignment semantics. The destructor is virtual because response must be at runtime and is dependent on the object's size, which can vary across the hierarchy. Finally, virtual public inheritance ensures that in MI schemes, we will not have multiple copies of the abstract base class.

8.7.2 Code Reuse

Private inheritance does not have a subtype, or is-a relationship. In private inheritance, we reuse a base class for its code. We will call private derivation a *like-a* relationship, or *implementation inheritance*, as opposed to interface inheritance. The like-a relationship comes in handy when diagramming the class relationships in a complicated software system. Because private and protected inheritance do not create type hierarchies, they have more limited utility than does public inheritance. In a first pass in understanding these concepts, nonpublic inheritance can be skipped.

Code reuse is often all you want from inheritance. The template methodology is simpler and more runtime efficient; it is simpler because instantiation requires only a single type placed in the template declaration. In inheritance, we need to derive the whole interface, substituting appropriate types. It is more runtime efficient because it often avoids indirection. Inheritance allows special cases to be developed for each type, if necessary; it does not lead to large object-code modules. Remember, each template instantiation is compiled to object code.

8.8 Runtime Type Identification

Runtime type identification (RTTI) provides a mechanism for safely determining the type pointed at by a base-class pointer at runtime. This mechanism involves `dynamic_cast`, an operator on a base-class pointer; `typeid`, an operator for determining the type of an object; and `type_info`, a structure providing runtime information for the associated type. The `dynamic_cast` operator has the form

```
dynamic_cast< type >( v )
```

where *type* must be a pointer or reference to a class type and *v* must be a corresponding pointer value or reference value.

This cast, used with classes having virtual functions, is implemented as follows:

```
class Base { virtual void foo(); ····· };
class Derived : public Base { ····· };

void fcn(Base* ptr)
{
    Derived* dptr = dynamic_cast<Derived*>(ptr);
    ·····
}
```

In this example, the cast converts the pointer value ptr to a Derived*. If the conversion is inappropriate, a value of 0, the NULL pointer, is returned. This is called a *downcast*. Dynamic casts also work with reference types.

The operator typeid() can be applied to a *typename* or to an expression to determine the exact type of the argument. The operator returns a reference to the class type_info, which is supplied by the system and is defined in the header file *typeinfo* (some compilers use *type_info*). The class type_info provides both a name() member function that returns a string that is the type name and overloaded equality operators. Remember to check the local implementation for the complete interface of this class.

In file typeid.cpp

```
Base* bptr;
·····
//print the type name of what bptr currently points at
cout << typeid(bptr).name() << endl;
·····
if (typeid(bptr) == typeid(Derived)) {
//do something appropriate for Derived
·····
}
```

Bad dynamic casts and typeid operations can be made to throw the exceptions bad_cast and bad_typeid, so the user can choose between dealing with the NULL pointer or catching an exception. (See Section 9.9, "Standard Exceptions and Their Uses," on page 318.)

8.9 Pragmatics

A difficulty in learning C++ is the many distinctions and rules pertaining to the use of functions. We have now described most of the extensions and shall mention some of the distinctions.

Function Use in C++

- A virtual function and its derived instances having the same signature must have the same return type, with some minor exceptions. The virtual function redefinition is called *overriding*. Notice that nonvirtual member functions with the same signature can have different return types in derived classes. (See exercise 6 on page 304.)

- All member functions except constructors and overloaded new and delete can be virtual.

- Constructors, destructors, overloaded operator=, and friends are not inherited.

- The operators =, (), [], and -> can be overloaded only with nonstatic member functions. Conversion functions that are operator *type*() must also be done only with nonstatic member functions. Overloading operators new and delete can be done only with static member functions. Other overloadable operators can be done with friend, member, or ordinary functions.

- A union may have constructors and destructors but not virtual functions. It can neither serve as a base class nor have a base class. Members of a union cannot require constructors or destructors.

- Access modification is possible, but using it with public inheritance destroys the subtype relationship. Access modification cannot broaden visibility. For example,

In file acc_mod.cpp

```
//Access modification

class B {
public:
    int  k;
protected:
    int  j, n;
private:
    int  i;
};

class D : public B {
public:
    int  m;
    B::n;        //illegal protected access can't be broadened
private:
    B::j;        //otherwise default is protected
};
```

8.10 Moving from C++ to Java

Like C++, Java has the inheritance mechanism, which extends a new class from an existing one, although Java does not have multiple inheritance and uses different terminology with respect to inheritance. The Java base class is called the *superclass.* The extended class adds to or alters the inherited superclass methods. This is used to share interface and to create a hierarchy of related types.

Consider designing a data base for a college. The registrar must track various types of students. The superclass we start with will be Person1. This class will be identical to Person in Section 5.13, "Moving from C++ to Java," on page 186, except that the private instance variables will be changed to have access protected. This access allows their use in the subclass but otherwise acts like private.

Here is an example of deriving a class:

```
// Note Person1 is Person with private instance variables
// made protected

class Student extends Person1 {
    private String college;
    private byte year;            //1 = fr, 2 = so, 3 = jr, 4 = sr
    private double gpa;           //0.0 to 4.0
    public void assignCollege(String nm) { college = nm; }
    public void assignYear(byte a) { year = a; }
    public void assignGpa(double g) { gpa = g; }
    public String toString()
        { return (super.toString() + "  College is " + college); }
    public Student()
        {super.assignName("Unknown"); college = "Unknown";}
    public Student(String nm)
        { super(nm); college = "Unknown"; }
    public Student(String nm, int a, char b)
        { name =nm; age =a; gender = b; }
};
```

In this example, Student is the subclass, and Person1 is the superclass. Notice the use of the keyword super, which provides a means of accessing the instance variables or methods found in the superclass.

The inheritance structure provides a design for the overall system. The superclass Person1 leads to a design whereby the subclass Student is derived from it. Other subclasses, such as GradStudent or Employee, could be added to this inheritance hierarchy.

In Java, polymorphism comes from both method overloading and method overriding. Overriding occurs when a method is redefined in the subclass. The toString() method is in Person1 and is redefined in Student extended from Person1.

```
//Overriding the printName() method
class Person1 {
    protected String name;
    protected int age;
    protected char gender;            //male == 'M' , female == 'F'
    public toString() {
        return(name + " age is " + age +
              " sex is " + (gender == 'F' ? "F": "M") );
    }
.....
};
```

```
class Student extends Person1 {
    private String college;
    private byte year;
    private double gpa;                //0.0 to 4.0
    public toString()
        { return(super.toString() + "  College is " + college); }
.....
};
```

The overridden method `toString()` has the same name and signature in both the superclass `Person1` and the subclass `Student`. Which one gets selected depends on what is being referenced at runtime. For example,

```
//StudentTest.java use Person1

public class StudentTest {
    public static void main (String[] args )
    {
        Person1 q1;
        q1 = new Student();
        q1.assignName("Charles Babbage");
        System.out.println(q1.toString());
        q1 = new Person1();
        q1.assignName("Charles Babbage");
        System.out.println(q1.toString());
    }
}
```

The variable q1 can refer to either `Person1` object or the subtype `Student` object. At runtime, the correct `toString()` will be selected. The `assignName()` method is known at compile time, since it is the superclass `Person1` method.

Summary

1. Inheritance is the mechanism of deriving a new class from old ones. That is, the existing classes can be added to or altered to create the derived class. Through inheritance, a hierarchy of related, code-sharing ADTs can be created.

2. A class can be derived from an existing class, using the form

   ```
   class class-name : (public|protected|private)opt base-name
   {
        member declarations
   };
   ```

   As usual, the keyword `class` can be replaced by the keyword `struct`, with the usual implication that members are by default `public`.

3. The keywords `public`, `private`, and `protected` are available as visibility modifiers for class members. A public member is visible throughout its scope. A private member is visible to other member functions within its own class and to friend functions. A protected member is visible to other member functions within its class, within friend functions, and within any class immediately derived from it. These visibility modifiers can be used within a class declaration in any order and with any frequency.

4. The derived class has its own constructors, which will invoke the base-class constructor. A special syntax is used to pass arguments from the derived-class constructor back to the base-class constructor:

   function header : base-classname (argument list)

5. A publicly derived class is a subtype of its base class. A variable of the derived class can in many ways be treated as if it were the base-class type. A pointer whose type is pointer to base class can point to objects of the publicly derived class type.

6. A reference to the derived class may be implicitly converted to a reference to the public base class. It is possible to declare a reference to a base class and to initialize it to a reference to an object of the publicly derived class.

7. The keyword `virtual` is a function specifier that provides a mechanism to dynamically select at runtime the appropriate member function from among

base- and derived-class functions. This specifier may be used only to modify member function declarations. This is called overriding. This ability to dynamically select a routine appropriate to an object's type is a form of polymorphism.

8. Inheritance provides for code reuse. The derived class inherits the base-class code and typically modifies and extends the base class. Public inheritance also creates a type hierarchy, allowing further generality by providing additional implicit type conversions. Also, at a runtime cost, it allows for runtime selection of overridden virtual functions. Facilities that allow the implementation of ADTs, inheritance, and the ability to process objects dynamically are the essentials of OOP.

9. A pure virtual function is a virtual member function whose body is normally undefined. Notationally, a pure virtual function is declared inside the class, as follows:

```
virtual function prototype = 0;
```

The pure virtual function is used to defer the implementation decision of the function. In OOP terminology, it is called a *deferred method*. A class that has at least one pure virtual function is an *abstract class*. It is useful for the base class in a type hierarchy to be an abstract class. As such, the base class would define the interface for its derived classes but cannot itself be used to declare objects.

Review Questions

1. In class X : Y { ... }, X is a _____ class and Y is a _____ class.

2. True or false: If D inherits from B privately, D is a subtype of B.

3. The term overriding refers to _____ functions.

4. An abstract base class contains a _____.

5. The subtyping relationship is called the _____.

6. True or false: Template classes cannot be base classes.

7. What is wrong with the following?

```
class A:B{...}; class B:C{...}; class C:A{...};
```

8. In multiple inheritance, why is virtual inheritance used?

9. The class `type_info` provides a `name()` member function that _____.

10. True or false: Constructors, destructors, overloaded `operator=`, and friends are not inherited.

Exercises

1. For `student` and `grad_student` code, input member functions that read input for each data member in their classes. (See Section 8.1, "A Derived Class," on page 275.) Use `student::read` to implement `grad_student::read`.

2. Pointer conversions, scope resolution, and explicit casting create a wide selection of possibilities. Using `main()`, discussed in Section 8.2, "Typing Conversions and Visibility," on page 277, which of the following work, and what is printed?

```
reinterpret_cast<grad_student *>(ps) -> print();
dynamic_cast<student *>(pgs) -> print();
pgs -> student::print();
ps -> grad_student::print();
```

Print out and explain the results.

3. Modify class D in Section 8.3, "Virtual Functions," on page 280, to be

```
class D2 : private B {
public:
   B::i;                    //access modification
   void  print_i()
   {
      cout << i << " inside D2 and B::i is "
            << B::i << endl;
   }
};
```

What is changed in the output from that program?

4. Derive an integer vector class from the STL class vector<int> that has 1 as its first index value and n as its last index value.

```
int_vector x(n);        //vector whose range is 1 to n
```

5. Generalize the previous exercise by deriving a template class that creates the index range 1 to n.

```
vec_1<double> x(n);     //vector whose range is 1 to n
```

6. For the following program, explain when both overriding and overloading take place.

```
class B {
public:
   B(int j = 0) : i(j) {}
   virtual void  print() const
      { cout << " i = " << i << endl; }
   void  print(char *s) const
      { cout << s << i << endl; }
private:
   int i;
};

class D : public B {
public:
   D(int j = 0) : B(5), i(j) {}
   void  print() const
      { cout << " i = " << i << endl; }
   int  print(char *s) const
      { cout << s << i << endl; return i; }
private:
   int  i;
};
```

```
int main()
{
    B   b1, b2(10), *pb;
    D   d1, d2(10), *pd = &d2;

    b1.print(); b2.print(); d1.print(); d2.print();
    b1.print("b1.i = "); b2.print("b2.i = ");
    d1.print("d1.i = "); d2.print("d2.i = ");
    pb = pd;
    pb -> print(); pb -> print("d2.i = ");
    pd -> print(); pd -> print("d2.i = ");
}
```

7. Define a base class person that will contain universal information, including
   name, address, birth date, and gender. Derive from this class the following
   classes:

```
class student : virtual public person {
// ····· relevant additional state and behavior
};

class worker : virtual public person {
// ····· relevant additional state and behavior
};

class student_worker : public student,public worker {
// ·····
};
```

Write a program that reads a file of information and creates a list of persons.
Process the list to create, in sorted order by last name, a list of all people, a list
of people who are students, a list of people who are employees, and a list of
people who are student-employees. On your system, can you easily produce a
list in sorted order of all students who are not employees?

8. *(Project)* Design and implement a graphical user interface (GUI) for the predator-
   prey simulation. It is beyond the scope of this book to describe various available
   GUI toolkits. The InterViews package works on top of X and is written in C++.
   The program should draw each iteration of the simulation on the screen. You
   should be able to directly input a "Garden of Eden" starting position. (See Section 8.4, "Abstract Base Classes," on page 283, for the game-of-life simulation.)
   You should also be able to provide other settings for the simulation, such as the
   size of the simulation. Can you allow the user to define other life-forms and

their rules for existing, eating, and reproducing? Make the graphical interface as elegant as possible. The user should be able to position it on the screen, resize it, and select icons for the various available life-forms.

9. *(Java)* Add `GraduateStudent` to the Java class hierarchy in Section 8.10, "Moving from C++ to Java," on page 300. Note how Java uses capitalization instead of an underscore to separate words in an identifier. This is stylistic. C++ derives its heritage directly from C and adopted C style. Java has a SmallTalk influence and has styles adopted from that culture.

10. *(Java)* Develop the Java version of the shape hierarchy in Section 8.3, "Virtual Functions," on page 282.

11. *(Java)* Develop the predator-prey simulation in Java, using the *awt* library to provide a graphical interface. (See Section 8.4, "Abstract Base Classes," on page 283 for the predator-prey C++ simulation.) This is one area that Java excels in. Section 10.6, "Moving from C++ to Java," on page 336, has some discussion of Java *awt*.

Chapter 9
Exceptions

This chapter describes exception handling in C++. *Exceptions* are generally unexpected error conditions. Normally, these conditions terminate the user program with a system-provided error message. An example is floating-point divide-by-zero. Usually, the system aborts the running program. C++ allows the programmer to attempt to recover from these conditions and to continue program execution.

Assertions are program checks that force error exits when correctness is violated. One point of view is that an exception is based on a breakdown of a contractual guarantee among the provider of a code, the code's manufacturer, and the code's client. (See Section 10.1.1, "ADTs: Encapsulation and Data Hiding," on page 328.) In this model, the client needs to guarantee that the conditions for applying the code exist, and the manufacturer needs to guarantee that the code will work correctly under these conditions. In this methodology, assertions provide the various guarantees.

9.1 Using the *assert* Library

Program correctness can be viewed in part as a proof that the computation terminated with correct output, dependent on correct input. The user of the computation had the responsibility of providing correct input. This was a *precondition*. The computation, if successful, satisfied a *postcondition*. Providing a fully formal proof of correctness is an ideal but is not usually done. Nevertheless, such assertions can be monitored at runtime to provide very useful diagnostics. Indeed, the discipline of thinking out appropriate assertions frequently causes the programmer to avoid bugs and pitfalls.

The C and C++ communities are increasingly emphasizing the use of assertions. The standard library *assert* provides a macro, `assert`, which is invoked as though its function signature were

```
void assert(bool expression);
```

If the *expression* evaluates as `false`, execution is aborted with diagnostic output. The assertions are discarded if the macro `NDEBUG` is defined.

Consider allocation to our safe array type db1_vect in Section 5.5, "The Class db1_vect," on page 163.

```
dbl_vect::dbl_vect(int n) : size(n)
{
   assert(n > 0);
   p = new int[size];
   assert(p != 0);
}
```

The use of assertions replaces the ad hoc use of conditional tests with a more uniform methodology. This is better practice. The downside is that the assertion methodology does not allow a retry or other repair strategy to continue program execution. Also, assertions do not allow a customized error message, although it would be easy to add this capability.

It is possible to make this scheme slightly more sophisticated by providing various testing levels, as are found in the Borland C++ *checks* library. Under this package, the flag _DEBUG can be set to

```
_DEBUG 0    no testing
_DEBUG 1    PRECONDITION tests only
_DEBUG 2    CHECK tests also
```

The idea is that once the library functions are thought to be correct, the level of checking is reduced to testing preconditions only. Once the client code is debugged, all testing can be suspended.

9.2 C++ Exceptions

C++ introduces a context-sensitive exception-handling mechanism. It is not intended to handle the asynchronous exceptions defined in *signal*, such as SIGFPE, which indicates a floating-point exception. The context for handling an exception is a try block. Handlers are declared at the end of a try block, using the keyword catch.

C++ code can raise an exception in a try block by using the throw expression. The exception is handled by invoking an appropriate handler selected from a list found at the end of the handler's try block. An example of this follows.

In file dbl_vect4.cpp

```
dbl_vect::dbl_vect(int n): size(n)
{
   if (n < 1) //1)                    //precondition assertion
      throw (n);
   p = new int[n];
   if (p == 0)                        //postcondition assertion
      throw ("FREE STORE EXHAUSTED");
}

void g(int n)
{
   try {
      dbl_vect  a(n), b(n);
      . . . . .
   }
   catch(int n) {·····}              //catches incorrect size
   catch(const char* error) {·····}  //catches no free store
}
```

The first `throw()` has an integer argument and matches the `catch(int n)` signature. This handler is expected to perform an appropriate action where an incorrect array size has been passed as an argument to the constructor. For example, an error message and abort are normal. The second `throw()` has a pointer to character argument and matches the `catch(const char* error)` signature.

9.3 Throwing Exceptions

Syntactically, *throw expressions* come in two forms:

```
throw expression
throw
```

The `throw` *expression* raises an exception. The innermost try block in which an exception is raised is used to select the `catch` statement that processes the exception. The `throw` with no argument can be used inside a `catch` to *rethrow* the current exception. This `throw` is typically used when you want a second handler called from the first handler to further process the exception.

The expression thrown is a static temporary object that persists until exception handling is exited. The expression is caught by a handler that may use this value, as follows:

In file throw1.cpp

```
void foo()
{
    int  i;
    //will illustrate how an exception is thrown
    i = -15;
    throw i;
}

int main()
{
    try {
        foo();
    }
    catch(int n)
        { cerr << "exception caught\n " << n << endl; }
}
```

The integer value thrown by throw i persists until the handler with the integer signature catch(int n) exits. This value is available for use within the handler as its argument.

When a nested function throws an exception, the process stack is "unwound" until an exception handler is found. This means that block exit from each terminated local process causes automatic objects to be destroyed.

In file throw2.cpp

```
void foo()
{
    int  i, j;
    .....
    throw i;
    .....
}
```

```
void call_foo()
{
   int  k;
   .....
   foo();
   .....
}

int main()
{
   try {
      call_foo();        //foo exits with i and j destroyed
   }
   catch(int n) { ..... }
}
```

9.3.1 Rethrown Exceptions

Using throw without an expression rethrows a caught exception. The catch that
rethrows the exception cannot complete the handling of the existing exception. This
catch passes control to the nearest surrounding try block, where a handler capable
of catching the still existing exception is invoked. The exception expression exists
until all handling is completed. Control resumes after the outermost try block that
last handled the rethrown expression.

An example of rethrowing of an exception follows.

```
void foo()
{
   try {
      ...
      throw i;
   }
   catch(int n)
   {
   if ( i > 0)        //handle for positive values here
   .....
      return;
   }
   else {             //handle i <= 0 partially
   ...
      throw;          //rethrown
   }
}
```

Assuming that the thrown expression was of integer type, the rethrown exception is the same persistent integer object that is handled by the nearest handler suitable for that type.

9.3.2 Exception Expressions

Conceptually, the thrown expression "passes" information to the handlers. Frequently, the handlers will not need this information. For example, a handler that prints a message and aborts needs no information from its environment. However, the user might want additional information printed so that it can be used to select or to help decide the handler's action. In this case, it is appropriate to package the information as an object.

```
class dbl_vect_error {
private:
    enum  error { bounds, heap, other } e_type;
    int  ub, index, size;
public:
    dbl_vect_error(error, int, int);    //out of bounds
    dbl_vect_error(error, int);         //out of memory
    . . . . .
};
```

Now, throwing an expression using an object of type dbl_vect_error can be more informative to a handler than just throwing expressions of simple types.

```
    . . . . .
    throw dbl_vect_error(bounds, i, ub);
    . . . . .
```

9.4 Try Blocks

Syntactically, a try block has the form

> try
> *compound statement*
> *handler list*

The try block is the context for deciding which handlers are invoked on a raised exception. The order in which handlers are defined determines the order in which a handler for a raised exception of matching type will be tried.

```
try {
    .....
    throw ("SOS");
    .....
    io_condition eof(argv[i]);
    throw (eof);
    .....
}

catch(const char*) {.....}
catch(io_condition& x) {.....}
```

Conditions Under Which Throw Expression Matches the Catch Handler Type

- An exact match

- A derived type of the public base-class handler type

- A thrown object type that is convertible to a pointer type that is the `catch` argument

It is an error to list handlers in an order that prevents them from being called. For example,

```
catch(void*)               //any char* would match
catch(char*)
catch(BaseTypeError&)      //always on DerivedTypeError
catch(DerivedTypeError&)
```

A try block can be nested. If no matching handler is available in the immediate try block, a handler is selected from its immediately surrounding try block. If no handler that matches can be found, a default behavior is used. This is by default terminate() (see Section 9.7, "terminate() and unexpected()," on page 315).

9.5 Handlers

Syntactically, a handler has the form

catch (*formal argument*)
compound statement

The catch looks like a function declaration of one argument without a return type.

In file catch.cpp

```
catch(char* message)
{
   cerr << message << endl;
   exit(1);
}

catch( ... )        //default action to be taken
{
   cerr << "THAT'S ALL FOLKS." << endl;
   abort();
}
```

An ellipsis signature matching any argument type is allowed. Also, the formal argument can be an abstract declaration. In other words, it can have type information without a variable name.

The handler is invoked by an appropriate throw expression. At that point, the try block is exited. The system calls clean-up functions that include destructors for any objects that were local to the try block. A partially constructed object will have destructors invoked on any parts of it that are constructed subobjects. The program resumes at the statement after the try block.

9.6 Exception Specification

Syntactically, an *exception specification* is part of a function declaration or a function definition and has the form

function header throw *(type list)*

The *type list* is the list of types that a throw expression within the function can have. The function definition and the function declaration must write out the exception specification identically.

If the list is empty, the compiler may assume that no throw will be executed by the function, either directly or indirectly.

```
void foo() throw(int, over_flow);
void noex(int i) throw();
```

If an exception specification is left off, the assumption is that an arbitrary exception can be thrown by such a function. Violations of these specifications are runtime errors and are caught by the function unexpected().

9.7 terminate() and unexpected()

The system-provided function terminate() is called when no handler has been provided to deal with an exception. The abort() function, called by default, immediately terminates the program, returning control to the operating system. Another action can be specified by using set_terminate() to provide a handler. These declarations are found in the *except* library.

The system-provided handler unexpected() is called when a function throws an exception that was not in its exception-specification list. By default, the terminate() function is called; otherwise, a set_unexpected() can be used to provide a handler.

9.8 Example Exception Code

In this section, we discuss some examples of exception code and their effects. Let us return to catching a size error in our `dbl_vect` constructor from Section 6.7, "Overloading Assignment and Subscripting Operators," on page 210.

In file dbl_vect4.cpp

```
dbl_vect::dbl_vect(int n): size(n)
{
   if (n < 1)                 //precondition assertion
      throw (n);
   p = new int[n];
   if (p == 0)                //postcondition assertion
      throw ("FREE STORE EXHAUSTED");
}

void g(int m)
{
   try {
      dbl_vect  a(m);
      .....
   }

   catch(int n)
   {
      cerr << "SIZE ERROR " << n << endl;   //retry g with
      g(10);                                //legal size
   }

   catch(const char* error)
   {
      cerr << error << endl;
      abort();
   }
}
```

The handler has replaced an illegal value with a default legal value. This may be reasonable in a system's debugging phase, when many routines are being integrated and tested. The system attempts to provide further diagnostics. It is analogous to a compiler's attempt to continue to parse an incorrect program after a syntax error. Frequently, the compiler provides additional error messages that prove useful.

The preceding constructor checks that only one variable has a legal value. It looks artificial in that it replaces code that could directly replace the illegal value with a default by throwing an exception and allowing the handler to repair the value. However, in this form, the separation of what is an error and how it is handled is clear. It is a clear methodology for developing fault-tolerant code.

More generally, one could have an object's constructor look like the following:

```
Object::Object(arguments)
{
    if (illegal argument1 )
        throw expression1;
    if (illegal argument2 )
        throw expression2;
    . . . . .
    //attempt to construct
    . . . . .
}
```

The `Object` constructor now provides a set of thrown expressions for an illegal state. The try block can now use the information to repair or to abort incorrect code.

```
    try {

    //· · · · · fault-tolerant code

    }
    catch(declaration1) { /* fixup this case */ }
    catch(declaration2) { /* fixup this case */ }
        . . . . .
    catch(declarationK) { /* fixup this case */ }
    //correct or repaired - state values are now legal
```

When many distinct error conditions are useful for the state of a given object, a class hierarchy can be used to create a selection of related types to be used as throw expressions.

```
Object_Error {
public:
   Object_Error(arguments);        //capture useful info
   members that contain thrown expression state
   virtual void repair()
      { cerr << "Repair failed in Object " << endl;
        abort(): }
};

Object_Error_S1 : public Object_Error {
public:
   Object_Error_S1(arguments);
   added members that contain thrown expression state
   void repair(); //override to provide repair
};

· · · · · //other derived error classes as needed
```

These hierarchies allow an appropriately ordered set of catches to handle exceptions in a logical sequence. Recall that a base-class type should come after a derived-class type in the list of catch declarations.

9.9 Standard Exceptions and Their Uses

C++ compilers and library vendors provide standard exceptions. For example, the exception type bad_alloc is thrown by the ANSII compiler if the new operator fails to return with storage from free store. The bad_alloc exception is in the *except* library.

Here is a program that lets you test this behavior on the Borland compiler.

In file except.cpp

```
int main()
{
    int *p, n;

    try {
        while (true) {
            cout << "enter allocation request:" << endl;
            cin >> n;
            p = new int[n];
        }
    }
    catch(bad_alloc x ) { cout << "bad_alloc caught" << endl; }
    catch(...) { cout << "default catch" << endl; }
}
```

This program loops until it is interrupted by an exception. On our system, a request for 1 billion integers will invoke the bad_alloc handler. In some systems, the exception class xalloc is provided for this purpose.

A frequent use of standard exceptions is in testing casts. The standard exception bad_cast is declared in file *exception*. The following program uses the *typeinfo* and *stdexception* libraries. The program also uses RTTI, as well as the bad_cast exception.

In file bad_cast.cpp

```
class A {
public:
    virtual void foo() { cout << "in A" << endl; }
};

class B: public A {
public:
    void foo() { cout << "in B" << endl; }
};
```

```
int main()
{
   try {
      A a, *pa; B b, *pb;
      pa = &b;
      pb = dynamic_cast<B*>(pa);        //succeeds
      pb -> foo();
      pa = &a;
      pb = dynamic_cast<B*>(pa);        //fails
      pb -> foo();
   }
   catch(bad_cast) { cout << "dynamic_cast failed" << endl; }
}
```

In systems that do not throw these exceptions, the pointer should be tested with an assertion to see that it is not converted to 0.

The standard library exceptions are derived from the base-class `exception`. Two derived classes are `logic_error` and `runtime_error`. Logic-error types include `bad_cast`, `out_of_range`, and `bad_typeid`, which are intended to be thrown as indicated by their names. The runtime error types include `range_error`, `overflow_error`, and `bad_alloc`.

The base class defines a virtual function.

```
virtual const char* exception::what() const throw();
```

This member function should be defined in each derived class to give more helpful messages. The empty throw-specification list indicates that the function should not itself throw an exception.

9.10 Pragmatics

Paradoxically, error recovery is concerned chiefly with writing correct programs. Exception handling is about error recovery. Exception handling is also a transfer-of-control mechanism. The client/manufacturer model gives the manufacturer the responsibility of making software that produces correct output, given acceptable input. The question for the manufacturer is how much error detection and, conceivably, correction should be built in. The client is often better served by fault-detecting libraries, which can be used in deciding whether to attempt to continue the computation.

Error recovery is based on the transfer of control. Undisciplined transfer of control leads to chaos. In error recovery, one assumes that an exceptional condition has corrupted the computation, making it dangerous to continue. It is analogous to driving a car after realizing that the steering mechanism is damaged. Useful exception handling is the disciplined recovery when damage occurs.

In most cases, programming that raises exceptions should print a diagnostic message and gracefully terminate. Special forms of processing, such as real-time processing and fault-tolerant computing, require that the system not go down. In these cases, heroic attempts at repair are legitimate.

What can be agreed on is that classes can usefully be provided with error conditions. In many of these conditions, the object has member values in illegal states—values it is not allowed to have. The system raises an exception for these cases, with the default action being program termination. This is analogous to the native types raising system-defined exceptions, such as SIGFPE.

But what kind of intervention is reasonable to keep the program running? And where should the flow of control be returned? C++ uses a termination model that forces the current try block to terminate. Under this regime, one will either retry the code or ignore or substitute a default result and continue. Retrying the code seems most likely to give a correct result.

Code is usually too thinly commented. It is difficult to imagine the program that would be too rich in assertions. Assertions and simple throws and catches that terminate the computation are parallel techniques. A well-thought-out set of error conditions detectable by the user of an ADT is an important part of a good design. An overreliance on exception handling in normal programming, beyond error detection and termination, is a sign that a program was ill-conceived, with too many holes, in its original form.

9.11 Moving from C++ to Java

Java has an exception-handling mechanism that is integral to the language and is heavily used for error detection at runtime. The mechanism is similar to the one found in C++. An exception is thrown by a method when it detects an error condition. The exception will be handled by invoking an appropriate *handler* selected from a list of handlers, or catches. These explicit catches occur at the end of an enclosing try block. An uncaught exception is handled by a default Java handler that issues a message and terminates the program. An exception is itself an object, which must be derived from the superclass Throwable.

As a simple example of all this, we will add an exception NoSuchNameException to our Person1 example class in Section 8.10, "Moving from C++ to Java," on page 300.

```
class NoSuchNameException extends Exception {
    public String str() { return name; }
    public String name;
    NoSuchNameException(String p) { name = p; }
};
```

The purpose of this exception is to report an incorrect or improperly formed name.
In many cases, exceptions act as assertions would in the C language. These exceptions determine whether an illegal action has occurred and report it. We now modify
the Person code to take advantage of the exception.

In file Person2.java

```
//Person2.class: Person with exceptions added

class Person2 {
    private String name;
    public Person2(String p)throws NoSuchNameException{
        if (p == "")
            throw new NoSuchNameException(p);
        name = p; }
    public String toString(){ return name;}
    public static void main(String[] args)
            throws NoSuchNameException
    {
        try{
            Person2 p = new Person2("ira pohl");
            System.out.println("PERSONS");
            System.out.println(p.toString());
            p = new Person2("");
        }
    catch(NoSuchNameException t)
        { System.out.println(" exception with name " + t.str()); }
    finally
        { System.out.println("finally clause"); }
};
```

The throw() has a NoSuchNameException argument and matches the catch() signature. This handler is expected to perform an appropriate action where an incorrect name has been passed as an argument to the Person2 constructor. As in this
example, an error message and abort are normal. The finally clause shown here is
code that is done regardless of how the try block terminates.

Summary

1. Exceptions are generally unexpected error conditions. Normally, these conditions terminate the user program with a system-provided error message. An example is floating-point divide-by-zero.

2. The standard library *assert* provides the macro

   ```
   assert(expression);
   ```

   If the *expression* evaluates as `false`, execution is aborted with diagnostic output. The assertions are discarded if the macro `NDEBUG` is defined.

3. The *signal* library provides a standard mechanism for handling system-defined exceptions in a straightforward manner. Some examples are

   ```
   #define   SIGINT    2     /*interrupt signal */
   #define   SIGFPE    8     /*floating-point exception */
   #define   SIGABRT   22    /*abort signal */
   ```

   The system can raise these exceptions. On many systems, for example, pressing control-C on the keyboard generates an interrupt. The normal action is to kill the current user process. These exceptions can be handled by use of the `signal()` function, which associates a handler function with a signal.

4. C++ code can raise an exception by using the throw expression. The exception is handled by invoking an appropriate handler selected from a list of handlers found at the end of the handler's try block.

5. Syntactically, throws come in two forms:

   ```
   throw
   throw expression
   ```

   The `throw` *expression* raises an exception in a try block. The `throw` with no argument may be used in a `catch` to rethrow the current exception.

6. Syntactically, a try block has the form

    ```
    try
    ```
    compound statement
    handler list

    The try block is the context for deciding which handlers are invoked on a raised exception. The order in which handlers are defined determines the order in which a handler for a raised exception of matching type is tried.

7. Syntactically, a handler has the form

    ```
    catch  (formal argument)
    ```
    compound statement

    The `catch` looks like a function declaration of one argument without a return type.

8. Syntactically, an exception specification is part of a function declaration and has the form

    function header `throw` (*type list*)

    The *type list* is the list of types that a throw expression within the function can have. If the list is empty, the compiler may assume that no throw will be executed by the function, either directly or indirectly.

9. The system-provided handler `terminate()` is called when no other handler has been provided to deal with an exception. The system-provided handler `unexpected()` is called when a function throws an exception that was not in its exception-specification list. By default, `terminate()` calls the `abort()` function. The default `unexpected()` behavior is to call `terminate()`.

Review Questions

1. True or false: In C++, `new` cannot throw an exception.

2. Asynchronous exceptions, such as `SIGFPE`, are defined in _____.

3. The context for handling an exception is a _____ block.

4. The system-provided handler _____ is called when a function throws an exception that was not in its exception-specification list.

5. A standard exception class is _____ and is used for _____.

6. The system-provided handler _____ is called when no other handler has been provided to deal with an exception.

7. Handlers are declared at the end of a `try` block, using the keyword _____.

8. The _____ is the list of types a throw expression can have.

9. Name three standard exceptions provided by C++ compilers and libraries.

10. What two actions should most handlers perform?

Exercises

1. The following bubble sort does not work correctly:

```
//Incorrect bubble sort

void swap(int a, int b)
{
   int  temp = a;

   a = b;
   b = temp;
}

void bubble(int a[], int size)
{
   int  i, j;

   for (i = 0; i != size; ++i)
      for (j = i ; j != size; ++j)
         if (a[j] < a [j + 1])
            swap (a[j], a[j + 1]);
}
```

```
int main()
{
    int  t[10] = { 9, 4, 6, 4, 5, 9, -3, 1, 0, 12};

    bubble(t, 10);
    for (int i = 0; i < 10; ++i)
        cout << t[i] << '\t';
    cout << "\nsorted? " << endl;
}
```

Place assertions in this code to test that it is working properly. Use this technique to write a correct program.

2. Use templates to write a generic version of the correct bubble sort, complete with assertions. Use a random-number generator to generate test data. On what types can this be made to work generically?

3. Code the member function `dbl_vect::operator[](int)` to throw an out-of-range exception if an incorrect index is used. (See Section 6.7, "Overloading Assignment and Subscripting Operators," on page 211.) Also, code a reasonable `catch` that prints out the incorrect value and terminates. To test the code, execute a try block in which the exception occurs. Write a `catch` that would allow user intervention at the keyboard to produce a correct index and to continue or to retry the computation. Can this be done in a reasonable manner?

4. Recode the `ch_stack` class to throw exceptions for as many conditions as you think are reasonable. (See Section 5.2, "Constructing a Dynamically Sized Stack," on page 155.) Use an enumerated type to list the conditions.

```
enum stack_error { overflow, underflow, ····· };
```

Write a `catch` that will use a `switch` statement to select an appropriate message and to terminate the computation.

5. Write a `stack_error` class that replaces the enumerated type of the previous exercise. Make this a base class for a series of derived classes that encapsulates each specific exception condition. The catches should be able to use overridden virtual functions to process the various thrown exceptions.

6. *(Java)* Recode in Java the `ch_stack` class, complete with exceptions. Java already throws exceptions if new fails to allocate storage, and Java automatically throws a range-error exception when an index is out of range.

Chapter 10
OOP Using C++

C++ is a hybrid language. The kernel language developed from C is classically used as a system-implementation language. As such, C++ is suitable for writing very efficient code. The class-based additions to the language support the full range of OOP requirements. Therefore, C++ is suitable for writing reusable libraries, and it supports a polymorphic coding style.

Object-oriented programming (OOP) and C++ were embraced by the industry very quickly. C++, as a hybrid OOP language, allows a multiparadigmatic approach to coding. The traditional advantages of C as an efficient, powerful programmer's language are not lost. The key new ingredients in C++ are inheritance and polymorphism, that is, its capability to assume many forms.

10.1 OOP Language Requirements

OOP Language Characteristics

- Encapsulation with data hiding: the ability to distinguish an object's internal state and behavior from its external state and behavior

- Type extensibility: the ability to add user-defined types to augment the native types

- Inheritance: the ability to create new types by importing or reusing the description of existing types

- Polymorphism with dynamic binding: the ability of objects to be responsible for interpreting function invocation

These features cannot substitute for programmer discipline and community-observed convention, but they can be used to promote such behavior.

Typical procedural languages, such as FORTRAN, Pascal, and C, have limited forms of type extensibility and encapsulation. These languages have pointer and record types that provide these features. C also has a scheme of file-oriented privacy, in its static file-scope declarations. Such languages as Modula-2 and Ada have more complete forms of encapsulation, namely, module and package, respectively. These languages readily allow users to build ADTs and provide significant library support for many application areas. A language such as pure LISP supports dynamic binding. The elements in OOP have been available in various languages for at least 25 years.

LISP, Simula, and SmallTalk have long been in widespread use in both the academic and research communities. These languages are in many ways more elegant than C and C++. However, not until OOP elements were added to C was there any significant movement to using OOP in industry. Indeed, the late 1980s saw a bandwagon effect in adopting C++ that cut across companies, product lines, and application areas; industry needed to couple OOP with the ability to program effectively at a low level.

Also crucial was the ease of migration from C to C++. PL/1, by contrast, is rooted in FORTRAN and COBOL; Ada is rooted in Pascal. But C++ had C as a nearly proper subset. As such, the installed base of C code need not be abandoned. These other languages required a nontrivial conversion process to modify existing code from their ancestor languages.

The conventional academic wisdom is that excessive concern with efficiency is detrimental to good coding practices. This concern misses the obvious, namely, that product competition is based on performance. Consequently, industry values low-level technology. In this environment, C++ is a very effective tool.

10.1.1 ADTs: Encapsulation and Data Hiding

To fully appreciate the OOP paradigm, we must view the overall coding process as an exercise in shared and distributed responsibilities. This text has used the terms *client* to mean a user of a class and *manufacturer* to mean the provider of the class.

A client of a class expects an approximation to an abstraction. A stack, to be useful, has to be of reasonable size. A complex number must be of reasonable precision. A deck of cards must be shufflable, with random outcome in dealing hands. The internals of how these behaviors are computed is not a direct concern of the client. The client is concerned with cost, effectiveness, and ease of operation, not with implementation. This is the *black box* principle, and it has two components.

Black Box for the Client

- Simple to use, easy to understand, and familiar
- In a component relationship within the system
- Cheap, efficient, and powerful

Black Box for the Manufacturer

- Easy to reuse and modify and difficult to misuse and reproduce

- Profitable to produce with a large client base

- Cheap, efficient, and powerful

The manufacturer competes for clients by implementing an ADT product that is reasonably priced and efficient. It is in the manufacturer's interest to hide details of an implementation. This simplifies what the manufacturer needs to explain to the client, and it frees the manufacturer to allow internal repairs or improvements that do not affect the client's use. It restrains the client from dangerous or inadvertent tampering with the product.

A data-hiding scheme that restricts access of implementation detail to manufacturers guarantees client conformance to the ADT abstraction. The private parts are hidden from client code, and the public parts are available. It is possible to change the hidden representation without changing the public access or functionality. If done properly, client code need not change when the hidden representation is modified. The two keys to fulfilling these conditions are inheritance and polymorphism.

10.1.2 Reuse and Inheritance

Library creation and reuse are crucial indicators of successful language strategies. Inheritance, or deriving a new class from an old one, is used for code sharing and reuse, as well as for developing type hierarchies. Inheritance can be used to create a hierarchy of related ADTs that share both code and a common interface, a feature critical to the ability to reuse code.

Inheritance influences overall software design by providing a framework that captures conceptual elements that become the focus for system building and reuse. For example, InterViews is a C++ package that supports building graphical user interfaces for interactive, text, and graphics objects. These categories are readily composed to produce various applications, such as a CAD system, a browser, or a WYSIWYG editor.

OOP Design Methodology

1. Decide on an appropriate set of ADTs.

2. Design in their relatedness, and use inheritance to share code and interface.

3. Use virtual functions to process related objects dynamically.

Inheritance also facilitates the black box principle and is an important mechanism for suppressing detail. It is hierarchical, and each level provides functionality to the next level that is built on it. In retrospect, structured programming methodology, with its process-centered view, relied on stepwise refinement to nest routines but did not adequately appreciate the need for a corresponding view of data.

10.1.3 Polymorphism

Polymorphism is the genie in OOP, taking instruction from a client and properly interpreting its wishes. A polymorphic function has many forms. Following Cardelli and Wegner, we make the following distinctions:

Types of Polymorphism

1. Coercion (ad hoc polymorphism): A function or operator works on several types by converting their values to the expected type. An example in ANSI C is assignment conversions of arithmetic types on function call.

   ```
   a / b            //divide determined by native coercions
   ```

2. Overloading (ad hoc polymorphism): A function is called, based on its signature, defined as the list of argument types in its parameter list. The C integer-divide operator and float-divide operator are distinguished, based on their argument list.

   ```
   cout << a        //function overloading
   ```

3. Inclusion (pure polymorphism): A type is a subtype of another type. Functions available for the base type will work on the subtype. Such a function can have various implementations that are invoked by a runtime determination of subtype.

   ```
   p -> draw()       //virtual function call
   ```

4. Parametric polymorphism (pure polymorphism): The type is left unspecified and is later instantiated. Manipulation of generic pointers and templates provides this in C++.

   ```
   stack <window*> win[40]
   ```

Polymorphism localizes responsibility for behavior. The client code frequently requires no revision when additional functionality is added to the system through manufacturer-provided code additions.

Polymorphism directly contributes to the black box principle. The virtual functions specified for the base class are the interface used by the client throughout. The client knows that an overridden member function takes responsibility for a specific implementation of a given action relevant to the object. The client need not know different routines for each calculation or different forms of specification. These details are suppressed.

10.2 OOP: The Dominant Programming Methodology

OOP using C++ gained dazzling acceptance in industry from 1986 on, despite acknowledged flaws and unfamiliarity with OOP strategies. The reason for this is that C++ brought OOP technology to industry in an acceptable way. C++ is based on an existing, widely used successful language. C++ allows tight, efficient, portable code to be written. Type safety is retained, and type extensibility is general. C++ coexists with standard languages and does not require special system resources.

C was designed as a system-implementation language and as such allows coding that is readily translated to efficiently use machine resources. Software products gain competitive advantage from such efficiency. Hence, despite complaints that traditional C was not a safe or robust language to code in, C grew in its range of application. The C community, by convention and discipline, used structured programming and ADT extensions. OOP made inroads into this professional community only when it was wed to C within a conceptual framework that maintained its traditional point of view and advantages. Key to the bandwagon move to C++ has been the understanding that inheritance and polymorphism gain additional important advantages over traditional coding practice.

Polymorphism in C++ allows a client to use an ADT as a black box. Success in OOP is characterized by the extent to which a user-defined type can be made indistinguishable from a native type. Polymorphism allows coercions to be specified that integrate the ADT with the native types. Objects from subtype hierarchies respond dynamically to function invocation, the messaging principle in OOP. Polymorphism also simplifies client protocols, and name proliferation is controlled by function and operator overloading. The availability of all four forms of polymorphism encourages the programmer to design with encapsulation and data hiding in mind. OOP is many things to many people. Attempts to define it are like the blind men's attempts to describe an elephant. Recall the equation describing object-orientation: *OOP = type-extensibility + polymorphism.*

In many languages and systems, the cost of detail suppression was runtime inefficiency or undue rigidity in the interface. C++ has a range of choices that allow both efficiency and flexibility. Also, the success of C++ was a precondition for the introduction of Java in 1995. Together, C++ and Java have established OOP as the dominant contemporary programming methodology.

10.3 Designing with OOP in Mind

Most programming should involve the use of existing designs. For example, the mathematical and scientific communities have standard definitions of complex numbers, rationals, matrices, and polynomials. Each of these can be readily coded as an ADT. The expected public behavior of these types is widely agreed on.

The programming community has widespread experience with standard container classes. Reasonable agreement exists as to the behavior of stack, associative array, binary tree, and queue. Also, the programming community has many examples of specialized programming language oriented to a particular domain. For example, SNOBOL and its successor language ICON have powerful string-processing features that can be captured as ADTs in C++.

OOP attempts to emphasize reuse, which is possible on several scales. The grandest scale is the development of libraries that are effective for an entire problem domain. The upside is that reuse contributes in the long run to more easily maintained code. The downside is that a particular application does not need costly library development.

OOP requires programmer sophistication. More sophisticated programmers are better programmers. The downside is high training cost and the potential misuse of sophisticated tools.

OOP makes client code simpler and more readily extensible. Polymorphism can be used to incorporate local changes into a large-scale system without global modification. The downside can be runtime overhead.

C++ provides programming encapsulations through classes, inheritance, and templates. Encapsulations hide and localize. As systems get bigger and more complex, there is an increasing need for such encapsulations. Simple block structure and functional encapsulation of such languages as Pascal are not enough. The 1970s taught us the need for the module as a programming unit. The 1980s taught us that modules need to have a logical coherence supported in the language and that they must be derivable from one another. When supported by a programming language, encapsulations and relationships lead to increased programmer discipline. The art of programming is to blend rigor and discipline with creativity.

Occam's Razor is a useful design principle: Entities should not be multiplied beyond necessity—or beyond completeness, invertibility, orthogonality, consistency, simplicity, efficiency, or expressiveness. Such ideals can be in conflict and frequently involve trade-offs in arriving at a design.

Invertibility means that the program should have member functions that are inverses. In the mathematical types, addition and subtraction are inverses. In a text editor, add and delete are inverses. Some commands, such as negation, are their own inverses. The importance of invertibility in a nonmathematical context can be seen by the brilliant success of the *undo* command in text editing and the *recover* commands in file maintenance.

Completeness is best seen in Boolean algebra, in which the nand operation suffices to generate all possible Boolean expressions. But Boolean algebra is usually taught with negation, conjunction, and disjunction as the basic operations. Completeness by itself is not enough to judge a design by. A large set of operators is frequently more expressive.

Orthogonality means that each element of a design should integrate and work with all other elements without overlapping or being redundant. For example, on a system that manipulates shapes, one should have a horizontal move, a vertical move, and a rotate operation. In effect, these operations would be adequate to position the shape at any point on the screen.

Hierarchy is captured through inheritance. Designs should be hierarchical. It is a reflection of two principles—decomposition and localization. Both principles are methods of suppressing detail, a key idea in coping with complexity. However, there is a scale problem in such a design. How much detail is enough to make a concept useful as its own class? It is important to avoid a proliferation of specialized concepts. Too much detail renders the class design difficult to master.

10.4 Class-Responsibility-Collaborator

Designs can be aided by a diagramming process. Several object-oriented design (OOD) notations exist, and a number have been incorporated in CASE (computer-assisted software engineering) tools. The most comprehensive of these are based on the Universal Modeling Language (UML) pioneered by Rational Software. This section describes a useful, related low-tech scheme: the Class-Responsibility-Collaborator (CRC) notecard scheme.

A responsibility is an obligation the class must keep. For example, complex number objects must provide an implementation of complex arithmetic. A collaborator is another object that cooperates with this object to provide an overall set of behaviors. For example, integers and reals collaborate with complex numbers to provide a comprehensive set of mathematical behaviors.

A CRC notecard is used to design a given class. The responsibilities of the class and the collaborators for that class are initially described. The back of the card is used to describe implementation detail. The front of the card corresponds to public behavior.

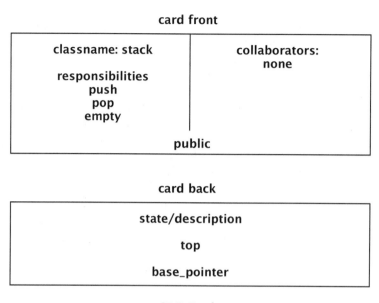

card front

classname: stack	collaborators: none
responsibilities push pop empty	

public

card back

state/description

top

base_pointer

CRC Card

As the design process proceeds, the cards are rewritten and refined. They become more detailed and closer to a set of member function headers. The back of the card can be used to show implementation details, including is-a, like-a, and has-a relationships.

The attractiveness of this scheme is its flexibility. In effect, it represents a pseudocode refinement process that can reflect local tastes. The number of revisions and the level of detail and rigor are a matter of taste.

10.5 Design Patterns

Reuse is a primary theme in modern programming. In early times, reuse was limited to simple libraries of functions, such as the math functions found in *math.h* or the string functions in *string.h*. In OOP, the class or template becomes a key construct for reuse. Classes and templates encapsulate code that conforms to certain designs. Thus, the iterator classes of STL are a *design pattern*. Recently, the concept of design pattern has proved very popular in defining medium-scale reuse. A design pattern has four elements.

Elements of a Design Pattern

1. The pattern terminology: for example, *iterator*

2. The problem and conditions: for example, *visitation* over a container

3. The solution: for example, pointer-like objects with a common interface

4. The evaluation: for example, the trade-off between defining an iterator on a vector or using a native array

A design pattern is an abstraction that suggests a useful solution to a particular programming problem. Often, reuse is inexpensive, as with STL container and iterator design patterns that require only instantiation. Sometimes, reuse is expensive, such as inventing a balanced-tree class with an interface conforming to STL sequence containers.

Design Patterns in This Text

1. *Iterator*, such as `vector::iterator`; organizes visitation on a container

2. *Composite*, such as `class grad_student`; composes complex objects out of simpler ones

3. *Template method*, such as the `quicksort()` template

OOP has stimulated reuse of *design patterns*. A design pattern is a software solution in search of a problem. Consider how the iterator logic of STL decouples visitation of container elements from specific details of the container. This idea is independent of computer language and is useful in C++, Java, and SmallTalk coding projects. This idea can be summarized as the *iterator* pattern.

The name is of great importance, as it increases the programmer's technical vocabulary. A name should be memorable and illuminate a key characteristic of the method. The problem identifies circumstances under which the pattern provides a solution. The solution shows how the pattern solves the problem. The consequences are a discussion of the cost-benefit trade-off in using the pattern.

When the pattern is discussed in a specific language context, it is often called a *programming idiom*. This is also sometimes used for smaller coding ideas. For example, in C++ or C, EOF is frequently used as a guard value to terminate file processing.

When the pattern is used in a wider context to provide a library of routines and components, it is called a *framework*. The STL can be considered a framework that makes heavy use of the iterator and template patterns, among others. In Java, the Java Foundation Classes, also known as Swing, support window development. They are implemented with the model-view-controller pattern.

10.6 Moving from C++ to Java

Java shares with C++ the use of classes and inheritance to build software in an object-oriented manner. Also, both languages use data hiding and have methods that are bundled within the class.

Unlike C++, Java does not allow for conventional programming. Everything is encapsulated in a class. This forces the programmer to think and to design everything as an object. The downside is that conventional C code is not as readily adapted to Java as it is to C++. Java avoids most of the memory-pointer errors that are common to C and C++. Address arithmetic and manipulation are done by the compiler and the system, not the programmer. Therefore, the Java programmer writes safer code. Also, memory reclamation is automatically done by the Java garbage collector.

Another important concept in OOP is the promotion of code reuse through the *inheritance* mechanism. In Java, this is the mechanism of *extending* a new class, called a *subclass*, from an existing one, called the *superclass*. Methods in the extended class override the superclass methods. The method selection occurs at runtime and is a highly flexible polymorphic style of coding.

Java, in a strict sense, is completely portable across all platforms that support it. Java is compiled to byte code that is run on the Java virtual machine. This is typically an interpreter—code that understands the Java byte code instructions. Such code is much slower than native code on most systems. The trade-off here is universally consistent behavior versus loss of efficiency.

Java has extensively developed libraries for performing Web-based programming. Java also has the ability to write graphical user interfaces that are used interactively. Its thread package has secure Web communication features that let the coder write distributed applications.

Java is far simpler than C++ in the core language and its features. In some ways, this is deceptive in that much of the complexity is in its libraries. Java is far safer because of very strict typing, avoidance of pointer arithmetic, and well-integrated exception handling. It is system independent in its behavior, so one size fits all. This combination of object orientation, simplicity, universality, and Web-sensitive libraries make it the language of the moment.

Java programs are classes. A `class` has syntactic form that is derived from the C `struct`, which is not in Java. Data and functions are placed within classes. When a class is executed as a program, it starts by calling the member function `main()`.

Java is known for providing applets on Web pages. A browser is used to display and to execute the applet. Typically, the applet provides a graphical user interface to the code. The following piece of code is an applet for computing the greatest common devisor for two numbers:

In file wgcd.java

```
//GCD applet implementations

import java.applet.*; //gets the applet superclass
import java.awt.*;    //abstract windowing toolkit
import java.io.*;

//derived from the class Applet

public class wgcd extends Applet {
   int x, y, z, r;
   TextField a = new TextField(10);        //input box
   TextField b = new TextField(10);        //input box
   TextField c = new TextField(10);        //output box
   Label l1 = new Label("Value1: ");
   Label l2 = new Label("Value2: ");
   Button gcd = new Button("   GCD: ");

//draws the screen layout such as the TextFields

   public void init() {
      setLayout(new FlowLayout());
      c.setEditable(false);
      add(l1); add(a);
      add(l2); add(b);
      add(gcd); add(c);
   }

//computes the greatest common divisor

   public int gcd(int m, int n) {
      while (n !=0) {
         r = m % n;
         m = n;
         n = r;
      }
      return m;
   }
```

```
//looks for screen events to interact with

    public boolean action(Event e, Object o) {
        if ("   GCD: ".equals(o)) { //press button
            x = Integer.parseInt(a.getText());
            y = Integer.parseInt(b.getText());
            z = gcd(x,y);
            //place answer in output TextField
            c.setText(Integer.toString(z));
        }
        return true;
    }
};
```

The code uses the graphics library *awt* and the applet class to draw an interactive interface that can be executed either by a special program called the *applet-viewer* or by a Java-aware browser, such as Microsoft Explorer or Netscape Navigator. Unlike ordinary Java programs, this program does not use a main() method to initiate the computation. Instead, the init() method draws the screen. Further computation is event driven and is processed by the action() method. The user terminates the applet by clicking on the *Quit* command in the applet pull-down menu.

Summary

1. Object-oriented programming (OOP) and C++ were embraced by industry very quickly. As a hybrid OOP language, C++ allows a multiparadigmatic approach to coding. The traditional advantages of C as an efficient, powerful programmer's language are not lost. The key new ingredient is polymorphism, or the ability to assume many forms.

2. Existing languages and methodology supported much of the OOP methodology by combining language features with programmer discipline. It is possible to create and to use ADTs in a non-OOP language. Three examples in the C community are string, boolean, and file, which are pseudotypes in that they do not enjoy the same privileges as true types. What is gained by looking at these examples is a better understanding of the limits of extensibility in non-OOP.

3. A black box for the client should be simple to use, easy to understand, and familiar; cheap, efficient, and powerful; and in a component relationship within

the system. A black box for the manufacturer should be easy to reuse and modify and difficult to misuse and reproduce; cheap, efficient, and powerful; and profitable to produce for a large client base. In brief, the OOP design methodology involves deciding on an appropriate set of ADTs, designing in their relatedness and using inheritance to share code and interface, and using virtual functions to process related objects dynamically.

4. Polymorphism directly contributes to the black box principle. The virtual functions specified for the base class are the interface used by the client throughout. The client knows that an overridden member function takes responsibility for a specific implementation of a given action relevant to the object.

5. As a hybrid OOP language, C++ can cause the programmer a dialectical tension headache. The penchant of C programmers to focus on efficiency and implementation conflicts with the penchant of objectivists to focus on elegance, abstraction, and generality. The two demands on the coding process are reconcilable but require a measure of coordination and respect for the process.

6. OOP is many things to many people. In many languages and systems, the cost of detail suppression was runtime inefficiency or undue rigidity in the interface. C++ has a range of choices that allow both efficiency and flexibility.

7. Occam's Razor, a useful design principle, states that entities should not be multiplied beyond necessity—or beyond completeness, invertibility, orthogonality, consistency, simplicity, efficiency, or expressiveness. These principles can be in conflict and frequently involve trade-offs in arriving at a design.

8. The Class-Responsibility-Collaborator (CRC) notecard scheme is used in OOD. A responsibility is an obligation the class must keep. A collaborator is another object that cooperates with this object to provide an overall set of behaviors. The responsibilities of the class and the collaborators for that class are initially described. The back of the card is used to describe implementation detail. The front of the card corresponds to public behavior.

9. OOP has stimulated reuse of *design patterns*. A design pattern is a software solution in search of a problem. Consider how the iterator logic of STL decouples visitation of container elements from specific details of the container. This idea can be summarized as the *iterator* pattern. The name is of great importance, as it increases the programmer's technical vocabulary. The name should be clever and should illuminate a key characteristic of the method. The problem identifies circumstances under which the pattern provides a solution. The solution shows how the pattern solves the problem. The consequences are a discussion of the cost-benefit trade-off in using the pattern.

Review Questions

1. Name three typical characteristics of an object-oriented programming language.

2. True or false: Conventional academic wisdom is that excessive concern with efficiency is detrimental to good coding practices.

3. Through _____, a hierarchy of related ADTs can be created that share code and a common interface.

4. Name three properties of a black box for the client.

5. Name three properties of a black box for the manufacturer.

6. _____ methodology has a process-centered view and relies on stepwise refinement to nest routines but does not adequately appreciate the need for a corresponding view of data.

7. _____ is the genie in OOP, taking instruction from a client and properly interpreting its wishes.

8. Give an example of ad hoc polymorphism.

9. Describe at least two separate concepts for the keyword `virtual` as used in C++. Does this cause conceptual confusion?

10. The package *string* is a pseudotype. It uses traditional C technology and programmer discipline to provide the ADT string. Why is it preferable to provide the standard library class `string`?

Exercises

1. Consider the following three ways to provide a Boolean type:

```
//Traditional C using the preprocessor

#define  TRUE   1
#define  FALSE  0
#define  Boolean int

//ANSI C and C++ using enumerated types
enum Boolean { false, true };

//C++ as a class
class Boolean {
    .....
public:
    //various member functions
    //including overloading  !  &&  ||  ==  !=
};
```

   Discuss the advantages and disadvantages of each style. Keep in mind scope, naming, and conversion problems. In what ways is it desirable for C++ to now have a native type `bool`?

2. C++ originally allowed the `this` pointer to be modifiable. One use was to have user-controlled storage management by assigning directly to the `this` pointer. The assignment of 0 meant that the associated memory could be returned to free store. Discuss why this is a bad idea. Write a program with an assignment of `this = 0`. What error message does your compiler give you? Can you get around this with a cast? Would this be a good idea?

3. The rules for deciding which definition of an overloaded function to invoke have changed since the first version of C++. One reason for this is to reduce the number of ambiguities. A criticism is that the rules allow matching through conversions that may be unintended by the programmer. This can cause difficult-to-detect runtime bugs. One strategy is to have the compiler issue a diagnostic warning in such cases; another is to use casting defensively to inform the compiler of the intended choice. Discuss these alternatives after investigating how the rules have changed.

4. *(Java)* Java and C++ have different casting rules. Investigate the differences. C++ allows a wider range of casting opportunities. Is this desirable?

5. List three things that you would drop from the C++ language. Argue why each would not be missed. For example, it is possible to have protected inheritance, although it was never discussed in this text. Should it be in the language for completeness' sake? Can you write code that uses protected inheritance that demonstrates that it is a critical feature of language as opposed to an extravagance?

6. *(Java)* Using *awt*, write a Java program that is a basic desktop calculator. Have buttons that indicate a series of operations, such as +, *, sqrt, and reciprocal; data fields to enter arguments; and a result field. If you have access to JFC (Swing), you use it. Document your design with CRC cards.

Appendix A
ASCII Character Codes

American Standard Code for Information Interchange									
	0	1	2	3	4	5	6	7	8	9
0	nul	soh	stx	etx	eot	enq	ack	bel	bs	ht
1	nl	vt	np	cr	so	si	dle	dc1	dc2	dc3
2	dc4	nak	syn	etb	can	em	sub	esc	fs	gs
3	rs	us	sp	!	"	#	$	%	&	'
4	(	)	*	+	,	–	.	/	0	1
5	2	3	4	5	6	7	8	9	:	;
6	<	=	>	?	@	A	B	C	D	E
7	F	G	H	I	J	K	L	M	N	O
8	P	Q	R	S	T	U	V	W	X	Y
9	Z	[	\	]	^	_	'	a	b	c
10	d	e	f	g	h	i	j	k	l	m
11	n	o	p	q	r	s	t	u	v	w
12	x	y	z	{	|	}	~	del		

Some Observations

- Character codes 0 through 31 and 127 are nonprinting.
- Character code 32 prints a single space.
- Character codes for digits 0 through 9 are contiguous.
- Character codes for letters A through Z are contiguous.
- Character codes for letters a through z are contiguous.
- The difference between an uppercase letter and the corresponding lowercase letter is 32.

The meanings for some of the abbreviations follow:

- bel—audible bell
- bs—backspace
- cr—carriage return
- esc—escape
- ht—horizontal tab
- nl—newline
- nul—null
- vt—vertical tab

Appendix B
Operator Precedence and Associativity

Operators	Associativity
:: (global scope) :: (class scope)	left to right
() [] -> . *(postfix)* ++ *(postfix)* --	left to right
++ *(prefix)* --*(prefix)* ! ~ sizeof*(type)* & *(address)* + *(unary)* - *(unary)* * *(indirection)* delete new	right to left
.* ->*	left to right
* / %	left to right
+ -	left to right
<< >>	left to right
< <= > >=	left to right
== !=	left to right
&	left to right
^	left to right
|	left to right
&&	left to right
||	left to right
?:	right to left
= += -= *= /= %= >>= <<= &= ^= |=	right to left
, *(comma operator)*	left to right

In case of doubt, use parentheses.

Appendix C
Language Guide

This concise guide to C++ summarizes many of the key language elements that are not found in older procedural languages, such as Pascal and C. This appendix is intended as a convenient guide to the language.

C.1 Program Structure

A program in C++ is a collection of functions and declarations, which may be declared in different files. Program execution begins with the function main().

```cpp
//The computation of circumference and area of circles.
//  Title: circles
//                  by
//            Geometrics Inc.
//            Version 2.2

#include <iostream>
using namespace std;

const  double pi = 3.14159;   //pi accurate to six places

inline double circum(double rad){ return (pi * 2 * rad); }
inline double area(double rad){ return (pi * rad * rad); }

int main()
{
   double  r;
   cout << "\nEnter radius: ";
   while ( cin >> r && r > 0.0 ) {
      cout << "\nArea is " << area(r);
      cout << "\nCircumference is " << circum(r) << endl;
      cout << "\nEnter radius > 0.0: ";
   }
}
```

C++ Program Organization

- C++ relies on an external standard library to provide input and output (I/O). The information the program needs to use this library resides in *iostream*.

- C++ uses a preprocessor to handle a set of directives, such as the `include` directive, to convert the program from its preprocessing form to pure C++ syntax. Directives start with the symbol #.

- A C++ program consists of declarations that may be in various files. Each function is on the external, or global, level and may not be declared in a nested manner. The files act as modules and may be compiled separately.

- The function `main()` is the starting point for program execution. This function obeys the C++ rules for function declaration. Normally, `main()` implicitly returns the integer value 0, indicating normal program completion. Other values need to be returned explicitly and indicate an error condition.

C.2 Lexical Elements

A C++ program is a sequence of characters that are collected into tokens, which comprise the basic vocabulary of the language. The six categories of tokens are keywords, identifiers, constants, string constants, operators, and punctuators.

The following characters can be used to construct tokens:

```
a b c d e f g h i j k l m n o p q r s t u v w x y z
A B C D E F G H I J K L M N O P Q R S T U V W X Y Z
0 1 2 3 4 5 6 7 8 9
+ - * / = () {} [] <> ' " ! # ~ % ∧ & _ : ; , . ? \ |
```
White space characters, such as blank and tab

In producing tokens, the compiler selects the longest string of characters that constitutes a token.

C.2.1 Comments

C++ has a rest-of-line comment symbol //. The C-style comment pairs /* */ are also available. Comments do not nest. Some examples of comments follow:

```
//OOP Using C++: Addison-Wesley Program GCD

const int N = 200;        //N is number of trials

/*    *   *   *   *   *   *
    Programmer:    Laura M. Pohl
    Compiler:      Borland 5.0
    Modifications: 5-2-96    Stack Overflow
*    *   *   *   *   *   *   */
```

Except for lengthy multiline comments, the rest-of-line comment should be used. This style is easier to use and is less error prone.

C.2.2 Identifiers

An identifier can be one character or more. The first character must be a letter or underscore. Subsequent characters can be letters, digits, or underscores. Although in principle, identifiers can be arbitrarily long, many systems distinguish only up to the first 31 characters. Identifiers that contain a double underscore or that begin with an underscore followed by an uppercase letter are reserved for system use.

Identifier Examples			Comments
multiWord	vector	flag_x	normal style
q213	sb3	abx1w	opaque
speed	Speed	speedy	distinct but confusing
_Sys1	__Adriver	__C__	reserved for system use
9illegal	wrong-2	il$form	illegal
typeid	this	register	keywords can't be used

C.2.3 Keywords

Keywords are explicitly reserved identifiers that have a strict meaning in C++. They cannot be redefined or used in other contexts. Some other keywords are specific to implementations, such as `near` and `far` in Borland C++. The following keywords are in use in most current C++ systems.

Keywords			
asm	else	operator	throw
auto	enum	private	true
bool	explicit	protected	try
break	extern	public	typedef
case	false	register	typeid
catch	float	reinterpret_cast	typename
char	for	return	union
class	friend	short	unsigned
const	goto	signed	using
const_cast	if	sizeof	virtual
continue	inline	static	void
default	int	static_cast	volatile
delete	long	struct	wchar_t
do	mutable	switch	while
double	namespace	template	
dynamic_cast	new	this	

C.3 Constants

C++ has constants for each basic type. These include integer, floating-point, and character constants. String constants are character sequences surrounded by double quotes. There is one universal pointer constant, namely 0.

Constants Examples			Comments
156 0156 0x156			integer: dec, oct, hex
156l 156u			integer: long, unsigned
'A' 'a' '7' '\t'			character: A, a, 7, tab
3.14f 3.1415 3.14159L			floating-point constants
"A string."			string constant
true false			bool constants

The suffixes u or U, l or L, and f or F are used to indicate unsigned, long, and float, respectively. The unsigned constants are positive numbers. The long constants have greater range than normal. The float constants are usually less precise than ordinary double constants.

The character constants are usually given in single quotes: for example, 's'. Some nonprinting and special characters require an escape sequence.

Character Constants	
'\a'	alert
'\\'	backslash
'\b'	backspace
'\r'	carriage return
'\"'	double quote
'\f'	formfeed
'\t'	tab
'\n'	newline
'\0'	null character
'\''	single quote
'\v'	vertical tab
'\101'	octal 101 in ASCII 'A'
'\x041'	hexadecimal ASCII 'A'
L'oop'	wchar_t constant

Floating-point constants can be specified with or without signed integer exponents.

Floating-Point Constants Examples			Comments
3.14f	1.234F		narrow `float` constants
0.123456	.123456		`double` constants
0.12345678L	0.123456781		`long double` constants
3.	3.0	0.3E1	all express `double` 3.0
300e-2	.03e2	30e-1	also 3.0

A string constant is a contiguous array of characters. String constants are considered `static char[]` constants. String constants that are separated only by white space are implicitly concatenated into a single string. A backslash character at the end of the line indicates string continuation. A backslash preceding a double quote makes the double quote part of the string. The compiler places a null character at the end of a complete string as a sentinel, or termination, character.

String Constants Examples	Comments
`""`	empty string is '\0'
`"OOP 4ME"`	'O' 'O' 'P' ' ' '4' 'M' 'E' '\0'
`"my \"quote \" is escaped"`	\" used for embedding "
`"a multiline string \` `is also possible"`	\ at end of line indicates string continuation

`"This is a single string, "`
`"since it is only separated "`
`"by whitespace."`
	implicitly concatenated

Enumerations define a collection of named constants called enumerators. The constants are a list of identifiers that are implicitly consecutive integer values, starting with 0. They can be either anonymous or distinct types.

Enumeration Constants	Comments
enum { off, on };	off == 0, on == 1
enum color { red, blue, white, green };	color is a type
enum { BOTTOM = 50, TOP = 100, OVER };	OVER == 101
enum grades { F = 59, D = 60, C = 70, B = 80, A = 90 };	all initialized

Enumeration constants are promoted to type int in expressions.

The keyword const is used to declare that an object's value is constant throughout its scope.

Using the const Keyword	Comments
const int N = 100;	N can't change
double w[N];	[uses constant expressions]
const int bus_stops[5] = { 23, 44, 57, 59, 83 };	element values, bus_stops[i], are constant

C++ uses a preprocessor to handle a set of directives, such as the include directive, to convert the program from its preprocessing form to pure C++ syntax. These directives are introduced by the symbol #.

The use of const differs from the use of #define, as in

```
#define  N  100
```

In the case of the const int N declaration, N is a nonmodifiable lvalue of type int. In the case of the define macro, N is a constant. Also, the macro replacement of N occurs as a preprocessor substitution without regard to other scope rules.

C.4 Declarations and Scope Rules

Declarations associate meaning with a given identifier. The syntax of C++ declarations is highly complex, incorporating many disparate, context-dependent elements. A declaration provides an identifier with a type, a storage class, and a scope. (See Section 2.4.1, "Initialization," on page 33.) A simple declaration is often a definition as well. For a simple variable, this means that the object is created and, possibly, initialized. For a function, it means that the function body—that is, the brace-enclosed statements the function executes—are written out.

```
const int n = 17;      //n is declared and defined
int sqrt(double);      //sqrt is declared not defined
void foo()             //foo is declared and defined
{
   int  i = 5;         //i is defined and initialized
   . . . . .           //i is automatic and local to foo
}
```

Complex declarations, such as those for classes, functions, and templates, are described in separate sections of this appendix.

The typedef mechanism can be used to create a synonym for the type it defines.

Typedefs Examples	Comments
typedef int BOOLEAN;	used prior to bool type
typedef char* c_string;	c_string pointer to char
typedef void (*ptr_f)();	pointer to void fcn()

C++ has file scope, function scope, block scope, class scope, function prototype scope, and namespace scope. File scope, also known as global scope, extends from the point of declaration in a file to the end of that file. Function prototype scope, the scope of identifiers in the function prototype argument list, extends to the end of the declaration. Blocks nest in a conventional way, and functions cannot be declared inside other functions or blocks.

Declarations can occur almost anywhere in a block. A declaration can also be an initializer in a for statement. For a code example, see file *for_test.cpp* in Section 2.8.5, "The for Statement," on page 48.

Selection statements, such as the if or switch statement, cannot merely control a declaration. In general, jumps and selections cannot bypass an initialization. This is not true in C.

```
if (flag)
    int  j = 6;                    //illegal
else
    j = 19;

if (flag) {
    int  j = 6;                    //legal within block
    cout << j;
}
```

C++ has a scope resolution operator ::. When used in the form :: *variable*, it allows access to the named global variable. Other uses of this notation are important for classes and namespaces. Class member identifiers are local to that class. The scope resolution operator can be used to resolve ambiguities. When used in the form *class-name* :: *variable*, it accesses the named variable from that class.

```
class A {
public:
    static void  foo();
};

class B {
public:
    void  foo() { A :: foo();  ····· }
};
```

A hidden external name can be accessed by using the scope resolution operator.

```
int  i;                //external i
void foo(int i)        //parameter i
{
    i = ::i;           //parameter i is assigned external i
    ·····
}
```

Classes can be nested. C++ rules scope the inner class within the outer class. This is a source of confusion, since the rules have changed and differ from C rules. For a code example, see file *nested.cpp* in Section 4.6.2, "Nested Classes," on page 124.

Enumerations declared inside a class give the enumerator's class scope, as in

```
class foo {
public:
   enum  button { off, on } flag;
};

int main()
{
   foo  c;

   c.flag = foo::off;
   .....
}
```

C.5 Namespaces

C++ traditionally had a single, global namespace. Since inadvertent name clashes may occur when programs written by different people are combined, and since C++ encourages multivendor library use, namespace scope was added.

In file iostream

```
//encapsulating a file in namespace std

namespace std {   //turn iostream.h into iostream
   #include <iostream.h>
}
//fully scoped resolved name would be
std::cout << "hello world" << std::endl;

//add your corporate name to your code

namespace LMPinc {    //LMP toy company software
   class puzzles { ····· };
   class toys { ····· };
   .....
}
//fully scoped resolved name would now be
LMPinc::puzzles x, y, z;
```

In effect, encapsulated declarations are given a qualified name. The `using` declaration allows these names to be used without the namespace identifier.

```
using namespace std;
using namespace LMPinc;
toys  top;                          //LMPinc::toys
```

The namespace declaration, like the class declaration, can be used as part of a scope resolved identifier.

Namespaces can nest. For a code example, see file *namespac.cpp* in Section 3.10, "Namespaces," on page 81. Namespaces can be used to provide a unique scope similar in effect to the use of static global declarations. This is done with an unnamed namespace definition.

```
namespace { int count = 0; }        //count is unique here
//count is available in the rest of the file
void  chg_cnt(int i) { count = i; }
```

The new ANSI-conforming library headers will no longer use the *.h* suffix. Files, such as *iostream* or *complex*, will be declared with the `namespace std`. Vendors will no doubt continue shipping old-style headers, such as *iostream.h* or *complex.h* as well, so that old code can run without change.

Most C++ programs will now begin with `includes` of standard library headers followed by a `using` declaration.

```
#include <iostream>    //std::cout is fully qualified name
#include <vector>      //STL vector templates
#include <cstddef>     //Old C libraries
using namespace std;
```

C.6 Linkage Rules

Modern systems are built around multifile inclusion, compilation, and linkage. For C++, it is necessary to understand how multifile programs are combined. Linking separate modules requires resolving external references. The key rule is that external nonstatic variables must be defined in only one place. Use of the keyword `extern`, together with an initializer, constitutes defining a variable. Using the keyword `extern` without an initializer constitutes a declaration but not a definition. If the keyword `extern` is omitted, the resulting declaration is a definition, with or without an initializer. The following example, in which these files would all be linked, illustrates these rules:

In file prog1.cpp

```
    char  c;              //definition of c
    .....
```

In file prog2.cpp

```
    extern char  c;       //declaration of c
    .....
```

In file prog3.cpp

```
    extern int  n = 5;    //definition of n
    .....
```

In file prog4.cpp

```
    char         c;       //illegal second definition
    extern float n;       //illegal type mismatch
    extern int   k;       //illegal no definition
    .....
```

Constant definitions and inline definitions at file scope are local to that file; in other words, they are implicitly static. Constant definitions can be explicitly declared extern. It is usual to place them in a header file to be included with any code that needs them.

A typedef declaration is local to its file. An enumeration constant declaration has linkage internal to its file. Enumerators and typedefs that are needed in a multifile program should be placed in a header file. Enumerators defined within a class are local to that class, and access to them requires the scope resolution operator.

Typically, declarations are placed in header files and are used in code files.

```
//LMPstack.h
#ifndef LMP_stack          //avoid reinclusion
#define LMP_stack
namespace LMP {
class stack { ..... };
}
#endif

//LMPstack.cpp
#include <LMPstack.h>      //include file above as source
using namespace LMP;
```

C.7 Types

The fundamental types in C++ are integral and floating-point types. The `char` type is the shortest integral type. The `long double` is the longest floating-point type.

The following table lists these types from shortest to longest. Reading across the table, the leftmost, topmost element is shortest, and the rightmost, bottommost element is longest.

Fundamental Data Types		
bool		
char	signed char	unsigned char
wchar_t		
short	int	long
unsigned short	unsigned	unsigned long
float	double	long double

Two of these data types, `bool` and `wchar_t`, were added by the ANSI committee.

The type `wchar_t` is intended for character sets that require characters not representable by `char`, such as the Japanese Kana alphabet. Literals of this type are wide character constants. This type is an integral type and in mixed expression follows the same rules for integral promotion.

The type `bool` is a break with C tradition. Over the years, many schemes have been used to achieve a Boolean type, and the new `bool` type removes these inconsistencies in practice. It is also an integral type. It becomes the type returned by relational, logical, and equality expressions. The `bool` constants `true` and `false` are promotable to 1 and 0, respectively. Nonzero values are assignment convertible to `true`, and 0 is assignment convertible to `false`. It is anticipated that as compiler vendors add this type, they will provide switches or options that allow the old practice of not using `bool`.

Types can be derived from the basic types. A simple derived type is the enumeration type. The derived types allow pointer types, array types, and structure types. A generic pointer type `void*` is allowed. Both anonymous unions and anonymous enumerations are allowed, and there is also a reference type. An anonymous union can have only nonstatic public data members. A file scope anonymous union has to be declared `static`. The `class` and `struct` types are structure types. Union, enumeration, and structure names are type names.

Types	Comments
`void*    gen_ptr;`	a generic pointer
`int      i, &ref_i = i;`	ref_i is an alias for i
`enum     button { off, on };`	enumeration
`button   flag;`	button is now a type name
`wchar_t  w = L'yz';`	new wide character type
`bool mine = false, yours = true;` `bool* p = &my_turn;`	new boolean type
`button   set[10];`	array

`class card {`
`public:`
`    suit  s;`
`    pips  p;`
`    void  pr_card();`
`private:`
`    int cd;`
`};`
	user-defined type
	
	public data member
	
	member function
	
	private data member

`suit card::* ptr_s = &card::s;`	pointer to member

There are five storage class keywords, as shown in the following table:

Storage Class Keywords	
`auto`	local to blocks and implicit
`register`	optimization advice and automatic
`extern`	global scope
`static`	within blocks, value retained
`typedef`	creates synonyms for types

The keyword `auto` can be used within blocks, but it is redundant and is normally omitted. Automatic variables are created at block entry and are destroyed at block exit. The keyword `register` can be used within blocks and for function parameters. It advises the compiler that for optimization purposes, the program wants a variable to reside in a high-speed register. The behavior of register variables is semantically equivalent to that of automatic variables.

The keyword `extern` can be used within blocks and at file scope. This keyword indicates that a variable is linked in from elsewhere. The keyword `static` can be used within blocks and at file scope. Inside a block, `extern` indicates that a variable's value is retained after block exit. At file scope, it indicates that declarations have internal linkage.

There are two special type-specifier keywords.

```
const               //nonmodifiable
volatile            //suppresses compiler optimization
```

The keyword `const` is used to indicate that a variable or a function parameter has a nonmodifiable value. The keyword `volatile` implies that an agent undetectable to the compiler can change the variable's value; therefore, the compiler cannot readily perform optimizations on code accessing this variable. Variables getting values from external agents would be `volatile`.

```
volatile const gmt;     //expect external time signal
```

C.8 Conversion Rules and Casts

C++ has both explicit conversions, called casts, and implicit conversions. The implicit conversions can occur in expressions, as well as in passing in arguments and returning expressions from functions. Many conversions are implicit, which makes C++ convenient but potentially dangerous for the novice. Implicit conversions can induce runtime bugs that are difficult to detect.

The general rules are straightforward.

Automatic Expression Conversion

1. Any `char`, `wchar_t`, `short`, `bool`, or `enum` is promoted to an `int`. Integral types unrepresentable as `int` are promoted to `unsigned`.

2. If, after the first step, the expression is of mixed type, then, according to the hierarchy of types,

```
int < unsigned < long < unsigned long
    < float < double < long double
```

the operand of lower type is promoted to that of the higher type, and the value of the expression has that type. Note that if `long` cannot contain all the values of `unsigned`, `unsigned` is promoted to `unsigned long`.

The new type `bool` is an integral type, with the `bool` constant `true` promoted to 1, and the `bool` constant `false` promoted to 0.

Implicit pointer conversions also occur in C++. Any pointer type can be converted to the generic pointer of type `void*`. However, unlike in ANSI C, a generic pointer is not assignment compatible with an arbitrary pointer type. This means that C++ requires that generic pointers be cast to an explicit type for assignment to a nongeneric pointer variable.

```
char*  mem;
void*  gen_p;

gen_p = mem;                          //C and C++
mem   = (char*)gen_p;                 //C and (obsolete) C++
mem   = static_cast<char*>(gen_p);    //C++
mem   = gen_p;                        //legal C and illegal C++
```

The name of an array is a pointer to its base element. The null-pointer constant can be converted to any pointer type.

```
char*  p = 0;                 //p is a null pointer
int*   x = p;                 //illegal need static_cast
int*   y = 0;                 //legal
```

A pointer to a class can be converted to a pointer to a publicly derived base class. This also applies to references.

In addition to implicit conversions, which can occur across assignments and in mixed expressions, there are explicit conversions, or casts. If `i` is an `int`, the expression `static_cast<double>(i)` will cast the value of `i` so that the expression has type `double`. The variable i itself remains unchanged. The `static_cast` is available for a conversion that is portable, well defined, and invertible. Some more examples are

```
static_cast<char>('A' + 1.0)
x = static_cast<double>(static_cast<int>(y) + 1)
```

Casts that are representation or system dependent use `reinterpret_cast`.

```
int i = reinterpret_cast<int>(&x)     //system dependent
```

System-dependent casts are undesirable and generally should be avoided.

Two other special casts exist in C++: `const_cast` and `dynamic_cast`. A useful discussion of `dynamic_cast` requires understanding inheritance (see Section C.13.5, "Runtime Type Identification," on page 398). The `const` modifier means that a variable's value is nonmodifiable. Very occasionally, it is convenient to remove this restriction. Known as casting away constness, this is done with the const_cast, as in

```
foo(const_cast<int>(c_var));     //used to invoke foo
```

Older C++ systems allow the following unrestricted forms of cast:

(type) expression   or   *type(expression)*

Some examples are

```
y = i/double(7);                 //would do division in double
ptr = (char*)(i + 88);           //int to pointer value
```

These older forms are considered obsolete and are not used in this text, but many older compilers and older source code still use them. The older casts do not differentiate among relatively safe casts, such as static_cast, and system-dependent unsafe casts, such as reinterpret_cast. The newer casts are self-documenting as well; for example, a const_cast suggests its intent through its name.

```
enum  peer { king, prince, earl } a;
enum  animal { horse, frog, snake } b;
. . . . .
a = static_cast<peer>(frog);
```

These new casts are safer and can replace all existing cast expressions. Still, casting should be avoided, as turning a frog into a prince is rarely a good idea.

Casts	Comments
x = float(i);	C++ functional notation
x = (float) i;	C cast notation
x = static_cast<float>(i);	ANSI C++
static_cast<char>('A' + 1.0)	ANSI C++
i = reinterpret_cast<int>(&x)	ANSI C++ system dependent
foo(const_cast<int>(c_var));	used to invoke foo() while casting away constness

A constructor of one argument is a de facto type conversion from the argument's type to the constructor's class type unless preceded by the keyword `explicit`. (See Section 5.1.3, "Constructors as Conversions," on page 152.) Consider the following example of a `my_string` constructor:

```
my_string::my_string(const char* p)
{
    len = strlen(p);
    s = new char[len + 1];
    assert (s != 0);
    strcpy(s, p);
}
```

This is automatically a type transfer from `char*` to `my_string`. These conversions are from an already defined type to a user-defined type. However, it is not possible for the user to add a constructor to a built-in type—for example, to `int` or to `double`. In the `my_string` example, you may also want a conversion from `my_string` to `char*`. You can do this by defining a special conversion function inside the `my_string` class, as follows.

```
operator char*() { return s; }       //char* s is a member
```

The general form of such a member function is

```
operator type()   { · · · · · }
```

These conversions occur implicitly in assignment expressions and in argument and return conversions from functions. Hidden temporaries can be created by the compiler to perform these operations and can affect execution speeds.

In systems implementing the `bool` type, implicit conversion to `bool` is required for expressions controlling the `if` or the `while` statement and for the first operand of the ternary `?:` operator. The obvious conversion of 0 to `false` and nonzero to `true` occurs.

C.9 Expressions and Operators

C++ is an operator-rich, expression-oriented language. The operators have 17 precedence levels. Operators can also have side effects. See Appendix B, "Operator Precedence and Associativity," on page 345 for the complete table of operator precedence and associativity.

C.9.1 `sizeof` Expressions

The `sizeof` operator can be applied to an expression or a parenthesized type name. This operator gives the size in bytes of the type to which it is applied. Its results are system dependent.

Declarations	
`int  a, b[10];`	
Expression	**Value on gnu C++ Running on a DECstation**
`sizeof(a)`	4
`sizeof(b)`	40 the array storage
`sizeof(b[1])`	4
`sizeof(5)`	4
`sizeof(5.5L)`	8

C.9.2 Autoincrement and Autodecrement Expressions

C++ provides autoincrement (++) and autodecrement (--) operators in both prefix and postfix form. The postfix form behaves differently from the prefix form by changing the affected lvalue after the rest of the expression is evaluated.

Autoincrement and Autodecrement	Equivalent Expression
`j = ++i;`	`i = i + 1; j = i;`
`j = i++;`	`j = i; i = i + 1;`
`j = --i;`	`i = i - 1; j = i;`
`j = i--;`	`j = i; i = i - 1;`

C.9.3 Arithmetic Expressions

Arithmetic expressions are consistent with expected practice. The following examples are grouped by precedence, highest first.

Arithmetic Expressions	Comments
-i +w	unary minus unary plus
a * b a / b i % 5	multiply divide modulus
a + b a - b	binary addition subtraction
a = 3 / 2.0;	a is assigned 1.5
a = 3 / 2;	a is assigned 1

The modulus operator % is the remainder from the division of the first argument by the second argument. The operator may be used only with integer types. Arithmetic expressions depend on the conversion rules given earlier. (See Section 5.1.3, "Constructors as Conversions," on page 152.) In the preceding table, see how the result of the division operator / depends on its argument types.

C.9.4 Relational, Equality, and Logical Expressions

This discussion is based on ANSI C++ adopting a bool type with constants false and true. Prior to the introduction of the bool type, the values 0 and nonzero were thought of as false and true and were used to affect the flow of control in various statement types. The following table contains the C++ operators that are most often used to affect flow of control.

Relational, Equality, and Logical Operators		
Relational operators	less than	<
	greater than	>
	less than or equal to	<=
	greater than or equal to	>=
Equality operators	equal	==
	not equal	!=
Logical operators	(unary) negation	!
	logical and	&&
	logical or	||

The negation operator ! is unary. All of the other relational, equality, and logical operators are binary. They operate on expressions and yield either `true` or `false`. Logical negation can be applied to an arbitrary expression, which is then converted to `bool`. When negation is applied to a `true` value, it results in `false`; when negation is applied to a `false` value, it results in `true`.

In the evaluation of expressions that are the operands of && and ||, the evaluation process stops as soon as the outcome `true` or `false` is known. This is called short-circuit evaluation. For example, suppose that *expr1* and *expr2* are expressions. If *expr1* has `false` value, *expr2* in

  expr1 && *expr2*

will not be evaluated, because the value of the logical expression is already determined to be `false`. Similarly, if *expr1* has `true` value, *expr2* in

  expr1 || *expr2*

will not be evaluated, because the value of the logical expression is already determined to be `true`.

On systems that do not implement the `bool` type, these expressions will evaluate to 1 and 0 instead of `true` and `false`.

Declarations and Initialization		
`int a = -5, b = 3, c = 0;`		
Expression	**Equivalent**	**Value**
`a + 5 && b`	`((a + 5) && b)`	`false or 0`
`!(a < b) && c`	`((!(a < b)) && c)`	`false or 0`
`1 || (a != 7)`	`(1 || (a != 7))`	`true or 1`

Note that the last expression always short-circuits to value `true`.

C.9.5 Assignment Expressions

In C++, assignment occurs as part of an assignment expression. The effect is to evaluate the right-hand side of the assignment and to convert it to a value compatible with the variable on the left-hand side. Assignment conversions occur implicitly and include narrowing conversions; simple variables are lvalues.

C++ allows multiple assignments in a single statement. Thus,

```
a = b + (c = 3);      is equivalent to      c = 3; a = b + c;
```

C++ provides assignment operators that combine an assignment and some other operator.

```
a op= b;          is equivalent to      a = a op b
```

Declarations and Initialization	
`int     a, i, *p = &i;` `double  w, *q = &w;`	
Assignment Expressions	**Comments**
`a = i + 1;`	assigns (`i + 1`) to `a`
`i = w;`	legal w value converted to `int`
`*q = i;`	legal integer value promoted to `double`
`*q = *p;`	legal
`q = p;`	illegal conversion between pointer types
`q = (double*)p;`	legal
`a *= a + b;`	equivalent to `a = a * (a + b);`
`a += b;`	equivalent to `a = a + b;`

C.9.6 Comma Expressions

The comma operator has the lowest precedence. It is a binary operator with expressions as operands. In a comma expression of the form

   expr1 , *expr2*

expr1 is evaluated first, then *expr2*. The comma expression as a whole has the value and type of its right operand. The comma operator is a control point. Therefore, each expression in the comma-separated list is evaluated completely before the next expression to its right. An example is

```
sum = 0, i = 1
```

If i has been declared an int, this comma expression has value 1 and type int. The comma operator associates from left to right.

C.9.7 Conditional Expressions

The conditional operator ?: is unusual in that it is a ternary operator. It takes as operands three expressions. In a construct such as

   expr1 ? *expr2* : *expr3*

expr1 is evaluated first. If it is true, *expr2* is evaluated, and its value is the value of the conditional expression as a whole. If *expr1* is false, *expr3* is evaluated, and its value is the value of the conditional expression as a whole. The following example uses a conditional operator to assign the smaller of two values to the variable x:

```
x = (y < z) ? y : z;
```

The parentheses are not necessary, because the conditional operator has precedence over the assignment operator. However, using parentheses is good style because they clarify what is being tested for.
   The type of the conditional expression

   expr1 ? *expr2* : *expr3*

is determined by *expr2* and *expr3*. If they are different types, the usual conversion rules apply. The conditional expression's type cannot depend on which of the two expressions is evaluated. The conditional operator ?: associates right to left.

C.9.8 Bit-Manipulation Expressions

C++ provides bit-manipulation operators. They operate on the machine-dependent bit representation of integral operands. It is customary that the shift operators be overloaded to perform I/O.

Bitwise Operators	Meaning
~	unary one's complement
<<	left shift
>>	right shift
&	and
^	exclusive or
|	or

C.9.9 Address and Indirection Expressions

The address operator & is a unary operator that yields the address, or location, where an object is stored. The indirection operator * is a unary operator that is applied to a value of type pointer. It retrieves the value from the location being pointed at. This is also known as *dereferencing*.

Declarations and Initialization	

`int   a = 5;`   `//declaration of a`
`int*  p = &a;`   `//p points to a`
`int&  ref_a = a;` `//alias for a`	

Expression	**Value**
`*p = 7;`	lvalue in effect a is assigned 7
`a = *p + 1;`	rvalue 7 added to 1 and a assigned 8

C.9.10 `new` and `delete` Expressions

The unary operators `new` and `delete` are available to manipulate free store, which is a system-provided memory pool for objects whose lifetime is directly managed by the programmer. Using `new` creates an object and using `delete` destroys it.

The `new` operator is used in the following simple forms:

new *type-name initializer*$_{opt}$
new *type-name*[*integer expression*]

The first form allocates an object of the specified type from free store. An initializing expression, if present, performs the initialization. The second form allocates an array of objects of the specified type from free store. A default initializer must be available for these objects.

The new Operator	Comments
new int	allocates an `int`
new char[100]	allocates an array of 100 `int`s
new int(99)	allocates an `int` initialized to 99
new char('c')	allocates a char initialized to c
new int[n][4]	allocates an array of pointers to `int`

In each case, there are at least two effects. First, an appropriate amount of store is allocated from free storage to contain the named type. Second, the base address of the object is returned as the value of the `new` expression. If `new` fails, either the null-pointer value 0 is returned, or the exception `bad_alloc` is thrown (see Section 9.9, "Standard Exceptions and Their Uses," on page 318). It is good practice to test for failure.

An initializer is a parenthesized list of arguments. For a simple type, such as an `int`, it would be a single expression. It cannot be used to initialize arrays, but it can be an argument list to an appropriate constructor. If the type being allocated has a constructor, the allocated object will be initialized.

The operator `delete` is used in the following forms:

delete *expression*
delete [ ] *expression*

In both forms, the expression is typically a pointer variable used in a previous `new` expression. The second form is used when returning storage that was allocated as an array type. The brackets indicate that a destructor should be called for each element of the array. The operator `delete` returns a value of type `void`.

The `delete` Operator	Comments
`delete ptr`	deletes the pointer to an object
`delete p[i]`	deletes object p[i]
`delete [] p`	deletes each object of type p

The operator `delete` destroys an object created by `new`, in effect returning its allocated storage to free store for reuse. If the type being deleted has a destructor, it will be called. There are no guarantees on what values will appear in objects allocated from free store. The programmer is responsible for properly initializing such objects. For a code example, see file *dynarray.cpp* in Section 3.20, "Free-Store Operators `new` and `delete`," on page 98.

Placement Syntax and Overloading

The operator `new` has the general form

> `::`$_{opt}$ `new` *placement*$_{opt}$ *type-name initializer*$_{opt}$

The global operator `new()` is typically used to allocate free store. The system provides a `sizeof(`*type*`)` argument to this function implicitly. Its function prototype is

```
void* operator new(size_t size);
```

The operator `new` can be overloaded at the global level by adding parameters and calling it, using placement syntax. THe operator can be overloaded and used to override the global versions at the class level. But when allocating an array of objects, only the default global `void* operator new(size_t size)` will be called.
   The `delete` operator also can be overloaded. The global version is

```
void operator delete(void* ptr)
```

A class-specific version can be declared as either of the following:

```
void operator delete(void* ptr)
void operator delete(void* ptr, size_t size)
```

However, only one of these forms can be used by any one class. When deallocating an array of objects, the global version will be called. This feature provides a simple mechanism for user-defined manipulation of free store. For example,

```
class X {
   . . . . .
public:
   void*  operator new(size_t size)
      { return (malloc(size)); }
   void   operator delete(void* ptr) { free(ptr); }
   X(unsigned size) { new(size); }
   ~X() { delete(this); }
   . . . . .
};
```

In this example, the class X provides overloaded forms of new() and delete(). When a class overloads operator new(), the global operator is still accessible, using the scope resolution operator ::. Note that the *stddef* library is required for *size_t* type, and malloc() is in the *stdlib* library.

The *placement* syntax provides for a comma-separated argument list that is used to select an overloaded operator new() with a matching signature. These additional arguments are often used to place the constructed object at a particular address. One form of this can be found in the *new* library.

Class new() and delete() member functions are always static. For a code example, see file *over_new.cpp* in Section 6.12, "Overloading new and delete," on page 221.

Error Conditions

In the absence of implemented exception handling, new returns a 0 value, indicating an allocation failure. The standard library *new* has the function set_new_handler(), which installs the function to be called when new fails. Calling this with value 0 means that a version of new that does not throw exceptions will be used. Otherwise, a bad_alloc exception will be thrown. The implementation of *new* can be system dependent.

C.9.11 Other Expressions

C++ considers *function call* () and *indexing* or *subscripting* [] to be operators. They have the same precedence as the member and structure pointer operators.

```
a[j + 6]           //means  *(a + j + 6)
sqrt(z + 15.5);    //returns a double
```

The global scope resolution operator is of highest precedence. The class scope resolution operator is used with a class name to qualify a local-to-class identifier.

```
::i                    //access global i
A::foo()               //invoke member foo() defined in A
```

C.10 Statements

C++ has a large variety of statement types and uses the semicolon as a statement terminator. Braces are used to enclose multiple statements and to treat them as a single unit. Statements are control points. Before a new statement is executed, the actions of the previous statements must be completed. Inside statements, the compiler has some liberty to pick which parts of subexpressions are evaluated first.

```
a = f(i);              //call f() and assign to a
a += g(j);             //call g() and add to a
a = f(i) + g(j);       //compiler decides calling order
```

C++ is a block-structured language in which declarations are often at the head of blocks. Unlike in C, declarations are statements and can be intermixed with other statements. Structured programming principles should still be followed when writing C++ code. Namely, the goto should be avoided, and care should be taken that the program's flow of control is easy to follow.

Because C++ has many possible side effects in expressions, care should be exercised in avoiding system-dependent effects. For example, the side effect operators autoincrement and autodecrement should be used sparingly in expressions where order-of-evaluation and possible compiler optimizations can lead to system dependencies.

In many cases, C++ statements are overly unrestrictive, and good programming discipline is required to avoid error-prone constructions. For example,

```
for (double x = 0.1; !(x == y); x += 0.1)
.....
```

is problematic because machine accuracy and round-off problems will in most cases cause a failure in the terminating condition.

The following table gives a summary of general C++ statements.

Statement	C++	Comments
empty	`;`	
expression	`i = i + k;`	assignment may use conversions
compound	`{ ·····` `}`	used for function definitions and structuring; same as block
`goto`	`goto l1;`	avoid
`if`	`if (p == 0)` `    cerr << "new error";`	one-branch conditional

if-else	`if (x == y)`
	`    cout << "same\n";`
	`else`
	`    cout << "unequal\n";`
		two-branch conditional

for	`for (i = 0; i < n; ++i)` `    a[i] = b[i] + c[i];`	declarations allowed in the first component
`while`	`while (x != y)`	zero or more iterations

do-while	`do`
	`    y = y - 1;`
	`while (y >= 0);`
		one or more iterations

switch	`switch (s) {`
	`case 1: ++i;   break;`
	`case 2: --i;   break;`
	`·····`
	`default: ++j;`
	`};`
		use `break` to avoid fall-through semantics and default as a last label

break	`break;`	used in `switch` and iteration
`continue`	`continue;`	used in iterations
declaration	`int i = 7;`	in a block, file, or namespace
try block	`try { ····· }`	see Section 9.4, "Try Blocks," on page 313
labeled	`error: cerr << "ERROR";`	target of goto
`return`	`return x * x * x;`	try for one `return` per function

C.10.1 Expression Statements

In C++, assignment occurs as part of an assignment expression. There is no assignment statement, since it is a form of expression statement.

```
a = b + 1;      //assign (b + 1) to a
++i;            //an expression statement
a + b;          //also a statement - but seemingly useless
```

C++ allows multiple assignments in a single statement.

```
a = b = c + 3;    is equivalent to    b = c + 3; a = b;
```

C.10.2 The Compound Statement

A compound statement in C++ is a series of statements surrounded by braces { }. The chief use of the compound statement is to group statements into an executable unit. The body of a C++ function is always a compound statement. In C, when declarations come at the beginning of a compound statement, the statement is called a block. This rule is relaxed in C++, and declaration statements may occur throughout the statement list. Wherever it is possible to place a statement, it is also possible to place a compound statement.

C.10.3 The `if` and `if-else` Statements

The general form of an `if` statement is

```
if (condition)
    statement
```

If *condition* is `true`, *statement* is executed; otherwise, it is skipped. After the `if` statement has been executed, control passes to the next statement. A condition is an expression or a declaration with initialization that selects flow of control. For a code example, see file *if_test.cpp* in Section 2.8.3, "The `if` and `if-else` Statements," on page 45.

The `if-else` statement has the general form

```
if (condition)
    statement1
else
    statement2
```

If *condition* is `true`, *statement1* is executed, and *statement2* is skipped; if *condition* is `false`, *statement1* is skipped, and *statement2* is executed. After the `if-else` statement has been executed, control passes to the next statement. Note that an `else` statement associates with its nearest `if`; this rule prevents the ambiguity of a dangling `else`. For a code example, see file *if_test.cpp* in Section 2.8.3, "The `if` and `if-else` Statements," on page 46.

C.10.4 The `while` Statement

The general form of a `while` statement is

```
while (condition)
    statement
```

First, *condition* is evaluated. If it is `true`, *statement* is executed, and control passes back to the beginning of the `while` loop. The effect of this is that the body of the `while` loop, namely, *statement*, is executed repeatedly until *condition* is `false`. At that point, control passes to the next statement. The effect of this is that *statement* can be executed zero or more times. For a code example, see file *while_t.cpp* in Section 2.8.4, "The `while` Statement," on page 47.

C.10.5 The `for` Statement

The general form of a `for` statement is

```
for (for-init-statement; condition; expression)
    statement
next statement
```

First, the *for-init-statement* is evaluated and is used to initialize a variable in the loop. Then *condition* is evaluated. If it is true, *statement* is executed, *expression* is evaluated, and control passes back to the beginning of the `for` loop, except that evaluation of *for-init-statement* is skipped. This iteration continues until *condition* is `false`, at which point control passes to *next statement*.

The *for-init-statement* can be an expression statement or a simple declaration. Where it is a declaration, the declared variable has the scope of the `for` statement. Note that this scope rule has changed from the previous rule, which gave such declarations scope outside the enclosing `for` statement.

The `for` statement is iterative and is typically used with a variable that is incremented or decremented. For a code example, see file *for_test.cpp* in Section 2.8.5, "The `for` Statement," on page 48.

The comma expressions can be used to initialize more than one variable.

```
for (factorial = n, i = n - 1; i >= 1; --i)
    factorial *= i;
```

Any or all of the expressions in a `for` statement can be missing, but the two semicolons must remain. If *for-init-statement* is missing, no initialization step is performed as part of the `for` loop. If *expression* is missing, no incrementation step is performed as part of the `for` loop. If *condition* is missing, no testing step is performed as part of the `for` loop. The special rule for when *condition* is missing is that the test is always `true`. Thus, the `for` loop in the code

```
for (i = 1, sum = 0 ; ; sum += i++)
    cout << sum << endl;
```

is an infinite loop.

The `for` statement is one common case in which a local declaration is used to provide the loop control variable, as in

```
for (int i = 0; i < N; ++i)
    sum += a[i];               //sum array a[0] + ... + a[N - 1]
```

The semantics are that the `int` variable `i` is local to the given loop. In earlier C++ systems, it was considered declared within the surrounding block. This can be confusing, and so it is reasonable to declare all automatic program variables at the heads of blocks.

C.10.6 The do Statement

The general form of a do statement is

```
do
    statement
while (condition);
next statement
```

First, *statement* is executed and then *condition* is evaluated. If it is `true`, control passes back to the beginning of the do statement, and the process repeats itself. When the value of *condition* is `false`, control passes to *next statement*. For a code example, see file *do_test.cpp* in Section 2.8.6, "The do Statement," on page 49.

C.10.7 The **break** and **continue** Statements

To interrupt the normal flow of control within a loop, the programmer can use the two special statements break and continue.The break statement, in addition to its use in loops, can be used in a switch statement. It causes an exit from the inner-most enclosing loop or switch statement.

The following example illustrates the use of a break statement. A test for a negative value is made; if it is true, the break statement causes the for loop to be exited. Program control jumps to the statement immediately following the loop. For a code example, see file *for_test.cpp* in Section 2.8.7, "The break and continue Statements," on page 50.

The continue statement causes the current iteration of a loop to stop and the next iteration of the loop to begin immediately. For a code example, see file *for_test.cpp* in Section 2.8.7, "The break and continue Statements," on page 50.

A break statement can occur only inside the body of a for, while, do, or switch statement. The continue statement can occur only inside the body of a for, while, or do statement.

C.10.8 The **switch** Statement

The switch statement is a multiway conditional statement generalizing the if-else statement. Its general form is

```
switch (condition)
    statement
```

where *statement* is typically a compound statement containing case labels and optionally a default label. Typically, a switch is composed of many cases, and the condition in parentheses following the keyword switch determines which, if any, of the cases are executed.

A case label is of the form

```
case constant integral expression:
```

In a switch statement, all case labels must be unique.

If no case label is selected, control passes to the default label, if there is one. No default label is required. If no case label is selected and if there is no default label, the switch statement is exited. The keywords case and default cannot occur outside a switch. For a code example, see file *switch_t.cpp* in Section 2.8.8, "The switch Statement," on page 51.

The Effect of a switch Statement

1. Evaluate the integral expression in the parentheses following switch.

2. Execute the case label having a constant value that matches that of the expression found in step 1. If no match is found, execute the default label; if there is no default label, terminate the switch.

3. Terminate the switch when a break statement is encountered or by "falling off the end."

A switch cannot bypass initialization of a variable unless the entire scope of the variable is bypassed.

```
switch (k) {
case 1:
   int   very_bad = 3; break;
case 2:                       //illegal: bypasses init of very_bad
   . . . . .
}

switch (k) {
case 1:
   {
      int  d = 3; break;
   }
case 2:                       //legal: bypasses scope of d
   . . . . .
}
```

C.10.9 The goto Statement

The goto statement is an unconditional branch to an arbitrary labeled statement in the function. It is considered a harmful construct in most accounts of modern programming methodology.

A label is an identifier. By executing a goto statement of the form

```
goto label;
```

control is unconditionally transferred to a labeled statement. Both the goto statement and its corresponding labeled statement must be in the body of the same function. For a code example, see file *goto_tst.cpp* in Section 2.8.9, "The goto Statement," on page 52.

A goto cannot bypass initialization of a variable unless the entire scope of the variable is bypassed.

```
if (i < j)
    goto max;        //illegal: bypasses init

int  crazy = 5;

max:
```

C.10.10 The return Statement

The `return` statement is used for two purposes. When it is executed, program control is immediately passed back to the calling environment. In addition, if an expression follows the keyword `return`, the value of the expression is returned to the calling environment as well. This value must be assignment convertible to the return type of the function-definition header.

A `return` statement has one of the following two forms:

```
return;
return expression;
```

Some examples are

```
return;
return 3;
return (a + b);
```

C.10.11 The Declaration Statement

The declaration statement can be placed nearly anywhere in a block. This lifts the C restriction that variable declarations are placed at the head of a block before executable statements. A declaration statement has the form

> *type variable-name;*

Normal block-structure rules apply to a variable so declared. Two examples are

```
for (int i = 0; i < N; ++i) {   //typical for loop
    a[i] = b[i] * c[i];
    int  k = a[i];               //k local - possibly inefficient
}
```

C++ imposes natural restrictions on transferring into blocks passed where declarations occur. These are disallowed, as are declarations that would occur in only one branch of a conditional statement.

C.11 Functions

Special features include the use of function prototypes, overloading, default arguments, and the effects of the keywords `inline`, `friend`, and `virtual`. This section restricts its discussion to basic functions, overloading, call-by-value, default arguments, and inlining. Member functions are discussed in Section C.12.2, "Member Functions," on page 389; friend functions in Section C.12.3, "Friend Functions," on page 389; and virtual functions in Section C.13.6, "Virtual Functions," on page 399. Generic functions are discussed throughout Appendix E, "STL and String Libraries."

In C++, function parameters are call-by-value unless they are declared as reference types.

Function Declaration	C++	Comments

function	```double cube(double x)```
	```{```
	   ```return x * x * x;```
	```}```
		parameters are call-by-value; return expression must be assignment compatible with return type

pure procedure	```void pr_int_sq(int i)```
	```{```
	   ```cout << i*i << endl;```
	```}```
		void return type denotes a pure procedure

empty argument list	```void pr_hi()```
	```{```
	   ```cout << "HI" << endl;```
	```}```
		can also be void pr_hi(void)

reference argument	```void```
	```swap(int& i, int& j)```
	```{```
	   ```int t = i;```
	   ```i = j; j = t;```
	```}```
		if invoked as swap(r, s), r and s exchange values

variable	```int``` ```scanf(const char*,...);```	matches any number of arguments

Function Declaration	C++	Comments
inline	`inline cube(int x);`	inline code
default argument	`int power(int x, int n = 2);`	power(4) yields 16 power(4, 3) yields 64
overload	`double power(double x, int n);`	signature is double, int

C.11.1 Prototypes

In C++, the prototype form is

   type name(*argument-declaration-list*) ;

Examples are

```
double sqrt(double x);                      //in math.h
double stats(const double data[], int size,
             double& max, double& min );
void print(const char* s);
int  printf(char* format, ...);             //in stdio.h
```

Prototypes make C++ functions type safe. When functions are called, the arguments are assignment converted to the formal arguments type. With the preceding `sqrt()` prototype definition, invoking `sqrt()` guarantees that, if feasible, an argument will be converted to type `double`. When variable-length argument lists are needed, the ellipsis symbol . . . is used.

C.11.2 Call-by-Reference

Reference declarations allow C++ to have call-by-reference arguments. Let us use this mechanism to write a function, `greater()`, that exchanges two values if the first is greater than the second.

```
int greater(int& a, int& b)
```

Now, if `i` and `j` are `int` variables,

```
greater(i, j)
```

will use the references to i and j to exchange, if necessary, their two values. In traditional C, this operation must be accomplished by using pointers and dereferencing. For a code example, see file *order1.cpp* in Section 3.11.2, "Pointer-Based Call-by-Reference," on page 83.

C.11.3 Inline Functions

The keyword inline suggests to the compiler that the function be converted to inline code. This keyword is used for the sake of efficiency, generally with short functions. It is implicit for member functions that are defined within their classes. A compiler can ignore this directive for a variety of reasons, including that the function is too long. In such cases, the inline function is compiled as an ordinary function. An example is

```
inline float circum(float rad) { return (pi * 2 * rad); }
```

Inline functions have internal linkage.

C.11.4 Default Arguments

A formal parameter can be given a default argument but only with contiguous formal parameters that are rightmost in the parameter list. A default value is usually an appropriate constant that occurs frequently when the function is called. The following function illustrates this point.

```
r_sqrd = pow(r);                    //return r*r
r_5th = pow(r, 5);                  //return r*r*r*r*r
```

For a code example, see file *powers.cpp* in Section 3.5, "Default Arguments," on page 70.

C.11.5 Overloading

Overloading is using the same name for multiple meanings of an operator or a function. The meaning selected depends on the types of the arguments used by the operator or function.

Consider a function that averages the values in an array of double versus one that averages the values in an array of int. Both are conveniently named avg_arr, as shown in the following program.

```
double avg_arr(const int a[], int size)
double avg_arr(const double a[], int size)
```

The function argument type list is called its *signature*. The return type is not a part of the signature, but the order of the arguments is crucial. For a code example, see file *avg_arr.cpp* in Section 3.7, "Overloading Functions," on page 72.

Consider the following overloaded declarations:

```
void  print(int i = 0);          //signature is int
void  print(int i, double x);    //int, double
void  print(double y, int i);    //double,int
```

When the print() function is invoked, the compiler matches the actual arguments to the various signatures and picks the best match. In general, there are three possibilities: a best match, an ambiguous match, and no match. Without a best match, the compiler issues an appropriate syntax error.

```
print('A');        //converts and matches int
print(str[]);      //no match, wrong type
print(15, 9);      //ambiguous
print(15, 9.0);    //matches int, double
print();           //matches int by default
```

The signature-matching algorithm has two parts. The first part determines a best match for each argument, and the second sees whether one function is a uniquely best match in each argument. This uniquely best match is defined as being a best match on at least one argument and a "tied-for-best" match on all other arguments.

For a given argument, a best match is always an exact match. An exact match also includes an argument with an outermost const or volatile. Thus,

```
void print(int i);
void print(const int& i);
```

is a redefinition error.

Whichever overloaded function is to be invoked, the invocation argument list must be matched to the declaration parameter list according to the function-selection algorithm.

Overloaded Function Selection Algorithm

1. Use an exact match if found.

2. Try standard type promotions.

3. Try standard type conversions.

4. Try user-defined conversions.

5. Use a match-to-ellipsis, if found.

Standard promotions are better than other standard conversions. These are conversions from `float` to `double` and from `char`, `short`, or `enum` to `int`. Standard conversions also include pointer conversions.

An exact match is clearly best. Casts can be used to force such a match. The compiler will complain about ambiguous situations.

C.11.6 Type-Safe Linkage for Functions

Linkage rules for non-C++ functions can be specified by using a linkage specification. Some examples are

```
extern "C" atoi(const char* nptr);   //C linkage

extern "C" {                         //C linkage all functions
#include  <stdio.h>
}
```

This specification is at file scope, with C and C++ always supported. It is system dependent if type-safe linkage for other languages is provided. Of a set of overloaded functions with the same number, one at most can be declared to have other than C++ linkage. Class member functions cannot be declared with a linkage specification.

C.12 Classes

Classes are forms of heterogeneous aggregate types and allow data hiding, inheritance, and member functions as a mechanism to provide user-defined types. An example is

```
//An implementation of a safe array type dbl_vect

class dbl_vect {
public:
    explicit dbl_vect(int n = 10);          //default constructor
    dbl_vect(const dbl_vect& v);            //copy constructor
    dbl_vect(const double a[], int n);      //init by array
    ~dbl_vect() { delete [] p; }            //destructor
    int  ub() const;                        //upper bound
    int& operator[](int i) const;           //indexing
    dbl_vect& operator=(const dbl_vect& v);   //assignment
    friend ostream& operator<<(ostream& out, const dbl_vect& v)
private:
    double  *p;                             //base pointer
    int  size;                              //number of elements
};
```

The keywords `public`, `private`, and `protected` indicate the access of members that follow. The default for `class` is `private`; for `struct`, `public`. In the preceding example, the data members p and `size` are `private`. This makes them accessible solely to member functions of the same class. For a code example, see file *ch_stac1.h* in Section 4.12, "A Container Class Example: ch_stack," on page 137.

C.12.1 Constructors and Destructors

A constructor, a member function whose name is the same as the class name, constructs objects of the class type. This involves initialization of data members and also frequently involves free-store allocation using `new`. If a class has a constructor with a `void` argument list, or a list whose arguments all have defaults, the class can be a base type of an array declaration, where initialization is not explicit. Such a constructor is called the default constructor.

```
dbl_vect::dbl_vect() { ····· }           //default constructor

dbl_vect::dbl_vect(int i = 0) { ····· }    //default constructor
```

A destructor is a member function whose name is the class name preceded by the tilde character ~. Its usual purpose is to destroy values of the class type. This is typically accomplished by using `delete`.

A constructor of the form

> *type::type*(`const` *type*`& x`)

is used to copy one *type* value into another, according to whether a type variable is initialized by a type value, a type value is passed as an argument in a function, or a type value is returned from a function. This is called the copy constructor; if not explicitly implemented, it is compiler generated. The default is member-by-member initialization of value.

Classes with default constructors can have a derived array type. For example, the `dbl_vect   a[5]` declaration uses the empty argument constructor to create an array a of five objects, each of which is a size 10 `dbl_vect`.

A special syntax exists for initializing subelements of objects with constructors. Initializers for structure and class members can be specified in a comma-separated list that follows the constructor parameter list and precedes the code body. An initializer's form is

> *member name* (*expression list*)

For example,

```
foo::foo(int* t):i(7), x(9.8), z(t)      //initializer list
{ //other executable follows here ····· }
```

When members are themselves classes with constructors, the expression list is matched to the appropriate constructor signature to invoke the correct overloaded constructor. It is not always possible to assign values to members in the body of the constructor. An initializer list is required when a nonstatic member is either a `const` or a reference. In the class `dbl_vect` example in the next section, the constructors use an initializer for the member `dbl_vect::size`.

Constructors cannot be virtual, although destructors can. Neither is inherited.

Constructors of a single parameter are automatically conversion functions. Consider the following class, whose purpose is to print nonvisible characters with their ASCII designations; for example, the code 07 (octal) is `alarm` or `bel`. The automatic creation of a conversion constructor from a single-parameter constructor can be disabled by using the keyword `explicit` to preface a single-argument constructor. For a code example, see file *string2.cpp* in Section 5.10, "Strings Using Reference Semantics," on page 181.

C.12.2 Member Functions

Member functions are functions declared within a class. As a consequence, they have access to private, protected, and public members of that class. If defined inside the class, they are treated as inline functions and are also treated, when necessary, as overloaded functions. In the class dbl_vect, the member function

```
int  ub() const { return (size - 1); }    //upper bound
```

is defined. In this example, the member function ub is inline, and it has access to the private member size.

Member functions are invoked normally by use of the . or -> operators, as in

```
dbl_vect   a(20), b;         //invoke appropriate constructor
dbl_vect*  ptr_v = &b;
int    uba = a.ub();         //invoke member ub
ubb = ptr_v -> ub();         //invoke member ub
```

Overloaded operator member functions, a special case of member functions, are discussed in Section C.11.5, "Overloading," on page 384.

C.12.3 Friend Functions

The keyword friend, a function specifier, allows a nonmember function access to the hidden members of the class of which it is a friend. A friend function must be declared inside the class declaration of which it is a friend. It is prefaced by the keyword friend and can appear anywhere in the class. Member functions of one class can be friend functions of another class. In this case, the member function is declared in the friend's class, using the scope resolution operator to qualify its function name. If all member functions of one class are friend functions of a second class, this can be specified by writing friend class classname.

The following declarations are typical:

```
class tweedledum {
   .....
   friend int  tweedledee::cheshire();
};

class node {
   .....
   friend class tree;
    //tree member functions have access to node
};
```

```
class complex {
    .....
    friend complex operator+(complex);
};                                        .
```

C.12.4 The this Pointer

The keyword this denotes an implicitly declared self-referential pointer that can be used only in a nonstatic member function. The this keyword provides for a built-in, self-referential pointer. It is as if clock implicitly declared the private member clock* const this. Early C++ systems allowed memory management for objects to be controlled by assignment to the this pointer. Such code is obsolete because the this pointer is nonmodifiable. For a code example, see file *clock.cpp* in Section 6.5, "Unary Operator Overloading," on page 205.

C.12.5 Operator Overloading

Operator overloading is a special case of function overloading. The keyword operator is used. Just as a function, such as print(), can be given a variety of meanings, depending on its arguments, so can an operator, such as +, be given additional meanings. This allows infix expressions of both user and built-in types to be written. The precedence and associativity remain fixed.

Operator overloading typically uses either member or friend functions, because both have privileged access. Overloading a unary operator using a member function has an empty argument list, because the single-operator argument is the implicit argument. For binary operators, member function operator overloading has, as its first argument, the implicitly passed class variable and, as its second argument, the lone argument-list parameter. Friend functions and ordinary functions have both arguments specified in the parameter list.

We expand the dbl_vect class from Section 6.7, "Overloading Assignment and Subscripting Operators," on page 210, to have overloaded operators for addition, assignment, subscripting, and output.

```
//Implementation of a safe array type dbl_vect

class dbl_vect {
public:
    .....
    int&  operator[](int i) const;
    dbl_vect&  operator=(const dbl_vect& v);
    friend dbl_vect  operator+(const dbl_vect&, const dbl_vect&);
    friend ostream&  operator<<(ostream& , const dbl_vect&)
private:
    double  *p;              //base pointer
    int  size;               //number of elements
};
```

This class overloads the assignment and subscript operators as member functions. The overloaded operator<<() (put to) is made a friend of dbl_vect so that it may access the private members of dbl_vect. The overloaded operator<<() should always return type ostream so that multiple put to operations may be executed in a single expression. The overloaded binary plus operator is a friend so that conversion operations can be applied to both arguments. Note that the overloaded assignment operator checks for assignment to itself. For a code example, see file *dbl_vect2.h* in Section 6.7, "Overloading Assignment and Subscripting Operators," on page 210.

The ternary conditional operator ?:, the scope resolution operator ::, and the two member operators . and .* cannot be overloaded.

Overloaded postfix autoincrement and autodecrement can be distinguished by defining the postfix overloaded function as having a single unused integer argument, as in

```
class T {
public:
    //postfix ++ invoked as t.operator++(0);
    void  operator++(int);
    void  operator--(int);
};
```

There is no implied semantic relationship between the postfix and prefix forms.

C.12.6 `static` and `const` Member Functions

An ordinary member function invoked as

```
object.mem(i, j, k);
```

has an explicit argument list i, j, k and an implicit argument list that contains the members of `object`. The implicit arguments can be thought of as a list of arguments accessible through the `this` pointer. In contrast, a `static` member function cannot access any of the members using the `this` pointer. A `const` member function cannot modify its implicit arguments.

```
class X{
public:
    void print() const { cout << "i = " << i << endl; }
    static void change_x_score(int i){ x_score = i; }
private:
    static int x_score;
    int i;
};
```

A `const` member function, such as `print()`, is not allowed to modify member variables of its class, such as i. A static member function, such as `change_x_score()`, is not given access to the nonstatic data members, such as i.

For a code example, see file *salary.cpp* in Section 4.8, "`static` and `const` Members," on page 130.

C.12.7 Mutable

The keyword `mutable` allows data members of class variables that have been declared `const` to remain modifiable. This reduces the need to cast away constness. This relatively new feature is not implemented on all C++ compilers. For a code example, see file *mutable.cpp* in Section 4.8.1, "Mutable Members," on page 132.

C.13 Inheritance

Inheritance is the mechanism of deriving a new class from an old one. The existing class, called a base class, can be added to or altered to create a new derived class. A class can be derived from an existing class by using the form

> class *class-name*: (`public`|`protected`|`private`)*opt* *base-name*
> {
>   *member declarations*
> };

As usual, the keyword `class` can be replaced by the keyword `struct`, with the implication that members are by default public. The keywords `public`, `private`, and `protected` are available as access modifiers for class members. A public member is accessible throughout its scope. A private member is accessible to other member functions within its own class. A protected member is accessible to other member functions within its class and any class immediately derived from it. These access modifiers can be used within a class declaration in any order and with any frequency.

A derived class must have a constructor if its base class lacks a default constructor. Where the base class has constructors requiring arguments, the derived class explicitly invokes the base-class constructor in its initializing list. The form of such a constructor is

> *class-name*(*arg-list*) : *base-name**opt*   (*base-class-arg-list*)
> {
>   . . . . .
> };

The *base-class-arg-list* is used when invoking the appropriate base-class constructor and is executed before the body of the derived-class constructor is executed.

A publicly derived class is a subtype of its base class. A variable of the derived class can in many ways be treated as if it were the base-class type. A pointer whose type is pointer to base class can point to objects having the publicly derived class type. A reference to the derived class, when meaningful, may be implicitly converted to a reference to the public base class. It is possible to declare a reference to a base class and to initialize it to an object of the publicly derived class.

In the following example, the `dbl_vect` class from Section 6.7, "Overloading Assignment and Subscripting Operators," on page 210, is used as the base class. The only modification to the base class is to make the private members protected. The following `dbl_vect_bnd` class is the derived class:

```
class dbl_vect_bnd : public dbl_vect {
public:
    dbl_vect_bnd(int = 0, int = 9);            //default 10 array
    dbl_vect_bnd(const dbl_vect_bnd& v);       //copy constructor
    dbl_vect_bnd(const dbl_vect& v);           //conversion
constructor
    dbl_vect_bnd(const double a[], int ne, int lb = 0);
    double&  operator[](int) const;
    int  ub() const { return (u_bnd); }
    int  lb() const { return (l_bnd); }
    dbl_vect_bnd& operator=(const dbl_vect_bnd& v);
private:
    int  l_bnd, u_bnd;
};

//default constructor
dbl_vect_bnd::dbl_vect_bnd(int lb, int ub) :
        dbl_vect(ub - lb + 1), l_bnd(lb), u_bnd(ub) { }

//conversion constructor
dbl_vect_bnd::dbl_vect_bnd(const dbl_vect& v) :
        dbl_vect(v), l_bnd(0), u_bnd(size - 1) { }

//copy constructor
dbl_vect_bnd::dbl_vect_bnd(const dbl_vect_bnd& v) :
        dbl_vect(v), l_bnd(v.l_bnd), u_bnd(v.u_bnd) { }

dbl_vect_bnd::dbl_vect_bnd(const double a[], int n, int lb) :
        dbl_vect(a, n), l_bnd(lb), u_bnd(lb + n) { }
```

In this example, the constructors for the derived class invoke a constructor in the base class, with the argument list following the colon.

C.13.1 Multiple Inheritance

Multiple inheritance allows a class to be derived from more than one base class. The syntax of class headers is extended to allow a list of base classes and their privacy designation. An example is

```
class shape {
   //class for shape interface
};

class tview {
   //class implementing text view
};

class tshape:public shape, private tview {
   //adapter of text view to shape view
};
```

In this example, the derived class tshape publicly inherits the shape base class, an interface, and privately inherits tview, an implementation of text view. This pattern of class design is called the *adapter pattern*. It uses multiple inheritance to combine an interface with an implementation; this technique is also known as using a *mixin* class.

In general, the parental relationship between classes is described by the inheritance directed acyclic graph (DAG). The DAG is a graph structure whose nodes are classes and whose directed edges point from base to derived class.

In deriving an identically named member from different classes, ambiguities may arise. These derivations are allowed, provided that the user does not make an ambiguous reference to such a member.

With multiple inheritance, two base classes can be derived from a common ancestor. If both base classes are used in the ordinary way by their derived class, that class will have two subobjects of the common ancestor. This duplication can be eliminated by using virtual inheritance. For a code example, see file *shape1.cpp* in Section 8.3, "Virtual Functions," on page 282.

C.13.2 Constructor Invocation

The order of execution for initializing constructors in base and member constructors is as follows: Base classes are initialized in declaration order; members are initialized in declaration order. Virtual base classes are constructed before any of their derived classes and before any nonvirtual base classes. Their construction order depends on their DAGs. It is a depth-first, left-to-right order. Destructors are invoked in the reverse order of the constructors.

C.13.3 Abstract Base Classes

A pure virtual function is a virtual member function whose body is normally undefined. Notationally, it is declared inside the class as follows:

```
virtual function prototype = 0;
```

A class that has at least one pure virtual function is an abstract base class. Variables of an abstract base class cannot exist, but pointers of such a class can be defined and used polymorphically. For a code example, see file *predator.cpp* in Section 8.4, "Abstract Base Classes," on page 283.

A pure virtual destructor must have a definition.

C.13.4 Pointer to Class Member

A pointer to class member is distinct from a pointer to class. A pointer to class member's type is $T::*$, where T is the class name. C++ has two operators that act to dereference a pointer to class member. The two pointer-to-member operators are .* and ->*. Think of *obj.*ptr_mem* and *pointer->*ptr_mem* as first accessing the object and then accessing and dereferencing the member that is specified.

The following code shows how to use these operators.

In file showhide.cpp

```
//Pointer to class member

class X {
public:
   int  visible;
   void print()
      { cout << "\nhide = " << hide
             << " visible = " << visible; }
   void reset() { visible = hide; }
   void set(int i) { hide = i; }
private:
   int  hide;
};

typedef void (X::*pfcn)();

int main()
{
   X   a, b, *pb = &b;
   int X::*pXint = &X::visible;
   pfcn pF = &X::print;

   a.set(8); a.reset();
   b.set(4); b.reset();
   a.print();
   a.*pXint += 1;
   a.print();
   cout << "\nb.visible = " << pb ->*pXint;
   (b.*pF)();
   pF = &X::reset;
   (a.*pF)();
   a.print();
   cout << endl;
}
```

The output is as follows:

```
hide = 8 visible = 8
hide = 8 visible = 9
b.visible = 4
hide = 4 visible = 4
hide = 8 visible = 8
```

The `typedef void (X::*pfcn)();` statement says that `pfcn` is a pointer to class X member whose base type is a function with no arguments that returns `void`. Member functions `X::print` and `X::reset` match this type.

The declaration

```
int X::*pXint = &X::visible;
```

declares `pXint` to be a pointer to class X member whose base type is `int`. It is initialized by `pfcn pF = &X::print` to point at the member `X::visible`. The pointer `pF` is initialized to point at the member function `X::print`. Given the pointer assignments in the program, the following equivalencies hold:

`a.*pXint += 1`	is equivalent to	`++a.visible`
`pb ->*pXint`	is equivalent to	`pb -> visible`
`b.*pF()`	is equivalent to	`b.print()`
`(a.*pF)()`	is equivalent to	`a.reset()`.

Consider the memory layout for representing an object. The object has a base address, and the various nonstatic members are offset relative to this base address. In effect, a pointer to class member is used as an offset and is not a true pointer; a true pointer has general memory addresses as values. A static member is not offset and, as such, a pointer to a static member is a true address.

C.13.5 Runtime Type Identification

Runtime type identification (RTTI) provides a mechanism for safely determining the type pointed at by a base-class pointer at runtime. RTTI involves `dynamic_cast`, an operator on a base-class pointer; `typeid`, an operator for determining the type of an object; and `type_info`, a structure providing runtime information for the associated type.

The `dynamic_cast` operator has the form

```
dynamic_cast< type >( v )
```

where *type* must be a pointer or a reference to a class type and *v* must be a corresponding pointer value or reference value. This operator is used with inherited classes having virtual functions, as follows.

```
class Base { ····· };
class Derived : Base { ····· };

void fcn(Base* ptr)
{
    Derived* bptr = dynamic_cast<Derived*>(ptr);
}
```

In this example, the cast converts the pointer value `ptr` to a `Derived*`. If the conversion is inappropriate, a value of 0 is returned or a `bad_cast` exception is thrown. Dynamic casts also work with reference types. Conceptually, the derived type object has a subobject that corresponds to the base type. The conversion replaces the derived-type pointer value or reference with an appropriate base-type pointer value or reference.

The operator `typeid()` can be applied to a *typename* or to an expression to determine the exact type of the argument. The operator returns a reference to the `class type_info`, which is supplied by the system and is defined in the header file *typeinfo* or *typeinfo.h*. The class `type_info` provides both a `name()` member function returning a string that is the type name and overloaded equality operators. Remember to check the local implementation for the complete class interface. Bad dynamic casts and `typeid` operations can be made to throw the exceptions `bad_cast` and `bad_typeid`, so the user can choose between dealing with the `NULL` pointer and catching an exception. For a code example, see file *typeid.cpp* in Section 8.8, "Runtime Type Identification," on page 296.

C.13.6 Virtual Functions

The keyword `virtual` is a function specifier that provides a mechanism for selecting, at runtime, the appropriate member function from among base- and derived-class functions. It may be used only to modify member function declarations. A virtual function must be executable code. When invoked, its semantics are the same as those of other functions. In a derived class, it can be overridden. The selection of which function to invoke from among a group of overridden virtual functions is dynamic. In the typical case, a base class has a virtual function and derived classes have their versions of this function. A pointer to a base-class type can point at either a base-class object or a derived-class object. The member function to be invoked is selected at runtime and corresponds to the object's type, not the pointer's. In the absence of a derived type member, the base-class virtual function is used by default. For a code example, see file *shape1.cpp* in Section 8.3, "Virtual Functions," on page 282.

One reason C++ is so complex is that it has many types of functions and many rule variations that apply to them. At this point, with inheritance and the introduction of virtual functions, we have seen most varieties of functions. There are also those functions that are generated by template syntax, as well as `catch()` handlers that are function-like and that are part of the exception mechanism. It is useful to summarize characteristics and rules applying to most of these by category. For example, inlined functions can be member or nonmember functions and can have or not have return types. Inlining forces local linkage.

Function Characteristics				
Function Category	**Member**	**Virtual**	**Return Type**	**Special**
constructor	yes	no	no	not inherited; default
destructor	yes	yes	no	not inherited; default
assignment	yes	yes	yes	not inherited
`->` `[]` `()`	yes	yes	yes	
`operator`	maybe	yes	yes	
conversion	yes	yes	no	no arguments
`new`	static	no	void*	
`delete`	static	no	void*	
`inline`	maybe	yes	maybe	local linkage
`catch`	no	no	no	one argument
`friend`	friend	no	yes	not inherited

C.14 Templates

The keyword `template` is used to implement parameterized types. Rather than repeatedly recoding for each type, the template feature allows instantiation to generate code automatically for each type.

```
template <class T>        //parameterize T
class stack {
public:
   stack();
   explicit stack(int s);
   T&  pop();
   void  push(T);
   .....
private:
   T*    item;
   int  top;
   int  size;
};

typedef stack<string> str_stack;
str_stack  s(100);        //explicit string stack variable
```

For a code example, see file *stack_t1.cpp* in Section 7.1, "Template Class stack," on page 240.

A template declaration has the form

template < *template arguments* > *declaration*

and a template argument can be

class *identifier*
argument declaration

The class *identifier* arguments are instantiated with a type. Other argument declarations are instantiated with constant expressions of a nonfloating type and can be a function or an address of an object with external linkage, as shown in the following code:

```
template<class T, int n >
class array_n {
   .....
private:
   T  items[n];              //n explicitly instantiated
   .....
};

array_n<complex, 1000>  w;       //w is an array of complex
```

Member function syntax, when external to the class definition, is as follows:

```
template <class T>
T& stack<T>::pop()
{
    return(item[top--]);
}
```

The classname used by the scope resolution operator includes the template arguments, and the member function declaration requires the template declaration as a preface to the function declaration.

C.14.1 Template Parameters

The preceding template can be rewritten with default parameters for both the int argument and the type. For example,

```
template<class T = int, int n = 100>
class array_n {
    .....
};
```

The default parameters can be instantiated when declaring variables or can be omitted, in which case the defaults will be used.

Templates can use the keyword typename in place of class. For example,

```
template<typename T = double, double* ptr_dbl>
```

This allows the template code to use a pointer to a double argument. Ordinary floating-point arguments are not allowed; only pointer and reference to floating-point arguments are allowed.

A template argument can also be a template parameter. For example,

```
template<typename T1, template<class T2> class T3>
```

This allows very sophisticated metatemplates—templates instantiated with templates—to be coded. Libraries, such as STL, can use such features.

C.14.2 Function Template

Until 1995, compilers allowed ordinary functions to be parameterized, using a restricted form of template syntax. Only `class` *identifier* instantiation is allowed. It must occur inside the function argument list.

```
//generic swap

template <class T>
void swap(T& x, T& y)
{
    T  temp;

    temp = x;
    x = y;
    y = temp;
}

//ANSI C++ but unavailable in many current compilers
template <class T, int n>
T foo()
{
  T  temp[n];
  .....
}

foo<char, 20>();        //use char, 20 and call foo
```

A function template is used to construct an appropriate function for any invocation that matches its arguments unambiguously.

```
swap(i, j);             //i j int - okay
swap(c1, c2);           //c1, c2 complex - okay
swap(i, ch);            //i int ch char - illegal
```

The overloading function-selection algorithm is as follows: exact match with trivial conversions allowed on a nontemplate function, exact match using a function template, and ordinary argument resolution on a nontemplate function. In the previous example, an ordinary function declaration `void swap(char, char)` would have been invoked on `swap(i, ch)`. For a code example, see file *swap.cpp* in Section 7.2.1, "Signature Matching and Overloading," on page 244.

C.14.3 Friends

Template classes can contain friends. A friend function that does not use a template specification is universally a friend of all instantiations of the template class. A friend function that incorporates template arguments is a friend only of its instantiated class.

```
template <class T>
class matrix {
private:
   friend void  foo_bar();                        //universal
   friend dbl_vect<T>  product(dbl_vect<T> v);   //instantiated
   .....
};
```

C.14.4 Static Members

Static members are not universal but are specific to each instantiation.

```
template <class T>
class foo {
public:
   static int  count;
   .....
};

foo<int>     a, b;
foo<double>  c;
```

The static variables foo<int>::count and foo<double>::count are distinct. The variables a.count and b.count reference foo<int>::count, but c.count references foo<double>::count. It is preferable to use the form foo<*type*>::count, which makes it clear that the variable referenced is the static variable.

C.14.5 Specialization

When the template code is unsatisfactory for a particular argument type, it can be specialized. A template function overloaded by an ordinary function of the same type—that is, one whose list of arguments and return type conform to the template declaration—is a specialization of the template. When the specialization matches the call, it, rather than code generated from the template, is called.

```
void maxelement<char*>(char*a[],char* &max,int size);
//specialized using strcmp() to return max string
```

This would be a specialization of the previously declared template for `template<class T>maxelement()`. Class specializations are also possible, as in

```
class stack<foobar_obj>   { /*specialize for foobar_obj */ };
```

For a code example, see file *swap.cpp* in Section 7.2.1, "Signature Matching and Overloading," on page 244.

C.15 Exceptions

Classically, an exception is an unexpected condition that the program encounters and cannot cope with. An example is floating-point divide-by-zero. Usually, the system aborts the running program.

C++ code is allowed to directly raise an exception in a try block by using the throw expression. The exception will be handled by invoking an appropriate handler selected from a list of handlers found in the handler's try block. A simple example of this follows:

```
dbl_vect::dbl_vect(int n)
{  //fault tolerant constructor
   try {
      if (n < 1)
         throw (n);
      p = new double[n];
      if (p == 0)
         throw ("FREE STORE EXHAUSTED");
   }
   catch (int n) { ····· }      //catches an incorrect size
   catch (const char* error) { ····· }
                               //catches free-store exhaustion
}
```

Note that new in this example is the traditional new returning 0 for an allocation error. C++ systems using exceptions within new can throw an xalloc or bad_alloc exception on failure. This replaces new returning 0 on failure to allocate. The older-style error handling can be retained by using set_new_handler(0). For a code example, see file *dbl_vect4.cpp* in Section 9.2, "C++ Exceptions," on page 309.

C.15.1 Throwing Exceptions

Syntactically, throw expressions come in two forms:

```
throw
throw expression
```

The throw expression raises an exception in a try block. The innermost try block is used to select the `catch` statement that processes the exception. The throw expression with no argument rethrows the current exception and is typically used when one wants a second handler called from the first handler to further process the exception.

The expression thrown is a static temporary object that persists until exception handling is exited. The expression is caught by a handler that may use this value. An uncaught expression terminates the program.

```cpp
void foo()
{
   int  i;
   //will illustrate how an exception is thrown
   i = -15;
   throw i;
}

int main()
{
   try {
      foo();
   }
   catch(int n)
      { cerr << "exception caught\n " << n << endl; }
}
```

The integer value thrown by `throw i` persists until the handler with integer signature `catch(int n)` exits. This value is available for use within the handler as its argument. For a code example, see file *throw1.cpp* in Section 9.3, "Throwing Exceptions," on page 310.

An example of rethrowing an exception follows:

```
catch(int n)
{
    . . . . .
    throw;        //rethrown
}
```

Assuming that the thrown expression was of integer type, the rethrown exception is the same persistent integer object that is handled by the nearest handler suitable for that type.

C.15.2 Try Blocks

Syntactically, a try block has the form

> try
> *compound statement*
> *handler list*

The try block is the context for deciding which handlers are invoked on a raised exception. The order in which handlers are defined is important, as it determines the order in which a handler for a raised exception of matching type will be tried.

```
try {
    . . . . .
    throw ("SOS");
    . . . . .
    io_condition eof(argv[i]);
    throw (eof);
    . . . . .
}

catch (const char*) { · · · · · }
catch (io_condition& x) { · · · · · }
```

Recall that a throw expression matches the catch if it is an exact match, a derived type of the public base-class handler type, or a thrown object type that is convertible to a pointer type that is the `catch` argument.

It is an error to list handlers in an order that prevents them from being called. For example,

```
catch(void*)              //any char* would match
catch(char*)
catch(BaseTypeError&)     //always for DerivedTypeError
catch(DerivedTypeError&)
```

C.15.3 Handlers

Syntactically, a handler has the form

catch (*formal argument*)
compound statement

The `catch` looks like a function declaration of one argument without a return type.

```
catch (const char* message)
{
   cerr << message << endl;
   exit(1);
}
```

An ellipses signature that matches any argument is allowed. Also, the formal argument can be an abstract declaration, meaning that it can have type information without a variable name. For a code example, see file *catch.cpp* in Section 9.5, "Handlers," on page 314.

C.15.4 Exception Specification

Syntactically, an exception specification is part of a function declaration and has the form

function header `throw` (*type list*)

The *type list* is the list of types that a `throw` expression within the function can have. The function definition and declaration must write out the exception specification identically.

If the list is empty, the compiler may assume that no `throw` will be executed by the function, either directly or indirectly.

```
void foo() throw(int, over_flow);
void noex(int i) throw();
```

If an exception specification is left off, the assumption is that an arbitrary exception can be thrown by such a function. Violations of these specifications are runtime errors. They are caught by the function `unexpected()`.

C.15.5 `terminate()` and `unexpected()`

The system-provided function `terminate()` is called when no handler has been provided to deal with an exception. The `abort()` function, called by default, immediately terminates the program, returning control to the operating system. Other action can be specified by using `set_terminate()` to provide a handler. These declarations are found in the *except* library.

The system-provided handler `unexpected()` is called when a function throws an exception that was not in its exception-specification list. By default, the `terminate()` function is called. Otherwise, `set_unexpected()` can be used to provide a handler.

C.15.6 Standard Library Exceptions

The standard library exceptions are derived from the base-class `exception`. Two of the derived classes are `logic_error` and `runtime_error`. The logic-error types include `bad_cast`, `out_of_range`, and `bad_typeid`, which are intended to be thrown as indicated by their names. The runtime error types include `range_error`, `overflow_error`, and `bad_alloc`.

The base class defines a virtual function

```
virtual const char* exception::what() const throw();
```

This member function is intended to return a meaningful diagnostic message and should be defined in each derived class to give more helpful messages. The empty throw-specification list indicates that the function itself should not throw an exception.

C.16 Caution and Compatibility

C++ is not completely upward compatible with C. In most cases of ordinary use, C++ is a superset of C. Also, C++ is not a completely stable language design. It is in the process of being standardized. The following sections note problematic features of the language.

C.16.1 Nested Class Declarations

The original scoping of nested classes was based on C rules. In effect, nesting was cosmetic, with the inner class globally visible. In C++, the inner class is local to the outer class enclosing it. Accessing such an inner class could require multiple uses of the scope resolution operator.

```
int outer::inner::foo(double w)        //foo is nested
    . . . . .
```

It is also possible to have classes nested inside functions.

C.16.2 Type Compatibilities

In general, C++ is more strongly typed than ANSI C is. Some differences are given in the following list.

Type Differences for ANSI C

- Enumerations are distinct types, and enumerators are not explicitly `int`. This means that enumerations must be cast when making assignments from integer types or other enumerations. Enumerations are promotable to integer. (See Section 2.6, "Enumeration Types," on page 38.)

- Any pointer type can be converted to a generic pointer of type `void*`. However, unlike in ANSI C, a generic pointer in C++ is not assignment compatible with an arbitrary pointer type. This means that C++ requires that generic pointers be cast to an explicit type for assignment to a nongeneric pointer variable. (See Section 3.13, "The Uses of `void`," on page 87.)

- A character constant in C++ is a `char`, but in ANSI C it is an `int`. The `char` type is distinct from both `signed char` and `unsigned char`. Functions may be overloaded based on the distinctions, and pointers to the three types are not compatible.

C.16.3 Miscellaneous

The old C function syntax, in which the argument list is left blank, is replaced in ANSI C by the explicit argument `void`. The signature `foo()` in C is considered equivalent to the use of ellipses and in C++ is considered equivalent to the empty argument list.

In early C++ systems, the `this` pointer could be modified and used to allocate memory for class objects. Although this use is obsolete, a compiler can continue to allow it. (See Section 4.9, "The `this` Pointer," on page 133.)

C++ allows declarations to be intermixed with executable statements. ANSI C allows declarations to be at the heads of blocks or in file scope only. However, in C++, goto, iteration, and selection statements are not allowed to bypass initialization of variables. This rule differs from ANSI C.

In C++, a global data object must have exactly one definition. Other declarations must use the keyword extern. ANSI C allows multiple declarations without the keyword extern.

C.17 New Features in C++

Most compilers have complete implementations of templates and exceptions. The behavior of new with exceptions implemented is to throw a bad_alloc exception. (See Section 9.9, "Standard Exceptions and Their Uses," on page 318.)

Mechanisms that dynamically determine object type have entered the language. This is called runtime type identification (RTTI). The new operator typeid() applies to either a *typename* or an *expression* and dynamic_cast<*type*>(*pointer*), whose effect is either to return 0 if the cast fails or to perform the cast. With exceptions in use, the standard library bad_cast exception is thrown when a conversion fails. In general, such casts will be allowed in polymorphic class hierarchies. (See Section C.13.5, "Runtime Type Identification," on page 398.)

The cast conversion operators static_cast and reinterpret_cast are also added. (See Section 2.5, "The Traditional Conversions," on page 34.)

Single-argument constructors may be prohibited from being conversion constructors with the use of the keyword explicit. (See Section 5.1.3, "Constructors as Conversions," on page 152.)

The keyword mutable allows data members of class variables that have been declared const to remain modifiable. (See Section 4.8.1, "Mutable Members," on page 132.)

Two new types, bool and wchar_t, were added to the simple types. (See Section 2.4, "Simple Types," on page 32.)

The existence of libraries that can lead to name clashes motivated the addition of a namespace scope. (See Section 3.10, "Namespaces," on page 80.) The standard library is encapsulated in the namespace std. This library includes the standard container classes, iterators, and algorithms of the STL.

See system manuals for a detailed description of what is implemented.

Appendix D
Input/Output

This appendix describes input/output in C++, using *iostream* and its associated libraries. The software for C++ includes a standard library that contains functions commonly used by the C++ community. The standard input/output library for C, described by the header *stdio.h*, is still available in C++. However, C++ introduces *iostream*, which implements its own collection of input/output functions. The header *stream* was used on systems before release 2.0 and is still available under many C++ systems.

The stream I/O is described as a set of classes in *iostream*. These classes overload the put to and get from operators << and >>. Streams can be associated with files, and examples of file processing using streams are discussed in this section. A lot of file processing requires character-handling macros, which are found in *ctype*. These are also discussed here.

In OOP, objects should know how to print themselves, and in this text we have frequently made `print()` a member function of a class. Notationally, it is also useful to overload << for user-defined ADTs. In this section, we develop output functions for the types `card` and `deck` to illustrate these techniques.

D.1 The Output Class `ostream`

Output is inserted into an object of type `ostream`, declared in the header file *iostream*. An operator << is overloaded in this class to perform output conversions from standard types. The overloaded left-shift operator is called the *insertion*, or *put to* operator. The operator is left associative and returns a value of type `ostream&`. The standard output `ostream` corresponding to `stdout` is `cout`, and the standard output `ostream` corresponding to `stderr` is `cerr`.

The effect of executing a simple output statement, such as

```
cout << "x = " << x << '\n';
```

is to print to the screen a string of four characters, followed by an appropriate representation for the output of x, followed by a new line. The representation depends on which overloaded version of << is invoked.

The class `ostream` contains public members, such as

```
ostream& operator<<(int i);
ostream& operator<<(long i);
ostream& operator<<(double x);
ostream& operator<<(char c);
ostream& operator<<(const char* s);
ostream& put(char c);
ostream& write(const char* p, int n);
ostream& flush();
```

The member function put() outputs the character representation of c. The member function write() outputs the string of length n pointed at by p. The member function flush() forces the stream to be written. Since these are member functions, they can be used as follows:

```
cout.put('A');                          //output A

char*  str = "ABCDEFGHI";
cout.write(str + 2, 3);                 //output CDE
cout.flush();                           //write buffered stream
```

D.2 Formatted Output and *iomanip*

The put to operator << produces by default the minimum number of characters needed to represent the output. As a consequence, output can be confusing, as seen in the following example:

```
int  i = 8, j = 9;

cout << i << j ;                        //confused: prints 89
cout << i << "    " << j;               //better: prints 8    9
cout << "i= " << i << " j= " << j;      //best: i= 8 j= 9
```

Two schemes that we have used to properly space output are to have strings separating output values and to use \n and \t to create new lines and tabbing. We can also use manipulators in the stream output to control output formatting.

A manipulator is a value or a function that has a special effect on the stream on which it operates. A simple example of a manipulator is endl, defined in *iostream*, which outputs a newline and flushes the ostream.

```
x = 1;
cout << "x = " << x << endl;
```

This immediately prints the line

```
x = 1
```

Another manipulator, flush, flushes the ostream, as in

```
cout << "x = " << x << flush;
```

This has almost the same effect as the previous example but does not advance to a new line.

The manipulators dec, hex, and oct can be used to change integer bases. The default is base 10. The conversion base remains set until it is explicitly changed.

In file manip.cpp

```
//Using different bases in integer I/O

int main()
{
    int  i = 10, j = 16, k = 24;
    cout << i << '\t' << j << '\t' << k << endl;
    cout << oct << i << '\t' << j << '\t' << k << endl;
    cout << hex << i << '\t' << j << '\t' << k << endl;
    cout << "Enter 3 integers, e.g. 11 11 12a" << endl;
    cin >> i >> hex >> j >> k;
    cout << dec << i << '\t' << j << '\t' << k << endl;
}
```

The resulting output is

```
10        16        24
12        20        30
a         10        18
Enter 3 integers, e.g. 11 11 12a
11        17        298
```

The reason that the final line of output is 11 followed by 17 followed by 298 is that the second 11 in the input was interpreted as hexadecimal, which is $16 + 1$, and the third input was hexadecimal 12a, which is decimal 298.

The preceding manipulators are found in *iostream*. Other manipulators are found in *iomanip*. For example, setw(int width) is a manipulator that changes the default field width for the next formatted I/O operation to the value of its argument.

This value reverts to the default. The following table briefly lists the standard manipulators, the function of each, and the location where each is defined.

I/O Manipulators		
Manipulator	**Function**	**File**
endl	outputs newline and flush	*iostream*
ends	outputs null in string	*iostream*
flush	flushes the output	*iostream*
dec	uses decimal	*iostream*
hex	uses hexadecimal	*iostream*
oct	uses octal	*iostream*
ws	skips white space on input	*iostream*
skipws	skips white space	*iostream*
noskipws	do not skip white space	*iostream*
boolalpha	prints "true" and "false"	*iostream*
noboolalpha	prints "1" and "0"	*iostream*
fixed	prints 123.45	*iostream*
scientific	print1.2345 e+02	*iostream*
left	fill characters to the right of value	*iostream*
right	fill characters to the left of value	*iostream*
internal	fill characters between sign and value	*iostream*
setw(int)	sets field width	*iomanip*
setfill(int)	sets fill character	*iomanip*
setbase(int)	sets base format	*iomanip*
setprecision(int)	sets floating-point precision	*iomanip*
setiosflags(long)	sets format bits	*iomanip*
resetiosflags(long)	resets format bits	*iomanip*

A further example will demonstrate the use of setw, setfill, and setprecision manipulators.

```
//Display use of formatting manipulators.

#include <iostream.h>
#include <iomanip.h>

const long double pi = 3.14159265358979323846L;//pi to 21 places

inline long double area(long double rad)
    { return (pi * rad * rad); }

int main()
{
   long double  r;

   cout << "\nEnter radius: ";
   cin >> r;
   cout << "\nArea is "  << setw(20) << area(r);
   cout << "\nArea is " << setw(20)
        << setprecision(10) << area(r);
   cout << "\nArea is "  << area(r);
   cout << "\nArea is " << setprecision(20) << area(r) << endl;
   cout << setfill('*');
   cout << setprecision(4) << setw(20) << r << endl;
}
```

The output from this program when 1.0 is entered for r is

```
Enter radius:
Area is             3.14159
Area is         3.141592654
Area is 3.141592654
Area is 3.141592653589793116
*******************1
```

As expected, the setprecision() yields a different number of decimal digits of floating-point precision. Be careful not to exceed the meaningful precision of the result. The fill character by default is blank, and here in the last line of output, 1 it was changed to the "star." The output widths are adjusted per each output value. Otherwise, the default width is the exact number of characters needed to display a result.

D.3 User-Defined Types: Output

User-defined types have typically been printed by creating a member function
print(). Let us use the types card and deck as an example of a simple user-
defined type. We write out a set of output routines for displaying cards.

In file pr_card1.cpp

```cpp
//card output

char  pips_symbol[14] = { '?', 'A', '2', '3', '4',
        '5', '6', '7', '8', '9', 'T', 'J', 'Q', 'K' };
char  suit_symbol[4] = { 'c', 'd', 'h', 's' };

enum suit { clubs, diamonds, hearts, spades };

class pips {
public:
    void  assign(int n) { p = n % 13 + 1; }
    void  print() { cout << pips_symbol[p]; }
private:
    int  p;
};

class card {
public:
    suit  s;
    pips  p;
    void  assign(int n)
        { cd = n; s = suit(n / 13); p.assign(n); }
    void  pr_card()
        { p.print(); cout << suit_symbol[s] << "  "; }
private:
    int  cd;                //a cd is from 0 to 51
};
```

```
class deck {
public:
   void  init_deck();
   void  shuffle();
   void  deal(int, int, card*);
   void  pr_deck();
private:
   card d[52];
};

void deck::pr_deck()
{
   for (int i = 0; i < 52; ++i) {
      if (i % 13 == 0)         //13 cards to a line
         cout << endl;
      d[i].pr_card();
   }
}
```

Each card will be printed out in two characters. If d is a variable of type deck, then d.pr_deck() will print out the entire deck, 13 cards to a line.

In keeping with the spirit of OOP, it would also be nice to overload << to accomplish the same aim. The operator << has two arguments—an ostream& and the ADT—and it must produce an ostream&. You want to use a reference to a stream and to return a reference to a stream, whenever overloading << or >>, because you do not want to copy a stream object. Let us write these functions for the types card and deck.

In file pr_card2.cpp

```
ostream& operator<<(ostream& out, pips x)
{
    return (out << pips_symbol[x.p]);
}

ostream& operator<<(ostream& out, card cd)
{
    return (out << cd.p << suit_symbol[cd.s] << "  " );
}
```

```
ostream& operator<<(ostream& out, deck x)
{
    for (int i = 0; i < 52; ++i) {
        if (i % 13 == 0)        //13 cards to a line
            out << endl;
        out << x.d[i];
    }
    return out;
}
```

The functions that operate on `pips` and `deck` need to be friends of the corresponding class, because they access private members.

D.4 The Input Class `istream`

An operator `>>` is overloaded in `istream` to perform input conversions to standard types. The overloaded right-shift operator is called the *extraction*, or *get from*, operator. The standard input `istream` corresponding to `stdin` is `cin`.

The effect of executing a simple input statement, such as

```
cin >> x >> i;
```

is to read from standard input, normally the keyboard, a value for x and then a value for i. White space is ignored.

The class `istream` contains public members, such as

```
istream& operator>>(int& i);
istream& operator>>(long& i);
istream& operator>>(double& x);
istream& operator>>(char& c);
istream& operator>>(char* s);
istream& get(char& c);
istream& get(char* s, int n, char c = '\n');
istream& getline(char* s, int n, char c = '\n');
istream& read(char* s, int n);
```

The member function get(char& c) inputs the character representation to c, including white space characters. The member function get(char* s, int n, int c = '\n') inputs into the string pointed at by s at most n - 1 characters, up to the specified delimiter character c or an end-of-file (EOF). A terminating 0 is placed in the output string. The optionally specified default character acts as a terminator but is not placed in the output string. If not specified, the input is read up to the next newline. The member function getline() works like get(char*, int, char = '\n'), except that it discards rather than keeps the delimiter character in the designated istream. The member function read(char* s, int n) inputs into the string pointed at by s at most n characters. It sets the failbit if an end-of-file is encountered before n characters are read. (See Section D.8, "Using Stream States," on page 427.) In systems that have implemented ANSI standard exceptions, the ios_base::failure may be thrown.

```
cin.get(c);            //one character
cin.get(s, 40);        //length 40 or terminated by '\n'
cin.get(s, 10, '*');   //length 10 or terminated by *
cin.getline(s, 40);    //same as get but '\n' discarded
```

Other useful member functions are

```
int gcount();                //number of recently extracted chars
istream& ignore(int n=1, int delimiter=EOF);  //skips
int peek();                  //get next character without extraction
istream& putback(char c);    //puts back character
```

When overloading the >> operator to produce input to a user-defined type, the typical form is

```
istream& operator>>(istream& p, user-defined-type& x)
```

If the function needs access to private members of x, it must be made a friend of class x. A major point is to make x a reference parameter so that its value can be modified.

D.5 Files

C systems have stdin, stdout, and stderr as standard files. In addition, systems may define other standard files, such as stdprn and stdaux. Abstractly, a file may be thought of as a stream of characters that are processed sequentially.

Standard Files			
C	**C++**	**Name**	**Connected to**
stdin	cin	standard input file	keyboard
stdout	cout	standard output file	screen
stderr	cerr	standard error file	screen
stdprn	cprn	standard printer file	printer
stdaux	caux	standard auxiliary file	auxiliary port

The C++ stream input/output ties the first three of these standard files to cin, cout, and cerr, respectively. Typically, C++ ties cprn and caux to their corresponding standard files, stdprn and stdaux. There is also clog, which is a buffered version of cerr. Other files can be opened or created by the programmer. We will show how to do this in the context of writing a program that double spaces an existing file into an existing or new file. The file names will be specified on the command line and passed into argv.

File I/O is handled by including *fstream*, which contains the classes ofstream and ifstream for output and input file-stream creation and manipulation. To properly open and manage an ifstream or ofstream related to a system file, you must first declare it with an appropriate constructor.

```
ifstream();
ifstream(const char*, int = ios::in,
        int prot = filebuf::openprot);
ofstream();
ofstream(const char*, int = ios::out,
        int prot = filebuf::openprot);
```

The constructor of no arguments creates a variable that will later be associated with an input file. The constructor of three arguments takes as its first argument the named file. The second argument specifies the file mode. The third argument is for file protection.

The arguments for file mode are defined as enumerators in class ios, as shown in the following table.

File Modes	
Argument	**Mode**
ios::in	input mode
ios::app	append mode
ios::out	output mode
ios::ate	open and seek to end of file
ios::nocreate	open but do not create mode
ios::trunc	discard contents and open
ios::noreplace	if file exists, open fails

Thus, the default for an ifstream is input mode, and the default for an ofstream is output mode. If file opening fails, the stream is put into a bad state. The mode can be tested with the !operator. In libraries built with exceptions, the failure exception can be thrown.

Other important member functions found in *fstream* include

```
//opens ifstream file
void open(const char*, int = ios::in,
        int prot = filebuf::openprot);

//opens ofstream file
void open(const char*, int = ios::out,
        int prot = filebuf::openprot);

void close();
```

These functions can be used to open and close appropriate files. If you create a file stream with the default constructor, you would normally use open() to associate it with a file. You could then use close() to close the file and to open another file, using the same stream. Additional member functions in other I/O classes allow for a full range of file manipulation. The following program uses both the *fstream* and the *stdlib* libraries.

In file dbl_sp.cpp

```cpp
//A program to double space a file.
//Usage: executable  f1 f2
//f1 must be present and readable
//f2 must be writable if it exists

void double_space(ifstream& f, ofstream& t)
{
   char  c;

   while (f.get(c)) {
      t.put(c);
      if (c == '\n')
         t.put(c);
   }
}

int main(int argc, char** argv)
{
   if (argc != 3) {
      cout << "\nUsage: " << argv[0]
           <<  "  infile  outfile" << endl;
      exit(1);
   }

   ifstream  f_in(argv[1]);
   ofstream  f_out(argv[2]);

   if (!f_in) {
      cerr << "cannot open " << argv[1] << endl;
      exit(1);
   }
   if (!f_out) {
      cerr << "cannot open " << argv[2] << endl;
      exit(1);
   }
   double_space(f_in, f_out);
}
```

D.6 Using Strings as Streams

The class `strstream` allows `char*` strings to be treated as `iostreams`. When using `strstreams`, the *strstream* library must be included. Newer libraries provide both `istringstream` and `ostringstream`, which support in-memory I/O, using the standard library type `string`. Check your system to determine which of these libraries is available.

The `istrstream` is used when input is from a string rather than from a stream. The overloaded `>>` get from operator may be used with `istrstream` variables. The forms for declaring an `istrstream` variable are

```
istrstream name (char* s);
istrstream name (char* s, int n);
```

where `s` is a string to use as input, `n` is the optional length of the input buffer, and *name* is used instead of `cin`. If `n` is not specified, the string must be terminated with a 0. The end-of-string sentinel is treated as an EOF. An example follows.

In file str_strm.cpp

```
char name[15];
int total;
char* scores[4] = { "Dave 2","Ida 5","Jim 4","Ira 8" };

istrstream ist(scores[3]);    //ist uses scores[3]
ist >> name >> total;         //name: Ira , total = 8
```

The `ostrstream` declarations have the following forms:

```
ostrstream();
ostrstream name(char* s, int n, int mode = ios::out);
```

where `s` is pointer to `buf` to receive string, `n` is the optional size of buffer, and `mode` specifies whether the data are to be put into an empty buffer (`ios::out`) or appended to the existing null-terminated string in the buffer (`ios::app` or `ios::ate`). If no size is specified, the buffer is dynamically allocated. The `ostrstream` variable may use the overloaded put to operator `<<` to build the string. The use of `ostrstream` is particularly useful when you want to construct a single string from information kept in a variety of variables. This technique is used in exception handling to build a single string variable to be used as an argument in a `throw()`. Our `vect` example, in Section 9.8, "Example Exception Code," on page 316, uses this technique. In the following example, note that `ost2` must contain an existing null-terminated string in order for the append to work correctly.

```
strstream ost1;
strstream ost2 (charbuf, 1000, ios::app);

ost1 << name << "  " << score << endl;
ost2 << address << city << endl << ends;
```

D.7 The Functions and Macros in *ctype*

The system provides a standard header file, *ctype* or *cctype*, which contains a set of functions used to test characters and a set of functions used to convert characters. These functions may be implemented as macros or as inline functions. This is mentioned here because of its usefulness in C++ input/output. Those functions that only test a character return an `int` value. The argument is type `int`.

ctype Function	Nonzero (true) Is Returned if c Is
isalpha(c)	a letter
isupper(c)	an uppercase letter
islower(c)	a lowercase letter
isdigit(c)	a digit
isxdigit(c)	a hexadecimal digit
isspace(c)	a white space character
isalnum(c)	a letter or digit
ispunct(c)	a punctuation character
isgraph(c)	a printing character, except space
isprint(c)	a printable character
iscntrl(c)	a control character
isascii(c)	an ASCII code

Other functions provide for the appropriate conversion of a character value. Note that these functions do not change the value of c stored in memory.

ctype Conversion Function	Effect
`toupper(c)`	changes c from lowercase to uppercase
`tolower(c)`	changes c from uppercase to lowercase
`toascii(c)`	changes c to ASCII code

The ASCII code functions are usual on ASCII systems.

D.8 Using Stream States

Each stream has an associated state that can be tested. The states on existing systems are

```
enum io_state { goodbit, eofbit, failbit, badbit };
```

ANSI systems propose the type `ios_base::iostate` to be a bitmask type defining these values. When the nongood values are set by an I/O operation, ANSI systems can throw the I/O standard exception `ios_base::failure`. Associated with this exception is a member function `what()` returning a `char*` message that gives a reason for the failure.

The values for a particular stream can be tested by using the public member functions in the following table.

Stream State Function	What It Returns
`int good();`	nonzero if not EOF or other error bit set
`int eof();`	nonzero if istream `eofbit` set
`int fail();`	nonzero if `failbit, badbit` set
`int bad();`	nonzero if `badbit` set
`int rdstate();`	returns error state
`void clear(int i = 0);`	resets error state
`int operator!();`	return `true` if `failbit` or `badbit` set
`operator void*() const;`	return `false` if `failbit` or `badbit` set

Testing for a stream's being in a nongood state can protect a program from hanging up. A stream state of good means that the previous input/output operation worked and that the next operation should also. A stream state of EOF means that the previous input operation returned an end-of-file condition. A stream state of fail means that the previous input/output operation failed but that the stream will be usable once the error bit is cleared. A stream state of bad means that the previous input/output operation is invalid but that the stream may be usable once the error condition is corrected.

It is also possible to directly test a stream. It is nonzero if it is in either a good or EOF state.

```
if (cout << x )          //output succeeded
   . . . . .
else
   . . . . .              //output failed
```

The following program counts the number of words coming from the standard input. Normally, this would be redirected to use an existing file. The program illustrates ideas discussed in this and the previous two sections.

In file word_cnt.cpp

```
//The word_cnt program for counting words
//Usage: executable < file

int  found_next_word();

int main()
{
   int  word_cnt = 0;

   while (found_next_word())
      ++word_cnt;
   cout << "word count is " << word_cnt << endl;
}
```

```
int found_next_word()
{
    char   c;
    int    word_sz = 0;

    cin >> c;
    while (!cin.eof() && !isspace(c)) {
        ++word_sz;
        cin.get(c);
    }
    return word_sz;
}
```

A nonwhite space character is received from the input stream and is assigned to c. The while loop calls the isspace() function in the *ctype* library to test that adjacent characters are not white space. The loop terminates when either an end-of-file character or a white space character is found. The word size is returned as 0 when the only nonwhite space character found is the end-of-file. One last point: The loop cannot be rewritten as

```
while (!cin.eof() && !isspace(c)) {
    ++word_sz;
    cin >> c;
}
```

because this would skip white space.

D.9 Mixing I/O Libraries

Throughout this text, *iostream* has been used. It is perfectly reasonable to want to continue using *stdio*. This is the standard in the C community, and it is well understood. Its disadvantage is that it is not type safe. Functions such as printf() use unchecked variable-length argument lists. Stream I/O requires, as arguments to its functions and overloaded operators, assignment-compatible types. You might also want to mix both forms of I/O. Synchronization problems can occur because the two libraries use different buffering strategies. This can be avoided by calling

```
ios::sync_with_stdio();
```

The following program coordinates the two libraries.

In file mix_io.cpp

```
//The mix_io program with syncronized I/O

unsigned long fact(int n)
{
   unsigned long  f = 1;

   for (int i = 2; i <= n; ++i)
      f *= i;
   return f;
}

int main()
{
   int n;

   ios::sync_with_stdio();

   do {
      cout << "\nEnter n positive or 0 to halt: ";
      scanf("%d", &n);
      printf("\n fact(%d) = %ld", n, fact(n));
   } while (n > 0);
   cout << "\nend of session" << endl;
}
```

Note that for integer values greater than 12, the results will overflow. It is safe to mix stdio and iostream, provided they are not mixed on the same file.

Appendix E
STL and String Libraries

The C++ standard template library (STL) provides generic programming for many standard data structures and algorithms. The STL provides containers, iterators, and algorithms that support a standard for generic programming. This appendix presents a brief description, emphasizing these three components.

The library is built using templates and is highly orthogonal in design. Components can be used with one another on native and user-provided types through proper instantiation of the various elements of the STL. Different header files are required, depending on the system. Examples here conform to the ANSI standard and are encapsulated in `namespace std`. For a code example, see file *stl_cont.cpp* in Section 7.5.1, "STL Example Code," on page 253.

E.1 Containers

Containers may be either sequence or associative. Sequence containers (vectors, lists, and deques) are ordered by having a sequence of elements. Associative containers (sets, multisets, maps, and multimaps) have keys for looking up elements. The map container is a basic associative array and requires that a comparison operation on the stored elements be defined. All varieties of containers share a similar interface.

STL Typical Container Interfaces

- Constructors, including default and copy constructors
- Element access
- Element insertion
- Element deletion
- Destructor
- Iterators

Containers are traversed by using iterators. These pointer-like objects are available as templates and are optimized for use with STL containers. For a code example, see file *stl_deq.cpp* in Section 7.6, "Containers," on page 254.

Container classes are designated as CAN in the following table.

STL Container Definitions	
CAN::value_type	type of value held in the CAN
CAN::reference	reference type to value
CAN::const_reference	const reference
CAN::pointer	pointer to reference type
CAN::iterator	iterator type
CAN::const_iterator	const iterator
CAN::reverse_iterator	reverse iterator
CAN::const_reverse_iterator	const reverse iterator
CAN::difference_type	represents the difference between two CAN::iterator values
CAN::size_type	size of a CAN

All container classes have these definitions available. For example, the vector container class vector<char>::value_type means that a character value is stored in the vector container. Such a container could be traversed with a vector<char>::iterator.

Containers allow both equality and comparison operators. These operators are as follows:

```
==   !=   <   >   <=   >=
```

Containers also have an extensive list of standard member functions.

STL Container Members	
`CAN::CAN()`	default constructor
`CAN::CAN(c)`	copy constructor
`c.begin()`	beginning location of CAN c
`c.end()`	ending location of CAN c
`c.rbegin()`	beginning for a reverse iterator
`c.rend()`	ending for a reverse iterator
`c.size()`	number of elements in CAN
`c.max_size()`	largest possible size
`c.empty()`	true if the CAN is empty
`c.swap(d)`	swap two CANs

E.1.1 Sequence Containers

The sequence containers (vector, list, and deque) have a sequence of accessible elements. In many cases, the C++ array type can also be treated as a sequence container. For a code example, see file *stl_vec2.cpp* in Section 7.6.1, "Sequence Containers," on page 255.

Sequence classes are designated as SEQ in the following table; these are in addition to the already described CAN interface.

STL Sequence Members	
`SEQ::SEQ(n, v)`	n elements of value v
`SEQ::SEQ(b_it, e_it)`	starts at b_it and goes to e_it - 1
`c.insert(w_it, v)`	inserts v before w_it
`c.insert(w_it, v, n)`	inserts n copies of v before w_it
`c.insert(w_it, b_it, e_it)`	inserts b_it to e_it before w_it
`c.erase(w_it)`	erases the element at w_it
`c.erase(b_it, e_it)`	erases b_it to e_it

Some examples of using these members follow:

```
double w[6] = { 1.1, 1.2, 2.2, 2.3, 3.3, 4.4 };
vector<double> v(15, 1.5);  //15 elements of value 1.5
deque<double> d(w + 2, w + 6);     //use 2.2 to 4.4
d.erase(d.begin() + 2);            //erase 3rd element
v.insert(v.begin() +1, w[3]);      //insert w[3]
```

E.1.2 Associative Containers

The associative containers (set, map, multiset, and multimap) have key-based accessible elements. These containers have an ordering relation, Compare, which is the comparison object for the associative container. For a code example, see file *stl_age.cpp* in Section 7.6.2, "Associative Containers," on page 257.

Associative classes are designated as ASSOC in the following table; these are in addition to the already described CAN interface.

STL Associative Definitions	
ASSOC::key_type	the retrieval key type
ASSOC::key_compare	the comparison object type
ASSOC::value_compare	the type for comparing ASSOC::value_type

The associative containers have several standard constructors for initialization.

STL Associative Constructors	
ASSOC()	default constructor using Compare
ASSOC(cmp)	constructor using cmp as the comparison object
ASSOC(b_it, e_it)	uses element range b_it to e_it using Compare
ASSOC(b_it, e_it, cmp)	uses element range b_it to e_it and cmp as the comparison object

What distinguishes associative constructors from sequence container constructors is the use of a comparison object.

STL Insert and Erase Member Functions	
`c.insert(t)`	inserts t if no existing element has the same key as t; returns `pair <iterator, bool>` with `bool` being `true` if t was not present
`c.insert(w_it, t)`	inserts t with w_it as a starting position for the search; fails on sets and maps if key value is already present; returns position of insertion
`c.insert(b_it, e_it)`	inserts the elements in this range
`c.erase(k)`	erases elements whose key value is k, returning the number of erased elements
`c.erase(w_it)`	erases the pointed-to element
`c.erase(b_it, e_it)`	erases the range of elements

The insertion works when no element of the same key is already present.

STL Member Functions	
`c.find(k)`	returns iterator to element having the given key k; otherwise, ends
`c.count(k)`	returns the number of elements with k
`c.lower_bound(k)`	returns iterator to first element having value greater than or equal to k
`c.upper_bound(k)`	returns iterator to first element having value greater than k
`c.equal_range(k)`	returns an iterator pair for `lower_bound` and `upper_bound`

Here are some examples of using these members.

```
int m[4] = { 1, 2, 3, 4 };
set<int, less<int> > s;       //set of ints ordered on less
set<int, less<int> > t(m, m +4);    //use 1, 2, 3, 4
s.insert(3);                  //place 3 in set s
t.insert(3);                  //no insertion as 3 is in set t
s.erase(2);                   //s had no such element
t.erase(4);                   //t now contains 1, 2, 3
```

E.1.3 Container Adapters

Container adapter classes modify existing containers to produce different public behaviors based on an existing implementation. Three provided container adapters are stack, queue, and priority_queue.

The stack, which can be adapted from vector, list, and deque, needs an implementation that supports back, push_back, and pop_back operations. This is a last-in-first-out data structure.

STL Adapted stack Functions	
void push(const value_type& v)	places v on the stack
void pop()	removes the top element of the stack
value_type& top() const	returns the top element of the stack
bool empty() const	returns true if the stack is empty
size_type size() const	returns the number of elements in the stack
operator== and operator<	equality and lexicographically less than

The queue can be adapted from list or deque. It needs an implementation that supports empty, size, front, back, push_back, and pop_front operations. This is a first-in-first-out data structure.

STL Adapted queue Functions	
void push(const value_type& v)	places v on the end of the queue
void pop()	removes the front element of the queue
value_type& front() const	returns the front element of the queue
value_type& back() const	returns the back element of the queue
bool empty() const	returns true if the queue is empty
size_type size() const	returns the number of elements in the queue
operator== and operator<	equality and lexicographically less than

The priority_queue, which can be adapted from vector or deque, needs an implementation that supports empty, size, front, push_back, and pop_back operations. A priority_queue also needs a comparison object for its instantiation. The top element is the largest element as defined by the comparison relationship for the priority_queue.

STL Adapted `priority_queue` Functions	
`void push(const value_type& v)`	places v in the `priority_queue`
`void pop()`	removes top element of the `priority_queue`
`value_type& top() const`	returns top element of the `priority_queue`
`bool empty() const`	checks for `priority_queue` empty
`size_type size() const`	shows number of elements in the `priority_queue`

We adapt the `stack` from an underlying `vector` implementation. Notice how the STL ADTs replace our individually designed implementations of these types. For a code example, see file *stl_stak.cpp* in Section 7.6.3, "Container Adapters," on page 258.

E.2 Iterators

Navigation over containers is by iterator. Iterators can be thought of as an enhanced pointer type. They are templates that are instantiated as to the container class type over which they iterate. There are five iterator types: input, output, forward, bidirectional, and random access. Not all iterator types may be available for a given container class. For example, random-access iterators are available for vectors but not for maps.

The input and output iterators have the fewest requirements and can be used for input and output. These iterators have special implementations, called `istream_iterator` and `ostream_iterator`, for these purposes. A forward iterator can do everything an input/output iterator can do and can additionally save a position within a container. A bidirectional iterator can go both forward and backward. A random-access iterator is the most powerful and can access any element in a suitable container, such as a `vector`, in constant time. For a code example, see file *stl_io.cpp* in Section 7.7.1, "The `istream_iterator` and `ostream_iterator`," on page 259.

E.2.1 Iterator Categories

Input iterators support equality operations, dereferencing, and autoincrement. An iterator that satisfies these conditions can be used for one-pass algorithms that read values of a data structure in one direction. A special case of the input iterator is the `istream_iterator`, which is derived from an `input_iterator` to work specifically with reading from streams. The template for `istream_iterator` is instantiated with a *<type, distance>*. This distance is usually specified by `ptrdiff_t`. As defined in *cstddef* or *stddef*, it is an integer type representing the difference between two pointer values. For a code example, see file *stl_io.cpp* in Section 7.7.1, "The `istream_iterator` and `ostream_iterator`," on page 259.

Output iterators support dereferencing restricted to the left-hand side of assignment and autoincrement. An iterator that satisfies these conditions can be used for one-pass algorithms that write values to a data structure in one direction. A special case of the output iterator is the `ostream_iterator`, which is derived from an `output_iterator` to work specifically with writing to streams. The `ostream_iterator` can be constructed with a `char*` delimiter, in this case "\t". Thus, the tab character will be issued to the stream `cout` after each `int` value is written. In this program, the iterator `out`, when it is dereferenced, writes the assigned `int` value to `cout`. For a code example, see file *stl_io.cpp* in Section 7.7.1, "The `istream_iterator` and `ostream_iterator`," on page 259.

Forward iterators support all input/output iterator operations and additionally support unrestricted use of assignment. This allows position within a data structure to be retained from pass to pass. Therefore, general one-directional multipass algorithms can be written with forward iterators.

Bidirectional iterators support all forward iterator operations, as well as both autoincrement and autodecrement. Therefore, general bidirectional multipass algorithms can be written with bidirectional iterators.

Random-access iterators support all bidirectional iterator operations and also address arithmetic operations, such as indexing. In addition, random-access iterators support comparison operations. Therefore, algorithms that require efficient random access in linear time, such as quicksort, can be written with these iterators.

Container classes and algorithms dictate the category of iterator available or needed, so `vector` containers allow random-access iterators, but `lists` do not. Sorting generally requires a random-access iterator, but finding requires only an input iterator.

E.2.2 Iterator Adapters

Iterators can be adapted to provide backward traversal and traversal with insertion. For a code example, see file *stl_io.cpp* in Section 7.7.1, "The `istream_iterator` and `ostream_iterator`," on page 259.

STL Iterator Adapters

- Reverse iterators—reverse the order of iteration.

- Insert iterators—insertion takes place instead of the normal overwriting mode.

Some adapters and their purpose as found in this library are as follows.

- ```
  template<class BidiIter,
     class T, class Ref = T&,
     class Distance = ptrdiff_t>
  class reverse_bidirectional_iterator;
  ```

  This reverses the normal direction of iteration. Use rbegin() and rend() for range.

- ```
  template<class RandAccIter,
     class T, class Ref = T&,
     class Distance = ptrdiff_t>
  class reverse_iterator;
  ```

  This reverses the normal direction of iteration. Use rbegin() and rend() for range.

- ```
  template <class Can>
     class insert_iterator;
  template <class Can, class Iter>
  insert_iterator<Can>
     inserter(Can& c, Iter p);
  ```

  The insert iterator inserts instead of overwrites. The insertion into c is at position p.

- ```
  template <class Can>
     class front_insert_iterator;
  template <class Can>
  front_insert_iterator<Can>
     front_inserter(Can& c);
  ```

  Front insertion occurs at the front of the container and requires the member push_front().

- ```
  template <class Can>
     class back_insert_iterator;
  template <class Can>
  back_insert_iterator<Can>
     back_inserter(Can& c);
  ```

  Back insertion occurs at the back of the container and requires a push_back() member.
  ```

E.3 Algorithms

The STL algorithms library contains the following four categories: sorting algorithms, nonmutating sequence algorithms, mutating sequence algorithms, and numerical algorithms. These algorithms generally use iterators to access containers instantiated on a given type. The resulting code can be competitive in efficiency with special-purpose codes.

E.3.1 Sorting Algorithms

Sorting algorithms include general sorting, merges, lexicographic comparison, permutation, binary search, and selected similar operations. These algorithms have versions that use either operator<() or a Compare object. They often require random-access iterators. Section 7.8.1, "Sorting Algorithms," on page 262.
   Some library prototypes for sorting algorithms follow.

▪   ```
    template<class RandAcc>
    void sort(RandAcc b, RandAcc e);
    ```

   This is a quicksort algorithm over the elements in the range b to e. The iterator type RandAcc must be a random-access iterator.

▪   ```
    template<class RandAcc>
    void stable_sort(RandAcc b, RandAcc e);
    ```

   This is a stable sorting algorithm over the elements in the range b to e. In a stable sort, equal elements remain in their relative same positions.

▪   ```
    template<class RandAcc>
    void partial_sort(RandAcc b, RandAcc m, RandAcc e);
    ```

   This is a partial sorting algorithm over the elements in the range b to e. The range b to m is filled with elements sorted up to position m.

▪   ```
    template<class InputIter, class RandAcc>
    void partial_sort_copy(InputIter b, InputIter e,
                           RandAcc result_b, RandAcc result_e);
    ```

   This is a partial sorting algorithm over the elements in the range b to e. Elements sorted are taken from the input iterator range and are copied to the random-access iterator range. The smaller of the two ranges is used.

- ```
  template<class RandAcc>
  void nth_element(RandAcc b, RandAcc nth, RandAcc e);
  ```

  The nth element is placed in sorted order, with the rest of the elements partitioned by it. For example, if the fifth position is chosen, the four smallest elements are placed to the left of it. The remaining elements are placed to the right of it and will be greater than it.

- ```
  template<class InputIter1, class InputIter2, class OutputIter>
  OutputIter merge(InputIter1 b1, InputIter1 e1, InputIter2 b2,
                   InputIter2 e2, OutputIter result_b);
  ```

  The elements in the range b1 to e1 and b2 to e2 are merged to the starting position result_b.

- ```
  template<class BidiIter>
  void inplace_merge(BidiIter b, BidiIter m, BidiIter e);
  ```

  The elements in the range b to m and m to e are merged in place.

The following table briefly lists other algorithms and their purposes as found in this library.

STL Sort-Related Library Functions	
binary_search(b, e, t)	true if t is found in b to e
lower_bound(b, e, t)	the first position for placing t while maintaining sorted order
upper_bound(b, e, t)	the last position for placing t while maintaining sorted order
equal_range(b, e, t)	returns an iterator pair for the range where t can be placed maintaining sorted order
push_heap(b, e)	places the location's e element into an already existing heap
pop_heap(b, e)	swaps the location's e element with its b element and reheaps
sort_heap(b, e)	performs a sort on the heap
make_heap(b, e)	creates a heap
next_permutation(b, e)	produces the next permutation
prev_permutation(b, e)	produces the previous permutation
  ```

STL Sort-Related Library Functions	
`lexicographical_compare` `(b1, e1, b2, e2)`	returns `true` if sequence 1 is lexico-graphically less than sequence 2
`min(t1, t2)`	returns the minimum of `t1` and `t2` that are call-by-reference arguments
`max(t1, t2)`	returns the maximum
`min_element(b, e)`	returns the position of the minimum
`max_element(b, e)`	returns the position of the maximum
`includes(b1, e1, b2, e2)`	returns `true` if the second sequence is a subset of the first sequence
`set_union (b1, e1, b2,` `            e2, r)`	returns the union as an output iterator *r*
`set_intersection (b1, e1,` `              b2, e2, r)`	returns the set intersection as an output iterator *r*
`set_difference (b1, e1, b2,` `            e2, r)`	returns the set difference as an output iterator *r*
`set_symmetric_difference` `       (b1, e1, b2, e2, r)`	returns the set symmetric difference as an output iterator *r*

These algorithms have a form that uses a `Compare` object replacing `operator<()`; for example,

- ```
  template<class RandAcc, class Compare>
  void sort(RandAcc b, RandAcc e, Compare comp);
  ```

  This is a quicksort algorithm over the elements in the range b to e, using `comp` for ordering.

E.3.2 Nonmutating Sequence Algorithms

Nonmutating algorithms do not modify the contents of the containers they work on. A typical operation is searching a container for a particular element and returning its position. For a code example, see file *stl_find.cpp* in Section 7.8.2, "Nonmutating Sequence Algorithms," on page 262.

The library prototypes for some nonmutating algorithms are as follows:

- ```
  template<class InputIter, class T>
  InputIter find(InputIter b, InputIter e, const T& t));
  ```

  This finds the position of t in the range b to e.

- ```
  template<class InputIter, class Predicate>
  InputIter find(InputIter b, InputIter e, Predicate p));
  ```

  This finds the position of the first element that makes the predicate true in the range b to e; otherwise, the position e is returned.

- ```
  template<class InputIter, class Function>
  void for_each(InputIter b, InputIter e, Function f));
  ```

  This applies the function f to each value found in the range b to e.

The following table briefly lists other algorithms and their purposes as found in this library.

STL Nonmutating Sequence Library Functions	
next_permutation(b, e)	produces next permutation
prev_permutation(b, e)	produces previous permutation
count(b, e, t, n)	returns to n the count of elements equal to t
count_if(b, e, p, n)	returns to n the count of elements that make predicate p true
adjacent_find(b, e)	returns the first position of adjacent elements that are equal; otherwise, returns e
adjacent_find(b, e, binp)	returns the first position of adjacent elements satisfying the binary predicate binp; otherwise, returns e
mismatch(b1, e1, b2)	returns an iterator pair indicating the positions where elements do not match from the given sequences, starting with b1 and b2
mismatch (b1, e1, b2, binp)	as above, with a binary predicate binp used instead of equality
equal(b1, e1, b2)	returns true if the indicated sequences match; otherwise, returns false
equal(b1, e1, b2, binp)	as above, with a binary predicate binp used instead of equality
search(b1, e1, b2, e2)	returns an iterator where the second sequence is contained in the first, if it is not e1
search (b1, e1, b2, e2, binp)	as above, with a binary predicate binp used instead of equality

E.3.3 Mutating Sequence Algorithms

Mutating algorithms can modify the contents of the containers they work on. A typical operation is reversing the contents of a container. For a code example, see file *stl_revr.cpp* in Section 7.8.3, "Mutating Sequence Algorithms," on page 263.

The library prototypes for some mutating algorithms follow.

- ```
  template<class InputIter, class OutputIter>
  OutputIter copy(InputIter b1, InputIter e1, OutputIter b2);
  ```

  This is a copying algorithm over the elements b1 to e1. The copy is placed starting at b2. The position returned is the end of the copy.

- ```
  template<class BidiIter1, class BidiIter2>
  BidiIter2 copy_backward(BidiIter1 b1, BidiIter1 e1,
                          BidiIter2 b2);
  ```

  This is a copying algorithm over the elements b1 to e1. The copy is placed starting at b2. The copying runs backward from e1 into b2, which are also going backward. The position returned is b2 - (e1 - b1).

- ```
  template<class BidiIter>
  void reverse(BidiIter b, BidiIter e);
  ```

  This reverses in place the elements b to e.

- ```
  template<class BidiIter, class OutputIter>
  OutputIter reverse_copy(BidiIter b1, BidiIter e1,
                          OutputIter b2);
  ```

  This is a reverse copying algorithm over the elements b1 to e1. The copy in reverse is placed starting at b2. The copying runs backward from e1 into b2, which are also going backward. The position returned is b2 + (e1 - b1).

- ```
  template<class ForwIter>
  ForwardIter unique(ForwIter b, ForwIter e);
  ```

  The adjacent elements in the range b to e are erased. The position returned is the end of the resulting range.

- ```
  template<class ForwIter, class BinaryPred>
  ForwardIter unique(ForwIter b, ForwIter e, BinaryPred bp);
  ```

  The adjacent elements in the range b to e with binary predicate bp satisfied are erased. The position returned is the end of the resulting range.

- ```
  template<class InputIter, class OutputIter>
  OutputIter unique_copy(InputIter b1, InputIter e1,
                         OutputIter b2);

  template<class InputIter, class OutputIter, class BinaryPred>
  OutputIter unique_copy(InputIter b1, InputIter e1,
                         OutputIter b2, BinaryPred bp);
  ```

The results are copied to b2, with the original range unchanged.

The remaining library functions are described in the following table.

STL Mutating Sequence Library Functions	
swap(t1, t2)	swaps t1 and t2
iter_swap(b1, b2)	swaps pointed-to locations
swap_range(b1, e1, b2)	swaps elements from b1 to e1 with those starting at b2; returns b2 + (e1 - b1)
transform(b1, e1, b2, op)	uses the unary operator op to transform the sequence b1 to e1, placing it at b2; returns the end of the output location
transform(b1, e1, b2, b3, bop)	uses the binary operator bop on the two sequences starting with b1 and b2 to produce the sequence b3; returns the end of the output location
replace(b, e, t1, t2)	replaces in the range b to e the value t1 by t2
replace_if(b, e, p, t2)	replaces in the range b to e the elements satisfying the predicate p by t2
replace_copy(b1, e1, b2, t1, t2)	copies and replaces into b2 the range b1 to e1, with the value t1 replacing t2
replace_copy_if(b1, e1, b2, p, t2)	copies and replaces into b2 the range b1 to e1, with the elements satisfying the predicate p replacing t2
remove(b, e, t)	removes elements of value t
  ```

STL Mutating Sequence Library Functions	
`remove_if`, `remove_copy`, `remove_copy_if`	similar to `replace` family except that values are removed
`fill(b, e, t)`	assigns t to the range b to e
`fill_n(b, n, t)`	assigns n ts starting at b
`generate(b, e, gen)`	assigns to the range b to e by calling generator `gen`
`generate_n(b, n, gen)`	assigns n values starting at b using `gen`
`rotate(b, m, e)`	rotates leftward the elements of the range b to e; element in position i ends up in position $(i + n - m) \% n$, where n is the size of the range, m is the midposition, and b is the first position
`rotate_copy(b1, m, e1, b2)`	as above, but copied to b2 with the original unchanged
`random_shuffle(b, e)`	shuffles the elements
`random_shuffle(b, e, rand)`	shuffles the elements, using the supplied random-number generator `rand`
`partition(b, e, p)`	partitions the range b to e to have all elements satisfying predicate p placed before those that do not satisfy p
`stable_partition(b, e, p)`	as above, but preserving relative order

E.3.4 Numerical Algorithms

Numerical algorithms include sums, inner product, and adjacent difference. For a code example, see file *stl_numr.cpp* in Section 7.8.4, "Numerical Algorithms," on page 264.

The library prototypes for numerical algorithms follow.

- ```
  template<class InputIter, class T>
  T accumulate(InputIter b, InputIter e, T t);
  ```

  This is a standard accumulation algorithm whose sum is initially t. The successive elements from the range b to e are added to this sum.

- ```
  template<class InputIter, class T, class BinOp>
  T accumulate(InputIter b, InputIter e, T t, BinOp bop);
  ```

  This is an accumulation algorithm whose sum is initially t. The successive elements from the range b to e are summed with sum = bop(sum, element).

The following table briefly lists other algorithms and their purposes as found in this library.

STL Numerical Library Functions	
inner_product(b1, e1, b2, t)	returns the inner product from the two ranges starting with b1 and b2; this product is initialized to t, which is usually 0
inner_product(b1,e1,b2,t,bop1,bop2)	returns a generalized inner product, using bop1 to sum and bop2 to multiply
partial_sum(b1, e1, b2)	starting at b2, produces a sequence that is the partial sum of terms from the range b1 to e1
partial_sum(b1, e1, b2, bop)	as above, using bop for summation
adjacent_difference(b1, e1, b2)	starting at b2, produces a sequence that is the adjacent difference of terms from the range b1 to e1
adjacent_difference(b1, e1, b2, bop)	as above, using bop for difference

E.4 Functions

It is useful to have function objects to further leverage the STL. For example, many of the previous numerical functions had a built-in meaning using + or * but also had a form in which user-provided binary operators could be passed in as arguments. Defined function objects can be either found in *function* or built. Function objects are classes that have operator() defined. These are inlined and are compiled to produce efficient object code.

In file stl_fucn.cpp

```
//Using a function object minus<int>.
#include <iostream>
#include <numeric>
using namespace std;

int main()
{
   double v1[3] = { 1.0, 2.5, 4.6 }, sum;

   sum = accumulate(v1, v1 + 3, 0.0, minus<int>());
   cout << "sum = " << sum << endl;      //sum = -7
}
```

Accumulation is done by using integer minus for the binary operation over the array v1[]. Therefore, the double values are truncated, with the result being –7.

There are three defined function object classes.

STL Defined Function Object Classes

- Arithmetic objects

- Comparison objects

- Logical objects

The following tables briefly list algorithms and their purposes as found in this library.

STL Arithmetic Objects	
`template <class T> struct plus<T>`	adds two operands of type T
`template <class T> struct minus<T>`	subtracts two operands of type T
`template <class T> struct times<T>`	multiplies two operands of type T
`template <class T> struct divides<T>`	divides two operands of type T
`template <class T> struct modulus<T>`	modulus for two operands of type T
`template <class T> struct negate<T>`	unary minus for one argument of type T

Arithmetic objects are often used in numerical algorithms, such as `accumulate()`.

STL Comparison Objects	
`template <class T> struct equal_to<T>`	equality of two operands of type T
`template <class T> struct not_equal_to<T>`	inequality of two operands of type T
`template <class T> struct greater<T>`	comparison by the greater (>) of two operands of type T
`template <class T> struct less<T>`	comparison by the lesser (<) of two operands of type T
`template <class T> struct greater_equal<T>`	comparison by the greater or equal (>=) of two operands of type T
`template <class T> struct less_equal<T>`	comparison by the lesser or equal (<=) of two operands of type T

The comparison objects are frequently used with sorting algorithms, such as `merge()`.

STL Logical Objects	
`template <class T> struct logical_and<T>`	performs logical and (&&) on two operands of type T
`template <class T> struct logical_or<T>`	performs logical or (||) on two operands of type T
`template <class T> struct logical_not<T>`	performs logical negation (!) on a single argument of type T

E.4.1 Function Adapters

Function adapters allow for the creation of function objects using adaption. In the following example, binder function `bind2nd` transforms an initial sequence of values to these values doubled.

In file stl_adap.cpp

```
//Use of the function adapter bind2nd.
#include <iostream>
#include <algorithm>
#include <functional>
#include <string>
using namespace std;

template <class ForwIter>
void print(ForwIter first, ForwIter last, const char* title)
{
   cout << title << endl;
   while (first != last)
      cout << *first++ << '\t';
   cout << endl;
}

int main()
{
   int data[3] = { 9, 10, 11};

   print(data, data + 3, "Original values");
   transform(data, data + 3, data,
             bind2nd(times<int>(), 2));
   print(data, data + 3, "New values");
}
```

STL Function Adapters

- Negators for negating predicate objects

- Binders for binding a function argument

- Adapters for pointer to a function

The following table briefly lists algorithms and their purposes as found in this library.

STL Function Adapters	

`template<class Pred>`
`unary_negate<Pred>`
`not1(const Pred& p)`
	returns `!p,` where p is a unary predicate

`template<class Pred>`
`binary_negate<Pred>`
`not2(const Pred& p)`
	returns `!p`, where p is a binary predicate

`template<class Op, class T>`
`binder1st<Op>bind1st`
`   (const Op& op,const T& t)`
	the binary op has a first argument bound to t; a function object is returned

`template<class Op, class T>`
`binder2nd<Op>bind2nd`
`   (const Op& op,const T& t)`
	the binary op has a second argument bound to t; a function object is returned

`template<class Arg,class T>` `ptr_fun(T (*f)(Arg))`	constructs a `pointer_to_unary_function<Arg, T>`

`template<class Arg1,`
`   class Arg2, class T>`
`ptr_fun(T (*f)(Arg1, Arg2))`
	constructs a
	`pointer_to_binary_function<Arg,T>`

E.5 Allocators

Allocator objects manage memory for containers. These allocators allow implementations to be tailored to local system conditions while maintaining a portable interface for the container class. Allocator definitions include `value_type`, `reference`, `size_type`, `pointer`, and `difference_type`.

The following table briefly lists allocator member functions and their purposes as found in this library.

STL Allocator Members	
`allocator();` `~allocator();`	constructor and destructor for allocators
`pointer address(reference r);`	returns the address of r
`pointer allocate(size_type n);`	allocates memory for n objects of `size_type` from free store
`void deallocate(pointer p);`	deallocates memory associated with p
`size_type max_size();`	returns the largest value for `difference_type`; in effect, the largest number of element allocatable to a container

Check your vendor's product for specific system-dependent implementations.

E.6 String Library

C++ provides a string type by including the standard header file *string*. It is the instantiation of a template class `basic_string<T>` with `char`. The string type provides member functions and operators that perform string manipulations, such as concatenation, assignment, or replacement. An example of a program using the string type for simple string manipulation follows.

In file stringt.cpp

```
//String class to rewrite a sentence

int main()
{
   string sentence, words[10];
   int pos = 0, old_pos = 0, nwords, i = 0;

   sentence = "Eskimos have 23 ways to ";
   sentence += "describe snow";
```

```
      while (pos < sentence.size()) {
         pos = sentence.find(' ', old_pos);
         words[i++].assign(sentence, old_pos, pos - old_pos);
         cout << words[i - 1] << endl;              //print words
         old_pos = pos + 1;
      }
      nwords = i;
      sentence = "C++ programmers ";
      for (i = 1; i < nwords -1; ++i)
         sentence += words[i] + ' ';
      sentence += "windows";
      cout << sentence << endl;
   }
```

The `string` type is used to capture each word from an initial sentence in which the words are separated by the space character. The position of the space characters is computed by the `find()` member function. Then, the `assign()` member function is used to select a substring from `sentence`. Finally, a new `sentence` is constructed, using the overloaded assignment, `operator+=()`, and `operator+()` functions to perform assignments and concatenations.

The representation for a string of characters follows. It is usual to have the instantiation `basic_string<wchar_t>` for a wide string type `wstring`. Other instantiations are possible as well.

String Private Data Members	
`char* ptr`	for pointing at the initial character
`size_t len`	for the length of the string
`size_t res`	for the currently allocated size or, for an unallocated string, its maximum size

This implementation provides an explicit variable to track the string length; thus, string length can be looked up in constant time, which is efficient for many string computations.

E.6.1 Constructors

Strings have six public constructors, which makes it easy to declare and initialize strings from a wide range of parameters.

String Constructor Members	
`string()`	default; creates an empty string
`string(const char* p)`	conversion constructor from a pointer to `char`
`string(InputIterator b,` `        InputIterator e)`	constructor from the `InputIterator` range from b to e
`string(const string& str,` `size_t pos = 0, size_t n = npos)`	copy constructor; `npos` is usually −1 and indicates that no memory was allocated
`string(const char* p, size_t n)`	copy n characters, where p is the base address
`string(size_t n, char c)`	construct a string of n cs

These constructors make it quite easy to use the string type initialized from `char*` pointers, which is the traditional C method for working with strings. Also, many computations are readily handled as a vector of characters. This is also facilitated by the `string` interface.

E.6.2 Member Functions

Strings have some members that overload operators, as described in the next table.

String Overloaded Operator Members	
`string& operator=(const string& s)`	assignment operator
`string& operator=(const char* p)`	assigns a char* to a string
`string& operator=(const char c)`	assigns a char c to a string
`string& operator+=(const string&s)`	appends string s
`string& operator+=(const char* p)`	appends a char* to a string
`string& operator+=(const char c)`	appends a char c to a string
`char operator[](size_t pos) const`	returns the character at pos
`char& operator[](size_t pos)`	returns the reference to the character at pos

The extensive set of public member functions lets you manipulate strings. In many cases, these functions are overloaded to work with string, char*, and char. A description of append() follows.

- `string& append(const string& s, size_t pos = 0, size_t n=npos);`

  Appends n characters, starting at pos from s to the implicit string object.

  ```
  //example s1 "I am " s2 "7 years old"
  s1.append(s2);              // s1 " I am 7 years old"
  s2.append(s1,0,4);          //s2 "7 years old I am"
  ```

- `string& append(const char* p, size_t n);`
  `string& append(const char* p);`
  `string& append(size_t n, char c);`

  In each case, a string object is constructed using the constructor of the same signature and appended to the implicit string object.

- `string& assign(const string& s, size_t pos = 0, size_t n=npos);`

  Assigns n characters, starting at pos from s to the implicit string object.

  ```
  //example s1 " I am " s2 "7 years old"
  s1.assign(s2);              // s1 "7 years old"
  ```

  The following signatures with the expected semantics are also overloaded:

  ```
  string& assign(const char* p, size_t n);
  string& assign(const char* p);
  string& assign(size_t n, char c);
  string& assign(InputIterator b, InputIterator e);
  ```

- `string& insert(size_t pos1, const string& str, size_t pos2 = 0, size_t n = npos);`

  The insert() function is an overloaded set of definitions that insert a string of characters at a specified position. This function inserts n characters taken from str, starting with pos2, into the implicit string at position pos1.

  ```
  //example s1 " I am " s2 " 7 years old"
  s1.insert(2,s2);            // s1 "I 7 years old am"
  ```

The following signatures with the expected semantics are also overloaded:

```
string& insert(size_t pos,const char* p, size_t n);
string& insert(size_t pos, const char* p);
string& insert(size_t pos, size_t n, char c);
iterator insert(iterator p, char c);
iterator insert(iterator p, size_t n, char c);
void insert(iterator p, InputIterator b, InputIterator e);
```

The inverse function is remove().

- `string& remove(size_t pos = 0, size_t n = npos);`

An n number of characters are removed from the implicit string at position pos.

The following table briefly describes further public string member functions.

String Members	
`string& replace(pos1, n1, str,` `    pos2 = 0, n2 = npos)`	replaces at pos1 for n1 characters, the substring in str at pos2 of n2 characters

`string& replace(pos,n,p,n2);`
`string& replace(pos,n,p);`
`string& replace(pos,n,c);`
	replaces n characters at pos, using a char* p of n2 characters, or a char* p until null, or a character c

`size_t length() const;`	returns the string length
`const char* c_str() const;`	converts string to traditional char* representation
`const char* data() const;`	returns the base address of the string representation
`void resize(n, c);` `void resize(n);`	resizes the string to length n; the padding character c is used in the first function, and the eos() character is used in the second
`void reserve(size_t res_arg);` `size_t reserve() const;`	allocates memory for string; returns the size of the allocation
`size_t copy(p, n, pos = 0) const;`	the implicit string starting at pos is copied into the char* p for n characters
`string substr(pos = 0, npos)const;`	a substring of n characters of the implicit string is returned

You can lexicographically compare two strings by using compare(), a family of overloaded member functions.

■ ```
int compare(const string& str, size_t pos = 0,
            size_t n = npos) const;
```

Compares the implicit string starting at pos for n characters with str. Returns 0 if the strings are equal; otherwise, returns a positive or a negative integer value indicating that the implicit string is greater or less than str lexicographically. The following signatures with the expected semantics are also overloaded:

```
int compare(const char* p,size_t pos, size_t n) const;
int compare(const char* p, size_t pos = 0) const;
```

Each signature specifies how the explicit string is constructed and then compared to the implicit string.

The final set of member functions perform a find operation. One group is discussed here; a table summarizes the rest of this group of member functions.

■ ```
size_t find(const string& str, size_t pos = 0) const;
```

The string str is searched for in the implicit string starting at pos. If it is found, the position it is found at is returned; otherwise, npos is returned, indicating failure.

The following signatures with the expected semantics are also overloaded:

```
size_t find(const char* p, size_t pos, size_t n)const;
size_t find(const char* p, size_t pos= 0) const;
size_t find(char c, size_t pos = 0) const;
```

Each signature specifies how the explicit string is constructed and then searched for in the implicit string. Further functions for finding strings and characters are briefly described in the following table.

String Find Members	

`size_t rfind(str, pos=npos) const;`
`size_t rfind(p, pos, n) const;`
`size_t rfind(p, pos=npos) const;`
`size_t rfind(c, pos=npos) const;`
	like `find()` but scans the string backward for a first match

`size_t find_first_of`
`        (str, pos = 0) const;`
`size_t find_first_of`
`        (p, pos, n) const;`
`size_t find_first_of`
`        (p, pos = 0) const;`
`size_t find_first_of`
`        (c, pos = 0) const;`
	searches for the first character of any character in the specified pattern: `str`, `char* p`, or `char c`

`size_t find_last_of`
`        (str, pos = npos) const;`
`size_t find_last_of`
`        (p, pos, n) const;`
`size_t find_last_of`
`        (p, pos= npos) const;`
`size_t find_last_of`
`        (c, pos = npos) const;`
	searches backward for the first character of any character in the specified pattern: `str`, `char* p`, or `char c`

`size_t find_first_not_of`
`        (str, pos = 0) const;`
`size_t find_first_not_of`
`        (p, pos, n) const;`
`size_t find_first_not_of`
`        (p, pos = 0) const;`
`size_t find_first_not_of`
`        (c, pos = 0) const;`
	searches for the first character that does not match any character in the specified pattern: `str`, `char* p`, or `char c`

`size_t find_last_not_of`
`        (str, pos = npos) const;`
`size_t find_last_not_of`
`        (p, pos, n) const;`
`size_t find_last_not_of`
`        (p, pos= npos) const;`
`size_t find_last_not_of`
`        (c, pos = npos) const;`
	searches backward for the first character that does not match any character in the specified pattern: `str`, `char* p`, or `char c`

E.6.3 Global Operators

The string package contains operator overloadings that provide input/output, concatenation, and comparison operators. These are intuitively understandable and are briefly described in the following table.

String Overloaded Global Operators	
`ostream& operator<<(ostream& o,` `                   const string& s);`	output operator
`istream& operator>>(istream& in,` `                   string& s);`	input operator
`string operator+(const string& s1,` `                 const string& s2);`	concatenates s1 and s2
`bool operator==(const string& s1,` `                const string& s2);`	true if string s1 and s2 are lexicographically equal
`<   <=   >   >=   !=`	as expected

The comparison operators and the concatenation `operator+()` are also overloaded with the following four signatures:

```
bool operator==(const char* p, const string& s);
bool operator==(char c, const string& s);
bool operator==(const string& s, const char* p);
bool operator==(const string& s, char c);
```

In effect, a comparison or concatenation of any kind can occur between string and a second argument that is a string, a character, or a character pointer.

References

Arnold, K. and J. Gosling, *The Java Programming Language.* 1996. Reading, Mass.: Addison-Wesley.

Boehm, H., and M. Weiser, "Garbage Collection in an Uncooperative Environment," *Software—Practice and Experience.* September 1988. pp. 807–820.

Booch, G., *Object-Oriented Analysis and Design with Applications, 2nd ed.* 1994. Reading, Mass.: Addison-Wesley.

Budd, T., *An Introduction to Object-Oriented Programming.* 1991. Reading, Mass.: Addison-Wesley.

Cardelli, L., and P. Wegner, "On Understanding Types, Data Abstraction, and Polymorphism." Computing Surveys, vol. 17, 1985. pp. 471–522.

Edelson, D., "A Mark and Sweep Collector for C++," in *Proceedings of Principles of Programming Languages* (January 1992).

Edelson, D., and I. Pohl, "A Copying Collector for C++," in *Usenix C++ Conference Proceedings.* 1991. pp. 85–102.

Ellis, M., and B. Stroustrup, *The Annotated C++ Reference Manual.* 1990. Reading, Mass.: Addison-Wesley.

Gamma, E., et al., *Design Patterns: Elements of Reusable Object-Oriented Software.* 1995. Reading, Mass.: Addison-Wesley.

Glass, G., and B. Schuchert, *The STL <Primer>.* 1996. Upper Saddle River, N.J.: Prentice Hall.

Kelley, A., and I. Pohl, *A Book on C, 3rd ed.* 1995. Reading, Mass.: Addison-Wesley.

Kernighan, B., and P. Plauger, *The Elements of Programming Style, 4th ed.* 1974. New York: McGraw-Hill.

Kernighan, B., and D. Ritchie, *The C Programming Language, 2nd ed.* 1988. Englewood Cliffs, N.J.: Prentice Hall.

Linton, M., J. Vlissides, and P. Calder, "Composing User Interfaces with InterViews," IEEE *Computer* v. 22, no. 2, 1989, pp. 8–22.

Lippman, S., *C++ Primer, 2nd ed.* 1991. Reading, Mass.: Addison-Wesley.

Meyers, S., *Effective C++: 50 Specific Ways to Improve Your Programs and Designs.* 1992. Reading, Mass.: Addison-Wesley.

Musser, D., and A. Saini, *STL Tutorial and Reference Guide: C++ Programming with the Standard Template Library.* 1996. Reading, Mass.: Addison-Wesley.

Pohl, I., *C++ for C Programmers, 2nd ed.* 1994. Reading, Mass.: Addison-Wesley.

Pohl, I., *C++ for Pascal Programmers, 2nd ed.* 1995. Reading, Mass.: Addison-Wesley.

Pohl, I., and D. Edelson, "A-Z: C Language Shortcomings," *Computer Languages*, vol. 13, no. 2. 1988. pp. 51–64.

Stroustrup, B., *The C++ Programming Language, 2nd ed.* 1991. Reading, Mass.: Addison-Wesley.

Stroustrup, B., *The Design and Evolution of C++.* 1994. Reading, Mass.: Addison-Wesley.

Taligent Press, *Taligent's Guide to Designing Programs: Well Mannered Object-Oriented Design in C++.* 1994. Reading, Mass.: Addison-Wesley.

Teale, S., *C++ IOStreams Handbook.* 1993. Reading, Mass.: Addison-Wesley.

Index

Symbols

! negation, 40, 366

!= not equal, 40, 366

% modulus, 366

& address, 43, 82, 135, 370

& and (bitwise), 43, 370

&& and (logical), 40, 366-367

() function call, 43, 216, 373

* dereferencing or indirection, 43, 83, 87, 370

++ autoincrement, 44, 204-206, 365, 391

, comma, 42

-- autodecrement, 44, 204, 365, 391

-> smart pointer, 236

-> structure pointer, 117, 219

. member operator, 8, 117, 204

.* member object selector, 204, 396

/* */ comment pair, 5, 24, 349

// comment, 5, 24, 349

// comment (Java), 15

:: scope resolution, 122, 204, 355, 410

< less than, 40, 366

<< left shift, 43, 370

<< put to, 29, 215, 413-414, 419

<= less than or equal, 40, 366

= assignment, 40, 44

== equal, 40, 366

> greater than, 40, 366

>= greater than or equal, 40, 366

>> get from, 29, 215, 420

>> right shift, 43, 370

?: conditional expression, 42, 204, 369

[] indexing or subscripting, 43, 90, 373

\ backslash, 27, 351

\" double quote, 27, 351

\' single quote, 27, 351

\0 end-of-string sentinel, 26, 158

^ exclusive or (bitwise), 43, 370

^ unary one's complement, 370

{} braces, 45

| or (bitwise), 43, 370

|| or (logical), 40, 366-367

~ complement, 43

->* pointer to member, 396

0 null pointer, 169

A

\a alert, 27, 351

AB_file program, 110

abort(), 315, 409

abstract base class, 283, 294, 396

abstract class, 283

abstract data type, 2, 6, 328-329

abstraction, 328

acc_mod program, 298

access keywords

private, 120-121, 138, 274, 387, 393

protected, 138, 274, 387, 393

public, 120, 138, 274-275, 387, 393

accessor function, 139, 154

accumulate() (STL), 253, 264, 447

ad hoc polymorphism, 195, 330

Ada, 327-328

adapter (STL)

container, 257

iterator, 260, 438

adapter pattern, 395

add_term(), 179

address &, 43, 82, 135, 370

address() (STL), 452

adjacent_difference() (STL), 447

adjacent_find() (STL), 443

ADT, 2, 6, 328-329

complex, 7-11

point, 118

polynomial, 213

string, 93, 158

student, 12

template stack, 240

template vector, 248

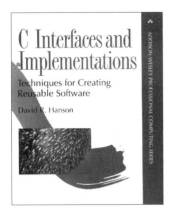

C Interfaces and Implementations
Techniques for Creating Reusable Software
David R. Hanson

Every programmer and software project manager must master the art of creating reusable software modules, which are the building blocks of large, reliable applications. Unlike some modern object-oriented languages, C provides little linguistic support or motivation for creating reusable application programming interfaces (APIs). While most C programmers use APIs and the libraries that implement them in almost every application they write, relatively few programmers create and disseminate new, widely applicable APIs. *C Interfaces and Implementations* shows how to create reusable APIs using interface-based design, a language-independent methodology that separates interfaces from their implementations. This methodology is explained by example. The author describes in detail twenty-four interfaces and their implementations, providing the reader with a thorough understanding of this design approach.

544 pages • Paperback • ISBN 0-201-49841-3
http://www.awl.com/cseng/titles/0-201-49841-3/

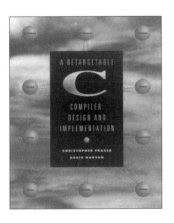

A Retargetable C Compiler
Design and Implementation
Christopher W. Fraser and David R. Hanson

This book examines the design and implementation of lcc, a production-quality, retargetable compiler for the ANSI C programming language designed at AT&T Bell Laboratories and Princeton University. The authors' innovative approach—a "literate program" that intermingles the text with the source code—gives a detailed tour of the code that explains the implementation and design decisions reflected in the software. And while most books describe toy compilers or focus on isolated pieces of code, the authors provide the entire source code for a real compiler, which is available via ftp. Structured as a self-study guide that describes the real-world tradeoffs encountered in building a production-quality compiler, this book is useful to individuals who work in application areas applying or creating language-based tools and techniques.

592 pages • Hardcover • ISBN 0-8053-1670-1
http://www.awl.com/cseng/titles/0-8053-1670-1/

C Programming FAQs
Frequently Asked Questions
Steve Summit

Steve Summit furnishes you with answers to some of the most frequently asked questions in C. Extensively revised from his popular FAQ list on the Internet, more than 400 questions are answered to illustrate key points and to provide practical guidelines for programmers. *C Programming FAQs* is a welcomed reference for all C programmers, providing accurate answers, insightful explanations, and clarification of fine points, along with numerous code examples.

432 pages • Paperback • ISBN 0-201-84519-9
http://www.awl.com/cseng/titles/0-201-84519-9/

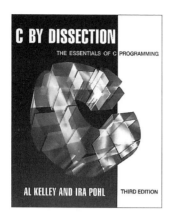

C By Dissection, Third Edition

The Essentials of C Programming

Al Kelley and Ira Pohl

This significantly revised edition has been carefully designed to meet the needs of readers new to C. The reader moves easily through the fundamentals of C and on to its latest applications by means of a time-tested explanatory tool called dissection, first developed by the authors in 1984. Dissection, a pedagogical method similar to a structured step-by-step walk-through, explains new programming elements and idioms as they are encountered in working code. Right from the start, the authors introduce the reader to complete programs, and at an early point in the text the reader learns to write functions, an important feature of structured programming.

720 pages • Paperback • ISBN 0-8053-3149-2
http://www.awl.com/cseng/titles/0-8053-3149-2/

C for COBOL Programmers

A Business Approach

Jim Gearing

Written by an experienced business data systems designer and programmer, this new tutorial provides an ideal introduction to C for the COBOL programmer who wants to become proficient in the powerful C language. Featuring side-by-side comparisons of the syntax and constructs of the two languages, *C for COBOL Programmers* uses the reader's knowledge of COBOL to build a framework for learning C quickly and easily. The book introduces coded examples in C early, and in the context of a business environment. A complete chapter is devoted to explaining the important differences between COBOL and C for data handling and I/O, while another chapter focuses on C programming standards as applied to business data processing. A valuable appendix cross-references COBOL commands to C commands, operators, and functions.

544 pages • Paperback • ISBN 0-8053-1660-4
http://www.awl.com/cseng/titles/0-8053-1660-4/

C++ For Fortran Programmers

Ira Pohl

Using your existing knowledge of Fortran, *C++ for Fortran Programmers* gets you up and running with C++ quickly. By showing how individual elements of a Fortran program compare and translate into C++, this book helps you make a smooth transition to C++ and object-oriented concepts. Best-selling author and C++ authority Ira Pohl uses his trademark dissection technique to illustrate the underlying structure of programs and to help you understand design trade-offs. Scientific and engineering coding examples are featured throughout the text.

560 pages • Paperback • ISBN 0-201-92483-8
http://www.awl.com/cseng/titles/0-201-92483-8/

C++ Distilled
A Concise ANSI/ISO Reference and Style Guide
Ira Pohl

In *C++ Distilled*, veteran teacher and programmer Dr. Ira Pohl condenses 700 pages of proposed ANSI standard into a concise road map to C++. Selecting the most important and commonly used language elements, Dr. Pohl provides syntax, semantics, and examples, as well as style tips that he has distilled from more than two decades of experience. *C++ Distilled* is a handy reference to the most recent additions to the language, many of which have yet to be covered in existing C++ books. All source code from the book is available via the World Wide Web.

224 pages • Paperback • ISBN 0-201-69587-1
http://www.awl.com/cseng/titles/0-201-69587-1/

Object-Oriented Programming Using C++, Second Edition
Ira Pohl

Object-Oriented Programming Using C++, Second Edition provides the experienced programmer with a clear and thorough introduction to the object-oriented paradigm using ANSI C++. Each chapter introduces you to specific C++ language features that support object-oriented programming concepts, including the most recent additions to the language such as STL, namespaces, RTTI, and the bool type. The book illustrates concepts by example, providing full working programs right from the start. All source code from the book is available via the World Wide Web.

576 pages • Paperback • ISBN 0-201-89550-1
http://www.awl.com/cseng/titles/0-201-89550-1/

A Book on C, Fourth Edition
Programming in C
Al Kelley and Ira Pohl

Now in its fourth edition, *A Book on C* retains the features that have made it a proven, best-selling tutorial and reference on the ANSI C programming language. This new edition includes new and updated programming examples and dissections (the authors' trademark technique!), multifile programming, Abstract Data Types, updated material on transitioning to C++, and new coverage on transitioning from C to Java. References to key programming functions and C features are provided in convenient tables. Beginners and professional programmers alike will benefit from the numerous examples and extensive exercises developed to guide readers through each concept.

752 pages • Paperback • ISBN 0-201-18399-4
http://www.awl.com/cseng/titles/0-201-18399-4/

Addison-Wesley Computer and Engineering Publishing Group

How to Interact with Us

1. Visit our Web site

http://www.awl.com/cseng

When you think you've read enough, there's always more content for you at Addison-Wesley's web site. Our web site contains a directory of complete product information including:

- Chapters
- Exclusive author interviews
- Links to authors' pages
- Tables of contents
- Source code

You can also discover what tradeshows and conferences Addison-Wesley will be attending, read what others are saying about our titles, and find out where and when you can meet our authors and have them sign your book.

2. Subscribe to Our Email Mailing Lists

Subscribe to our electronic mailing lists and be the first to know when new books are publishing. Here's how it works: Sign up for our electronic mailing at http://www.awl.com/cseng/mailinglists.html. Just select the subject areas that interest you and you will receive notification via email when we publish a book in that area.

3. Contact with Us via Email

cepubprof@awl.com

Ask general questions about our books.
Sign up for our electronic mailing lists.
Submit corrections for our web site.

bexpress@awl.com

Request an Addison-Wesley catalog.
Get answers to questions regarding your order or our products.

innovations@awl.com

Request a current Innovations Newsletter.

webmaster@awl.com

Send comments about our web site.

cepubeditors@awl.com

Submit a book proposal.
Send errata for an Addison-Wesley book.

cepubpublicity@awl.com

Request a review copy for a member of the media interested in reviewing new Addison-Wesley titles.

We encourage you to patronize the many fine retailers who stock Addison-Wesley titles. Visit our online directory to find stores near you or visit our online store: http://store.awl.com/ or call 800-824-7799.

Addison Wesley Longman
Computer and Engineering Publishing Group
One Jacob Way, Reading, Massachusetts 01867 USA
TEL 781-944-3700 • FAX 781-942-3076